The commercial project manager

The commercial project manager

Managing owners, sponsors, partners, supporters, stakeholders, contractors and consultants

J. Rodney Turner

McGRAW-HILL BOOK COMPANY

London · New York · St Louis · San Francisco · Auckland
Bogotá · Caracas · Lisbon · Madrid · Mexico · Milan
Montreal · New Delhi · Panama · Paris · San Juan
São Paulo · Singapore · Sydney · Tokyo · Toronto

Published by
McGRAW–HILL Book Company Europe
Shoppenhangers Road, Maidenhead, Berkshire, SL6 2QL, England
Telephone 01628 23432
Fax 01628 770224

British Library Cataloguing in Publication Data
Turner, J. Rodney (John Rodney),
    The commercial project manager: managing owners, sponsors,
partners, supporters, stakeholders, contractors and
consultants/J. Rodney Turner.
        p. cm.
    Includes index.
    ISBN 0-07-707946-9:
    1. Industrial project management.   2. Industrial project
management–Finance.   3. Contracts.   4. Partnership.   I. Title.
HD69.P75T848   1995
658.4'04–dc20   94-40491
                                                                                CIP
Library of Congress Cataloging-in-Publication Data
Turner, Rodney
    Commercial Project Manager: Managing Owners, Sponsors, Partners,
    Supporters, Stakeholders, Contractors and Consultants
    I. Title
    658.404

    ISBN 0-07-707946-9

12345 BL 98765

Typeset by BookEns Ltd, Royston, Herts.
and printed and bound in Great Britain by Biddles Ltd., Guildford.

Printed on permanent paper in compliance with the ISO Standard 9706.

To my father, to whom I do not write enough letters

Contents

Foreword

Dr Martin Barnes
Coopers & Lybrand
Vice-President of the Association of Project Managers

Not all projects are commercial and many projects are not managed with proper consideration of commercial aspects. Only in the last few years have many people realized, for example, that only the most trivial projects are completed without needing well-designed contracts between the contributing people and organizations. Similarly, risk management was, until recently, regarded as a 'bolt-on extra' to project management technique, not as part of the core.

This book comprises a comprehensive description of practice and of good practice in all the areas which were formerly regarded as peripheral or even disconnected and which should now be regarded as core.

It is conventional to say that a new book 'fills a gap'. Perhaps the better new books, as this one, first demonstrate an unrecognized gap and then fill it. Rodney Turner and his team have not taken up space with descriptions of the traditional techniques of project management. There is nothing here about time, cost and quality control. But, for the first time, almost everything which sets the context within which these basic project management functions have to be performed is here. Reading *The Commercial Project Manager* starkly demonstrates how important the surrounding commercial considerations are to successful project management. Integration of the commercial aspects with the basic technology has often not been achieved. Full integration, based on a clear understanding, makes a big difference to the success of the completed project. Strangely, this applies whether the objectives of the project are themselves intensely commercial or not.

Much of this book is about people. It is about how to decide *who* you need, *how* you decide *what* they should do and *how* to organize their relationships. We are even told what to do if any of the people fall into dispute. It is refreshing and exciting that an important new book in project management should focus on these and other commercial issues. The days of project management being only about the words and numbers on programmes, budgets and specifications are happily now gone. *The Commercial Project Manager* belongs to the mature phase of project management into which we have now moved. Taking an analogy from the book itself, project management is no longer an island; when placed within its surrounding commercial context, it becomes a valuable part of nearly everything we do.

Preface

This book investigates the financial, commercial and legal relationships between the parties involved in a project. It describes how project managers can apply commercial skills to manage the project's context.

Many traditional books on project management almost treat the project as an island, totally isolated from other projects and operations undertaken by the parent organization. The project manager has within his or her control all the resources needed to undertake the project. The resources may not be enough to do the project in the shortest possible time, but the project manager has control over their prioritization to deliver the project in the optimum time. Indeed, this is the view I took in a previous book (*The Handbook of Project-based Management*, McGraw-Hill, 1993), although at several points I qualified the text to say that I was making this assumption.

In reality, no one organization has all the available resources to undertake a project in its entirety. Either material must be procured, or labour, or professional services, or all three. Even for the simplest projects, such as decorating our homes, we need to buy paint, wall paper and tools. Sometimes we may pay a decorator to do the actual work, and less frequently we will pay someone to design the work. In the early part of this century organizations did try to undertake all their work for themselves. The Cadbury visitors' centre in Bourneville has a row of fabrication shops which are now a children's play area. This practice survived into the 1980s in the pseudo-public sector. I was involved in the privatization of the Royal Dockyards in 1986–87, and at the time they had some fairly specialized workshops, such as chain making, mattress repair, motor winding, etc. However, most organizations in the private sector, and many in the public sector, find it most effective to keep to their core business, and procure other services from outside. Some people call this 'Keeping to the knitting'.

This is just as true for projects as for the routine of organizations, perhaps more so, since projects by their very nature being non-routine involve more work, goods and services from outside the organization's mainline business. Hence, project managers must develop the commercial, financial and legal skills to manage the relationships with external parties involved in a project, and the project's links with its context and environment. These parties involved will include the following people:

- owners and sponsors
- partners
- supporters
- stakeholders.

In addition, to be able to work together these groups of people need to form an understanding of how the relationship will work, and this they do through contracts.

This book is divided into five parts. Each of the first four parts addresses each of the above groups in turn, and the fifth describes the formation and management of contractual relationships.

Before continuing I should like to say that throughout this book we differentiate between the environment and the context of a project.

- *The environment* is a physical concept. It is the neighbourhood in which the facility produced by the project is built
- *The context* is an abstract concept, but includes the environment. It is the complete economic, human, social and ecosystem in which the project exists.

Part One: Owners and sponsors

Part One looks at the organizations that make the investment in projects, and in particular why they make the investment, how they make the decision to invest and how they raise the finance. In a very simple model, a project is an endeavour in which work is done to build a facility, and that facility is operated to produce a profit or benefit (Fig. 0.1). Doing the work to build the facility costs money, and so an organization must make the money available to buy the facility. That organization becomes the *owner* of the facility. In almost all cases, the facility will be operated on behalf of the owner, by users, to produce benefit for the owner, which over time will (hopefully) repay the cost of building the facility. The facility may be operated to make a product which will be sold on to external consumers, which is the case of many engineering and construction products. Alternatively, it may be operated to remove an inefficiency, in which case the users will also be the consumers. This is typical of many IT and management development projects.

There are cases in which the owner makes money available to a project for purely altruistic reasons, receiving no benefit from the operation of the facility. Examples might be the Sainsbury wing of the National Gallery, and Bob Geldof and the Band Aid concerts in 1984. In both cases, the owners achieved some benefit in that some kudos accrued to them, but it is doubtful if that will or did ever repay the investment.

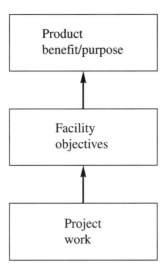

Figure 0.1 Simple model of a project

Often, the owner does not have sufficient financial resources to buy the facility on his or her own, and so must seek external funding from *sponsors*. They may be shareholders or banks. Even where the owner organization does have sufficient internal funds to buy the facility, it is common to identify a sponsor as the person or group who takes the ultimate decision to commit the money. That may be the managing director or board of directors. The sponsor should not be confused with the *champion*, a senior user, who argues the case for the investment, and wins priority for it over other demands for available funds.

Part One investigates owners and sponsors, how projects contribute to the value of an organization, the drivers in markets and technologies which lead them to undertake projects, how to estimate the costs and revenues from projects, how to assess the value of a project and whether it is likely to repay the investment and what the risks are that it will not, and possible sources and costs of finance to pay for the project.

Part Two: Partners

Often one organization has insufficient sources of funds or resources to undertake a project alone. Similarly, the organization may not be large enough to bear all the loss should the project turn out badly. In these cases, companies may enter into partnerships or joint ventures to share the costs and risks with other organizations. Partnerships often cross international boundaries, and these are also considered.

The concept of partnerships is also being widened beyond the traditional joint ventures or collaboration, into more novel arrangements. These include:

- *Partnering* organizations recognize that to undertake projects regularly they need access to resources which are outside their main line of business. For example ICI is in the business of making chemicals, not designing and building chemical plants; Marks and Spencer's is in the business of selling clothes and food, not making and distributing them. Traditionally, companies like ICI maintained large design and construction departments to build new plants. These could become large overheads, which were often an embarrassment between projects, especially during a recession. However, companies are now recognizing that they no more need to maintain these departments than Marks and Spencer's needs to maintain factories and distribution companies, and so they are entering into long-term relationships with potential suppliers, called partnering. This has the added benefit that working together becomes collaborative, rather than confrontational as it has traditionally been.
- *Build–own–operate(–transfer), (BOO(T))* this goes a step further. The consuming organization recognizes it does not need to own and operate the facility. It can buy the product, and sell it on, having another organization, more skilled or with access to greater resources or funds, build, own and operate the facility on its behalf. Depending on the expected life of the facility, it will be either scrapped or transferred to the client organization at the end of the agreed collaborative period. BOOT is being used on infrastructure projects in both Western and developing countries. It is being used in the West to make the private sector take responsibility for infrastructure projects which can be made self-financing. The Channel Tunnel is an example. In developing countries it is seen as an answer to Third World debt. However, money still has to be exported from the countries to pay the owners. Again, Marks and Spencer's effectively use BOO on its distribution network because it is not seen as part of the business, and British Steel uses it for the supply of oxygen to its smelting plants.

A similar, partial arrangement is buy-and-lease-back, or build-own-lease. One organization builds and owns the facility, and another operates it and pays a rental to the owner. This is fairly common on property development projects, but is now used in other areas. In the early 1980s, parts of ICI considered using this arrangement for new chemical plants, and radar systems are sometimes supplied to merchant navy ships in this way. The benefit in this last case is one supplier keeps a stock of spares rather than each operator. It has even been suggested that the Royal Navy should buy its ships in this way. This proposal appeared again in the 'Front Line First' defence review in early 1994.

Each of these two types of partnership arrangement is considered in Part Two.

Part 3: Supporters

Seldom does an owner organization have all the skills required to undertake its projects, and in fact where organizations have built them up, either deliberately, or mistakenly, or without realizing what they were doing, they have usually found that this is inefficient, as was implied above. It is better to concentrate on what you are good at, and to employ experts for what they are good at: 'Keep to the knitting'.

Therefore almost every project, from the smallest DIY job at home, to the construction of the Channel Tunnel, requires the support of external organizations. The roles fulfilled by these organizations may be:

– *Contractors* who supply labour to build some or all of the facility.
– *Managing contractors* who manage the construction of the facility on behalf of the owner. If the managing contractor also fulfils another contracting role then they are sometimes called the *prime contractor.*
– *Suppliers* who supply completed materials to be consumed in the construction of the facility, or plant and equipment to be used to help in the construction of the facility.
– *Consultants* who provide expertise which the owner lacks, perhaps providing an audit or quality control check on other supporters, or providing focused technical or managerial skills to naive owners.
– *Designers* consultants who design the facility for the owner.
– *Shippers* consultants who arrange for the transport of materials, plant and equipment from suppliers to the construction site.
– *Financiers* who provide the funds to the owner.
– *Insurers* who buy some of the risk from the owner, primarily risk which is one-sided and so will lead to loss only.
– *Government* who manage the economic and social system within which the project exists, and can therefore help or hinder any of the above relationships, or increase, reduce or even remove risk.

Part Three deals with the supporters, and describes the roles they fulfil in greater detail, how they can support the owner, the potential benefits and threats from the arrangement to both parties, and how the relationship is managed to maximize the benefit and minimize the risk.

Part 4: Stakeholders

The first three parts deal with the parties to a project who are willingly involved, who have a choice about whether or not they contribute to the project, and who usually expect to make a financial return out of their involvement.

There is also a group of people who are often involved without their prior agreement, sometimes against their will, and who often view the project as being a disbenefit because it somehow distracts from their local environment. These are the *stakeholders*. It is only since the late 1960s, that investors in projects have begun to consider the stakeholders in a project, and it is only over the last decade, since the 1980s, that truly adequate notice has been given to their requirements. Unfortunately, due to earlier neglect, the pendulum may now have swung too far, and local pressure groups are able to block projects which are for the overall benefit of the nation, but which the pressure group feels may have an adverse effect on their environment. Often, the response is emotional, and based on an imagined rather than a real impact.

However, many project sponsors and champions have still not learnt the lesson, and pay scant regard to the requirements of the local community. If more effort and expense is put in at the start of the project managing the needs of the stakeholders, then the overall cost can be lower, and the duration of the project shortened. The proposed railway line through Kent from the Channel Tunnel to the centre of London appears to be one example of where this mistake has been made. If British Rail had spent more time consulting local communities before designing their route, they may have found one which was slightly longer, but which was more acceptable to the people of Kent. As it is, modifications to the route, running it through tunnels, have almost made it commercially non-viable. The routes proposed by the two private consortia are longer, and would add about 20 minutes to the travel time, but have found much more local favour, although this may be partly due to the fact that they run through economically less affluent parts of Kent and Essex.

Furthermore, the environment itself may have a value, in one of two ways:

1. It has a value in that it can provide enjoyment or pleasure. Advertisements on the television encouraging people to move to Milton Keynes or Telford acknowledge this value.
2. It also has a value in that it can generate revenue. Damaging the environment can reduce that commercial value, as the people of the Adriatic Coast of Italy found to their cost during the early 1990s.

Part Four investigates the impact of projects on the environment, how to manage the needs of the stakeholders, how to make projects environmentally more sensitive by conducting an environmental impact assessment, and taking steps to overcome any issues identified, and how to manage the planning and inquiry process which is necessary on many projects. It may seem strange to include environmental issues in a book on the commercial issues of projects. However, I believe it is the right place for them. The impact of projects on the environment affects the local economy, and managing the environmental impact is a cost to the project which can be optimized. It is precisely because organizations view environmental matters as an unnecessary overhead, a cost rather than an opportunity for additional benefit, that they rile the local community and make the sort of mistake that British Rail appears to have done over the Channel Tunnel link through Kent.

Part 5: Contracting

Up to now, we have addressed the economic aspects of the relationships between the parties involved in a project, what benefits each party expects from their involvement and the involvement of others, what risks there are in their joint relationship, and how the relationship can be managed to the best advantage of both parties. The final part of the book deals with the legal aspect of the relationships: the contracts. With the best will in the world, we have to come to a formal agreement with the people we are working with as to how the relationship will work. This may be for the following reasons:

- Both parties must know in advance that they have the same perception of the relationship.
- Both parties must agree how the relationship will work.
- The parties must understand how they are to be rewarded by the relationship.
- There must be protections against default by either party: one party or the other may default for reasons beyond their control, and so that must be accounted for.
- There must be protections against unscrupulous behaviour by either party.
- The parties must agree how to handle changes in the scope of the work.

The British political and legal systems are both based on confrontation, and this is often built into the relationships between clients and contractors. Contractual relations do not have to be built on confrontation, they do not have to be win/lose relationships. The move towards partnering has shown that contracts can be built on mutual trust and cooperation, on win/win relationships. However, even in those circumstances proper protection must be built into the relationship to allow for involuntary default by either party.

Part Five addresses contractual relationships from both the client's and the contractor's viewpoints. The client may be the owner of the facility, or may be a managing contractor, managing the contract on behalf of the owner, or may be a contractor letting part of the work to a subcontractor. We consider how the clients analyse their requirements for using external resources on a job and use that information to determine a procurement and contract strategy. We give a brief overview of contract law and European law as it relates to contracts and procurement, and describe standard forms of contract. We describe how contractors are selected to do the work through a process of issuing an invitation to tender, and reviewing the subsequent bids; we consider how contractors manage the bid process to maximize the chance of winning the bid, from first hearing of the opportunity, through receipt of the invitation to tender and preparation of the bid, to the final negotiation with the client. We consider how clients use consultants. We then describe the processes of administering contracts, the use of claims procedures if the contract goes wrong, and the use of Alternative Dispute Resolution (ADR) procedures to avoid protracted and messy claims.

Acknowledgements

My primary thanks go to all the people who have contributed to the text of this book, including: Roger Mills, Susan Foreman, Dan Remenyi, Chris Chapman, John Aston, John Dingle, Ashok Jashapara, Colin Smith, David Topping, Chris Benjamin, Steve Tonks, Peter Morris, Ernie Torbet, Norman Dunlop, Malcolm Watkinson, Jeffrey Blum, Bian Yong-Qian, Stuart Calvert, Dennis Burningham, John Stringer, Paul Kersey, Bart Bernink, Geoff Quaife, Frank Thomas and Tim Adams. I should also like to thank those who did additional background research, or provided guidance, including: Patrick Hodgson, Kevin Herriot, John White, Eleri Evans, Clive Mason, Richard McGrane and Robert Chambers.

With the modern PC there is no need to thank a typist. However, Alison Pyper and Tricia Hyde have done the modern-day equivalent, scanning a series of articles for me where the author had been unable to send a disk, or I had lost it.

As ever, my wife Beverley and son Edward continue to support me. They are the ultimate owners, sponsors, partners, supporters and stakeholders.

Rodney Turner
East Horsley

Authors' profiles

Rodney Turner is Director of Project Management at Henley Management College, where he is a professor with responsibility for masters' degrees, short courses and research in project management. He is also tutor for fellows sponsored on to the College's masters programme by the Engineering Construction Industry Training Board. After graduating from the University of Oxford, he spent several years with ICI working on engineering design, construction and maintenance projects in the petro-chemical industry. He worked as a consultant in Project Management with Coopers and Lybrand before joining Henley Management College in 1989. He still works as a Project Management consultant, he lectures world-wide, and has published several books and papers on Project Management, including contributions to the INTERNET International Expert seminars. Professor Turner edits the *International Journal of Project Management*, and is a Council member of the Association of Project Managers and a former Deputy Chairman and Treasurer.

Previous books by Professor Turner include: *Goal Directed Project Management*, Kogan Page (1987; reprinted 1988, 1989, 1990, 1991 and 1992 (twice)), with E. S. Andersen, K. V. Grude and T. Haug; *The Handbook of Project-based Management: Improving the processes of achieving your strategic objectives*, McGraw-Hill (1993; reprinted 1993 (twice)).

Tim Adams is a construction manager with Foster Wheeler Energy, and a former fellow on the Engineering Construction Industry Fellowship Scheme at Henley Management College.

John Aston is a tutor in Accounting at the West London Institute, and a visiting tutor at Henley Management College. Previously he was secretary to the Institute of Chartered Accountants.

Chris Benjamin works for C Itoh and Cie (Europe), and is a former under-secretary at the Department of Trade and Industry.

Bart Bernink is Director of HJB Project Consultancy, a Dutch-based firm specializing in Project and Bid Management. Previously he worked as a project manager for Digital in The Netherlands.

Bian Yong-Qian works for HWW Enterprises in the Asian Games Village in

Beijing, and was previously a master's student in Project Management at Henley Management College, sponsored by the British Council. Before coming to Henley, he was a project manager with China Power and Light, working on the construction of a major hydroelectric power station on the Yangtse River.

Jeffrey Blum is a shipbroker at the Baltic Exchange, and also works as a consultant and lecturer.

Dennis Burningham is a consultant in Project and Environmental Management to the oil, gas and petrochemical industry, and he lectures world-wide on those subjects.

Stuart Calvert is a Project Services Manager in the Major Projects Division of Railtrack.

Chris Chapman is Professor of Management Science and Head of the Department of Accounting and Management Science at the University of Southampton. For about 20 years his consultancy and research has centred on the management of risk. He has concentrated primarily on the energy sector in Europe and North America, but has also worked in IT and financial industries.

John Dingle is a consultant and trainer for the oil, gas and petrochemical industries. He previously worked as a project manager in those industries, and is an associate of the College of Petroleum and Energy Studies, Oxford.

Norman Dunlop is a Managing Director of Foster Wheeler Energy Ltd, design and construction contractors to the engineering construction industry. He has spent his career as a design and construction project manager in the oil, gas and petrochemical industries. Mr Dunlop is also Chairman of the Engineering Construction Energy Training Board.

Susan Foreman is a lead tutor in Marketing at Henley Management College. Her research interests are in the areas of marketing in the services industries and internal marketing.

Ashok Jashapara is a senior lecturer at the University of Westminster, where he teaches and researches in construction management, and is undertaking research and study towards a DBA at Henley Management College.

Paul Kersey is a project manager in the IT industry, and a master's graduate from Henley Management College.

Roger Mills is Professor of Accounting and Financial Management at Henley Management College. His research includes the areas of shareholder value analysis and post-completion audits of major projects.

Dr Peter Morris is a Group Director at Bovis, with responsibility for special projects. He is an Associate Fellow of Templeton College, Oxford, where he was previously Executive Director of the Major Projects Association. He is a visiting speaker at Henley Management College, and is Chairman of the Association of Project Managers.

Geoff Quaife is a quantity surveyor, and works as a consultant in contract management with Bucknall Austin.

Dan Remenyi is Professor of Information Systems Management at the University of Witwatersrand in Johannesburg, and Director of TechTrans Ltd, an international firm based in Britain providing training and consultancy in Information Systems, their use and management.

Colin Smith is a construction project manager with Foster Wheeler Energy. He spent one year at Henley Management College on the Engineering Construction Industry Fellowship Scheme, and undertook work on joint ventures and partnering.

John Stringer is an Emeritus Professor of Management at the Australian Graduate School of Management. He is a Visiting Professor at the University of Southampton, and has undertaken research on behalf of the Major Projects Association into the planning and inquiry process.

Frank Thomas has retired after a career spent in design, construction and project management in the engineering construction industry.

Stephen Tonks is a construction project manager with Press Steel Construction, a subsidiary of the AMEC Group. He spent one year at Henley Management College on the Engineering Construction Industry Fellowship Scheme, and undertook research work on partnering.

David Topping is a civil engineer working in Malaysia. He has worked in design and project management in the construction industry in the United Kingdom and overseas.

Ernie Torbet is a consultant project manager and trainer with Nichols Associates, project management consultants to the construction industry.

Malcolm Watkinson is a Procurement Director with Railtrack.

PART ONE
OWNERS AND
SPONSORS

Part One looks at the organizations which make the investment in projects, and in particular why they make the investment, how they make the decision to invest, and how they raise the finance.

In Chapter 1, Roger Mills and Rodney Turner explain the key role of projects in building the value of organizations to their owners. The modern view is that the stock market values companies from the value of their future cash flows. Projects are the medium through which organizations invest in new assets to generate future cash. The concepts of shareholder value analysis identify seven drivers of the value of a company. We show how this approach can be used to value a business, and consider the important role of projects in achieving shareholder value, the influence project managers have over these seven drivers, and hence what contribution they have to the value of their companies.

In Chapter 2, Susan Foreman describes strategic marketing, how it helps organizations to identify customers' future needs, and thereby invest in appropriate projects to meet those needs. These projects may lead the organization to develop new products, exploit new markets, adopt new technologies, or change the organization structure to make it better able to respond to the competitive environment.

In Chapter 3, Rodney Turner describes how to estimate the costs of projects. Cost estimating methods are presented from the IT, building and engineering construction industries. Estimating methods are most well developed in these three industries, and it is proposed that readers should be able to develop estimating methods for their own industries by comparison with these. There is a short discussion on how to estimate benefits from information systems projects written by Dan Remenyi.

In Chapter 4, Chris Chapman describes how to analyse the impact of risk on our projects. The processes discussed can be used for planning, scheduling or control purposes, for costing purposes, or to address economic or financial issues. They therefore support many of the processes described in other chapters.

In Chapter 5, John Aston describes how to assess the financial viability of projects. He presents several techniques, and compares their utility. In reality a portfolio of techniques will be used to assess any one project. The case study was developed by Rodney Turner from an idea of John Aston.

In Chapter 6, John Dingle and Ashok Jashapara describe how to raise finance for a project. The chapter compares debt and equity, introduces many versions and sources of these two primary types of finance, and describes several more sophisticated approaches to financing projects.

1
Projects for shareholder value

Roger Mills and Rodney Turner

1.1 Introduction

Why do organizations invest in projects? The simple answer is to make a profit; that is they expect the financial returns from the project to be greater than the money invested. However, there are many ways of measuring 'financial returns', and they give different answers as to the value of a project to the parent organization.

The traditional accounting-based approach to financial measurement, which measures the development of an organization in terms of short-term profit growth tends to work against investment in projects. It is possible to increase profits in the short term, at the expense of long-term growth. It has been traditional wisdom to blame the decay of British industry, and its failure to invest, on the 'short-termism' of the London stock market. Managers have said that they find the need to increase profits year on year a tyranny they find burdensome. This *stewardship reporting*, as it is called, is backward and inward looking. It requires the allocation of costs between discrete, short periods of time. However, management decision making, especially the decision to invest in a project, is judgemental, forward looking, and concerned with outcomes over a longer period of time. It would therefore seem as though the investors in organizations work against long-term investment and hence against projects.

However, recent research has shown that conventional wisdom may be flawed, and that the pressure on managers may be more perceived that real.[1,2,3] Marsh[1] has reviewed the evidence relating to short-termism. In particular, he considered the notion that short-term investment decisions has dulled Britain's and America's competitive edge, and that this is the fault of the financial institutions. He has found no support for this. Shares are not mis-priced, and markets do not give too much weight to near-term earnings and dividends. Indeed, research in the United States has shown that the stock market tends to react to announcements of capital

3

expenditure on projects (which will reduce short-term earnings) by marking share prices up. Good projects are viewed by the stock market as increasing the value of the organization, and hence shares. The financial institutions appear to value companies (and hence their shares) as the *present value*, PV, of their future cash flows. This is the basis of an approach to valuing companies called *shareholder value analysis*.[2,3]

By contrast, it is management which takes the short-term view, aiming to increase short-term profits at the expense of medium-term growth. Businesses are milked, and research and investment neglected, because managers perceive the need to respond in the ways listed in Table 1.1. This view has been supported by a number of other studies.[4]

Table 1.1   Drivers to short-termism

Drivers
Increase short-term profits
Enlarge the dividend
Increase the share price
Respond to fund managers
Respond to owners who are speculators rather than investors
Ward-off the takeover threat

In this chapter we take a strategic view of the question posed at the start – Why should an organization invest in a project? The answer is to generate a return at least equal to the cost of the funds required by the project (the cost of capital). We consider what this means and describe some of the challenging issues associated with measuring the cost of the funds in practice. We then describe shareholder value analysis as a way of valuing companies. We introduce the seven drivers of project value, and illustrate their use through a worked example. We highlight the contribution of projects to these drivers, and consider the influence project managers have over them.

1.2 The cost of capital

A project will be worth while if it generates a return greater than the cost of the funds invested in it. There is a real challenge in measuring the required rate of return not only for the whole organization, but also for various parts of the business. Furthermore, it is important to appreciate that the cost of funds is an issue that concerns organizations of all types. Whether an organization is for-profit or not-for-profit, the funds it uses will have an opportunity cost, that is an alternative use cost. This is what the cost of funds, otherwise known as the cost of capital, represents. The cost of capital is one of those areas that can become extremely complex and upon which a good deal has been written. For our purposes it will be reviewed in relatively simple terms.

Determining the cost of capital

What actually is the cost of capital? It is simply the opportunity cost of funds to an organization, which seen from the perspective of the providers of those funds represents their required rate of return. Of course, organizations may have more than one source of financing, in which case the cost of capital has to reflect in some way the breadth of different interests. For example, for a commercial organization this is achieved by weighting the relative contributions to the total cost of financing made by each component part. So, for example, a business with 60 per cent equity and 40 per cent debt and with a cost of equity of 12 per cent and a cost of debt of 8 per cent would have a weighted average cost of capital of 10.4 per cent. The calculation of the costs associated with each component part of the cost of capital also represents a challenge.

$$\text{Cost of capital } =$$
$$\text{Cost of equity } \times \text{ Ratio of equity } + \text{ Cost of debt } \times \text{ Ratio of debt}$$

Cost of debt

The cost associated with any debt is typically calculated by estimating the yield on the cash flows paid out by way of interest after tax and any redemption payment on maturity. Its calculation is conceptually straightforward relative to the cost of equity.

$$\text{Cost of debt } = \text{ Interest rates } \times (1 - \text{Tax rate})$$

Cost of equity

For calculating the cost of equity, there are two main alternative approaches. One way is by assessing the future dividend streams required by shareholders, making an allowance for future growth. The alternative can be thought of in terms of relating the required return to the level of risk associated with the investment. A risk-free investment will be the starting point for any investment decision. Thus, anyone contemplating investing in the United Kingdom would require at the very minimum the return available on a government security. For any level of risk above this some compensation would be required by way of a premium. Such a premium can be calculated in many ways, but one popular approach is to use the *capital asset pricing model*, known as CAPM. According to CAPM the cost of equity is found from:

Cost of equity = Risk-free rate + (Beta × Equity risk premium)

There are three parameters in the CAPM formula:

- The beta value of a share
- The risk-free rate (referred to above)
- The equity risk premium.

- *The beta* This measures the risk premium in CAPM. The risk is called systematic, market, or non-diversifiable risk. This risk is caused by macroeconomic factors like inflation, or political events, which affect the returns of all companies. If a company is affected by these macro-economic factors in the same way as the market is, then the company will have a beta of 1, and will be expected to have returns equal to the market. Similarly, if a company's systematic risk is greater than the market, then the company will be priced such that it is expected to have returns greater than the market.
  Perhaps it is easier to think of the beta as being a relative measure of volatility, the relative volatility being determined by comparing a share's returns with the market's returns. The greater the volatility, the more risky the share is said to be which relates directly into a higher beta. For example, if a share has a beta of 2.0, then on average for every 10 per cent that the market index has returned above the risk-free rate, the share will have returned 20 per cent. Conversely, for every 10 per cent the market index has returned below the risk-free rate, the share will have returned 20 per cent below.
  How are betas measured? The answer is by measuring the variance of an individual share relative to the variance of a market portfolio like the FTSE All Share in the United Kingdom, or Standard & Poor's 500 index in the United States. The most common method of estimating beta is with standard regression techniques based on historical share price move-ments. The historical period or estimation period generally accepted is five years, using monthly returns. This standard method is used in the United Kingdom and is provided by the London Business School's Risk Measurement Service.
- *The risk-free rate* This represents the most secure return that could be achieved. Anyone wishing to sleep soundly at night could invest all available funds in government bonds which are largely insensitive to what happens in the share market and, therefore, have a beta of nearly zero. The risk-free rate within CAPM is theoretically defined as an investment

that has no variance and no covariance with the market. This means a perfect proxy is a difficult task, in fact it is empirically impossible. So the best tactic is to find a proxy that meets these requirements as closely as possible. Government guarantees payment.

- *The equity risk premium* This represents the excess return above the risk-free rate that investors demand for holding risky securities. It is the excess return above a risk-free rate that investors demand for holding risky securities. The risk premium in the CAPM is the premium above the risk-free rate on a portfolio assumed to have a beta equal to 1.0. If an individual security is more or less risky, then it will have a higher or lower risk premium. Research has revealed the market risk premium for the US and UK to be between 5.5 per cent and 11 per cent historically, depending upon the time period chosen and the method used, and approximately 3 per cent to 4 per cent taking a forward looking view.

Once the beta, the risk-free rate and the equity risk premium have been determined, the cost of equity can be found using the CAPM formula above. For example, with a risk-free rate of 8 per cent, a beta of 1.2, and an equity risk premium of 4 per cent, the cost of equity would be:

$$
\begin{aligned}
\text{Cost of equity} \quad &= \quad 8\% + (1.2 \times 4\%) \\
&= \quad 12.8\%
\end{aligned}
$$

Unlike the risk captured in the beta, risk that is isolated to an individual company but not the market as a whole is called unsystematic, specific, or diversifiable risk. Company-specific risk can be eliminated by company-specific action and it is an assumption of the CAPM approach that such risk does not have to be priced and compensated for. Why? It is considered that all investors can carry diversified portfolios. Investors who choose not to be fully diversified will not be compensated for the total risk of their holdings, because the only risk which is priced and compensated for in the market is systematic.

Cost of capital to business units

The process we have described so far concerns the estimation for the cost of capital for a corporation as a whole. It is not unusual for organizations to have a number of business units, each of which may have a different rate of return required by investors to reflect differences in systematic risk. This can also be so for projects and the estimation of divisional or project costs of capital can represent a real challenge.

1.3 Valuing the business

The fundamental assumption in shareholder value analysis is that the value of a business can be determined by discounting its future cash flows using an appropriate cost of capital. In fact, there are many features of this approach which makes it seem very much like the net present value approach which has long been used in evaluating capital projects. (Discounted cash flow and net present value techniques are covered in greater detail in Chapter 5.)

What is particularly noteworthy about the approach is that it allows trade-offs associated with strategic planning to be viewed holistically. For example, the immediate cash flows associated with significant capital investment are able to be weighed up against longer term cash flows. These are captured within seven key value drivers (Table 1.2) which can be expanded and adapted to suit specific situations.

Table 1.2   Seven value drivers for shareholder value analysis

Value drivers
Sales growth rate
Operating profit margin
Cash tax rate
Fixed capital investment
Working capital investment
Planning period
Cost of capital

Future cash flows can be determined from the first five value drivers. These can again be divided into two groups corresponding with decisions about managing operations and investment within a business.

Group 1: consisting of three value drivers, sales growth rate, operating profit margin, and cash tax rate, is instrumental in determining cash inflows.
Group 2: consisting of two value drivers, fixed and working capital investment, is instrumental in determining cash outflows.

The difference between cash inflows and cash outflows is what is known as free cash flow and represents the cash available to the providers of finance. This free cash flow recognises the long-term implications associated with short-term actions and may be positive or negative. For example, in developing and introducing a new product significant fixed and working capital investment may often be required. This may represent a significant drain on immediate cash flow. However, the intention in incurring such expenditure will be to benefit from a larger cash flow from operations in the future than would otherwise be the case. In other words, long term benefit is intended to be driven from a decision with immediate implications.

Applying cash flow drivers

How can the future cash flows associated with a strategic plan be estimated? This involves estimating potential growth in sales and the margin to be made on those sales from which it is relatively straightforward to estimate likely future cash inflows. Associated with these estimated cash inflows there will be cash outflows in the form of taxation and also the capital to be invested to support current and future sales.

To see how the five cash flow drivers can be used to provide a free cash flow estimate, let us consider the following example.

Assume a business with sales revenue today of £100 million and sales growth rate, operating margin and tax expectations as shown in Table 1.3.

Table 1.3 Group 1 value drivers for a fictional company

Year	0	1	2	3	4	5
Sales growth rate (%)		5	10	10	15	15
Operating profit margin (%)	10	10	12	12	14	
Cash tax rate (%)		30	30	30	30	30

Table 1.4 shows how these Group 1 value drivers can be used to generate a forecast of operating profit. This can be converted into cash flow terms by adding back depreciation and any other provisions, which in this case we have assumed to be £5 million for each of the five years. The result of adding back this depreciation is the operating cash flow, but this is not yet free cash flow because it does not take account of important cash outflows that will need to be incurred to support the intended sales growth. In order to achieve the intended sales growth rates, fixed and working capital investment will often need to be incurred.

What about the Group 2 value drivers, fixed capital investment (RFCI and IFCI) and working capital investment (IWCI)?

– *Fixed capital investment* This is made up of two components: replacement and incremental. Replacement fixed capital investment (RFCI) is required to maintain the existing capital stock and has been assumed to be the same as the annual depreciation charge. Without maintenance and replacement the ability to meet current levels of demand let alone increases will prove impossible. Incremental fixed capital investment (IFCI) is quite simply the amount of incremental fixed capital that will be

Table 1.4 Operating profit and free cash flow

Year		0	1	2	3	4	5
Sales receipts	£m	100.00	105.00	115.50	127.05	146.11	168.03
Operating profit margin			×10%	×10%	×12%	×12%	×14%
Operating profit	£m		10.50	11.55	15.25	17.53	23.52
Cash tax rate			−30%	−30%	−30%	−30%	−30%
Profit after tax	£m		7.35	8.09	10.68	12.27	16.46
Add: Depreciation	£m		5.00	5.00	5.00	5.00	5.00
Operating cash flow	£m		12.35	13.09	15.68	17.27	21.46
Subtract: RFCI	£m		(5.00)	(5.00)	(5.00)	(5.00)	(5.00)
IFCI	£m		(0.20)	(0.63)	(0.35)	(0.38)	(0.44)
IWCI	£m		(0.15)	(0.32)	(0.35)	(0.76)	(0.88)
Free cash flow	£m		7.00	7.14	9.98	11.13	15.14

required to support incremental sales, and an estimate has to be made of this. One way to make such an estimate is to assume that for every £ of sales to be generated some fixed capital investment will need to be incurred, albeit that it may not occur in even increments but rather in 'lumps'.

– *Working capital investment* This is needed because additional sales will be difficult to sustain without incurring incremental working capital. More stock may be required and it may only be possible to achieve a growth in sales by extending credit and increasing debtors. In common with incremental fixed capital it can be assumed that for every additional £ of sales to be generated, some working capital investment will be required. In other words, any increase in sales can only be incurred by taking on more stocks of raw materials and, possibly, by increasing accounts receivable (debtors).

For purposes of our example we will assume incremental fixed capital investment and incremental working capital investment to be as shown in Table 1.5.

To find IFCI and IWCI in money terms, these percentages are applied to the change in sales receipts from period to period. Therefore, in year 1:

IFCI = (£105 million–£100 million) × 4% = £0.2 million
IWCI = (£105 million–£100 million) × 3% = £0.15 million

Table 1.5 Group 2 value drivers for a fictional company

Year	0	1	2	3	4	5
IFCI(%)		4	6	3	2	2
IWCI(%)		3	3	3	4	4

The Group 2 value drivers represent the investment in projects. Without them there would be no increase in sales, and hence no increase in the value of the business. Indeed, without the RFCI, sales would decrease, and the business would wither and die. Unfortunately, without the investment in projects, managers are able to increase short-term cash flows (and accounting profits) and hence respond in the ways listed in Table 1.1.

Relationship between cash flow drivers

In reviewing the cash flow drivers, factors that may limit future plans are often identified. At this point it is important to recognize that there is a relationship between the cash inflows and outflows. To achieve sales growth, expenditure will usually have to be incurred, the amount of which will depend on the magnitude of the sales growth and the capacity of the business to expand. The relationship between the five cash flow drivers is vital to understand. The ability to achieve the targets set for one of them may well be dependent on another, like, for example, the relationship between the sales growth rate and incremental fixed and working capital investment. Without adequate fixed assets and working capital it may be impossible to achieve a certain growth rate, let alone sustain it.

A problem with fixed capital investment is it may often be 'lumpy', that is beyond a certain level of production it may be impossible to produce more without investing in completely new plant and equipment. Thus, a linear relationship between sales growth and investment is an assumption which may not always be relevant.

Forecasting the future can be very difficult and even when a satisfactory balance between the five cash flow drivers at last looks in sight it may well slip away. Why? Well, there may be yet one other limiting factor which, if it arises, will typically necessitate re-forecasting free cash flows. Quite simply, financing costs are omitted in determining free cash flows. Such costs in the form of dividends and interest are important and may often be subject to limited discretion. There has to be cash available to meet the perceived requirements of the providers of funds. In other words, a company typically has to ensure that sufficient free cash is available to meet financing requirements. This may well constrain ambitious plans such as that to achieve substantial future sales growth via the immediate purchase of plant and equipment and incremental working capital investment, if it results in unsatisfactory cash flows in the near term.

Value and free cash flow

Let us summarize the position we have reached. To estimate the free cash flow associated with a strategic plan we can use five cash flow drivers. Furthermore, we can test the impact upon the estimated cash flows by changing the assumptions relating to any of the five. However, we can go further than this and review a strategic plan in terms of any value that will be created.

In order to calculate value from such cash flows we must discount them. So, in terms of our example, we need to express the future cash flows for the five years in present value terms by discounting them at the required rate of return (cost of capital). Let us assume that the cost of capital after tax and when appropriately adjusted for inflation is 10 per cent. With knowledge of this cost of capital we can calculate the present value of the cash flows for the five year planning period as being £36.83m (Table 1.6).

Table 1.6   Present values of cash flows for the five-year planning period

Year		1	2	3	4	5
Free cash flow	£m	7.00	7.14	9.98	11.13	15.14
Discount factor		0.91	0.84	0.75	0.68	0.62
Present value, PV	£m	6.36	5.97	7.50	7.60	9.40
Cumulative PV	£m	6.36	12.33	19.83	27.43	36.83

The planning period

Strategic planning is concerned with the long term. Corporate strategies that deal with establishing a market share, building brand name values, or deciding upon the most beneficial areas for research and development need to be evaluated over the long term and, as you will see, the most significant part of value can often be generated beyond the point at which managers are comfortable with forecasting.

It cannot be ignored that once a market has been established, cash receipts could conceivably be indefinite – as long as marketing or research and development expenditure is undertaken to maintain market share. Just because new market entrants threaten market dominance free cash flow can still be generated, but the return on it will be eroded. A key question therefore is – how can we capture any future value as realistically as possible? The time horizon, or planning period, is yet another variable in the evaluation of strategic plans. It may therefore be regarded as a sixth value driver. Let us focus our attention around issues associated with the sixth of the seven value drivers introduced earlier – the planning period.

One key issue that must always be considered in undertaking a business valuation is how far one should look into the future. So far we have looked at five years, but should we look at a shorter or longer time horizon? In evaluating a capital project, normal practice is to select a time period for evaluating a project that is consistent with its useful economic life. In our experience, time periods selected are often very arbitrary and not typically very long term. For example, many organizations are loathe to extend their analysis beyond five years. Furthermore, any value at the end of the time period used tends to be recaptured in assumed disposal values for fixed assets and the liquidation of stocks and debtors.

However, where a project is under consideration for strategic reasons a good case can be made for saying that an investment could have an indefinite life, providing any necessary capital expenditure, say for replacement, is undertaken. The argument here is that if an investment is undertaken because a potential opportunity has been identified, and hence a competitive advantage, then this advantage will not necessarily be completely eroded at the end of the time period.

Let us put this within the context of one indicator of competitive advantage, sales growth rate. An organization that has identified the potential for substantial sales growth will eventually be limited in its ability to continue growing. Depending upon the conditions within the market in which it operates, like barriers to entry created by patents and trademarks, there will come a time when competitors' action will drive down growth potential, and the likely premium able to be charged for products and/or services. However, a case can be made for assuming that the organization will still be able to generate revenues and earn its required rate of return, if it ensures the quality of what it provides in the long term is maintained by capital expenditure to replace old or obsolete assets.

The implications of this are that sometimes a case can be made for a very long-term, even an indefinite, cash flow stream based upon this assumption that the quality of the underlying asset base can and will be maintained. If this is so, it raises yet another important question – how can business value be calculated from a potentially indefinite cash flow stream? Does it mean that 'forever' type net present value calculations have to be undertaken upon the basis of assumptions about cash flows into infinity? Fortunately, no! The principles of finance can be applied to the problem if we can separate infinity into two parts that we will refer to as the planning period, and the continuing period.

The planning period can be viewed as the period over which competitive advantage prevails which, in simple terms, we would equate with sales growth potential and the achievement of a positive net present value. Beyond this period lies the continuing period in which we will assume that no sales growth can be achieved. In terms of competitive dynamics we are assuming that a company able to generate returns above the cost of capital will eventually attract competitors, whose entry into the business will drive returns down to the minimum acceptable, or cost of capital, rate. In this continuing period the business will earn, on average, the cost of capital on new investments.

Free cash flow in the planning and continuing periods

In our earlier example a planning period of five years was used. A breakdown of the components of free cash flow for both the planning period and the years comprising the continuing period is shown in Table 1.7. Because sales growth has been assumed to cease at the end of the planning period, sales and hence operating profit remain the same in each year of the continuing period as in year 5. Similarly, with depreciation assumed to be unchanged, operating cash flow remains the same in the continuing period as in the last year of the planning period. However, where there is a noteworthy change is in the level of investment. While RFCI remains unchanged because such investment will need to be undertaken to maintain the quality of existing assets, IFCI and IWCI fall off to zero. These you will remember were forecast upon the basis of sales growth – no sales growth, no IFCI or IWCI!

Table 1.7 Operating profit and free cash flow beyond the planning horizon

Year		1	2	3	4	5	6 Plus
Sales receipts	£m	105.00	115.50	127.05	146.11	168.03	168.03
Operating profit margin		× 10%	× 10%	× 12%	× 12%	× 14%	× 14%
Operating profit	£m	10.50	11.55	15.25	17.53	23.52	23.52
Cash tax rate			−30%	−30%	−30%	−30%	−30%	−30%
Profit after tax	£m	7.35	8.09	10.68	12.27	16.46	16.46
Add: Depreciation	£m	5.00	5.00	5.00	5.00	5.00	5.00
Operating cash flow	£m	12.35	13.09	15.68	17.27	21.46	21.46
Subtract: RFCI	£m	(5.00)	(5.00)	(5.00)	(5.00)	(5.00)	(5.00)
IFCI	£m	(0.20)	(0.63)	(0.35)	(0.38)	(0.44)	
IWCI	£m	(0.15)	(0.32)	(0.35)	(0.76)	(0.88)	
Free cash flow	£m	7.00	7.14	9.98	11.13	15.14	16.46

The result is that the free cash flow beyond year 5 is greater than that for year 5 by £1.32m, the value of IFCI and IWCI in year 6. But, while we know how to put a value on the free cash flows for the planning period, how can we value the free cash flows for the continuing period which may be assumed in principle to be received indefinitely? One answer is that we might view the free cash flow for year 6 and beyond as being a perpetuity, that is a constant cash flow to be received in perpetuity. What is the value of this cash stream to the business? Well, the minimum amount of capital required to fund this stream is the net cash value divided by the cost of capital.

Perpetuity value = Free cash flow/Cost of capital

Applying this to our earlier example produces the following result:

Perpetuity value = Free cash flow/Cost of capital
£16.46 million/0.10
£164.6 million

However, this assumes that the perpetuity is measured at the end of the planning period. It is not the present value of the perpetuity. Given that we have the discount rate of 10 per cent we can calculate the present value of the perpetuity by discounting it at the relevant discount factor, that is 10 per cent at the beginning of year 6. Thus, the present value of such a perpetuity is found from:

PV of perpetuity = £164.6 million × 0.62
= £102.2 million

To determine a business value where there is a given planning period, the present value of the planning period has to be combined with the present value of the value to be derived from the business beyond it. In the case of our example, assuming a five year planning period and a cost of capital of 10 per cent, the result is that the company has a present value of:

PV of company = PV of cash flows for planning horizon +
PV of perpetuity
= £36.8 million + £102.2 million
= £139.0 million

This is the value of the company to its sponsors (shareholders). The size of the value from the continuing period, often known as the residual value, is the largest contributor to total value. In fact, in this case the residual value represents 71 per cent of the total value, which is quite logical when one considers that it represents a period of infinity, *less* the five years accounted for by the planning period. Not surprisingly, the further into the future that the planning period extends the lower is the relative contribution made by the continuing period.

1.4 Influence of project managers on the value drivers

We have seen that the value of a business is dependent on seven value drivers. Project managers have influence over four of them:

- *Sales growth rate* Project managers will not influence the sales of the product as it is made. However, they can have an influence over the rate at which new production facilities are brought on line. If the facilities are late, then sales will not grow at the rate expected. A report by the consultants, McKinsey,[5] showed that if a product development project is late delivering a product to market, then the amount by which the overall profitability of the new product is reduced is magnified several times. Hence, project managers can have a considerable influence on future sales growth.
- *Operating profit margin* The design of the facility can have an impact on the operating profit of the resultant business, especially through its availability, reliability and maintainability. Some decisions affect the overall operating profit of the future business, e.g. whether the facility and the product it produces are designed for:
  Minimum capital investment
  Minimum operating cost
  Minimum maintenance cost
  Minimum life-cycle cost.
- *Fixed and working capital investment* Likewise, project managers influence capital investment through the cost of their projects. The report by McKinsey[5] showed that this had a much smaller impact on profitability. Any overspend on a project development project had a reduced impact on overall profitability. Many people forget about working capital investment in their project appraisal. However, no products can be produced until minimum levels of working capital are in place. These levels will comprise:
  Raw materials
  Work in progress
  Finished goods in store.

1.5 Concluding remarks

We have seen that the value of a business to its shareholders is related to its ability to generate future cash, and that is related to its future sales growth. Maintaining existing sales, and achieving future sales growth, both require an investment in projects.

Before a company can begin to consider what projects it should invest in, it must decide is where that future sales growth will come from; that is what products, markets and technologies will provide it, and what organizational systems, structures and skills the organization must adopt to exploit it. Strategic marketing helps to provide the answers to these questions. That is the topic of the next chapter.

1.6 Summary

1. Shareholder value analysis predicts that the value of a company is the net present value of its future cash flows. Empirical evidence from the United Kingdom and the United States stock markets supports this view. The corollary is that investing in projects increases the future value of a company.
2. A project must deliver returns higher than the cost of capital for the parent organization, where:

$$\text{Cost of capital} = \text{Cost of equity} \times \text{Ratio of equity} + \text{Cost of debt} \times \text{Ratio of debt}$$

where

$$\text{Cost of debt} = \text{Interest rate} \times (1 - \text{Marginal tax rate})$$
$$\text{Cost of equity} = \text{Risk-free rate} + \text{Beta} \times \text{Equity risk premium}$$

3. The seven value drivers of shareholder value are:
   - Sales growth rate
   - Operating profit margin
   - Cash tax rate
   - Fixed capital investment
   - Working capital investment
   - Planning period
   - Cost of capital.
4. Project managers can influence the first five of these.

References

1. Marsh, P., *Short-termism on Trial*, Institute of Fund Managers Association, 1989.
2. Mills, R.W., 'Strategic value management: towards a financial framework for developing the general manager', in *Journal of General Management*, **18**(4), Summer 1993.
3. Mills, R.W., 'Strategic Financial Analysis', in *Treasury Today*, **2**(12), 1992.
4. Coopers & Lybrand, *Shareholder Value Analysis Survey*, Coopers & Lybrand, 1991.
5. Dumaine, B., 'How managers can succeed through speed', *Fortune*, 1989.

2

Project selection: markets and technologies

Susan Foreman

2.1 Introduction

Marketing is the management function by which organizations predict their future product requirements, the markets to which their products are to be sold, and the technologies needed to deliver them. Hence, many project requirements are first identified by the marketing function. Marketing, both as a concept and in its function, should complement the overall business ethos of an organization. The Chartered Institute of Marketing has outlined the role of marketing in its traditional definition:

> Marketing is the management process responsible for identifying, anticipating, and satisfying customer requirements profitably.

The key features of this definition are the identification, anticipation and satisfaction of customer needs. In the current competitive environment, organizations must do more than satisfy existing customer demands with products, services, projects and associated secondary services. They must be proactive in scanning the marketplace to identify and ultimately to develop project-based activities which the customer will find beneficial.

Marketing's strength lies in its ability to anticipate new project opportunities, and in directing the course of the organization into the future. This is often referred to as *strategic marketing*, a process which enables an organization to look beyond the existing situation and encourages an outward approach to decision making. Unfortunately, the current trading situation does not necessarily provide the most satisfactory conditions for anticipating the nature and source of future projects.

However, a strategic approach provides the creative framework for management and thus the subsequent impact on project selection. The basic prerequisites and requirements for the implementation of this course of action are outlined in this chapter. We describe the role of strategic marketing in setting future business direction. We identify the need of organizations to make a commitment to strategic orientation, and describe how they achieve it. The role of technology in competitiveness is identified, and the key elements of Strategic Marketing are described.

2.2 Strategic marketing

Strategic marketing is essentially concerned with those business decisions which indicate the future direction of the organization. There are a number of definitions of strategic marketing.[1] An interesting definition is offered by Cravens:[2]

> Strategic marketing management is the analytical process of seeking a differential advantage through:
> - the analysis of the product–market relationships with a view toward developing the best yield configuration in terms of financial performance; and
> - the formulation of management strategies that create and support viable product–market relationships consistent with the enterprise capabilities and objectives.

In essence, strategic marketing is a process which enables managers to consider business decisions and tasks in a structured rather than an *ad hoc* manner. The ideal future position is to maintain and develop differential advantage – a much sought after, yet elusive, goal.

Many people consider that strategic marketing is merely another term to describe those activities which come under the remit of marketing management. However, it is the degree of environmental uncertainty in the marketplace which requires the application of a strategic approach and associated processes in the organization, and more specifically, in this instance, to the selection of project opportunities. An organization which operates in a stable environment where change is gradual and/or moderate may be able to operate on an operational level with a short-term perspective. However, in an increasingly complex and caustic climate, firms of all sizes or sectors need to match market uncertainties with appropriate parallel strategies. The strategic implications, in this instance, are to focus all the internal skills, knowledge and resources on identifiable and anticipated market opportunities.

2.3 Strategic commitment

Organizational commitment to a strategic orientation is becoming a necessary prerequisite for survival in a turbulent environment. It is suggested that those organizations which do not seize the opportunity to be

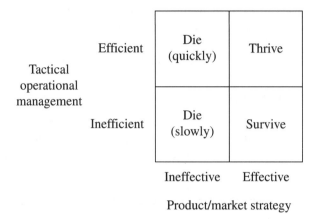

Figure 2.1   The planning matrix
Source: After McDonald (1987).

proactive and have a vision for the future will produce average performance. In order to illustrate the need for organizations to be proactive and to consider the combination of day-to-day management issues with a perspective which endures beyond a one year planning horizon, McDonald[3] uses the marketing planning matrix (Fig. 2.1). This matrix, suggests that the activities of an organization can be broken into two dimensions: operational management and strategic development. The matrix suggests that with an over-emphasis on operational and short-term management decisions the firm will stagnate and ultimately 'die'. The matrix shows the level of commitment needed by an organization if it wishes to 'thrive'. In order to achieve this desired status, efficient strategy needs to be combined with effective strategy development.

2.4 Technology and competitiveness

When considering the nature of markets and technological developments, it is important to remember that organizations do not operate in a vacuum. Invariably they have a large number of competitors each attempting to offer superior value satisfactions to the customer.

Competitiveness is a relative term. Georgiou[4] described it as a race in which the participants are trying to get ahead, and the ability to stay in the lead is the critical factor. Those organizations which create a sustainable lead tend to be those who are classed as truly competitive companies. In the race between competitors to develop new project-based activities, technological innovation will play a leading role. Indeed it has been considered a key determinant of industrial competitiveness. Georgiou[4] considers that:

> Industrial competitiveness depends on a process in which new products and processes are continually introduced, improved and replaced.

The link between technological newness and competitive success is well documented. This close relationship is seen as a key determinant of success for all organizations, whether they are providing tangible products, or whether their offering to the marketplace is less tangible, such as service- or consultancy-based activities. The constant drive to be one step ahead of the anticipated demand of the marketplace will be a key determinant of the identification of successful projects.

The role of technology in determining the nature of competition depends on the position technology plays in each organization. The prevailing attitudes towards technology are based on traditions and organizational evolution. The decision to use technological innovation as a competitive tool is often built into the ethos of the organization. Their commitment to technology is used as means of categorization, such as: leaders; followers; dependants; and reactionaries.

2.5 The role of strategic marketing

The selection of new product opportunities, either by introducing new ones or by exploiting new markets, must be supported internally by a structured approach. There are three key ingredients:

- Organizational climate
- The planning process
- Organizational capabilities.

Organizational Climate

The prevailing climate in an organization is conveyed in the formal systems, procedures and structures which exist, as well as those informal aspects of behaviour, expressed in traditions, rituals, ethos, stories and symbols. Commitment to the principles of strategic marketing needs to be accompanied by a culture which supports this orientation. The continuous search to find the best fit between the organization and the marketplace involves a degree of risk, and so there needs to be a 'cultural congruence' of views internally which supports the external activities.[5] A strategic orientation is an amalgamation of inspiration and perspiration. In addition to creativity this approach requires consistent effort on a continuous basis.

Its use lies in its combination of realism and creativity, in an attempt to satisfy organizational objectives within a supportive climate.

The planning process

The need to adopt a future orientation in the selection of project opportunities is acceptable in principle. Actually putting the concept into action needs to be addressed. Planning ensures that an organization has the inbuilt capability to target and select lucrative project opportunities. Three simple yet fundamental questions need to be asked at this stage:

Q1: Where are we now?
Q2: Where do we want to go?
Q3: How are we going to get there?

The planning aspects of the strategic marketing process help to anticipate and satisfy opportunities by using established frameworks creatively in a formal process. There are seven steps to this process:

STEP ONE: ORGANIZATIONAL CONTEXT

Plans need to be in keeping with the sentiment expressed in the mission statement (if one exists) and compatible with the corporate objectives. Furthermore, marketing plans need to be compatible with all other functions and thereby enhance overall performance.

STEP TWO: THE MARKETING AUDIT/ENVIRONMENTAL ANALYSIS

The environment can be broken down into two sections: the internal environment and the external environment. The marketing audit forms the basis for understanding the current commercial performance of the organization. It is a necessary prerequisite for the satisfactory completion of the latter stages. All data collected are in an unrefined state, and should not be used as the basis for decision making.

STEP THREE: SITUATIONAL ANALYSIS/SWOT ANALYSIS

At this step, the unrefined data gathered in the audit are used to develop an understanding of the operating conditions. Data provide the opportunity to identify the company's strengths and weaknesses, and compare these with the prevailing opportunities and threats in the marketplace. The situational analysis is often illustrated in abbreviated table format referred to as a SWOT analysis (Strengths, Weaknesses, Opportunities and Threats). All issues should be discussed in comparison with the other players in the marketplace, with explanations for any performance which is perceived to be good or bad.

STEP FOUR: SETTING MARKETING OBJECTIVES

An objective essentially establishes what an organization wants to achieve. Many companies use the obvious marketing roles to assign appropriate objectives. For example objectives are set for marketing research, distribution, communication, pricing, etc. Unfortunately this approach does not satisfy our previously stated desire to identify opportunities and examine project selection decisions within a strategic manner. In an attempt to exert some control over the environment techniques have been developed to support a future orientation. These include:

- The Ansoff matrix
- The product portfolio matrix
- Gap analysis.

(These three techniques are described in Section 2.6.) We should stress the importance of this stage in the planning process. Any product/market anomalies which occur, unbalanced portfolios, and gaps identified in the performance are critical as they reveal not problems, but opportunities for the development of new project applications complementary to the existing range of products and the ability to match future customer needs.

STEP FIVE: MARKETING STRATEGIES

In simple terms, if an objective is what you want to achieve, then a strategy is the *means* by which the objectives are achieved. Management activity tends to concentrate on the development of the strategy according to the basic tenets of the marketing mix – called the *four Ps*: product, price, place and promotion.[3] However as the market is made up of a large number of customers, which are heterogeneous in nature, it would be impossible to satisfy all customers with one strategy. Customers need to be segmented into meaningful groups with similar characteristics. Segments of customers which are thus relatively homogeneous in nature can be used as the basis for matching project opportunities with appropriate marketing strategies. Three broad strategies emerge:

- Mass marketing
- Differentiated marketing
- Concentrated marketing.

The overriding aim is to ensure that the best possible synergy exists between project applications and anticipated market demand. The identification and targeting of segments which match organizational capabilities must be analysed to ensure that they can be approached on a profitable basis. Some common assessment criteria for examining the feasibility of segments include:

C1: How accessible are they?
C2: How measurable are they?
C3: How substantial are they?

These strategies for the marketing mix, product, price, place and promotion will all lead to the need for programmes of projects.

STEP SIX: MARKETING PROGRAMMES

As the planning develops it is evident that the process is becoming more concerned with implementation issues. Using the strategies outlined above, programmes for implementation can be developed aimed at operational activities used to move the organization towards meeting its objectives. Depending on the organizational structure, programme development tends to be allocated to the relevant functional areas. In some instances responsibility may fall to project teams to develop tactics which are complementary to the overall strategy. The tactical plans often revert back to traditional responsibilities related to the marketing mix, promotional plans, pricing plans, product plans and so forth. It is at this stage that the budgetary considerations take on a renewed significance. Although the ideal situation may involve designing budgets based on the objectives without consideration of potential constraints, in reality budgets often dictate the process of selection of objectives and subsequent strategy development. To be effective budgets should be action-oriented and flexible.

STEP SEVEN: FORECASTING

In an environment in a constant state of flux forecasting with accuracy is an almost impossible task. Forecasting has two main components: qualitative and quantitative. There is a wide range of statistical packages available which are used to examine the micro and macro environment, and they are often used in isolation. However, it is necessary to balance statistical evidence with qualitative evidence. The latter, though less scientific, none the less remains a useful instrument, and it includes instinct, opinion and analogy. Although much maligned, forecasting is essential, not only in the identification of new project opportunities, but as a starting point for measuring the implications of strategies and programmes and analysing achievements. This is a continuous process, as the data gathered are used to prepare updated forecasts for application to future planning horizons.

Organizational capabilities

In addition to the strategic commitment it is necessary to have the organizational capability to anticipate and capitalize on opportunities. It is not sufficient to be inspirational, an organization must have the processes and procedures which ensure innovation is an accepted mode of working and subsequent opportunities are adopted. The responsibility for the development of a future orientation is often allocated to a remote group who rarely have contact with the ultimate customer. In order to formalize and coordinate this role some organizations have 'Futures Committees' whose task is to monitor future opportunities. Futures committees will comprise senior managers for research, engineering, production and marketing. Ideally, those charged with the responsibility should be in tune with the environmental changes. It is necessary to develop an orientation with scope for freedom, as the future is fraught with uncertainties and is unpredictable so that desired conditions are rarely achieved. Thus, there is a necessity to accept the need to balance creativity with contingencies and incremental decision making.

Strategic marketing goes beyond the traditional scope of marketing management, emphasizing the need not only to match the current needs of the marketplace but also to anticipate future customer requirements. Thus it is insufficient to base future business plans on the current business situation – in essence the plans would be out-of-date. It is necessary to do more than merely react to the changing conditions and the opportunities this provides – companies must be proactive. Marketing is a continuous activity.

2.6 Techniques for setting marketing objectives

In this section we describe the three techniques for setting marketing objectives:

- The Ansoff matrix
- The product portfolio matrix
- Gap analysis.

The Ansoff matrix

The Ansoff matrix (Fig. 2.2) suggests that objectives should be considered on the basis of technological (product) newness and market newness.

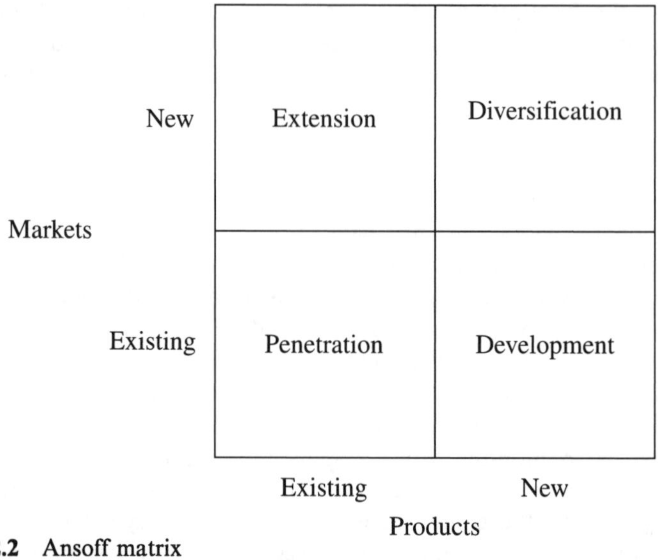

	Extension	Diversification
New		
Existing	Penetration	Development

New

Markets

Existing   Penetration   Development

Existing   New

Products

Figure 2.2   Ansoff matrix

Essentially, in order to survive, the firm must match its offering to the customer (such as projects) with the customer's identified and anticipated needs.

The four quadrants of the Ansoff matrix outline different objectives which can be perused at this stage. A company could opt for:

- *Penetration* Selling more of existing products in existing markets.
- *Development* Developing new products in existing markets.
- *Extension* Selling existing products in new markets.
- *Diversification* Developing new products for new markets.

If a comparison is made between a product development strategy and a market extension strategy it is possible to see the implications of each course of action.

If project selection is based on the development of new products, such as product design, facility construction or consultancy services, the implications for strategy are quite significant. The nature of new product development (NPD) creates a number of planning problems, as the whole NPD process needs to be managed. The crucial stage is to embrace the organizational implications and the sequence of events from idea generation to ultimate commercialization. Product development without a customer orientation is not sufficient to promote growth.

In contrast, the decision to maintain the existing product range creates a different range of problems. A market extension policy commonly seen in the expansion of geographical boundaries requires an evaluation of different sectors or potential foreign markets, culminating in the development of appropriate entry strategies for each target market.

The product portfolio matrix

The product portfolio matrix (Fig. 2.3) was developed in the 1960s by the Boston Consultancy Group as a means of understanding the current position of Specific Business Units, SBUs (such as products, services, projects, etc.), in the marketplace. It is also useful as a forecasting tool and can inject a note of realism into the development of objectives by management.

The matrix can tabulate SBUs on two axes, according to relative market share (measured in comparison with competitors) and relative market growth (measured against GDP). Each SBU is plotted on the matrix according to its size and position. SBUs are categorized in four ways;

1. *A problem child* is a product which has not yet achieved a dominant position in the marketplace, and so tends to be a high user of cash while not generating any replacement funds.
2. *A star* is a relatively new product in the portfolio with a comparatively high market share, and so tends to be self financing in cash terms.

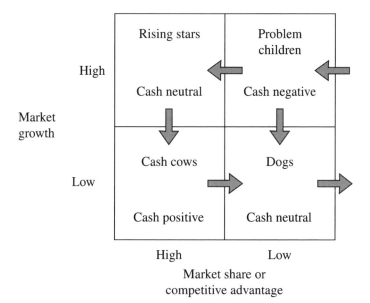

Figure 2.3   The product portfolio matrix

3. *A cash cow* is a leader in a stable marketplace, but with little additional growth, and so in terms of cash generation the performance is excellent.
4. *A dog* has a limited future in a potentially shrinking marketplace.

Once a company has developed a matrix it can identify whether it has a balanced portfolio. In essence the objective is to create a balanced portfolio which minimizes risk by offsetting short-term secure activities with potentially risky high return opportunities. The most commonly accepted objectives emerging from this approach are:

– Build
– Hold
– Harvest
– Divest.

An unbalanced portfolio could have serious repercussions in the future as a disproportionate number of problem children could result in low growth and poor profit performance. Instability may be created by an over-preponderance of stars due to the strain on company resources. Furthermore a large number of cash cows may provide plentiful cash flow but at the expense of growth. Finally, if a large number of SBUs are considered to be dogs, a situation may be created of poor cash flow, low growth and inadequate product performance.

Gap analysis

Gap analysis (Fig. 2.4) is used as a method to focus attention on the future by drawing one's attention to creative ways of improving performance. A company establishes that if objectives set for sales and profit are not achieved in a particular planning horizon then a 'Gap' will occur between the actual and desired situation.

Several broad opportunities exist, including:

– To develop existing business activities and encourage further growth (similar to market penetration in the Ansoff matrix).
– To develop or acquire related business activities (similar to product development).
– To acquire unrelated business activities (that is diversification).

2.7 Summary

1. Strategic marketing can help organizations identify the need for projects, to develop new products, to introduce new technology, to exploit new

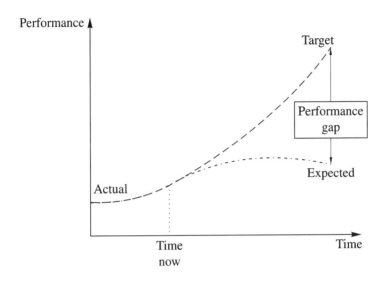

Figure 2.4   Gap analysis

markets, or to streamline the organization itself, in order to respond to changing customer requirements and to remain ahead of the competition.
2. In order to survive, organizations must have a planning horizon beyond the current year.
3. Technological development is a key element of competitive strategy.
4. There are three key ingredients to strategic marketing:
   – Organizational climate
   – The planning process
   – Organizational capabilities.
5. There are three fundamental questions in the planning process:
   – Where are we?
   – Where do we want to go?
   – How do we get there?
6. There are seven steps in the planning process:
   – Organizational context
   – Marketing audit/environmental analysis
   – Situational analysis/SWOT analysis
   – Setting marketing objectives
   – Marketing strategies
   – Marketing programmes
   – Forecasting.
7. There are three tools for setting marketing objectives:
   – The Ansoff matrix

– Product portfolio matrix
– Gap analysis.

References

1. See for instance:
   Kerrin, R.A. and Peterson, R.A., *Perspectives on Strategic Marketing Management*, 2nd edition, Allyn and Bacon, 1983.
   Aaker, D.A., *Strategic Marketing Management*, Wiley, 1984.
   Day, G.S., *Strategic Market Planning: the pursuit of competitive advantage*, West Publishing, 1984.
   Kotler, P., *Marketing Management: Analysis, planning and control*, 5th edition, Prentice-Hall, 1984.
   Luck, D.J. and Ferrell, O.C., *Marketing, Strategy, and Plans*, 2nd edition, Prentice-Hall, 1984.
2. Cravens D.W., *Strategic Marketing*, Irwin, 1982.
3. McDonald, M.B. *Marketing Plans: How to prepare them, how to use them*, Heinemann, 1987.
4. Georgiou, L., *Post Innovation Performance, Technological Development, and Competition*, Macmillan, 1986.
5. Brown, R., 'Marketing: a function and a philosophy', *Quarterly Review of Marketing*, Spring/Summer, 1988.

3
Estimating costs and revenues

Rodney Turner and Dan Remenyi*

3.1 Introduction

Having identified project opportunities, the owner must decide whether the cost of undertaking the project will be repaid by the potential benefit. There are several steps in that process:

1. The owner determines the expected cost of undertaking the project (the cost of delivering the facility) and the expected benefit to be obtained from the exploiting the opportunity (the revenue stream expected from operating the facility and selling the product).
2. They should then assess the risks of the project. That is they must consider the likelihood that the cost will turn out higher than expected, and the benefits lower, and determine what impact that will have on the profitability of the project. They may also try to find ways to reduce those risks.
3. Finally they must determine if the benefits do justify the costs, taking account of all the risks, and so determine the expected profitability of the project through a formal process of investment appraisal.

This chapter describes the first step. We start by considering methods for estimating the cost of projects, starting with the engineering construction industry, where techniques are highly developed. We then describe techniques developed in the building and IT industries. The estimates of likely revenues will usually be determined from marketing or efficiency studies, and will be calculated as part of a feasibility study.[1] We describe work on estimating expected benefits from IT systems. The timing of expenditure and returns must be determined, as part of investment

---

*Additional research was undertaken by Kevin Herriot and John White on estimating in the building industry and by Eleri Evans and Clive Mason on estimating in the IT industry.

appraisal, to optimize the returns from the project, and to determine the cash flow requirements. We consider the scheduling of estimates. The estimates must also be adjusted to allow for inflation, currency changes or different costs in different locations. We begin by showing how the accuracy of an estimate (the quality of the answer) is dependent on the amount of effort put into reaching the estimate, and what costs are estimated.

The next two chapters describe the subsequent two steps in turn.

3.2 Types of estimate

It costs money (in the form of human effort) to estimate the cost of a project. It is usually neither possible nor realistic to go straight to a highly detailed and accurate estimate for a project, without first taking a view whether the effort expended in estimating is likely to be worth while. Therefore the estimate on a project is evolved through several stages. Projects go through several stages of development,[1] typically:

− Proposal and initiation
− Design and appraisal
− Execution and control
− Finalization and close-out.

There are five types of estimate, of varying accuracy, associated with the first three stages of this life cycle (Table 3.1). The reason for producing these various estimates is that it requires increasing effort to produce each one. Each estimate is therefore used to justify the effort in producing the next, until the sanction estimate is used to justify the execution of the project (including the full, detailed design or control estimate).

Table 3.2 and Fig. 3.1 illustrate the relationship between the accuracy of the estimates and the effort in their production. Figure 3.1 is derived from figures measured in the engineering construction industry in the 1960s.[2] In the IT industry it may require four times as much effort to produce an

Table 3.1 Types of estimate − purpose and stage of production

Type of estimate	Stage of production	Purpose
Proposal	Pre-proposal and initiation	Appraise viability to start feasibility study
Budget	End-proposal and initiation	Appraise viability to start systems design
Sanction	End-design and appraisal	Appraise viability to approve project, obtain funding, allocate resources
Control	Pre-execution and control	Measure progress, assign resources
Tender	Via-execution and control	Prepare tender

Table 3.2   Accuracy of estimates and the level of effort in their production

Type of estimate	Accuracy (%)	Level of effort as % of project cost
Proposal	±30 to ±50	0.02–0.1
Budget	±20 to ±35	0.1–0.3
Sanction	±10 to ±25	0.4–0.8
Control	±5 to ±15	1–3
Tender	±2 to ±5	5–10

estimate of similar accuracy. Figure 3.1 shows a typical learning curve, following an inverse square law, that is to double the accuracy of the estimate requires four times as much effort. The way to achieve increasing accuracy is to estimate at lower and lower levels of work breakdown (Table 3.3). Table 3.4 gives an example for a large engineering project. At any level of the work breakdown structure (WBS), there is no point calculating and quoting the estimates to a greater degree of accuracy than the figure in the right-hand column, and any contingency added at that level of the WBS must be at least of this amount as a level of contingency is already included through the accuracy to which the figures are calculated.

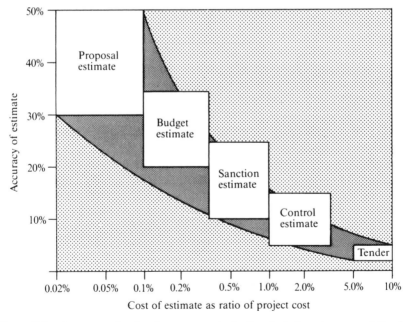

Figure 3.1   Accuracy of estimate versus cost of estimate (a learning curve following an inverse square law)

Table 3.3 Types of estimate versus level in work breakdown structure

Type of estimate	Lowest level of Estimating in WBS	Accuracy of estimate of			
		Project	Work area	Work pack	Activity
Proposal	Areas of work	±50%	±100%	–	–
Budget	Work packages	±20%	±40%	±100%	–
Sanction	Work package scoping	±10%	±20%	±50%	(±150%)
Control	Activities	±5%	±10%	±25%	±75%
Tender	Tasks	±2%	±4%	±10%	±30%
Assumed number per project		1	4	25	200

Table 3.4 Levels of estimating in a large engineering project

Level of WBS	Number in project	Average cost	Accuracy (ratio)	Accuracy (value)
Project	1	£100 000 000	±1%	±£1 000 000
Area of work	100	£1 000 000	±10%	±£100 000
Work package	1 000	£100 000	±30%	±£30 000
Activity	10 000	£10 000	±100%	±£10 000

3.3 Structuring the estimate

We consider the components of cost on a project and how these components are incorporated into the cost control cube.

Cost components

The cost of a project may consist of several components,[1] including:

- *Labour* The cost of people employed by the parent company involved in executing project tasks, including people designing and delivering the facility.
- *Materials* The cost of all materials bought via the parent company and consumed in delivering the facility. This may be materials contained in the final product or consumables used on project tasks.
- *Plant and equipment* Materials used in delivering the facility, but not consumed, but can be reused on subsequent projects. They may be bought or hired, but either way each project only pays a part of their price new. This component should only include the cost of plant and equipment born by the parent company.
- *Subcontract* The cost of labour and materials as above provided by

outside contractors. Costs will be included in this heading where their control is not within the scope of the parent organization.

- *Management* The cost of people and materials involved in managing the project. They are directly attributable to the project, but not to specific tasks. The cost of management becomes a smaller proportion of the total cost as the size grows. Typically it is about 5 per cent on a project of £10 million, and 1 per cent on a project of £1 billion.[2]
- *Overhead and administration* The cost of administering items included in labour, materials and subcontract, including costs directly attributable to some items such as transport, but also including costs shared between items such as procurement, storage and absorption of some parent company overheads
- *Fees and taxation* The cost of insurance, finance, licence agreements. Taxation may be regarded as a special type of fee.
- *Inflation* This may or may not be ignored in the estimates.

  Two cases when it is ignored are on publicly funded infrastructure projects, and projects where project costs, raw material costs and revenues are expected to inflate at the same rate.

  Two cases where it is not ignored is where there is expected to be differential inflation between project costs, raw material costs and revenues and by contractors preparing fixed price tenders.
- *Contingency* This may be added as blanket figures or calculated according to risk. In the copy of the estimate shown to the owner, contingency is usually distributed among the other headings. In the copy shown to the team, the manager should keep contingency back in a *project manager's reserve*, and show them just the raw estimates. Given that 'work done expands to fill the time available', if contingency is included in the sub-budgets given to work-package managers and subcontractors, then they will spend up to that amount. It is common for project managers to maintain three estimates:[1]

  The baseline or estimated prime cost: the amount communicated to the project team.

  The most likely out-turn: the amount the project manager expects to spend.

  The budget: the amount the owner is willing to spend.

On a typical engineering project the budget will be 10–20 per cent higher than the baseline, with the most likely out-turn half-way between. On information systems and R&D projects the contingency may be much higher.

Structuring the estimate

These seven or eight headings constitute the *cost breakdown structure*

(CBS)[1]. The three breakdown structures, work breakdown structure (WBS), organization breakdown structure (OBS), and cost breakdown structure (CBS), combine to form the *cost control cube* (Fig. 3.2.). The concept of the cost control cube was developed by the United States Department of Defenses, (DOD) in the 1950s, as the basis of its C/SPEC methodology for controlling project costs (sometimes called C/SCSC). All costs can be assigned to a cell of the cube, and through the cube all costs have a position in each of the three breakdown structures. A project aggregate can then be prepared by summing along any of the three directions.

Of course a large number, often the majority, of cells in the cube will contain no costs. For instance:

– A work element may be wholly assigned to one subcontractor, a single entity in both the OBS and CBS.
– A work element may consume labour only and of one type only.
– A work element may be created to assign management costs.

The cost control cube provides a structure for the estimate, used to create the estimate, and in the subsequent control of costs. The WBS and OBS are evolved to the current lowest level according to the estimate being produced (Tables 3.1–3.3) and costs assigned to each element in the WBS/OBS matrix

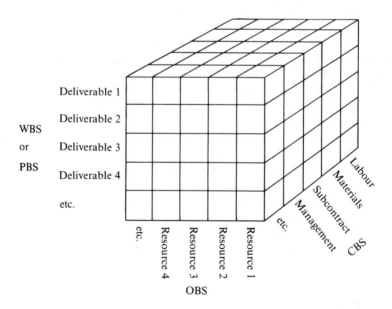

Figure 3.2   Cost control cube

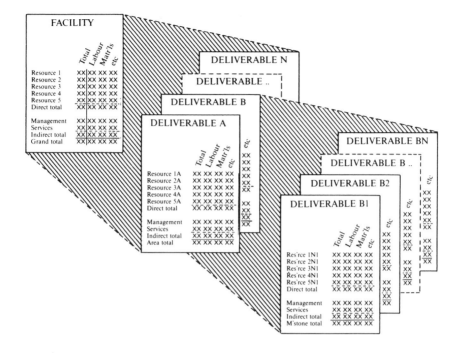

Figure 3.3 Cascade of estimates through the WBS, OBS and CBS

against each cost element. This provides a cascade of estimates through the WBS/OBS (Figure 3.3). The estimate is then aggregated to the project level.

Figure 3.4 shows a typical OBS for a chemical plant. A page like this would be prepared for the facility as a whole, that is aggregated from similar pages for each subassembly (intermediate product) of the facility, and those in turn for each component of the subassembly. Figure 3.5 is a page at the plant area level for the plant in Fig. 3.4.

3.4 Estimating methods

There are several ways of preparing estimates for the various cost components. The most direct is to break the work down to a lower level of detail, estimate the cost at that level and sum back up. However, the arguments of Section 3.2 imply that level of detail cannot always be justified, especially at earlier stages of the project life cycle. It is therefore necessary to use other methods which enable estimates to be produced at higher levels of work breakdown. We consider methods used in the engineering construction, building and information systems industries. It must be recognized that

PROJECT ESTIMATE   NORTHERN ENERGY AND CHEMICAL INDUSTRIES PLC   02-Jan-9X

PROJECT:	Petrochemical Plant	CODE:	THNS	ISSUE:	A
WORK AREA:	....	CODE:	....	AUTHOR:	JRT
WORK PACKAGE:	....	CODE:	....	APPRVD:	CME
ACTIVITY:	....	CODE:	....	DATE:	02-Jan-9X

| | 1000 tonne per day plant | | | | SCALE EXPONENT | COST FACTOR | 1500 tonne per day plant | | | |
	Material £,000	Erection £,000	Function £,000	Plant £,000	n	1.5^n	Material £,000	Erection £,000	Function £000	Plant £000
Main plant items										
– Vessels	13.33	0.63	13.96		0.65	1.30	17.35	0.82	18.17	
– Furnace and boiler	2.89	0.14	3.03		0.70	1.33	3.84	0.18	4.02	
– Machines and drives	9.73	0.46	10.19		0.75	1.36	13.19	0.62	13.81	
– Vendor packages	6.77	0.32	7.09		0.75	1.36	9.18	0.43	9.61	
– Other	0.00	0.13	0.13		0.70	1.33	0.00	0.17	0.17	
MPI total: Materials	32.72	–	32.72				43.55	–	43.55	
MPI total: Erection	–	1.67	1.67				–	2.22	2.22	
Bulk Items										
– Piping	1.22	1.88	3.10		0.70	1.33	1.62	2.50	4.12	
– Instruments	0.64	1.10	0.74		0.60	1.28	0.82	0.13	0.94	
– Computer control system	1.56	0.88	2.44		0.70	1.33	2.07	1.17	3.24	
– Electrical	1.82	0.53	2.35		0.70	1.33	2.42	0.70	3.12	
– Structural		0.26	0.26		0.65	1.30	0.00	0.34	0.34	
– Civil		2.11	2.11		0.65	1.30	0.00	2.75	2.75	
– Painting		0.10	0.10		0.65	1.30	0.00	0.13	0.13	
– Insulation		1.50	1.50		0.65	1.30	0.00	1.95	1.95	
– Buildings		0.12	0.12		0.65	1.30	0.00	0.16	0.16	
– Plant modification		0.70	0.70		0.70	1.33	0.00	0.93	0.93	
Bulk items total	5.24	8.18	13.42				6.93	10.75	17.68	
TOTAL DIRECT COSTS				47.81						63.45
Engineering – Design			8.40		0.50	1.22			10.29	
– Software			0.53		1.20	1.63			0.86	
Construction – Management			3.22		0.65	1.30			4.19	
– Services			1.50		0.65	1.30			1.95	
Works – Start-up			6.70		0.65	1.30			8.72	
– Working capital			9.56		1.00	1.50			12.69	
Contingency			4.78						6.34	
TOTAL INDIRECT COSTS				34.69						45.05
CAPITAL COST OF ERECTED PLANT				82.50						108.50
Inflation			4.13						5.42	
Licence fees and royalties			0.41						0.54	
Insurance			0.83						1.08	
TOTAL OVERHEADS				5.36						7.05
TOTAL CAPITAL COST				87.86						115.55

Figure 3.4   Sample OBS for a chemical plant (plant level)

PROJECT ESTIMATE		NORTHERN ENERGY AND CHEMICAL INDUSTRIES PLC					02-Jan-9X
PROJECT:	Petrochemical Plant	CODE:	THNS	ISSUE:	A		
WORK AREA:	Synthesis	CODE:	THNS5	AUTHOR:	JRT		
WORK PACKAGE:	....	CODE:	....	APPRVD:	CME		
ACTIVITY:	....	CODE:	....	DATE:	02-Jan-9x		

	Material £,000	Erection £,000	Function £,000	Plant £,000		Parametric ratio Function %MPI	Plant %MPI
Main plant items							
– Vessels	4.85	0.23	5.08				
– Furnace and boiler	0.00	0.00	0.00				
– Machines and drives	3.67	0.17	3.84				
– Vendor packages	1.55	0.07	1.62				
– Other	0.00	0.00	0.00				
MPI Total: Materials	10.07	–	10.07			100.0%	
MPI Total: Erection	–	0.47	0.47			4.7%	
Bulk Items							
– Piping			1.21			12.0%	
– Instruments			0.23			2.3%	
– Computer control system			0.82			8.1%	
– Electrical			0.81			8.0%	
– Structural			0.09			0.9%	
– Civil			0.76			7.5%	
– Painting			0.03			0.3%	
– Insulation			0.50			5.0%	
– Buildings			0.06			0.6%	
– Plant modification			0.24			2.4%	
Bulk items total			4.74			0.47	
TOTAL DIRECT COSTS				15.29			1.52
Engineering – Design			1.72			17.1%	
– Software			0.09			0.9%	
Construction – Management			0.80			7.9%	
– Services			0.33			3.3%	
Works – Start-up			1.43			14.2%	
– Working capital			3.06			30.4%	
Contingency			1.53			15.2%	
TOTAL INDIRECT COSTS				8.96			0.89
CAPITAL COST OF ERECTED PLANT				24.24			2.41
Inflation							
Licence fees and royalties							
Insurance							
TOTAL OVERHEADS				0.00			
TOTAL CAPITAL COST				24.24			

Figure 3.5 Sample OBS for a chemical plant (plant area level)

all these methods will give an estimate of the cost of the work. The actual *price* charged by a contractor will depend on the current market conditions.

Methods in the engineering construction industry

The engineering construction industry has well-advanced methods of estimating at all levels of work breakdown[2] (Table 3.5). These rely heavily on historical data and include:

Table 3.5   Estimating methods used to prepare types of estimate

Type of estimate	Accuracy	Estimating methods
Proposal estimate	± 50%	Step counting
		Exponential (plant level)
Budget estimate	± 20%	Exponential (MPI level)
		Parametric (plant level)
Sanction estimate	± 10%	Parametric (MPI level, vendor quotes)
Control estimate	± 5%	Parametric (MPI level, firm prices)
Tender estimate	± 2%	Detailed estimating

- *Step counting methods* These assume cost is function of the number of functions and plant throughput. In the engineering construction industry standard formulae and tables have been derived from empirical data. Some of these formulae are still valid after 20 years, because of the stability of the technology. The formulae exist at several levels of the WBS, the plant level, plant area level or main plant item (MPI) level.
- *Exponential methods* These assume cost is proportional to the size of the facility, to some power. In the engineering construction industry, this is called the *two thirds power law* because the exponent is usually between 0.6 and 0.75. If you know the cost of a plant of standard size, the cost of a larger or smaller one can be derived. The law can be applied at several levels of WBS or OBS; the lower the level, the more accurate the estimate at the plant level. Figure 3.4 contains exponents from George[2] for chemical plant, applied at the first level of OBS, showing how they can be used to convert from a 1000 tonne/day plant to a 1500 tonne/day plant.
- *Parametric methods* These assume all costs are proportional to some core cost. On chemical plants this is the MPI. Tables of ratios exist giving the cost of other items as ratios the MPI, dependent on the value of the MPI, its type and the severity of duty. These tables exist at several levels of WBS. Figure 3.5 contains data at the plant area level.[2] The techniques are so advanced in the engineering construction industry that estimates based on prices of placed order and derived at the equipment levels are

sufficiently accurate for the control estimate. It is in this way that the cost of estimating is being reduced.

- *Detailed estimates* They are prepared by contracting companies tendering for work, where the level of accuracy is of the same order of magnitude as the expected profit margin. At the lowest levels the costs are derived from standard cost books or from parametric data.
- *Computer-aided estimating* This has have been derived to support parametric estimating and detailed estimating. These are often based on a bill of materials (BOM) or a bill of quantities (BOQ) for standard components.

Possible sources of data for preparing estimates are:
Suppliers' quotations (typical, budget, detailed)
Trade literature, technical literature, textbooks
Company historical data, standard costs
Computer systems
Black books
Government figures.

Estimating methods in the building industry

Table 3.6 shows when, by whom and how estimates are made in the building industry. Methods of estimating include:

Table 3.6   Method of estimating versus stage of use

Level	WBS type	Estimate	User	Method	Design stage
1	Unit	Pre-proposal	QS	Functional	Brief
2	Space	Proposal	QS	Approximate	Sketch
3	Element	Budget	QS	Elemental	Sketch/detail
4	Feature	Sanction	QS	Empirical	Detail
5	Item	Control	QS	BOQ	Detail/working
6	Operations	Tender	Contractor	Network	Working
7	Resources	Work	Contractor	SOR	Working

QS   Quantity surveyor.
BOQ   Bill of quantities.
SOR   Schedule of rates.

- *Approximate methods* The cost is assumed to be proportional to the lettable floor area of a building of appropriate type, use and quality. Tables of figures are given, for instance, in Spon.[3] The figures given include costs not only for the whole building but also for individual services within the building (all related back to the area of the whole building). The cost given, in £/m^2, can range by a factor of three for a given type of building, and so it is important to be aware of the use and quality. The user must also be aware of what services are and are not included in the costs calculated. However, the figures give estimates accurate enough for proposal estimates. The figures given are also only valid in Outer London at a certain time. Tables are given to update the estimates for other locations and other times (see Section 3.6 below).

- *Functional methods* A coarser method of approximate estimating some-times used is to estimate in terms of the functional requirements, that is cost per bed in a hospital, the cost per pupil in a school, the cost per seat in an office building. These estimates have the same validity in terms of location and time as the approximate methods, and will be prepared at an earlier stage of the project than the approximate methods.
- *Elemental estimating* In this approach the building is broken down into major elements, and the cost estimated as a ratio of the assumed duty or floor area of that element. The essential difference between this and the previous method is that the cost of each service is calculated from the size of that service, not the floor area of the whole building. This method can produce an estimate accurate enough for budget, or even sanction, purposes. Once this estimate has been accepted, it can be used to generate a complete bill of quantities.
- *Empirical estimating* In this approach, costs are extrapolated from the cost of schemes of similar size, scope and type. Historical data are used to establish overall parameters and indicators which influence cost. These can be arrived at by regression analysis or curve fitting, from established data or industry standard formulae.[4]
- *Schedule of rates* This is not so much an estimating method, as a detailed breakdown of the cost of doing individual tasks on a building or construction site. A schedule of rates can be used for building up a detailed estimate. Or they can be used for building up costs associated with small projects, or even individual, isolated tasks, such as maintenance projects and maintenance jobs respectively. A schedule of rates will often be used on cost plus contracts (see Chapter 17).
- *Bill of quantities* This is equivalent to the computerized estimate described above. It will often be built up from a CAD drawing of the building, using standard bills of quantities for repeated elements.

Estimating methods in the IT industry

The IT industry has developed a set of estimating techniques to meet its own particular needs. There are major differences between estimating on software projects versus construction projects, for the following reasons:

1. Software projects are not mechanistic (though neither is engineering design). The activities are indeterminate and cannot be measured by simple means. Task size and complexity can be assessed by experts, but this is not normally reliable. The more complex the project, the less reliable the estimate.
2. Because of the rapid change of technology, there is not a wealth of historical data. The COCOMO model described later was based on information from 63 projects. While it gives a good base estimate for software projects, it is only applicable to programming using 3GLs.

Techniques for estimating on software projects are described by many authors,[5] and include:

- *Analogy* Estimates are made by comparison to previous, similar projects. This is probably the most valid technique for many organizations, but does rely on historical records. The technique relies on the use of a consistent software development life cycle.[1] Using the technique to extrapolate between projects of different size can also be fraught with danger, given the non-linear relationship between size, effort and time-scale.
- *Top-down estimating* The estimate is made against stages of a standard life cycle,[1] and activities within the life cycle, often applying fixed percentage allocations to each stage. This approach has several advantages:
  A detailed design of the final system is not required, so the approach can be used at an early stage.
  The technique is comparatively inexpensive.
  It does not constrain the use of other techniques.
- *Bottom–up estimating* This is the detailed estimate built up from a knowledge of the design of the system. It is most effectively used to provide an estimate of the next stage of a project prepared on completion of the current stage. The technique is expensive, and has several disadvantages which mean it must almost always be used in conjunction with other techniques:
  Errors tend to compound, usually resulting in underestimation of the total cost of a system
  It takes no account of the shortened project time-scales – two people do not take half the time of one person to do a job.[6]
- *Mathematical models* These relate effort and time to lines of code, similar to step counting and exponential methods. These methods rely on historical data, and must be tailored to an organization's needs. The models only apply to the development stage of a project. In many of the models, the equations take the following form:

$$\text{effort} = A * (\text{size})^b$$
$$\text{time} = C * (\text{effort})^d$$

where size is measured in thousands of lines of code, effort is measured in man-months, and time in months. Table 3.7 contains coefficients for several models.[7] In most cases the exponent b is greater than one, giving relatively larger cost for bigger systems. These models take no account of the effects of time compression. The constraint models provide correction factors. Table 3.7 also shows the effort and time predicted by the different methods for a system of 40 000 lines of code, and software development costs of £4000 per man month. The figures vary quite wildly. Each model was developed in a different organization, and therefore represent the characteristic of that organization. This means that organizations should develop their own models. It also means that organizations should question their software development environment if their estimates are uncompetitive.

Table 3.7   Mathematical estimating models

Model	A	b	C	d	Effort (m-mths)	Duration (months)	Cost (£,000)
Watson Felix (IBM)	5.2	0.91	2.47	0.35	149	14.2	592
Nelson (SDC)	4.9	0.98	3.04	0.36	192	19.8	728
COCOMO (organic)	2.4	1.05	2.5	0.38	115	15.2	462
COCOMO (semi-d)	3.0	1.12	2.5	0.35	187	15.6	747
Frederic	2.4	1.18	-	-	186		746
COCOMO (embed'd)	3.6	1.20	2.5	0.32	301	15.5	1205
Phister	1.0	1.275	-	-	110		441
Jones	1.0	1.40	-	-	175		700
Halstead	0.7	1.50	-	-	177		708

– *Function point analysis* The mathematical models apply only to the development stage of the project (cutting code), which typically accounts for only 50 per cent of the cost. Function point analysis counts the function points, which represent the total functionality of the system.[7] Function points include:
   Inputs: forms and screens
   Outputs: reports and screens
   End-user enquiries
   Logical data files
   Interfaces to other systems.
Function points are converted to an estimate by:

comparison with previous systems – applicable to the whole life cycle; converting to lines of code – applicable to the development stage only.
- *Constraint models* The models above take no account of the reducing efficiency caused by decreasing duration.[6] Reducing duration increases costs.[1] Constraint models have been developed in an attempt to calculate the effects of time-scale compression. They are still relatively new.

Most of the models above were developed for Third Generation Languages (3GLs) such as COBOL and FORTRAN. However, all bar the mathematical models are applicable to Fourth Generation Languages (4GLs), but with suitable new historical data.

3.5 Estimating and measuring benefits

The expected returns from the project will be determined by the feasibility and marketing studies (see for instance Turner[1] and Chapter 2). For an engineering project this may simply be a matter of estimating (guessing) the levels of sales, and the price and profitability of the product. To this income stream must be added any increased revenue due to increased efficiency from eliminating old products and any lost revenue from sales of old products must be subtracted.

For IT and organizational change projects, the benefits may be more obtuse, arising from increased efficiency and facilitation of operations.[8] Estimating them relies on subjective assessment rather than quantitative calculation – although it can be argued that sales and price forecasts are also subjective. The remainder of this section is devoted to estimating the benefits from IT projects.

Measuring and managing IT benefits

Many firms have little idea whether the money they spend on their computers is well spent or not. They do not know whether they could find cheaper sources of computing, but, more importantly, they do not know whether they are actually getting the right level of benefits from their systems. In fact some systems have actually been known to produce more disbenefits than benefits, and so called intangible benefits sometimes do not amount to anything of value to the business. Also the risks which the firm faces due to its computer system are often not properly understood, provided for, controlled or assessed. However this need not be the case. Current research clearly indicates that there are various ways that firms can assess the performance of their information system department. Research findings clearly show that benefit measuring techniques must be chosen to match the type of system under review. Therefore the first step is to categorize the firm's systems. The main categories used are automate systems, informate systems and transformate systems, and different approaches to systems assessment are required for each type. Automate systems require a relatively straightforward approach using traditional cost-benefit analysis, while informate systems require detailed decision analysis. The evaluation of transformate systems involves a much wider perspective of the business and the role of information in the firm. To justify a transformate systems a proper business case must be made in exactly the same way as if the firm intended to enter a new market, launch a new product or acquire a new business.

The above benefit measuring techniques may be regarded as single point evaluation procedures. By this it is meant that each individual system has to be evaluated, and the sum of their values or benefits aggregated to be able to ascertain the overall effectiveness of the IS function. This can be a long and tedious job. However some firms prefer using a holistic approach to their systems' effectiveness, and user surveys form the main approach in this case. The type of survey is referred to as a GAP survey, which attempts to measure the difference between what the users think is important to help them with their work and what they feel is being delivered by the ISD. The GAPs measured in this way can point to where expenditure is being well spent or not. This survey approach is becoming more and more popular as firms strive to answer the question of how well the ISD is performing. GAP analysis by the survey is relatively inexpensive and may be performed in a reasonably short period of time.

Every firm can improve the performance of their information systems department, not to mention spend their IT budgets more efficiently. In some cases the IT expenditure may be reduced, but in nearly every case it can be fine-tuned so that benefits available through the use of computers are optimized.

The techniques used to measure IT performance are not necessarily difficult. In some cases cost–benefit analysis (CBA) is applied which is fairly straightforward except for perhaps the analysis of intangible benefits. Cost displacement, cost avoidance, decision analysis, time release and breakeven projections are the most popular form of CBA. In other cases opinion surveys are used to find the level of user satisfaction.

3.6 Scheduling the estimate

The timing of both expenditure and returns must be determined. There are three reasons for this:
1. To assess the viability of the project.
2. To optimize the returns from the project.
3. To schedule the cash flow requirements during the delivery of the project.

The timing of the returns will be determined as part of the marketing or feasibility study by which they were determined. They may not be constant, but they will usually be assumed to be fairly uniform.

The timing of project expenditure will be determined using standard project scheduling techniques. These are well known, and well written up elsewhere,[1] and so it is not our intention to describe them further here. Scheduling of the expenditure will usually lead to the classic S-curve shape of cumulative project expenditure (Fig. 3.6).

However, it is worth commenting on the three reasons for scheduling the expenditure.

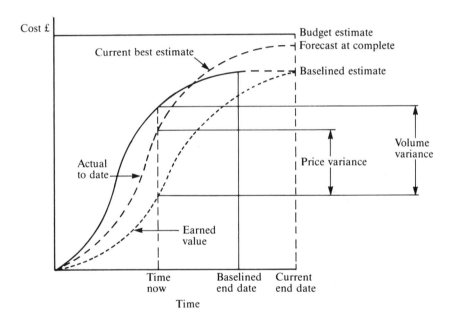

Figure 3.6 Classic S-curve of project expenditure

Assessing viability

Financing charges must be paid from the day money is borrowed, and yet cannot be repaid until the facility delivered by the project begins to earn revenue. Hence the relative timing of expenditure and revenue will have an impact on the viability of the project. It may be worth while delaying the procurement of large items of equipment to install them just before the facility is commissioned. Alternatively, it may be preferable to spend money more quickly, in order to complete the project earlier (Fig 3.7). Most of the modern financial appraisal techniques take account of the timing of expenditure and revenue (see Chapter 5) by allowing for the time value of money, that is by accounting for the financing charges. However, these techniques usually only take an annual view, and so if the work of the project is wholly contained within one financial year, they will not differentiate between different build profiles with the same total cost. However, you are still paying your financing charges from the day you borrow the money.

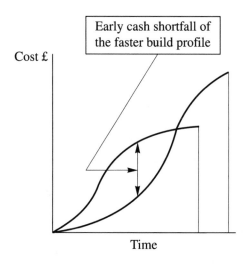

Figure 3.7   Different build profiles for a project

Optimizing the returns

We have just said that you may be able to vary the overall cost of the project by adopting different build profiles. Figure 3.7 shows the project being achieved earlier and at a cheaper overall cost, by undertaking more expensive work at an earlier stage. However, without changing the sequence of the work, you can change the overall cost just by varying the time taken to do it.

There is in fact an optimum time-scale for a project. If you try to do it more quickly or more slowly, the project will cost you more (Fig. 3.8). The explanation for this is that there are two elements to the cost of a project: a time-dependent one and a time-independent one. Though one is nominally time independent, if you try to do the work too quickly, inefficiencies creep in. For example, 100 man-days is the same whether 5 people take 20 days or 10 people take 10 days. However, if you try to use 20 people, you may find it

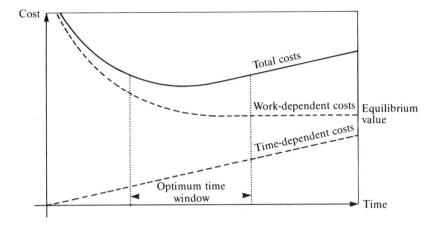

Figure 3.8   Timing of minimum cost of a project

takes 6 days and so consumes 120 man-days. The time dependent costs are mainly overhead costs. You have only one project manager. If the project takes 100 days, that is 100 man-days; if it takes 200 days that is 200 man-days. Add these two costs together and you get the optimum time window of cost (Fig 3.8). However, optimizing cost may not be your key criterion – it may be optimizing profit, and the returns may also be time dependent. Usually the later you deliver the project, the less return you get. There are two reasons:

– There may be only a limited time window for the project.
– Because of the time value of money, money earned later is worth less than money earned earlier.

Hence, the project duration which gives maximum profit may not correspond with the time that gives minimum cost (Fig. 3.9). In this figure, it is assumed the market for the product does not start until a certain point, and this is the timing of project duration which gives maximum profit. However, if the market window were to extend earlier, this is the time that would give you maximum profit, because the increased cost of earlier completion is greater than the increased profit.

Timing of finance
It is critical to be able to predict the timing of the cash flow requirements of

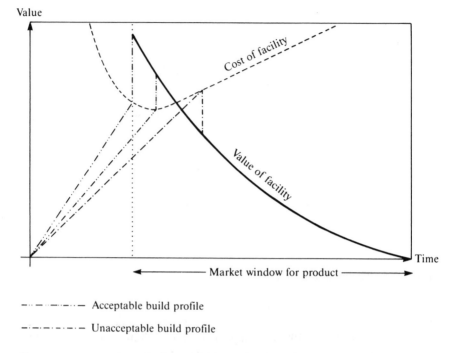

---··—··—··— Acceptable build profile

—·—·—·—·— Unacceptable build profile

Figure 3.9 Timing of optimum return from a project

your project, so this can be agreed with the financiers, and money made available at the rate at which it is spent. There are stories of 'smart' project managers driving their organizations to bankruptcy by trying to complete their projects ahead of schedule. If you had agreed the slower more expensive spend profile in Fig 3.7, and you then achieved the faster cheaper one, your company would need to finance the higher earlier expenditure. If it was not able to, it could go into liquidation. Scheduling the spend profile is critical – keeping to it is even more critical.

3.7 Updating estimates

Estimating data are only valid at a certain time, in a certain place and in a given currency. It will almost certainly be necessary to allow for inflation. It may also be necessary to convert from one country to another and from one currency to another. Tables of ratios exist for these conversions.[2] For example, to calculate the cost in one year given the cost in the second, you merely need to multiply by the ratio of the price index in the two years, (usually calculated with respect to a base year):

$$\frac{\text{Cost in year 1}}{\text{Cost in year 2}} = \frac{\text{Price index in year 1}}{\text{Price index in year 2}}$$

Without any other guidance you can use the retail price index, RPI. However tables exist for many industries giving inflation rates different to RPI. Tables are published for most countries of the world. They also exist for ratios of exchange rates for years past, and for differences in labour and material costs between different countries. Therefore, given the price of a project in one country in its local currency in a year past you can calculate the cost of the same project in another country in its local currency in another year past. The tables also predict future rates.

3.8 Summary

1. There are five types of estimate of increasing accuracy obtained through the project life cycle:
   - Proposal estimate
   - Budget estimate
   - Sanction estimate
   - Control estimate
   - Tender estimate.
2. Estimating costs time and effort. To double the accuracy of the estimate quadruples the effort required. Estimates of increasing accuracy are obtained by working at lower levels of work breakdown.
3. The cost components of a project include:
   - Labour
   - Materials
   - Plant and equipment
   - Subcontract
   - Management
   - Overhead and administration
   - Fees and taxation
   - Inflation
   - Other contingency.
4. These constitute a cost breakdown structure (CBS). When combined with the work breakdown structure (WBS) and organization breakdown structure (OBS) the WBS × OBS × CBS constitute the cost control cube, a tool for estimating and controlling costs.
5. Estimating methods in the engineering construction industry include:
   - Step counting methods
   - Exponential methods
   - Parametric methods
   - Detailed and computerized methods.

6. Estimating methods in the building industry include:
   - Approximate methods
   - Functional methods
   - Elemental prices
   - Empirical studies
   - Schedule of rates
   - Priced bill of quantities.
7. Estimating methods in the IT industry include:
   - Analogy methods
   - Top–down estimating
   - Bottom–up estimating
   - Mathematical models
   - Function point analysis
   - Constraint models.
8. Reasons for scheduling the estimates of expenditure and returns include:
   - To assess the viability of the project
   - To optimise the returns from the project
   - To schedule the cash flow requirements during the delivery of the project.
9. Once obtained, estimates must be updated to allow for the following:
   - Location
   - Currency
   - Inflation.

References

1. Turner, J.R., *The Handbook of Project-Based Management*, McGraw-Hill, 1993.
2. George, D.J. (ed.), *A Guide to Capital Cost Estimating*, Institution of Chemical Engineering, 1988.
3. Spon, E.&F.N., *Mechanical and Electrical Services Price Book*, 22nd edition, E.&F.N. Spon, 1991.
4. Spon, E.&F.N., *Budget Estimating Handbook*, 1st edition, E.&F.N. Spon, 1990.
5. For instance, see:
   Boehm, B.W., *Software Engineering Economics*, Prentice-Hall, 1981.
   DeMarco, T., *Controlling Software Projects: Management, measurement and estimation*, Yourdon Monograph, Prentice-Hall, 1982.
   Londeix, B., *Cost Estimation for Software Development*, Addison-Wesley, 1987.
   Pressman, R.S., *Software Engineering*, McGraw-Hill, 1987.
6. Brooks, F.P., *The Mythical Man-Month*, Addison-Wesley, 1982.
7. Albrecht, A., 'Software function, source lines of code, and development effort prediction', *IEEE Transactions on Software Engineering*, November 1983.
8. Remenyi, D.S., Money, A.H. and Twite, A., *Measuring and Managing IT Benefits*, NCC-Blackwell, 1991.

4
Risk analysis

Chris Chapman and Rodney Turner

4.1 Introduction

Managing risk effectively and efficiently can be a highly intuitive art. For example, successful sports men and women are very skilled at managing instinctively risks inherent in their sport, part of their expertise being that they do not need to think about the issues in a direct or formal manner. Players at Wimbledon can react before the ball has been struck by the opposing player. Managing risk associated with projects is a different matter. Some degree of formal analysis is highly desirable. This chapter outlines processes which will help you consider risk effectively and efficiently.

In the previous chapter we described cost estimating, and treating the estimates as deterministic point estimates, single value estimates obtained by combining several single value estimates. However, in reality, the estimates are only some form of mid-range value, a sample of the actual out-turn, which can be almost guaranteed to be different from the estimate.

Traditional methods of risk analysis, such as PERT and Monte Carlo,[1] apply probability distributions to the likely out-turn, and use probabilistic combination to determine the uncertainty of the overall outcome of the project. That is one approach, but not the only one, nor a necessary one. Here we describe an approach called SCERT (Synergistic Contingency Evaluation and Review Technique), developed initially for planning North Sea oil projects and subsequently adopted by BP world-wide for planning and costing.[2] The SCERT approach was later developed to be applied by other organizations to the determination of availability, reliability and maintainability (ARM) and technical choices,[3,4] and for planning and costing.[5,6] Incorporating these adapted forms, it can be viewed as a framework which includes the traditional methods such as PERT and Monte Carlo analysis, and other top-down and bottom-up approaches, as special cases. The chapter follows the structure of the SCERT approach (see Table 4.1).

Table 4.1   Risk analysis and management using SCERT

Stage	Phase	Steps
Qualitative analysis	Scope phase	Component breakdown
		Identification of sources of risk
		Identification of responses
		Identification of secondary risk
		Identification of secondary responses
	Structuring phase	Risk and response links
		Major and minor risks
		Focus of risks and responses
		Sequence of decision making
Quantitative analysis	Parameter phase	Deciding when to quantify
		Quantifying uncertainty
		Combining risks
Risk management		Identifying data and response needs
		Managing these needs as part of project risk
		Interpretation of results
		Developing risk reduction strategies and responses

4.2 Qualitative analysis – scope phase

Component breakdown

The first step is to break the project into component parts. The type of breakdown chosen will depend on the type of risk thought to be important:

- To consider risk associated with a project's schedule or duration, a project needs to be decomposed into a set of component activities.
- To consider risk associated with the capital cost of a project, the project needs to be decomposed into a set of cost components.
- If both schedule and cost risk are important, these costs components may be activity durations and associated cost rates plus material costs.
- To consider risk associated with the economic desirability or the financial feasibility of a project, the full life cycle cash flow analysis needs to be decomposed into a set of components, one being capital cost.
- To consider risk associated with contractual issues, ownership becomes a key issue.

In any of these cases, the key to effective risk analysis is to keep the component breakdown structure as simple as possible, with 5 components a guideline lower bound, and 20 components a guideline upper bound even for very large projects.

We illustrate the approach by using the example of the design and

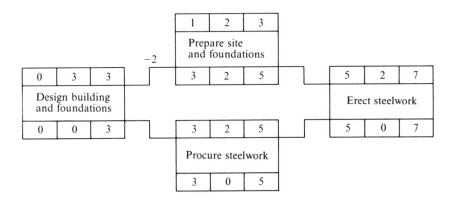

Figure 4.1 Network for the construction of a warehouse

construction of a warehouse. Figure 4.1 shows a four activity network for the project. The times shown are all in months. Design is due to start on the 1 October – thus month 1 is October. The two months' lead time shown against the start of the foundation work reflects the fact that the foundation design is completed after one month, and work could start straight away. (Figure 4.1 uses the networking conventions described by Turner.[1])

Identification of sources of risk

The second step is to identify potential sources of risk associated with each component in the breakdown. In traditional approaches to risk analysis, variability in the value of a component may be assigned without reference to the reasons for that variability. For example, a PERT analysis associates activity durations with probability distributions directly, and a similar approach can be taken to a life cycle cash flow analysis. If the associated variability cannot be managed, and if it does not involve dependence between components, this may be appropriate. Otherwise it is important to identify all key sources of risk associated with each component, the reasons why variability is possible. For example, costs and revenues may rise because of general inflation or because of demand/supply market conditions, on a short-term or a long-term basis. Short-term forecasting and management of demand/supply factors is a viable proposition which can be very important. Long-term inflation involves quite different forecasting and evaluation issues.

On the warehouse project, the risks are:

1. The design will take more or less time than expected. In particular there

may be some rework as one area of the design impacts on another already completed. Of particular concern is the design of the foundations being changed by the design of the steelwork.

2. The foundation work may be held up by inclement weather, especially snow. Snow is most likely in January and February, which is when the foundation work would take place if we wait for completion of all design before starting work.

3. The procurement of the steelwork may take more or less time. In particular, there may be a more expensive supplier who is likely to take less time, and a cheaper one who is likely to take longer.

4. The erection of the steelwork may be held up by inclement weather. In particular, wind in March or rain in April are problems. March and April are when erection of the steelwork is scheduled in the initial plan.

Identification of responses

The third step is to identify the responses associated with the sources of risk. Responses can be of four types:

1. *Purely after the event* A contingency plan is drawn up and enacted should the risk occur, but no action is taken prior to the event. This amounts to repairing any damage, and procuring parts to effect the repair only after the risk event has occurred.

2. *After the event, but with essential prior action* A contingency plan is drawn up, and enacted should the risk occur. However, to be effective, the plan requires some preparation before beginning work on the project. For example, spare parts required to repair damage may have a long lead time, and if the risk is reasonably likely to occur, it may be essential to buy the spare parts with the original equipment.

3. *Prior action which mitigates the impact of the after the event action* A contingency plan is drawn up, but the design of the facility or method of project working is changed to reduce the impact of that contingency plan (in terms of time or cost or whatever). For instance the design might be changed to make repair and maintenance easier: capital cost increased against the reduced cost should the risk occur. This also depends on the likelihood of the risk.

4. *Purely prior action* Ways are found to eliminate the risk, or reduce its likelihood or the damage of its impact. Again this may require a balance of up-front capital cost versus the cost of the risk's occurring.

For important sources of risk it is important to identify all key responses.

For the warehouse project the responses might be:

- Delaying foundation work until all design is complete, or sequencing the design to minimize the likelihood of rework (both prior action).
- Trying to start foundation work early, in November, to avoid snow (prior action), but this requires effective sequencing of the design work (essential prior action).
- Choosing a supplier in response to risks encountered to that point (after the event, but also prior action which mitigates the after the event action – see below).
- Allow a contingency in the programme for expected delays, but if work has progressed quickly, use the more expensive supplier to try to start in February, or if work has been delayed, use the cheaper supplier and plan to start in April (after the event with essential prior action).

Secondary risks and responses

If the planned response to a key risk may not work, it is important to appreciate this, and to consider higher order responses if necessary. For example, using a fixed price contract is often assumed to provide protection against cost variations, but such protection may be far from effective or efficient. It is important not to overlook any key secondary risks and responses. The extent to which it is worth while identifying higher order risks and responses is a matter of judgement and experience, dependent on a variety of issues. The essential skill is not to overlook any critical issues. Claims are a secondary response on a fixed price contract. However, one client organization initiating a claim found that the claim was passed on to a subcontractor owned by themselves – a devastating secondary risk. Second-order risks on the warehouse project may relate to penalties imposed on the suppliers of the steelwork. Also some of the identified risks are affected by the earlier risks, as discussed.

Documentation

It is important to document this analysis. Experience shows that the documentation can be extensive, even with a 20 component breakdown. For example, documentation for North Sea oil fields has been known to exceed 600 pages, and that for a simple office block 200 pages. However, though there may be temptation to ignore it, the documentation is important for five reasons:

- It clarifies thinking.
- It aids communication.
- It can be used in project start-up and to brief new staff.

- It captures expertise for future projects.
- It provides an audit trail if decisions prove unlucky.

4.3 Qualitative analysis – structuring phase

The identification of components, risks, responses, secondary risks and responses provides an initial structure of the issues. However, further structuring is necessary to clarify what is involved. This process identifies:

- Links between the risks and responses
- Major and minor risks
- The focus of responses
- The decision-making process.

- *Links between risks and responses* Some may make other risks more likely to occur, and where this occurs it must be taken account of in the analysis. We showed above links between the risks on the warehouse project.
- *Major and minor risks* At some stage we must classify the risks as major and minor. There is a natural tendency to do this very early, and to dismiss potentially damaging risks as unimportant. However, it is useful to develop the discipline of leaving this decision to this stage, because:
  having identified risk–response links, some apparently major risks become minor because they have effective response strategies;
  some apparently minor risks with no effective strategy become major, and must be dealt with.
- *Focus of responses* Some responses may deal more with only one source of risks, while others may deal with a broad range of risks. Preparing a contingency plan for repair of a failure, may allow parallel working if a delay occurs elsewhere.
- *Moving from simple decisions to complex decisions* With too much data and analysis, you can confuse yourself with the facts: paralysis by analysis. Efficient and effective risk analysis requires a structured approach to gathering the data, defining the options and taking the decisions (Fig. 4.2). The analysis and management decision making process has to start with the simpler decisions and move to the more complex. We also have to move from the strategic to the tactical, to the extent this is appropriate.

To help in this structuring, it can be useful to draw simple diagrams, using decision tree and probability tree conventions or some simplification of such conventions, to understand complex structuring issues.[1] This analysis is still qualitative in the sense that no estimates of component values or associated probabilities have been considered.

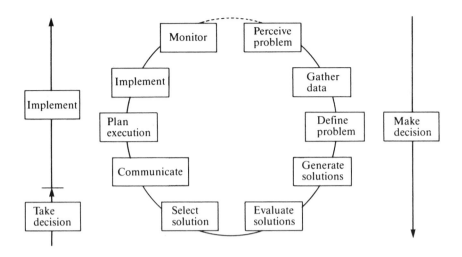

Figure 4.2   A structured approach to decision making and taking

4.4 Quantitative analysis

The third phase of the analysis is the use and combination of probability distributions Sometimes it is useful to associate all sources of risk for all components with probability distributions, and combine these distributions to gain an understanding of the joint effect of each source of risk. This is the basis of the bottom-up approaches to risk analysis, such as PERT and Monte Carlo analysis. Sometimes this is not very helpful, because the sources of risk are related in very complex ways and no responses can be used to manage them. In such cases it may suffice to identify critical values of key parameters in relation to a decision like accept or reject a proposed project, assessing these critical values in terms of how likely it is that actual values will be above or below the critical values. The approach to the quantitative analysis involves:

1. *Deciding when to use the quantitative analysis*, and to what extent Risk-averse organizations may concentrate on avoiding risks, or transferring them to others. However, usually some element of quantitative analysis is necessary.
2. *Quantification of uncertainty* For some risks there will be very precise historical data which will enable precise probability estimates. For instance, we can say with some precision for how many days we expect outside working to be held up due to snow in January or wind in March. Often precise data are not available. In this case, some people argue the

analysis is a waste of time. However, it makes the analysis difficult, but *more* important. It is possible, in these cases to turn the analysis around, by:

conducting sensitivity analysis, to see what is the impact of the risk should it occur;

asking what the probability of the risk must be before spending money to eliminate it is worth while.

3. *Combining the risks* We can determine the impact of all the risks individually on the project. However, they need to be combined to determine the overall impact of all the risks together. The bottom-up approach to this is PERT or Monte Carlo analysis. The top-down approach will be by conducting a joint sensitivity analysis, combining risks in pairs, triplets, and so on, taking account of their interaction, identified previously, to build up an overall picture of their combined effect on duration, cost and viability of the project.

Figure 4.3 shows the result of combining risks on the warehouse project. (This was obtained using very simplistic data,[1] not reproduced here.) It shows a probability distribution of potential outcomes for the duration. Note, the median outcome (half of the expected outcomes are higher and half lower), is in excess of eight months, compared to the predicted outcome without risk analysis of seven months. The chance of achieving seven months or less is only 18 per cent. This belies sensitivity analysis, which would calculate all outcomes around a 'norm' of seven months.

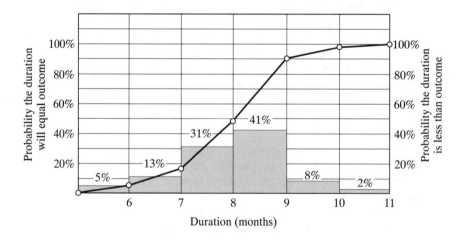

Figure 4.3   Range of outcomes for the warehouse project

4.5 Risk management

The primary rationale for the analysis undertaken thus far is to develop an understanding of risks and responses in order to manage the risk. This may involve reducing risk by doing things differently, or transferring risk to others. It may involve increasing risk in order to reduce expected cost or increase expected profit. Once identified, the risks need to be managed. Turner[1] suggests a three step process:

Step 1: Draw up a risk management plan This is the culmination of what we have discussed so far. The documentation is important for recording this. A risk item tracking form can help in this process (Fig. 4.4).
Step 2: Monitor risks As the project progresses, monitor the risks as they occur (or not). This should be done at regular intervals (weekly, fortnightly or monthly). A top ten hit list can focus attention (Fig. 4.5).
Step 3: Take action That is, implement your responses as appropriate.

4.6 Summary

1. There are four phases of risk analysis:
   - Qualitative analysis – scope phase
   - Qualitative analysis – structuring phase
   - Quantitative analysis – parametric phase
   - Risk management.
2. There are four steps to the qualitative analysis – scope phase:
   - Component breakdown
   - Identification of sources of risk
   - Identification of responses
   - Identification of secondary risks and responses.
3. There are four issues in the quantitative analysis – structuring phase:
   - Risk and response links
   - Major and minor risks
   - Focus of risks and responses
   - Sequence of decision making.
4. There are three issues in the quantitative analysis – parametric phase:
   - Deciding when to quantify
   - Quantifying uncertainty
   - Combining risks.
5. There are three steps of risk management:
   - Draw up a risk management plan
   - Monitor results
   - Take action.

TRIMAGI COMMUNICATIONS BV

RISK ITEM TRACKING FORM

PROJECT: CODE

WORK PACKAGE   CODE

ACTIVITY   CODE

RISK NUMBER: RISK IDENTIFIER

NATURE OF RISK

SOURCE: EU/EP/IT/IN/L   TYPE: BUSINESS/INSURABLE

CATEGORY   CONTRACTUAL/MANAGEMENT/TECHNICAL/PERSONNEL

DESCRIPTION:

IMPACT DATE: LIKELIHOOD   LOW/MEDIUM/HIGH

SUBSIDIARY RISKS

ACTIVITY   RISK IDENTIFIER

ACTIVITY   RISK IDENTIFIER

RISK IMPACT

SEVERITY: VL/L/M/H/VH   SEVERITY SCORE   ..../5

LIKELIHOOD SCORE   ..../3   RISK SCORE   SS * LS = .../15

IMPACT AREA

SCHEDULE:

COST:
PERFORMANCE:

RISK MONITORING

MONTH											
RANK											

Figure 4.4 Risk item tracking form

TRIMAGI COMMUNICATIONS BV

RISK ITEM TRACKING FORM   PAGE 2 of 2

CORRECTIVE ACTION   PROPOSED/APPROVED

DESCRIPTION:

RISK REDUCTION COST

RESPONSIBLE MANAGER

REVISED DATE   LIKELIHOOD   LOW/MEDIUM/HIGH

START DATE: CLOSURE DATE:

REVISED IMPACT

SEVERITY: VL/L/M/H/VH   SEVERITY SCORE   ..../5

LIKELIHOOD SCORE   ..../3   RISK SCORE   SS * LS = .../15

IMPACT AREA

SCHEDULE:

COST:

PERFORMANCE:

MONTH	ACTION TAKEN	NEXT ACTION	BY WHOM

ISSUE: DATE: AUTHOR   APPROVED

Figure 4.4   Risk item tracking form (cont.)

TRIMAGI COMMUNICATIONS BV
MONTHLY TOP RISK ITEM REPORT

PROJECT: CRMO RATIONALIZATION PROJECT   MANAGER: RODNEY TURNER

WORK AREA: TECHNOLOGY   DATE: 26 FEBRUARY 1999x

RANK THIS MONTH	RANK LAST MONTH	MONTHS ON LIST	RISK ITEM	POTENTIAL CONSEQUENCE	RISK RESOLUTION PROGRESS
1	4	2	Replacement for team leader for MIS software development team	Lack of expertise in team. Delay in code production, with likelihood of lower quality – less reliable operation even after testing	Chosen replacement unavailable
2	6	2	Requested changes to user-interface	Now realized may impact h/w-s/w interface definition. If not cleared up at next week's user evaluation of prototype, will delay delivery date	User evaluation of latest prototype set for next week – attendance of some key users still to be confirmed
3	2	5	Resolution of network diagnostic software problems	Delay in completion of software detailed design and coding	New version of diagnostics appears to clear most problems but still to be fully checked
4	3	6	Availability of workstations for main test phase	Lack of sufficient workstations will restrict progress on testing	Delay in deliveries being discussed with supplier
5	5	3	Testbed interface definitions	If not finalized by end of next month, will delay availability of testbed	Delayed items now being worked on. Review meeting scheduled
6	1	3	Tighter fault tolerance requirements impact on performance	Performance problems could require change to h/w-s/w architecture with major impact on cost and schedule	Latest prototype demonstrates performance within specification
7	–	1	Delay in specification of network data transmission	Could delay availability of hardware subsystems for integration	Meeting scheduled to consider alternatives
8	8	4	Tech author required	Insufficient time for programming staff to produce quality manuals	Requirement with agency
–	7	4	CM assistant required	Inadequate effort for rising CM workload with resulting costly errors	CM assistant joined team full-time
–	9	4	Reusable database software uncertainties	Potential increase in estimates of coding effort	Uncertainties resolved in latest prototype

Figure 4.5   Top ten risk item report

References

1. Turner, J.R., *Handbook of Project-based Management*, McGraw-Hill, 1993.
2. Chapman, C.B., 'Risk', in *Proceedings of the First RICS National Research Project*, E. & F.N. Spon, 1991.
3. Chapman, C.B., Cooper, D.F. and Cammaert, A.B., 'Model and situation specific OR methods: risk engineering reliability analysis of an LNG facility', *Journal of the Operational Research Society*, **35**(1), 27–35, 1984.
4. Chapman, C.B., Cooper, D.F., Debelius, C.A. and Pecora, A.G., 'Problem-solving methodology design on the run', *Journal of the Operational Research Society*, **36**(9), 769–778, 1985.
5. MOD(PE)–DPP(PM), *Risk Management in Defence Procurement*, PECAG, Ministry of Defence Procurement Executive, Directorate of Procurement Policy (Project Management).
6. CCTA, *Practical Risk Guidelines for IS/IT Managers*, Information Systems Library, HMSO (forthcoming).

5

Investment appraisal

John Aston and Rodney Turner

5.1 Introduction

Investment in capital assets and projects contributes to future output of the economy. Given resources are usually scarce (there is never sufficient to satisfy all our needs), it is important that they are used in the most efficient and effective way. It is therefore necessary to develop analytical techniques which help decision makers to prioritize the application of resources, especially money, in chosing between alternative, competing projects. Proposals need to be split into those considered worth while and those which should be discarded, and those proposals considered worth while need to be ranked in priority order. Investment appraisal techniques provide a useful tool for performing this analysis. The main types of technique are examined in this chapter. However, managers must be aware that although the financial appraisal techniques fulfil an important role in decision making they should not lose sight of the many non-financial factors which influence the decision. These factors might include:

- The presence of outside influences, often constraining management, such as government, the EEC, public opinion, etc.
- The effect on customers and staff
- The effect on the environment
- Social consequences.

The essential problem when making capital investment decisions is the allocation of scarce resources towards competing ends. There are normally many alternatives available for evaluating projects. How many methods are used, and which ones must be a matter of judgement. Research reveals that payback is the most popular, but it is almost always linked to one other. In this chapter we describe the common techniques, including:

- Accounting rate of return

- Payback
- Discounted cash flow
- Net present value
- Internal rate of return
- Profitability index.

As we describe the techniques, we illustrate them with the same case study. In this way we provide a comparison between them.

Case study 5.1

An organization has four potential projects in which to invest. These projects labelled A, B, C and D, are shown in Table 5.1. Projects A, B and C each have an initial capital outlay of £100 000 in year 0. Project D has an initial capital outlay of £10 000. Each project has a life of four years. The first column in each case shows the net income for each project; that is the gross income, *less* the raw material costs direct labour costs and maintenance costs. The second column is the profit before taxation, calculated by deducting depreciation from the net income. Because each project has a life of four years, depreciation is one-quarter of the initial capital outlay. You will notice the figures for Project D are one-tenth those of Project B. These are very simplistic examples. In reality the calculation of net income and profit will be more complex, and may involve many other costs (and cost savings). However, they serve to illustrate the points.

Table 5.1 Net income and profit before tax for three projects: A, B, C and D

Year	Project A Net inc £'000	Project B Profit £'000	Project C Net inc £'000	Project D Profit £'000	Net inc £'000	Profit £'000	Net inc £'000	Profit £'000
0	−100		−100		−100		−10.0	
1	45	20	65	40	75	50	6.5	4.0
2	45	20	45	20	25	0	4.5	2.0
3	45	20	35	10	25	0	3.5	1.0
4	45	20	35	10	25	0	3.5	1.0

5.2 Accounting rate of return

This method aims to quantify the profits expected from investment projects under consideration. The accounting rate of return (ARR), expresses the profit forecast as a percentage of the capital expenditure involved. There are

Table 5.2   Accounting rate of return for Projects A, B and C

Year	Project A Profit £'000	Project B Profit £'000	Project C Profit £'000
1	20	40	50
2	20	20	0
3	20	10	0
4	20	10	0
TOTAL	80	80	50

Calculating the accounting rate of return (ARR) on:

(a)   Initial capital outlay

Average profits	=	$\dfrac{80}{4}$	$\dfrac{80}{4}$	$\dfrac{50}{4}$
or	=	20 p.a.	20 p.a.	12.5 p.a.
ARR	=	$\dfrac{20}{100} \times 100$	$\dfrac{20}{100} \times 100$	$\dfrac{12.5}{100} \times 100$
or	=	20% p.a.	20% p.a.	12.5% p.a.

(b)   Average capital

Average capital	=	$\dfrac{100}{2}$	$\dfrac{100}{2}$	$\dfrac{100}{2}$
or	=	50	50	50
ARR	=	$\dfrac{20}{50} \times 100$	$\dfrac{20}{50} \times 100$	$\dfrac{12.5}{50} \times 100$
or	=	40% p.a.	40% p.a.	25% p.a.

different methods of calculating the ARR. In some methods the profit is taken before tax, and in some after. Capital employed may be taken as the initial capital outlay of the project, or the average capital employed over the project life. Table 5.2 shows how to calculate the ARR for Projects A, B and C. (Project D will be the same as Project B). The ARR is calculated as a ratio of:

– The initial capital outlay.
– The average capital employed over the four years (depreciated on a

straight line basis). Average capital is calculated on the basis that it steadily erodes over the life of the project. The mid-point is therefore taken.

The advantages of ARR are as follows:

- It is popular with many organizations.
- The percentage return can be compared with the firm's target return or hurdle rate.

However, the disadvantages of ARR are as follows:

- The different methods of calculation can cause confusion.
- It does not allow for the time factor of profits – in the three examples, projects are ranked equally, even though there are major differences in the timing of profits.
- The profit element contains some subjective element – it is not as appropriate as cash flows.

5.3 Cash flows

All methods of investment appraisal relate future receipts from the investment to its capital cost. Cash receipts must be estimated whether they vary from year to year, or they are a fixed sum each year. The investor must always make an estimate of the income generated from the project. Whereas the accounting rate of return (ARR) uses *profits* as a basis for income measurement, other methods of investment appraisal use net cash flows. The latter has no element of fixed costs or depreciation. The use of future cash flows for investment appraisal is now considered more appropriate. Future projects should add to shareholder value, and modern methods of assessing the value of shares assess the present value of future cash flows, not profits.[1,2] In calculating the net cash inflows from an investment, you should add in any savings from maintenance of old plant replaced by the new, and subtract any lost revenue from lost sales from the old plant. That is you calculate the cash flow as the difference between the cash inflow with the new investment and the cash inflow without it. You do not consider just the cash inflow from the new investment in isolation.

Consider this example. A company buys an item of plant with a four year life for £100 000. For each of the four years, it hires the item out, generating fee income of £75 000 per year. The company pays maintenance costs of £10 000, £30 000, £40 000 and £40 000 over the four years respectively. Table 5.3 shows how to calculate the net cash flow. This is Project B.

Table 5.3   Net cash flows and profit

Year	Hire fees	Depreciation	Maintenance	Cash flow	Profit
1	£75 000	£25 000	£10 000	£65 000	£40 000
2	£75 000	£25 000	£30 000	£45 000	£20 000
3	£75 000	£25 000	£40 000	£35 000	£10 000
4	£75 000	£25 000	£40 000	£35 000	£10 000

5.4 Payback

This method calculates the period (normally expressed in years and months) it takes for the project's net cash inflows to equal the capital outlay. The payback periods on Projects A, B and C are:

Project A   2.2 years, or 2 years 3 months
Project B   1.8 years, or 1 year 9 months
Project C   2.0 years, or 2 years 0 months

The advantages of payback are:

- It is simple.
- It is a useful technique in high risk situations.
- The method favours projects with a fast return which favours company liquidity.
- It is used world-wide.

However, the disadvantages of payback are:

- It ignores the time value of money (although you can calculate payback using discounted cash flows).
- It does not take into consideration cash flows after the payback period.

Although Project C has a shorter payback period than Project A, the latter is considerably more profitable. Hence payback must never be used on its own, but in conjunction with other investment appraisal techniques.

5.5 Discounted cash flow techniques

In this section we look at discounted cash flow (DCF) or present value techniques. We consider three:

- Net present value (NPV)

– Internal rate of return (IRR)
– Profitability index (PI).

Discounted cash flow (DCF)

DCF techniques are based on the concept that £1000 received today is worth £1000, whereas £1000 received in one year's time is worth substantially less (say £870 assuming a notional interest rate of 15 per cent). The future value of money is calculated from present value tables, or by formula:

$$PV = \frac{P}{(1+r)^n}$$

where   PV   =   the present value of sum P
         r =   notional interest rate, or cost of capital
         n =   number of years time in which the sum P is received.
So
$$\frac{1000}{1.15} = £870$$

assuming a notional interest rate, or cost of capital of 15 per cent.

The discount factor is usually calculated from the organization's cost of capital, that is its cost of borrowing, (see Chapter 1).

Net present value (NPV)

The first discounted cash flow technique for comparing projects is net present value (NPV). The net present value is the sum of the present values of all the cash inflows, *less* the present values of all the cash outflows. Projects with high NPV are deemed to be preferable to projects with lower NPV. Table 5.4 shows how to calculate the net present value of Projects A, B, C and D, to determine which is the most profitable. A discount factor of 15 per cent is used. It can be seen from these figures that Project B has the highest NPV, and so would be the most profitable option.

Internal rate of return (IRR)

The second discounting approach is to find the interest rate which an investment of capital will return, or putting it another way, find the discount rate which will give zero net present value. This interest rate is known as the internal rate of return (IRR). The IRR for a project is compared to a target rate or hurdle for the company to establish whether the project will go ahead. A particular company's hurdle rate is set by senior management. Table 5.5 shows how to find the IRR for Projects A, B, C and D. Projects B and D have the highest internal rates of return at 33.3 per cent.

Table 5.4 Calculation of discounted cash flow and net present value

	Project A			Project B		
Year	Cash flow £'000	Discnt factor @15%	Present value £'000	Cash flow £,000	Discnt factor @15%	Present value £'000
0 Inflow	−100	1.00	−100.0	−100	1.00	−100.0
1	45	0.87	39.1	65	0.87	56.5
2	45	0.76	34.0	35	0.76	34.0
3	45	0.66	29.6	35	0.66	23.0
4	45	0.57	25.7	35	0.57	20.0
TOTAL	80		128.5	80		133.6
Net present value (NPV) =	28.5					33.6

	Project C			Project D		
Year	Cash flow £'000	Discnt factor @15%	Present value £'000	Cash flow £'000	Discnt factor @15%	Present value £'000
0 Inflow	−100	1.00	−100.0	−10.0	1.00	−10.0
1	75	0.87	65.2	6.5	0.87	5.7
2	25	0.76	18.9	4.5	0.76	3.5
3	25	0.66	16.4	3.5	0.66	2.3
4	25	0.57	14.3	3.5	0.57	2.0
TOTAL	50		114.9	8.0		13.4
Net present value (NPV) =	14.9					3.4

Table 5.5   Calculation of discounted cash flow and internal rate of return

	Project A			Project B		
Year	Cash flow £'000	Discnt factor @28.5%	Present value £'000	Cash flow £'000	Discnt factor @33.3%	Present value £'000
0	−100	1.00	−100.0	−100	1.00	−100.0
Inflow						
1	45	0.78	35.0	65	0.75	48.8
2	45	0.61	27.3	35	0.56	25.3
3	45	0.47	21.2	35	0.42	14.8
4	45	0.37	16.5	35	0.32	11.1
TOTAL	80		100.0	80		100.0
Net present value (NPV) =	0.0			0.0		

	Project C			Project D		
Year	Cash flow £'000	Discnt factor @24.2%	Present value £'000	Cash flow £'000	Discnt factor @33.3%	Present value £'000
0	−100	1.00	−100.0	−10.0	1.00	−10.0
Inflow						
1	75	0.80	60.3	6.5	0.75	4.9
2	25	0.65	16.2	4.5	0.56	2.5
3	25	0.52	13.0	3.5	0.42	1.5
4	25	0.42	10.5	3.5	0.32	1.1
TOTAL	50		100.0	8.0		10.0
Net present value (NPV) =	0.0			0.0		

Profitability index (PI)

The third discounting technique is the profitability index, which combines the NPV and IRR techniques. The profitability index is the ratio of the present value of the cash inflows to the present value of the cash outflows. The profitability indexes of Projects A, B, C and D are:

$$\text{Project A, PI} \quad = \quad \frac{128.5}{100} \quad = \quad 1.285$$

$$\text{Project B, PI} \quad = \quad \frac{133.6}{100} \quad = \quad 1.336$$

$$\text{Project C, PI} \quad = \quad \frac{114.9}{100} \quad = \quad 1.149$$

$$\text{Project D, PI} \quad = \quad \frac{13.4}{10.0} \quad = \quad 1.34$$

Projects B and D have the highest profitability index, and so are the better choice.

5.6 Choosing a project

The reader must be aware that all these techniques are optional. The final decision to go ahead for any project will often be made on management judgement (intuition or 'gut feel'), supported by the investment appraisal techniques described in this chapter. However, to close this chapter, we can ask ourselves which projects, A, B, C or D, would an organization choose to invest in if it had amounts of £100 000, £115 000, £125 000 or £200 000 to spend:

- £100 000: It would probably choose Project B as this gives the best returns against all the criteria.
- £115 000: It would probably choose Projects B and D as together they give the best returns against all the criteria – £5000 would be left to invest elsewhere.
- £125 000: It may choose B and D again, leaving £15 000 to invest elsewhere. It may choose Project C, if the opportunity for B will not go away, as at the end of the first year there should be enough returns to invest in B, and to continue to get returns from C.
- £200 000: It would probably choose A and B. Even though A gives worse returns than D, A can work the capital better than investing in D and leaving £90 000 on deposit. However, you may choose B and C. Even though C appears inferior to A it has shorter payback, and is therefore less risky. It gives the money back for reinvestment earlier, and is still reasonably respectable in terms of the returns it gives.

5.7 Summary

1. Methods of investment appraisal enable us to compare the relative profitability of projects, to enable us to decide which projects to give priority to when assigning scarce resources.
2. Methods of investment appraisal include:
   - Accounting rate of return
   - Payback
   - Discounted cash flow
   - Net present value
   - Internal rate of return
   - Profitability index.

References

1. Mills, R.W., 'Strategic value management: towards a financial framework for developing the general manager', in *Journal of General Management*, **18**(4), Summer 1993.
2. Turner, J.R., *The Handbook of Project-based Management*, McGraw-Hill, 1993.

6
Raising project finance

John Dingle and Ashok Jashapara*

6.1 Introduction

Project managers are rarely responsible for arranging the financing of their projects, even though the financial arrangements can exert a strong influence on a project's chances of success. Consequently, although they will seldom get involved in the details, project managers do need to contribute to the development of a project's financial strategy: a vital segment of the overall project strategy.

The financing of projects is a broad subject, which means that if we are to cover the ground in a relatively short space, we will concentrate on a limited number of key issues which project sponsors and other parties involved must keep in mind. By choosing to emphasize some issues, we will inevitably appear to neglect others. In the financing of projects, nothing is more important than flexibility, so that any generalization is bound to sound controversial in the context of a particular project.

Most projects will be financed out of the capital of the parent organization – that is long-term loans or shareholders' reserves – and we will consider some of these sources of finance.

We will also consider *project financing*. This is a specialist type of financing where an organization (or a group of organizations in a joint venture), raise money to pay for a specific project, and the loan is repaid out of the income stream from that project. It is only larger projects which will require dedicated project financing. (Sometimes the parent organization may be created for the specific purpose of undertaking the project. In these cases the parent organization may be funded by venture capital – see Chapter 12. The largest example of this in the recent past was Eurotunnel Plc, established to build, own and operate the Channel Tunnel. In that case,

---

*The bulk of Chapter 6 was written by John Dingle. It incorporates material previously written by Ashok Jashapara.

however, much of the money was raised by project financing.) Projects large enough to require project financing share several common features, regardless of industry:

– They are usually very large, whatever the yardstick used.
– They often cross national boundaries – while parts of a project may be national in scope, the impact of a major project as a whole is often international.
– They often exceed the capacity of any single organization to plan, supply and construct, which implies coordination, sometimes internationally, of contracting activities.
– They are technically complex, demanding resources with skills which are not widely available – some projects require items of equipment or materials for which sources of supply are very limited.
– They are often dedicated to a single purpose. A good example is a liquefied natural gas plant, which will comprise gas collection, liquefaction, storage, delivery to market by a fleet of specialized vessels, reception facilities, more storage, regasification and distribution facilities. None of these constituent parts can be used for any other purpose without significant additional investment.
– They are often located at remote sites, demanding substantial additional investment in infrastructure work, which is not in itself productive.
– They are capital intensive, needing substantial financial investment in comparison with other inputs.
– The time for project development and implementation is quite long, so that return on the investment is deferred for some years after it is committed.

It is not surprising, therefore, if the planning of finance and the eventual financial structure reflect these features of the project in terms of their own complexity. Nor is it surprising that the suppliers of finance to the project will be very much concerned to analyse the risks associated with the project.

In this chapter, we consider the characteristics of project financing. We identify sources of finance, and describe the markets for raising finance and how to approach them. We close by explaining some of the pitfalls in raising finance and the implications for project managers.

6.2 Characteristics of project financing

In addition to the characteristics listed above, each project will have specific features which will affect the design of its particular financing strategy. There may be very many such features to be taken into account. However, in general, there are four which have rather wide application:

- There is no project without sufficient finance.
- The cost of financing is a significant proportion of the total project cost.
- Financial planning should begin at the feasibility study or earlier.
- Financing adds to the complexity of even quite complex projects.

No project without adequate finance

There will be no project no matter what the technical merit, without finance in some form or other. Of the three projects in Table 6.1, only C can proceed.

Table 6.1   Status of three projects

Project	A	B	C
Technical evaluation (%)	100	95	60
Finance availability (%)	90	95	100

Cost of project finance as a ratio of project cost

The design, implementation and management of the financing demand the same level of commitment of planning and management resources as the project itself. For example, consider a project in which 15 per cent of the total investment is for engineering design and management, 55 per cent is for the purchase of equipment and materials, 30 per cent is for construction and start-up. Assume the investment is financed by credit over 10 years at 15 per cent p.a. interest. You can calculate that the cost of financing the debt is a little in excess of 60 per cent of the total investment, which is more than the major cost element in the project. Hence the total cost of finance may amount to about the same as the unfinanced total cost, and so it is clear that good *financial management* is at least as important as good *project management*.

Financial planning begins at the feasibility study

Financial planning should begin at the same time as, or earlier than, technical project planning. Regrettably, financial planning for the project is often begun at the last minute, when most if its other features are already 'cast in concrete'. Conversely, it could be said that the most successful projects are often those where the original inspiration is financial!

Financing adding to the complexity of projects

While the financial package will reflect the complexity of the project, finance has some inherent characteristics which themselves add to the complexity of the undertaking. Three of these should be emphasized because they do exert a significant influence on financial planning, and hence on the structure of the eventual financial package, its negotiation, and the implementation of the project:

1. It is not always clear which comes first:
   - identifying sources of supply for finance; or
   - preparing technical specifications for equipment and services, etc.
   Finance, or more often lack of it, imposes the need to develop a sense of compromise. One needs to be able to detect as early as possible when compromise is required.
2. The availability of finance, and terms on which it is available for a particular project, may be subject to significant and rapid change for reasons quite beyond the control of the sponsor or project manager.
3. The structuring, and eventually the acceptability, of the financial package depends largely on one's point of view. Obviously, a lender is likely to have a different point of view, at least initially, from a would-be borrower. Also, a package which appears attractive to, say, the project contractor who wants an order, may not be so attractive to the project sponsor or his government authorities. For example, low interest rates may have to be traded off against high exchange rate risks.

In what follows, we will see that these characteristics continually influence our discussion of project financing.

6.3 Setting a financial strategy for the project

We said above, and it is so obvious as to be an axiom, that without finance there could be no project. Yet many projects around the world are begun and not completed (or run into long delays and huge cost escalation) because the project sponsor failed to identify sources for 100 per cent of the finance needed to implement the project. Note also, that until sources for 100 per cent of the finance have been identified, there is no point spending a lot of time worrying about the cost of finance, the terms and conditions upon which it may be made available, or the methodology for evaluating financial packages. At an early stage the project manager and sponsor need to develop a financial strategy for the project, and this should identify:

- The main categories of finance.

– The relationship between project activities and sources of finance.
– The cost of capital.

Categories of finance: debt, equity and aid

Finance for projects falls into three main categories:[1]

1. *Equity* This is defined broadly as funds subscribed in a project (or a company undertaking a project) by shareholders from their own resources. There is no guarantee that a dividend will be paid, so the investors may lose their money if the project fails to perform. Equity investors have the last claim if the project (or the parent company) goes into liquidation.

2. *Debt* This has the essential characteristic of representing an obligation on the borrower to repay. Debt also usually carries an obligation to pay interest, and to adhere to a prearranged repayment schedule. The lender has a priority claim if the borrower goes into liquidation. There are three major types of debt:
   – Subordinate debt
   – Senior debt (secured)
   – Senior debt (unsecured).

   Subordinate debt (or quasi-equity) is repayable only after all the senior debt has been repaid. It is seen rather like equity, where different parties to a project, such as the owner, suppliers, users or government provide capital for the project to attract greater third party lenders. It can often be treated as equity when calculating debt to equity ratios in negotiations with senior lenders (see below).

   Senior debt is borrowing from commercial banks in the form of secured or unsecured loans. Secured loan is debt secured by collateral or assets easily convertible into cash. Unsecured debt is backed by the general creditworthiness of the borrower established through good reputation with the financial community. Unsecured debt is sometimes called *project financing*, or *non-recourse financing*, and the lender primarily relies for repayment on the revenue stream generated by the project.

3. *Grant aid* This is a direct gift of money normally made by one government (or a multinational supra-government agency such as the World Bank) to another. Grant aid is usually intended to help less developed countries meet social or community welfare objectives. It is seldom entirely free from obligations on the recipient government, and although strings may not be directly attached to the project, they may influence the way the project can be managed.[2] (Other forms of aid, such as subsidized credit for exports, or aid-plus-credit packages (*credit mixte*) are best considered as forms of debt financing.)

Debt and equity are available in a wide variety of forms, as described in the next section. They are distinguished by:

- The cost of the finance
- The terms upon which it is available
- Its use for certain purposes or project activities
- The obligations of the respective parties to one another.

Project activities and their relation to sources of finance

It is essential, at an early stage of project financial planning, to relate project activities to sources of finance, perhaps in the form of a matrix. Initially, this will serve to distinguish those activities which could be financed by equity from those which would be financed by debt.

Because debt implies an obligation to repay, it is usual practice that it is not available for high risk activities such as minerals exploration, research, or project development planning.

Equity, on the other hand, is usually applicable to all project-related activities, provided the shareholders are prepared to bear the cost. In practice, however, it may happen that all the project costs cannot be met by equity. For example, the equity finance available for a project may be denominated in a currency which cannot be converted to currencies which contractors or equipment suppliers are willing to accept.

As soon as possible in the planning of finance, sources of debt and equity should be put into specific categories. We need to know whether a specific source of debt (or equity) exists for a particular project expenditure, and whether, given the characteristics of the project under consideration, it can be made available when it is needed. Methods of providing debt and equity finance are described in the next section, and potential sources in Chapter 12.

Cost of capital

Generally speaking, the cost and terms on which finance is made available always reflect the financiers' views about the riskiness of the project. However, equity is usually scarcer than debt. Once the available equity is committed to financing a particular element of a project, it is usually extremely difficult to obtain additional equity to finance other elements for which debt finance has not been foreseen, or not planned in advance, or to pay for cost over-runs. The cost of borrowing for a project (called the cost of capital) depends on the proportion of equity to debt, which therefore has important consequences for the appraisal of the project. It also influences the way investors and lenders perceive the commitment of the project sponsor to the project. The debt/equity ratio would be expected to conform to certain accepted norms, which depend on national, industrial and financial practice, and which tend to change with time, so that selecting the appropriate ratio for a particular project calls for considerable specialized knowledge.

We showed in Chapter 1 that the cost of capital can be calculated as:

Cost of capital = (Cost of equity) × (Ratio of equity)
                    + (Cost of debt) × (Ratio of debt) × (1 − Marginal tax rate).

The cost of equity will be higher than the cost of debt, reflecting the higher risk involved to the shareholder (Chapter 1). The cost of debt is the interest rate charged by the lender. Interest on debt is paid out of gross profits before deduction of tax, whereas the cost of equity (dividends and capital appreciation) is paid out of taxed income. Hence the third multiplier on the second line.

A company has an equity to debt ratio of 1 : 4. Its cost of equity is 15 per cent, its overdraft rate is 18 per cent, and its marginal tax rate is 33 per cent.

Cost of capital = (20)% × (15)% + (80)% × (18)% × (1 − 33 per cent.
                = 12.6%

6.4 Raising finance – the markets

The majority of people will be involved in raising finance for domestic projects, and many familiar sources of finance exist for these. (The sources may be both domestic and international.) Some sources of finance exist specifically to finance exports of goods and services for projects. There are also some unconventional sources of financing.

Conventional sources – domestic projects

There are three conventional sources of finance for domestic projects. The providers of these types of finance are described further in Chapter 12.

1. *Shareholders and other subscribers* They may be public or private institutions or individuals who provide equity for use directly in the financing of certain project activities or, perhaps more usually, as collateral for obtaining debt finance. Sources of equity include:
   – Corporate cash flow generated by existing business operations
   – Corporate or individual investors, or funds raised through the stock markets
   – Joint venture partners

- Venture capital companies
- Government subscriptions
- International investment institutions, such as the World Bank.

2. *Banks* Banks and other financial institutions, provide debt normally against security (for example, the borrower must provide collateral or convertible assets or, in the case of unsecured loans, must have a financial reputation for creditworthiness acceptable to the lender). Many banks offer debt financing, and hence keen competition between them helps to keep costs low. Internationally active merchant banks often act as agents for arranging project finance by international investors.

3. *International sources of finance* These can be advantageous, providing lower costs, less government regulation, lower taxes, deposit requirements and political risk. The main sources of international finance are Euromarkets (Eurocurrency, Eurobonds) for financial resources held outside by their country of origin. Euromarkets offer lower interest rates as well as certain other advantages to large, highly creditworthy corporate borrowers.

Conventional sources – export projects

Some special arrangements exist for financing export projects. Here, additional risks influence the choice of financing method, including:

- The status of the buyer of the project
- The international market for projects of that type (and implications for the exporting country's balance of trade)
- The structure of the proposed export deal
- The required length of credit and periods of grace
- The complexity that can be managed by the buyer's side (as well as by the seller).

Many financial instruments have been developed to facilitate export trade. We will consider only a few from the project manager's point of view of ease of access and use, cost and risk sharing.

LETTER OF CREDIT

These are also called bills of exchange. The buyer's banker issues a letter of credit as proof that the seller will be paid (subject to specified terms). Letters of credit are negotiable, for example they can be traded for cash. They are relatively low risk instruments suitable for short duration deals involving relatively small sums, are easy to organise and cost relatively little.

EXPORT CREDITS

These are financed by banks backed by insurance cover. The bank has no recourse to the exporter if the buyer defaults. Export credits usually mean that the greater part of the supply must be obtained from the supplier's country. The proportions which are admissible vary from country to country, and are subject to international agreements which often seem in practice to be more honoured in the breach than in the practice. In general, however, export credits are a popular way of financing both large and small export projects, provided care is taken with the terms of credit insurance. There are two types of export credit, supplier's credit and buyer's credit.

SUPPLIER CREDIT

These are arrangements in which the exporter obtains a loan from a bank and insurance cover from a specialized insurer, (Fig. 6.1). The terms of these arrangements are often subsidized by governments to promote export trade. The exporter should therefore be able to negotiate a competitive contract with the buyer. An additional advantage to the buyer is that he or she has only the exporter to deal with: the exporter makes all other arrangements. A disadvantage is that the supply contract is subject to approval by the supplier's government.

Supplier credit is probably the most popular form of project financing, due in part at least to the following features:

- The buyer has to deal only with the seller, who makes all the other arrangements.
- The loan is tied to the supply contractor via approval by the supplier government (or its agency such as the Export Credit Guarantee Department, ECGD, in the United Kingdom) with its backing up to typically 85 per cent of the financed value.
- The credit is usually insured by the seller's government agency – although private sector insurance is also possible – and requires security in the form of Letter of Guarantee by the buyer's government or national bank.
- The credit terms, interest, draw down and repayment schedule are ultimately subject to approval by the seller's government.
- Aid may also be available, for example to help with down payments, which usually results in tied supply (as in *credit mixte*).

BUYER CREDIT

These are arrangements in which the buyer, usually a government or a para-statal agency, borrows direct from a lender in the seller's country (Fig. 6.2).

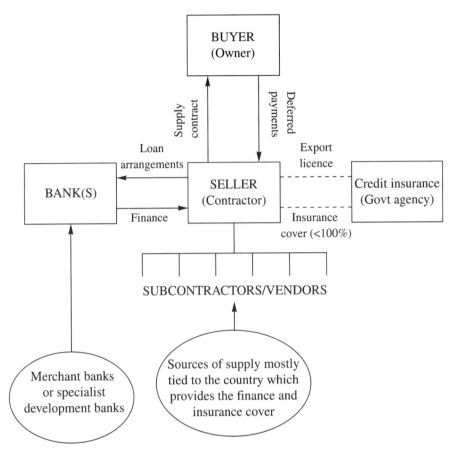

Figure 6.1 Supplier credit

The seller is paid by the lending institution against evidence of satisfactory supply. Buyer's credit often falls within a government-to-government line of credit which enables the buyer to negotiate contracts for any good or services in the lending country. However, the buyer now has two channels of negotiation to manage: with the seller, and with the lending institution in the seller's country.

The features of buyer credit are:

- The buyer (government or para-statal agency) borrows direct from a financial institution, (either a government or government supported institution) in the seller's country.
- The seller is paid by the financial institution, against specific evidence of supply.

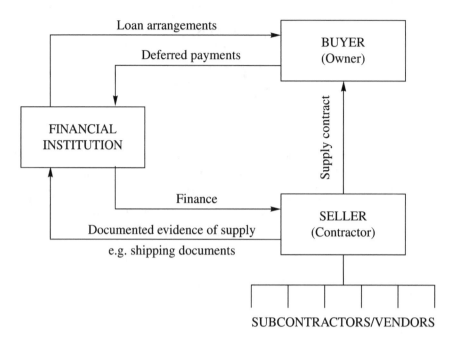

Figure 6.2   Buyer credit

– They are usually operated under government to government agreements, such as 'Line of Credit', enabling the buyer to negotiate supply contracts for any goods or services from the lending country.

AID

Export credits are sometimes combined with forms of aid (as in '*credit mixte*' or the UK 'Aid and Trade' provision) (Fig. 6.3). Such arrangements are suitable for large prestigious projects where government support need to be mobilized to establish a position against international competition. While the eventual terms may be exceptionally favourable, the project promoters will have to commit a lot of senior management effort to satisfying bureaucratic requirements. This is true of mobilizing aid finance in general. There are basically two forms of aid:

– *Project aid* for specific projects, highly structured and formalized in accordance with the donor institution's project appraisal procedures.
– *Programme aid*, intended to finance imports (including projects, though usually small ones) in return for sectoral policy reform. Programme aid

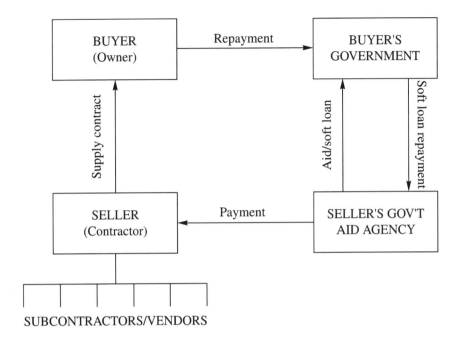

Figure 6.3   Aid for developmens such as infrastructure projects

leads to shopping lists of imports which may be specific, allowing individual projects to be identified, or may include only general aims.

Aid finance is normally government to government (bilateral), when it is usually, but not always, tied to supplies from the donor country, or is from a multilateral institution, when use is not tied to a particular supplier. There is a tendency for the multilaterals to blur the distinction between development aid and commercial lending through low-interest (soft) loans and grant aid used to dilute interest payments, or by co-financing, which involves the participation of other donor agencies working with the multilateral institutions.

This multiplicity of options and sources serves to increase the management effort needed to secure the financing of a project involving an aid component. Nevertheless, aid provides a useful niche market for financing some projects, especially those where open competitive bidding is deemed inappropriate. Examples included those where only one supplier is thought capable of carrying out the project, certain high risk projects, and specialized project areas such as maintenance, emergency or training projects.

Less conventional financing

A number of unconventional methods of raising finance for projects have evolved in order to try to overcome the disadvantage of the conventional markets discussed above. Their aims include:

- Simplicity.
- To generate convertible currency.
- To gain access to markets which are otherwise limited.
- To avoid a drain on balance of payments.
- To accelerate development of technical skills.
- To comply with political or cultural/religous requirements.
- Above all, to reduce or shift the balance of risk.

Like other attempts to alleviate risk, they incur costs, and it is a matter of judgement as to whether they are actually efficient. These methods include:

- Leasing
- Forfaiting
- Counter-trade
- Switch trading
- Offset
- Build-operate-transfer
- Franchise financing
- Debt/equity swapping
- Islamic banks.

LEASING

Makes available use of project assets through off-balance sheet financing, and may attract favourable tax allowances. However, tax laws are subject to change at short notice under the influence of arbitrary changes in government policy, so leasing may prove to be an unattractive option.

FORFAITING

Finance is made available through the sale of financial instruments due to mature at some time in the future. The cost in terms of fees and discounting can be very high.

COUNTER-TRADE

The seller accepts (or arranges for a third party to accept) goods or services in lieu of cash. Counter-trade may take the form of simple exchange or barter, or the project may be paid for with its own output, as in buyback (Fig. 6.4). There are many ways of effecting counter-trade, all expensive, cumbersome and tricky to negotiate. Hence, counter-trade is unloved by project contractors and the financial community. There are also issues to do with interference with free trade which are often believed to be undesirable aspects of counter-trade. However, buyback is said by its proponents, usually politicians in developing countries, to be a satisfactory means of encouraging technology suppliers to commit themselves to the long-term transfer of their technology in complex projects. Features of buyback arrangements are:

- The seller is paid by the development bank(s).
- The development bank(s) are paid from the Escrow Account.
- The Escrow Account receives payments from the sale of the product.
- After the banks have been paid, the surplus from the Escrow Account goes to the buyer.
- These arrangements are usually for very large, long-term projects in developing countries, but where the seller country needs long-term energy imports.

SWITCH TRADING

This is a technique for making use, via a third party, of uncleared credit surplus arising from bilateral trade arrangements (Fig. 6.5). For example, if country B has a credit surplus with country C, exports from A and B may be financed by payments effected through a switch trader from C to A. Needless to say, this can lead to some very complex and expensive arrangements.

OFFSET

This requires the exporter of a technically advanced project to incorporate an agreed value of materials, equipment and/or services supplied by the importer. Offset may be extended to require the exporter, as owner of the technology, to set up local production facilities associated with the project. The idea is again to provide evidence of the supplier's long-term commitment to the development aims of the importer.

BUILD–OPERATE–TRANSFER (BOT)

This is a relatively new approach to the problem of raising money and ensuring that technology transfer is adequately effected in complex projects

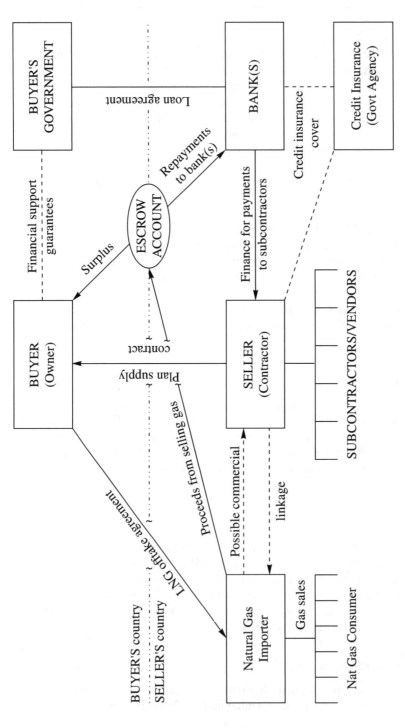

Figure 6.4 Typical buyback arrangement – LNG export project

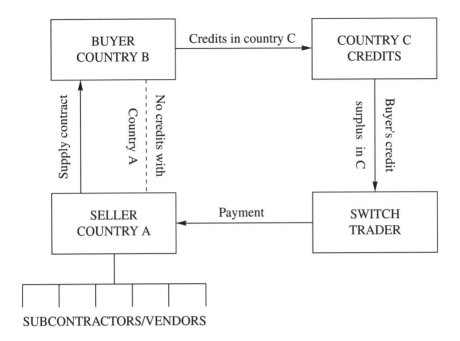

SUBCONTRACTORS/VENDORS

Figure 6.5   Switch trade

(see Chapter 9). The project is financed, constructed and then operated by the supplier (more usually, by a consortium of suppliers), who have rights to recover their costs and profits from the income generated by the project over an agreed period of time. After this, the project is taken over and operated by the buyer. BOT schemes are difficult to put together and, because of the exceptionally long-term commitment required, are vulnerable to currency depreciation and political risks.

FRANCHISE FINANCING

This requires engineering and construction contractors to become equity joint venture partners in projects they design and build, and thus to remain associated with implementation and operation of the project over a number of years. A hoped-for consequence is that this will result in better quality projects, because the contractors and/or licensors will share responsibility for efficient long-term management.

DEBT/EQUITY SWAPPING

This is a device to encourage investment by technology owners. Typically, a multinational technology owner buys host country debt at a discount. The debt is redeemed in local currency at a favourable rate of exchange for the purpose of setting up a local company, which uses the transferred technology to generate foreign exchange, replace imports and create local employment.

ISLAMIC BANKS

Islamic banks provide finance according to the precepts of Shary'ah law, which takes a significantly different view of the function of investment and profit than do Western commercial banks. Finance for projects in Islamic countries can be available to non-Islamic contractors. Negotiations can be expected to be complex and time consuming.

6.5 Raising finance – the approaches

The justification

Because there are many possible sources of debt and equity, it is usually possible to identify, at least in principle, a mix of potential source for all the various financial components of a project. The problem is to secure the financial requirements on terms which promote the project's chance of success. As a first step, recall the purpose of the financing: it is simply to improve the project's financial performance. Consider the project in Tables 6.2 and 6.3, one financed 100 per cent by equity and the other with a mixture of equity and debt.

Table 6.2 No debt, project with 100% equity

	Year 0	Year 1	Year 2	Year 3	Year 4	Total
Capex	(100)					(100)
Net revenue	0	20	40	50	60	170
Cash flow	(100)	20	40	50	60	170

IRR = 21.0%

Table 6.3 Debt 60% and equity 40%

	Year 0	Year 1	Year 2	Year 3	Year 4	Total
Capex	(100)					(100)
Net revenue	0	20	40	50	60	170
Loan	60					60
Repayments		(15)	(15)	(15)	(15)	(60)
Interest @ 10%	(6)	(4.5)	(3)	(1.5)		
Cash flow	(40)	(1)	20.5	32	43.5	55

IRR = 31.2%

Clearly, the higher the debt to equity ratio, the more impressive will be the project's financial performance in relation to the equity employed. Note also that the project's financial performance will be very strongly affected by taxation; though consideration of these effects is outside the scope of this book. The project sponsor's requirements in raising finance may be summarized as follows:

- To raise the necessary amount of money at the times and in the currencies required by the project.
- To minimize costs.
- To share risks.
- To maintain flexibility and control, including the possibility of rescheduling if necessary.
- To be able to pay dividends to shareholders.

The lender's requirements are rather different:

- The lender needs to be satisfied that debts (and interests and fees) will be repaid on time.
- There must be adequate security and resource in the event that the borrower defaults on payment.
- Shareholders will want to be sure that satisfactory dividends will be paid.

These differences in viewpoint are least when the project is financed from corporate resources. If external financing is needed in addition, the lender (or investor) will take a view that the corporation is backing the project, so the main risk is of the corporation defaulting. For financing raised by established corporations, this is normally the minimum cost scenario as well.

More complex issues are raised by project financing. Now the lender must consider the creditworthiness of the project as well as that of the project sponsor. The lender's recourse is to the cash flow generated by the project, and the lender may have no recourse (in a 'non-recourse' financing) or only limited recourse to the borrower. Consequently, the lender will seek very detailed information about the project when approached for a project financing facility. Typical questions are:

- What is the basis on which cash flows depend? The nature of the business or market for the products?
- How robust are the size and duration of the project's cash flows?
- Can cash flow be assigned to other parties?
- Are the project's assets dedicated to the project?
- Can the project's assets be isolated, leased or pledged as security?
- What is the true market value of the project's assets?

- What provisos for insurance, or maintenance, exist?
- Who will be the owners, operators and contractors?
- What are the political risks, especially as regards ownership?
- What are the currency risks (for example inflation or exchange rate)?
- What are the economic risks, and what is the balance of risk between lenders and investors?

These are essentially the same kinds of questions as are raised by prudent project sponsors during the feasibility study phase of project development. However, their interpretation of the answers, and especially of sensitivity analyses, may differ from the interpretation placed on them by project financiers.

The status of the project sponsor and the location of the project site have a fundamental influence on the process of planning, structuring and implementing finance for the project. Obviously, a well-established corporation, located in a stable part of the world, and having wide-ranging international connections, is likely to be in a much stronger position to arrange finance for a large project than a small company located in a country experiencing radical political change or economic problems. This is not to say that the great multinationals never have project financing problems. They, after all, are the organizations which usually take on the biggest and most technically difficult projects at the frontiers of management capability. It does, however, point to the fact that the issues to be faced in the planning of finance are likely to be rather different.

The project sponsor needs to understand the lender's concerns. Information to support answers to the lender's questions listed above should be prepared. For example, the project sponsor should be able to demonstrate a satisfactory feasibility study and project development plan based on adequate market research and projections of economic factors including inflation and interest. Aspects often omitted which should be addressed include: the logistics of moving products to the market; the availability of local materials for construction; good communications between the project site and the offices of all parties involved; the experience and capability of the proposed project manager. Lenders normally expect to see evidence of satisfactory agreements between partners in a joint venture, and that key partners have made adequate contributions to equity in the project. Lenders dislike projects involving new technology. They like to see that serious project management problems have been considered: in particular, the consequences of delay, cost over-runs and *force majeure*; and they will require adequate insurance cover. Satisfying the lenders on these points helps to make the sponsor's approaches fruitful. Evidently, every project raises its own problems, and calls for its own financial mix. Development of the financial strategy therefore calls for very good contacts with the international financial community, and for understanding of financial mechanisms as well as the technical complexities of the industry.

Seeking financial proposals

Having identified the potential mix of financing sources and justified the need does not solve the problem of financing the project. We now have to convert the potential mix in the commitment, or at least into proposals capable of being accepted. This step is especially important if there are difficulties about the location of the project, or the status of the project sponsor. First of all, we have to distinguish between sources of finance which can only be approached by the project sponsor (or in some cases, by a government authority acting on behalf of the project sponsor), and those which may be approached by parties other than the project sponsor, such as contractors or equipment suppliers. The World Bank, and regional development banks such as ADB, AFDB, IADB, can be approached only by governments, or project sponsors who are acting as the agent of a government body. Export credit is available only in support of exports from the country of the suppliers, and is normally obtained through the suppliers or contractors concerned. Commercial bank finance can be accessed by project sponsors, or by suppliers or contractors in support of their bids. Aid is arranged through a combination of project sponsor, suppliers and their respective governments.

The project sponsor's ability to get good terms for finance is considerably enhanced if he or she has a 'borrowing base'; for example a portfolio of projects. Lenders may be inclined to accept the portfolio as a risk dilution device which reduces the cost of borrowing to the project sponsor. If a project sponsor intends to ask suppliers or contractors for supporting finance, it is crucially important for the enquiry documents to specify this, and the nature of the support requested. The relevant sections of the enquiry documents are best prepared by specialists to ensure that the project sponsor's freedom of action is maximized, and at the same time to motivate the support of the suppliers or contractors and their respective financial institutions. The project sponsor will do well to cultivate contacts with several potential sources of finance before making a formal enquiry. In default of this, the project sponsor has no alternative but to 'cold call'. Because financing depends primarily on confidence, this is the approach least likely to be successful. Once contact is established, finalization of financial arrangements is a matter for negotiation. Each project is unique: the terms for its financing will be special, though based on precedent to the extent that the lender's experience allows. This general background was discussed above, and it should help the sponsor to orient his or her approach. It is perhaps useful to remember Keynes's dictum that 'if you owe a bank £100, you have a problem. If you owe it £1 million, it has a problem.' Allow two orders of magnitude for project borrowing today.

One final point about approaches to financial institutions. Money lending, like all other trades based on art rather than science, relies on jargon to mystify and impress clients. Be sure you know precisely what is meant by bankers' jargon: many words have technical meanings different from their meanings in ordinary speech. If in doubt, ask for clarification. The *Pocket Economist*, published by Economist Publications, is a handy reference.

6.6 Financing problems – implications for project managers

Although there are many and varied sources of finance for projects, that is it is usually possible to find potential lenders, establishing a workable financial package is difficult, and fraught with pitfalls. Project managers are wise to take note of these, for the pitfalls snare their feet more often than they trip up corporate money men.

DEBT SERVICING

This is repayment of the sum borrowed (that is, the 'principal') plus interest repayments. In the final feasibility study, project cash flows will be shown to accommodate debt servicing requirements comfortably. If for any reason they do not, then the project, and the project manager, are in serious trouble, for the cost of financing unforeseen adverse cash flows is very high. Note that unexpected adverse cash flows are most likely to arise between the final stages of construction and completion of project implementation, which is also the time when, very often, major debt servicing payments fall due.

FEES

Fees are payable to the financial institutions which arrange and provide the money for the project. Often, more than one institution is involved, for example, as agent for the borrower, or as actual providers of finance. Fees are payable for a wide range of services, which may not be immediately apparent when the project's financial planning is being considered. In particular, if the project go-ahead is deferred, standby fees are payable to the financial institutions involved in keeping the finance available. Almost certainly, standby fees will not have been foreseen in the original financial plan.

INSUFFICIENT FUNDS

Insufficient funds may be in place when the project is launched. Despite the obvious problems, it is very tempting for enthusiastic project promoters to get the project started in anticipation of a final tranche of finance being available at some later date. It may not be, or it may be available only on extravagant terms. Other causes for insufficient finance include:

— Miscalculation of the actual capital costs required.
— Poor definition of actual work scope.
— Changes to work scope accepted without considering cost implications (a frequent problem arises from a decision to fast-track the project in the belief this has little or no effect on costs).
— Underestimating the cost of working capital and/or spares and other consumables.
— Project delay. Even when finance for the total cost of the project is available, if money is not available at the required TIME, the project will suffer from insufficient funding.

CURRENCY

Project costs are denominated in one or more specific currencies. If financial input and output are denominated in different currencies, exchange rate fluctuations may cause difficulty. For example, petroleum industry revenues are usually based on the US dollar. Project finance in a currency which tends to appreciate against the US dollar will embody an exchange risk which may be extremely costly for project implementation.

Most exchange rate risks can be hedged by using currency forward markets, interest rate swaps, options, and other instruments. Hedge mechanisms are themselves risky, especially so in the hands of amateur money managers. They are also expensive. Project managers should try to ensure that, so far as possible, project input and output are denominated and balanced in the same currencies.

Inflation raises similar issues if not adequately accounted for in planning. In particular contractors' 'overnight' cost estimates: 'overnight' excludes inflation during the period of design and construction.

SECURITY

Security is normally required, in some form, for debt-finance. In addition to conventional types of collateral, there is increasing use of project assets, rights to project resources (such as oil or gas in the ground) and rights to project outputs as security. Another form of security much used in industrialization projects in developing countries is the sovereign guarantee of the government of the country where the project is located.

In recent years, in some parts of the world, sovereign guarantees have lost some of their virtue because of debt crises which colour the judgement of some finance ministries. This has moved financial institutions to pay more attention to the assets represented by the project, and its value as a means of exploiting natural resources or developing markets. Although this is sometimes considered to be a novel development, it is of course the way in which historically most large projects were financed: a fact possibly obscured by the increasing sophistication of both projects and the financial markets.

POLITICAL RISK

Political risk exercises the providers of finance for projects perhaps more than project sponsors. Part of their concern arises from the perceived risk of expropriation. Part arises from the ease or difficulty of obtaining authorizations from government agencies for the project. Political risk can be lessened by arranging several agreements between the project sponsor and the various government bodies involved with the project (but note that competition among departments of government is a fact of bureaucratic life everywhere), and by arranging finance through lenders in several countries.

Political risks can be insured against although it is expensive. The World Bank has set up the Multilateral Investment Guarantee Agency (MIGA), the purpose of which is to provide insurance to companies investing in the Third World against the expropriation of their assets, and to cover the certain other political risks.

Another risk-diluting mechanism is 'guaranteed recovery of investment principal' (GRIP), under which investors would place funds with International Finance Corporation (IFC), which in turn provides equity as a minority partner in developing country projects. On maturity of the loan, the investors may choose to reclaim their principal (for example, if the project has failed to come up to expectations) or they can take up the investment itself. IFC takes a share in any dividends in return for taking most of the project risk.

6.7 Summary

1. The characteristic features of projects impose special requirements for financing project capital. While project managers are seldom responsible for making the financial arrangements, these arrangements can influence the manageability of the project, and their implications should be understood by project managers.

2. The financing strategy is a crucial component of project development strategy. Financing adds to the complexity of the project. It demands early consideration and management commitment if a satisfactory outcome is to be achieved.
3. Many different types of finance, from many sources, are potentially available, including:
   - Equity
   - Subordinate debt
   - Senior debt – secured
   - Senior debt – unsecured
   - Grant aid
   - Less conventional forms.
4. The suitability of a particular type is coloured by the source's perception of project risk, which may well be different from the perception of the project sponsor. Usually, a mix of various types of finance proves more suitable, though the terms upon which each type of finance is made available are always a matter of negotiation with the various sources.
5. The response of potential sources of finance is essentially the response of a market. Sources (or markets) respond to different kinds of project in terms of relative ease of access to finance, its use, cost and risk sharing largely as a function of the project type, scale, and whether it is an export project.
6. Accessing finance inevitably involves justification of project activities. Project financiers expect project sponsors to justify their projects in terms understandable and acceptable to financiers. Usually, this requires extensive information about how the project will be managed, as well as estimates and forecasts of its expected performance. The approach and subsequent detailed negotiations will be time-consuming – another reason for early and careful preparation on the part of the project manager.
7. At the same time, indeed as part of their preparation, project managers must be aware of, and alert for, problems in financing and their implications for the manageability of the project, since insufficiency or untimely availability of finance for any phase of the project, or situations that increase project risk, will inevitably reduce the chance of project success.

References

1. Nevitt, P., *Project Financing*, Euromoney Publications, 1989.
2. Turner, J.R., *The Handbook of Project-based Management*, McGraw-Hill, 1993.

PART TWO
PARTNERS

Part Two considers collaborative arrangements between organizations to undertake projects together. In reality, most projects require several organizations to work together. No one organization has the skills, technologies or range of services to undertake anything but the smallest of projects on its own. However, the relationship is usually as a client and contractor or supplier. These relationships are described in Parts Three and Five of the book. What characterizes partnerships is the sharing of risk between the parties to their mutual benefit. We consider a range of collaborative arrangements including joint ventures, partnering and build–own–operate(-transfer) projects.

In Chapter 7, David Topping starts by describing a range of collaborative arrangements. Colin Smith then considers joint ventures, explaining why organizations enter into them, and how they are formed and managed. Chris Benjamin ends by describing special features of international collaborative arrangements, and how they might be addressed.

In Chapter 8, Colin Smith and Steve Tonks describe partnering. This is a looser arrangement than a joint venture, where a client and contractor work together in closer harmony, to avoid conflict on projects thereby increasing both their profits. The arrangement may be for a single project (single project partnering), or for several projects undertaken over a specified time-scale. The latter maximizes the opportunity for joint learning, but organizations are finding the single project arrangements almost as effective, while maintaining flexibility.

In Chapter 9, Peter Morris describes build–own–operate(–Transfer), BOO(T), projects. These are projects where the private sector finances and builds infrastructure projects on behalf of governments. The project sponsors are repaid by charging a toll for the use of the facility, that is they are repaid out of the revenue streams. The private sector thereby takes the risk on the success of the project.

7
Joint ventures

Colin Smith, David Topping and Chris Benjamin

7.1 Collaborative arrangements

Simple definitions of collaborative arrangements are rarely attempted. When they are, they tend to reflect the writer's perspective. There are several types of strategic cooperative arrangement:

1. *Supply contracts* These are the simplest. A detailed specification of exactly what is required is drawn up, tendered for by a number of organizations, and once the contract is fulfilled, formal connections ceases for the time being. Supply contracts are the subject of Parts Three and Five.
2. *Vertical integration* A company, recognizing the benefit of working with one supplier over others, enters a long-term supply arrangement with that supplier. Marks and Spencer's has this with many suppliers, and it is increasingly happening in manufacturing, in particular the motor industry, where Just-in-Time, Total Quality Management, and subcontracting of several inputs through a small number of coordinating suppliers are becoming the norm. A degree of managerial interrelationship becomes important, and strategic decisions by both supplier and purchaser begin to be influenced by the contracts between them. As the span of control extends up the supply chain to subcontractors, and down to customers, the approach becomes known as *supply chain management*. This is more appropriate to routine manufacturing than projects. However, many of the benefits are being incorporated into projects through the approach know as *partnering* (Chapter 8).
2. *Joint ventures* These involve closer integration, and follow from a recognition that each party has something the other needs, perhaps not of equal importance, but of such significance that it is in both parties' interest to ensure longer term cooperation between them. The relationship will be a key element of the corporate strategy of each partner and a necessary component of achieving the mission. The emphasis is on

achieving objectives for the business as a whole, rather than at the project or product level, which is dealt with by short- or long-term supply arrangements.

4. *Mergers* The ultimate cooperative arrangement, where two companies become one. A merger may follow from a successful joint venture. The decision to merge depends on the degree of common interest. Two companies with widely differing portfolios may find that in one area a joint venture provides mutual benefit, but they have little common interest elsewhere. Where the majority of business sectors they serve are common, a merger is possible. A takeover, friendly or otherwise, arises from the recognition of business fit by one or both parties.

This range of collaborative arrangements suggests the essential features of joint ventures:

- They require two or more autonomous parties to work together;
- They rely on mutual trust, understanding and assistance.
- They require careful formation and management.
- They require each party to reveal its covert objectives.
- They should be undertaken for a specific business purpose.
- They should be essential to the mission of both parties.

There are three basic formats:

1. *Consortia* are groups of companies who combine resources, typically for a one-off project, without disguising their individual involvements. Consortia do not consolidate liability, and so leave individual companies exposed. They give certain tax advantages. There are two types of consortia:
   - *open consortium* where each company contracts with the client;
   - *closed consortium* which is an internal agreement between the companies with only one contracting with the client.
2. *Partnerships* are similar to consortia. They allow closer cooperation, but, importantly, each company is liable for any debt incurred, action taken or default incurred by any of the others. They have certain tax considerations.
3. *Incorporation* is the establishment of a separate legal identity for a partnership, as a limited liability company. This gives the venture a separate identity, which enables it to operate independently and raise finance in its own right.

7.2 Objectives of joint ventures

Joint ventures are more difficult to operate than the usual main contractor/subcontractor and direct labour approaches to projects. Therefore, the objectives must provide sound reason for the more difficult approach. Possible reasons for forming a joint venture include:

1. *Political risk sharing* Notably in unstable regions for tying together the interests of a foreign contractor with a local company.
2. *Commercial risk sharing* Especially in the case of substantial projects requiring large financial commitment over a number of years, to improve prospects for capital expenditure, commercial risk and therefore insurance and guarantee prospects.
3. *Investment of surplus capital and assets* Enabling participation in a prestigious project, by a contractor with an existing reasonably full order book.
4. *Overcoming host government discrimination* Notably where foreign governments apply a premium to non-local company tenders. Also used during transition from multinational dominance in a country developing its own industry.
5. *Combining resources credibility and commitment* Necessary where client requirements are greater than the capabilities of a tenderer and also to enable direct control by the client as opposed to a hierarchy of subcontractors.
6. *Competition* In specialist work the availability of an expert company to competitors will be reduced. It also may be used as a first step to future purchase of a selected company.
7. *Tax consideration* Certain advantages exist based on the legal entity of a company.

7.3 Operational difficulties

There are two major areas of operational difficulty in joint ventures:

– Conflict
– Culture.

Conflict

Joint Ventures are frequently short term in outlook, conflicting with partners long term views.[1]

Potential areas of conflict on a joint venture include:

1. *Management styles* Decision making responsibility and authority even with minority share partners who must have some ability to protect their interests.
2. *Management board composition* Regular participation of senior personnel is necessary. However, this conflicts with the personal diaries and often duties are delegated to less senior personnel.
3. *Implications of project failure* The prospect of failure and its effect on reputations poses different considerations for each party.
4. *Profit distribution policy* A foreign partner would probably wish to transfer profits out of a host country. However, early removal of funds will limit the financial capabilities of a venture. Retention of profits in the venture may erode the influence of minority share partners.
5. *Personnel* Allocation of key personnel especially the project manager guarantees influence.
6. *Conflict of interests* Overt and covert goals exist and conflict in most ventures and must be learnt through experience.
7. *External factors* Government pressures limit the ability for global integration of companies, thus restricting the growth of any joint venture.
8. *Scale of works* The forced involvement of numerous competing partners may be a necessity.

Culture

The degree to which personnel accommodate the ways of others may prove critical to partner interests. However, there are barriers programmed into us by our own culture. Our own norms and standards are not always applicable to others. It is important therefore to invest time and effort in familiarizing personnel with the culture of the prospective partner. This need is amplified for work in a foreign country.[2,3] The most obvious area for concentration is communication, language, alphabet, context, etc., and a cautious, patient approach is to be recommended. Sometimes the pitfalls are greater where there is a supposed 'common' language, but the cultures are quite different. This is covered further in Section 7.7.

7.4 Organizational structures

Basic formats

There are three basic formats for joint venture arrangements:

- *Forward integration* where two companies form a joint venture to perform works.

- *Backward integration* where a joint venture contracts work back to the individual partners.
- *Multi-stage arrangement* where a joint venture contracts works to other companies.

A symmetrical arrangement is where equal shares are held.

Operational structures

The structure determines the active involvement of each partner. There are essentially two types of operating structure:

- Integrated
- Non-integrated.

INTEGRATED

Staff from the two parties to the venture are seconded into a new task force for the duration of the project. This approach is favoured where it is impractical to divide the project into neat packages of work, or where the scope is so complex that it requires a highly structured and authoritative management. Benefits include a reduction in inter-company rivalry and a degree of management flexibility.

NON INTEGRATED

Each party works separately on its designated share of the work. This approach is of benefit where the project works lend themselves to breakdown on a technical or geographical basis.

The sponsor

The vast majority of joint ventures entail some aspects of the integrated and non-integrated approaches, and it is common practice for one party to assume a dominant role. This party is often called the *sponsor*. Adopting a sponsor and the sponsor's organization, systems and management structure enables a faster start to a project. However, the sponsor will be in a position to exert a considerable amount of influence on the future running of the venture, possibly resulting in conflict with equal share partners.

Usually the sponsor provides the basic management infrastructure to support project operations, administration, client liaison, accounting, etc. Previous input may have included provision of pre-tender teams for estimating, planning and pre-contract negotiation. It is important at the outset to make agreement provision for sponsor. It is vital for the protection of both the sponsor and the other partners, that the agreement clearly lays down the following:

- The responsibility and authority of the sponsor to act on behalf of the joint venture participants.
- The liability to which the sponsor will be accountable while acting on behalf of the participants.
- Reimbursement provision, in lump sum or profit percentage terms, for the additional services provided.

7.5 Forming the venture

Partner selection

Compromise is important when choosing a partner and the process must start by definition of reasons and a statement of goals. In Section 7.2 we listed objectives of joint ventures, and these should be related to the choice of partner:

Political risk may be reduced if a joint venture is perceived to contain a high degree of local content. If this is not possible the following must be considered:

- Is the political risk unacceptable?
- Are the existing allegiances of the local companies open to review?
- Is it feasible to partner local companies outside your industry?
- Is it feasible to partner influential companies outside the host country?

Commercial risk may be reduced by combining practical, financial or other expertise in a venture. Level of input and areas of reliance must be predetermined. Selection must therefore involve detailed financial appraisal of prospective partners' resources and capabilities together with the possible attitude to adversity. Ideally, four criteria should be fulfilled:

- Previous involvement in similar projects
- Previous experience in proposed host country
- Adequate financial capability and stability
- Compatible management attitudes.

Host government discrimination may be overcome if prospective partners have substantial influence in the host country. The main question in this case is the share to be held by the local company.

Increased credibility and commitment requires prospective partners to be appraised as follows to ensure they have genuine capability:

- *Financial resources* must be sufficient to meet project needs and may be determined by analysis of accounting data.
- *Track record* should be established by references over previous ten years. It is important to investigate key management personnel who will be actively involved with the venture.

Competition strategy requires care to be taken to understand fully the overt and covert goals of any prospective partner. One reason for joint venturing is as an initial step towards takeover.

Tax advantage may be the main reason for joint venturing. Then, it is probable that the company name and country of registration are the primary concerns.

Initial agreement

It is important to set out clearly the basis of the proposed relationship in an initial agreement. Notably when joint ventures are formed there is little time to formulate a comprehensive document and therefore a statement of general agreements should be constructed referring to principles, management structure, financial, commercial and resource matters. In a typical format, the document would normally refer to the following:

- Declaration of intention to joint venture.
- Works description.
- Recognition in principle of the responsibilities, liabilities, obligations and rights of each party.
- A declaration of shareholding and allocation of profit and losses.
- A statement regarding the nature of the proposal, i.e. consortium, partnership or incorporation.
- Recognition of the role and reimbursement of the sponsor.
- Agreement to a third party arbitrator.
- A basis for contract termination.
- A statement regarding resolution of possible future conflicts of interests.

Legality will depend on the wording so contained. It must be determined whether the document will form a contract in its own right or whether it is merely a statement of future intent to contract.

Law should be that of the country in which work is to be undertaken.

Formal agreement

Ideally any contract should be established, then restricted to use as a reference point only. Reference should be made to the following areas which may cause concern:

- *Capital requirement* is usually fulfilled in proportion to the intended shareholdings. Frequently, joint ventures are best served by financial loans from individual partners. A clause is usually necessary to prevent unilateral withdrawal of capital.
- *Operational structure* should be defined. State whether an integrated or non-integrated approach is to be adopted and where overall control and guidance will be administered. This covers: appointments to the executive board, nomination procedures, chairman election, and board jurisdiction; management structure, the appointment of project manager, key managerial positions, accountability and the provision of support resources.
- *Sponsor's* role, authority and reimbursement for additional activities must be specified.
- *Marketing and tendering costs* must be allocated to each party in the venture.
- *Bonds and guarantees* will require the backing of partners individually until a joint venture has established sufficient credibility in its own right.
- *Individual services* must be specified with reference to specialist resources and their remuneration.
- *Profit distribution* is usually distributed in accordance with shareholding although a mechanism should be included to allow for possible change.
- *Plant and equipment* must be procured. Direction should be given regarding purchase, leasing or loans from individual partners. Disposal should also be addressed.
- *Accounting standards and practices* should be specified, typically including:
  - Open bookkeeping
  - Fiscal year dates
  - Depreciation methods
  - Nomination of auditors
  - Frequency and type of management acounting reports.
- *Duration* is specified by stating whether the contract is work related or time related.

7.6 Managing the venture

Executive board

Effectively a joint venture board is much the same as a company board of directors.

Composition and appointments generally reflect shareholding of each partner, however deviations may be applicable in special circumstances. Numbers must be kept to a manageable level if numerous partners are involved and this may mean certain members possessing enhanced voting power. The position of chairman should be rotated and purely perfunctory. To comply with the Companies Act, the board of an incorporated venture may fulfil the two roles of board of directors and shareholders' representatives.

Jurisdiction of the board is to direct the venture without involvement in daily routine operations. Matters of importance may include:

- Tendering policy
- Financing and budgeting
- Capital contributions
- Bonds and guarantees
- Strategic planning
- Major procurement
- Key personnel appointments.

Joint venture staff, via the project manager, should only be responsible to the board. The board officially acts as the only responsible body to report progress to the partners.

Management

Joint ventures are often created due to competitive motives which may in turn be responsible for their termination. Trust and open communications must be developed between project manager, executive board and partners. One potential limitation in use of enhanced resources is that this need arises before a time when trust and confidence has been firmly established. To ensure long-term success, compromise must be perceived by all parties as being a mutual effort. Personal allegiance of staff must primarily be with the venture to maintain credibility with all partners. In developing countries ventures should be locally staffed as managing requirements include dealing with the local community.

7.7 International projects

One of the most demanding situations arises when your customers or partners in a joint venture have a cultural or institutional structure different from your own. This often happens on projects involving international collaboration, where the financial and credibility risks are often high. With fewer shared cultural and commercial assumptions, let alone language, the chances of a damaging misunderstanding are greater, and so previous experience in dealing with these parties, maintaining contacts and communication and having a continuing presence in the countries concerned become important. So much so that serious players in international projects have a permanent presence in the countries where they operate, preferring not to rely on local agents. This will give local clients, government authorities and business interests confidence that your participation in a project, which may have local significance far greater than its relative financial importance, is part of a continuing relationship, and that local concerns will be handled rapidly by direct contact with a senior level in your organization. This requires continuing commitment of resources, including finance and quality managers, but is indispensable if success, and not tears, is to result. It follows that care must be taken in choice of market, taking account of consultant/contractor advantages and the potential project demands, not least the extra supply, transportation and site management needs imposed by geographical distance. International projects carry a set of special problems, and should be approached with an open and frank mind being aware of the following:

- The special demands of the client and market.
- The calibre and motivation of both oneself and prospective partners.
- The need to prepare and negotiate a satisfactory contract and sharing arrangement with partners.
- The need to establish an effective project team and liaison locally, with the necessary senior backing to respond to sudden changes.

Characteristics of international projects

The market environment of international projects poses several special issues:

CLIENT GOVERNMENT PROCEDURE

Many projects, especially in developing nations relying on aid or government guaranteed financing, will be contracted with local government agencies, and so the allocation of resources, including local currency for civil works, will require authorization of a central finance ministry. For all decisions to be made promptly, the following need to be established in advance:

- The decision-making structure
- The levels of responsibility
- The participants involved in the process
- Any necessary stipulations and limitations on the client to carry out their responsibilities.

In general, these can involve procedures and conditions with which the average contractor may not be familiar from his or her own domestic experience. You need to think carefully from the standpoint of the various partners involved, and conduct a dialogue relationship with them to avoid unnecessary offence. Disagreements on apparently trivial issues can lead to attitude changes with damaging consequences. Assume nothing.

LEGAL STRUCTURE AND PAYMENT CONDITIONS

In order to avoid ambiguity, and the imposition of unexpected conditions in subsequent negotiations, the following need to be clarified at an early stage:

- Contract conditions
- Payment triggers
- The legal status of parties to the contract
- Default stipulation and arbitration
- The designation of local subcontractors.

PERFORMANCE OF LOCAL SUBCONTRACTORS

The conduct of a project, especially time-scale and cost, can be radically affected by the performance of local participants. Careful and tactful supervision of them is therefore required, but with good local advice to avoid damaging offence or loss of face.

CHARACTERISTICS OF THE CLIENT

The status, personalities, professional standing and aspirations of key local client staff should be recognized and respected. The basic rule in carrying out the project is 'make sure the buck stops on the other side of the table'; that is any pretexts for delay or change should be with the clients or their agencies.

LOCAL ADMINISTRATIVE DEMANDS

To maintain a continuing interface and feedback with the client and other local interests affecting the outcome of the project, a stable and professional group of people must be established at the earliest stage. They must be equipped with adequate hardware, software and communications systems, and there must be minimal changes of personnel during the project. To be convincing, the local team must have genuine, devolved authority, and where reference to a senior level is necessary, this should be seen to be rapid and effective. Local client confidence is crucial. Even though local specifics may vary, these essentials need to be established, particularly to cope with the inevitable uncertainties and problems of doing the project.

Characteristics of international partners

A similar set of issues need to be borne in mind for a sound confident relationship with project partners.

NATURE OF THE COMPANY

Since your fortunes are linked to how well partners do their job and respond to the unpredictable, a clear-sighted view is needed of their reliability in the face of risks. There should therefore be a thorough review of their financial strength, backing, track record in the technology and markets, and their strengths and weaknesses. This is especially important with new partners.

RELATIONSHIP WITH GOVERNMENT

Since most overseas projects involve export credit guarantees, Third World aid, or other financial aspects impinging on government relationships, the effectiveness of a partner's relationships with its own government could be crucial. For particularly large or controversial projects, it may be necessary to create contacts between national governments, in which case it is vital to have good links established at both company and government level.

ATTITUDE TO RISK

Risks on international projects include normal contractual risks such as bid and performance bonds, penalties, damages, but also major additional risks such as climatic conditions, delays and damage in port and freight handling, and security of storage. The most important interface with partners is their readiness to tolerate the extra cost of responding to these risks. An essential prerequisite to agreeing the scope of shared work, is to define clearly roles and responsibilities, and the channels of communications on solving joint problems. The awkward issues lie in ensuring precise monitoring and identification of problems early enough for joint management decisions.

MARKET AND LOGISTICS CAPABILITY

In the context of the market, the partner's competence in handling an international project should complement and be integrated with one's own, so that actions to clients, authorities, local interests and government agencies are consistent and tactfully effective.

Why Collaborate?

Overseas collaborative projects are far more risky than those in one's own backyard. In addition, reputation is more publicly at stake. You must be sure of your motives in entering into international collaborative ventures. Given the effort and resources required, a single opportunistic project alone is unlikely to justify the risks, so such endeavours should be part of a coherent strategy with the full backing of senior management. There are dangers on all sides. Before entering an international venture, you should ask yourself the following questions:

- Are you really sure of what you want to achieve, and the real risks involved?
- Do you have confidence based on real knowledge of other participants?
- Are you sure of the acceptable conditions and terms to do your job?
- Have you secured the necessary conditions to enable you to be sure of other participants?
- Is your negotiating team up to the job? The outcome is significantly decided before contract signing.
- Are you prepared to deploy the resources to undertake often protracted negotiations, and to have a professional team to participate in these, and be on the spot for the start of the project?

Kind of projects

If the answer to the majority of these questions is a clear yes, it is worth moving to the starting gate. Much will depend on how the project is to take place:

1. If funds are available and the project is being let by orthodox competitive tender, as is the case in Hong Kong, Indonesia and Taiwan, competition will be fierce. You will often have competitors with a local base. An

important purpose of collaboration will then be to gain access to good local contractors, with expertise on prevailing legislation and procedures. However, margins are bound to be tight, and clarity of motives, particularly in looking to a longer term advantage, is essential.

2. If there is a sound project languishing for lack of funds, a collaborative proposal where two governments combine export credit and aid funds to bring it forward, offers scope for a negotiated contract without open competitive bidding. On the other hand, the client and funding governments will need to be satisfied that there is reasonable value for money. In this case, the preliminary work to establish the project's technical feasibility, its priority in the client government's request for aid and financial support, and acceptability to funding governments, will require much more preparatory work and liaison with the project partners. However, success in identifying the opportunity, and working it up into a viable project, will depend on established and continuing local presence.

7.8 Summary

1. Types of cooperative agreement include:
   - Supply contract
   - Vertical integration
   - Joint venture
   - Merger.
2. The essential features of a joint venture are as follows:
   - They require two or more autonomous parties to work together.
   - They rely on mutual trust, understanding and assistance.
   - They require careful formation and management.
   - They require each party to reveal its covert objectives.
   - They should be undertaken for a specific business purpose.
   - They should be essential to the mission of both parties.
3. Objectives of forming a venture include:
   - Political risk sharing
   - Commercial risk sharing
   - Investment of surplus capital and assets
   - Overcoming host government discrimination
   - Combining resources, credibility and commitment
   - Tax advantages.
4. Conflict within a joint venture can be caused by:
   - Management styles
   - Management board composition
   - Project failure implications
   - Profit distribution

- Personnel
- Conflict of interest
- External factors
- Scale of works.

5. There are three basic formats and two types of organizational structure for a joint venture, respectively:
   - Forward integration
   - Backward integration
   - Multi-stage arrangement
   - Integrated versus non-integrated.

   One party is usually dominant in a venture, and assumes the role of sponsor. The sponsor often provides the basic management infrastructure.

6. In forming the venture, partner selection should be linked to the objectives of the venture. There should be an initial agreement and a final agreement. The final agreement should cover the following:
   - Capital requirement
   - Operational structure
   - Sponsor
   - Marketing and tendering costs
   - Bonds and guarantees
   - Individual services
   - Profit distribution
   - Plant and equipment
   - Accounting structures and practices
   - Duration of the agreement.

7. Partners to international projects must consider:
   - Host government procedure
   - Legal structure and payment conditions
   - Performance of local subcontractors
   - Characteristics of the client
   - Local administrative demands.

8. When about to start working overseas you need to ask yourself the following questions:
   - What do you want to achieve, and what are the risks?
   - Are you confident of other participants?
   - Are terms and conditions acceptable?
   - Is your negotiating team up to the job?
   - Do you have the resources to undertake protracted negotiations, and to start the project?

References

1. Schaan, J.L. and Beamish, P.W., 'Joint venture general managers in less developed countries', in *Proceedings of Colloquium on Co-operative Strategies in International Business*, 1988.
2. Jessen, S.A., 'Can project dynamics be modelled?', in *Proceedings of the 1988 International Conference of the System Dynamics Society*, La Jolla, California, Systems Dynamics Society, 1988.
3. Turner, J.R., *The Handbook of Project-based Management* (Chapter 21), McGraw-Hill, 1993.

Bibliography

1. Armitt, J.A., 'Joint Ventures: formation and operation', in *Management of International Construction Projects*, Thomas Telford, 1984.
2. Harrigan, K., *Managing for Joint Venture Success*, Lexington, 1986.
3. Ohmae, K., *The Coming Shape of Global Competition*, Free Press, 1985.
4. Walmsley, J., *Handbook of International Joint Ventures*, Graham and Trotman, 1982.

8

Partnering

Colin Smith and Steve Tonks*

8.1 Introduction

Examples of long-term associations between clients and contractors may be quoted from the last century. It is not a new philosophy. 'Partnering' is merely the 1990s name for an old idea. Possibly the most prominent partnering relationship in UK construction is that between Marks and Spencer and Bovis, dating from the 1920s. Partnering is a way of doing business which recognizes that common goals exist which can be achieved through cooperation and open communications. However, it is more than a set of goals and procedures; it is a philosophy, a state of mind that demands commitment to respect, trust, cooperation and excellence for all stakeholders involved. This revitalized form of cooperation has its roots in the United States, but has established itself in various forms, significantly in the UK process engineering and construction industry. [1,2,3,4,5]

In this chapter, we describe partnering as an approach to contracting. We describe why organizations enter partnering arrangements, the forms they take, how to go about establishing such an arrangement, and commercial and legal issues.

8.2 Why partnering?

Partnering can be viewed as a contractual technique for motivating all participants (individuals and organizations) involved in a project jointly to achieve an enhancement of their competitive position. If benefits are to be justified, partnering needs to be viewed on a long-term basis. Cost minimization and profit maximization must be viewed as the secondary results of less tangible primary benefits such as:

---

*The original version of Chapter 8 was written by Colin Smith. The material on this rapidly changing field was revised and brought up to date by Stephen Tonks.

- Application of total quality management
- Security against the effects of industry recession
- Training improvements
- Industrial relations stability
- Safety enhancement.

Motivation for companies to take part in partnering include the following:

- Clients achieve value for money.
- Contractors achieve income stability.
- Both achieve a reduction in confrontation.

Value for money for clients

Clients can gain financially by closer cooperation with contractors. Value for money by effective partnering may be achieved by:

- Reducing overheads
- Cutting excessive bidding and contract selection costs
- Providing flexible response to market demands
- Allowing clients to concentrate on core business.

However, to enable the above to be achieved, consideration should be given to the use of integrated or complementary, client-contractor teams, or trustworthy contractors working unsupervised.

Contractors' income stability

Implications, to the contractors, from partnering over a period of time are likely to include the following:

- Planning and resource building
- Training, and R&D
- Must provide resources for client's cyclical demands
- May lose work with other clients.

Confrontation reduction

NEDO[6] proposes the reduction in the current level of confrontation in the industry as one of the main benefits to be gained from partnering. Consideration of the following concepts would help achieve this:

- Promotion of a free flow of information.

- Careful selection of contractors after full appraisal of capabilities, availabilities and other qualities.
- Greater emphasis on avoidance of problems rather than solutions.
- Penalties focused on failure to provide information and response to remedial measures, rather than narrow performance of contracted service.
- Substitute contractors' current perceived commercial advantages with protection from worst aspects of blind competition.
- Remove 'the engineer' from his or her current position and promote realities of client/contractor relations, for example by using a 'facilitator' to sponsor agreement rather than enforce it.

8.3 Responding to the changing environment

In a contractual relationship, initial contracts, legal statements or agreements often focus attention on the wrong set of issues. Later, this becomes apparent to management and creates conflict in the relationship between the parties.

When two firms negotiate a partnering agreement, they have a concept of fairness in sharing and in relative benefit. Each perceives benefits from a set of overt and covert goals. The expectation of the partners is that they will get what they bargained for, given the environment they had predicted, and that they will satisfy at least part of their hidden agenda.

If the environment changes, then that can cause unexpected results from a contractual relationship. However, partnering will evolve even when the environment is stable. This is because the partners, the task and the goals all evolve with time. This can be the cause of instability in the partners' expectations, the partnering structure and possibly the partnering arrangement itself. The cyclical nature of project-based industries contributes significantly to this instability. Partnering arrangements which looked good to client organizations in the boom time of the late 1980s, seemed a curse in the recession of the early 1990s. However, the client organizations should remember that one objective of the partnering arrangement was to transfer client exposure to the business cycles to the contractors.

The current practice is for companies to measure their success against the initial negotiated agreement, the overt and the covert goals. Consequently, unexpected outcomes may be an underlining cause of dissatisfaction and conflict. Differences in organizations also represent potential areas of conflict. For example, the culture of each organization or group is different; protocols and languages may be different. Furthermore, participants are likely to have different agendas and be subject to different reward systems. Merging these divergent talents into an effective team can prove to be extremely challenging.[1,2] Therefore, it is important that certain processes are adopted by participants to manage the changes:

- *Learning* Gaining knowledge of the partner's organization, operational practices, business and environment.
- *Bargaining and balancing the revised perceptions and goal sharing* The process must enable renegotiation to an acceptable degree over time or an adjustment of expectations to actual values.
- *Leveraging of partnering values* This affects the values of changing goals to each participant. The value of a specific joint goal to one partner may not be the same to another.

The learning process

Partnering companies must address various areas of learning. Three key areas are recognized:

1. *The partner* It is unlikely that in partnering between a client and a contractor either company will know the other more than superficially upon commencement. This may be in spite of previous experience of working together. Information is also initially restricted due to mistrust and apprehension, by formal transactions, negotiating situations and concern over covert goals. Misrepresentation may well be common. As such, learning may be more difficult in cases where organizational structures differ greatly.
2. *The projects* Formation of a partnering arrangement may result from, or coincide with, the commencement of a particular project. The very reasons for partnering conception may often make the project difficult to plan precisely at the outset. Joint learning about a project is a great medium for binding two companies, as the experience gives the participants the perception of a shared fate, which encourages cooperation.
3. *The goals* The benefits of goals are usually overstated in the initial bargaining process. Also, where learning is a real objective of one partner, this may decay over time as fulfilment is reached. If partners do not continue to expand, a 'dependency spiral' may result as the more static partner depletes an existing inventory of skills to maintain the interest of the other partner.[7]

The bargain and balance process

This process takes place in adjusting perception and sharing outcomes in the partnering agreement. The risk is that often the one-sided need for restoring the balance is found in the partner who has the weaker bargaining position, or more limited extra partnership alternatives. However, the perception of one party of a 'balanced exchange' may not correspond with the other. This is one area where an independent facilitator contractually agreed by all parties can anticipate or resolve disputes.

The leverage process

Leveraging of values created in the partnering arrangement will not affect the set of results, but their value to each partner individually on an absolute, relative, differential or company-specific basis.

Two companies in a partnering arrangement may be satisfied with their gains when the direct gain from the arrangement is clearly asymmetrical.

8.4 Partnering variations

Partnering has a tendency to mean 'all things to all people' and there is considerable variation in the degree to which these arrangements are formalized. However, a general classification of the forms includes:

– Framework agreements
– Coordination agreements
– Full partnering agreements.

1. *Framework agreements* These establish cooperation in its loosest sense. A client will select one or more contractors or suppliers with whom it will enter into standard contracts in the future with no actual commitment to let or take the work from either party. A basic understanding of general concepts and requirements is maintained and advance information may be provided on the client's requirements to facilitate advanced planning.
2. *Coordination agreements* These are essentially defined by an agreement to cooperate in avoiding problems. The relationship is voluntary and is overlaid on a standard contract for project implementation. The duration of the relationship may vary from single project to long-term agreements with the provision for the negotiation of a series of contracts.
3. *Full partnering agreements* These provide for unsupervised provision of services, usually for a specified term. The partnering agreement is the contract and is not subordinated by any other. A joint organization, containing personnel from all parties involved, is normally set up specifically to provide the service.

The beneficial development from general cooperation agreements to more definite associations will occur as long as both parties perceive the arrangement to be the most commercially advantageous. This must regularly be demonstrated, for example by selected competitive tendering. The degree to which the relationship between client and contractor permeates through each project will depend on the client's own capability. The choices are limited to:

- *Minimum client involvement* Whereby the client's input is limited, or consciously reduced.
- *Integration or complementing resources* Clients with large experienced engineering capability are able to give substantial input to projects, with additional resources and expertise provided by contractors.

In either case, the factors essential for achieving success are:

- Selecting the right partner
- Selecting the right personnel
- Mutual trust and respect
- Commitment at all levels
- Team building and training
- Joint problem resolution mechanisms.

8.5 Establishing a partnering arrangement

The partnering arrangement must be established to ensure these key success factors. However, the process must at all times be client led.

Partnering is client led

While in no way inferring that contractors can only be reactive, few contractors would significantly involve themselves in areas which may not fit in with the current thinking of those on whom they are dependent. The following should therefore be considered:

- Client organizations set the strategies and hold the purse strings.
- High pressure promotion to clients, by contractors, of a concept of this magnitude will not work.
- Partnering involves a fundamental strategic rethinking by clients.
- It is necessary for clients to finance the transition, as contractors have a relatively small asset base and therefore cannot raise the necessary initial finance.

Establishing the key success factors

To ensure a successful partnering arrangement, the key success factors listed above must be put in place.

PARTNER SELECTION

Must be carried out with due care, by both clients and contractors. Without careful consideration either party may lock itself into a prospective uncompetitive contract. Clients risk loss of commercial advantage in the contracting marketplace and contractors risk loss of opportunities elsewhere. It is important that both sides understand the extent of workload available for development, and the culture of the prospective partners prior to commencement. Therefore, clients are unlikely to select partners by open competition, but rather as a development from previous successful projects. Clients should spend time developing their cultural knowledge of all prospective collaborators.

PERSONNEL SELECTION

This is critical because it is not formal contracts which make successful relationships; people do. The success of a collaboration depends upon the quality and compatibility of the staff allocated to the association.[8] This is because any project team is the primary contact point in the collaborative process. Most of the inter-organizational communication, decision making and problem solving will take place within this group.[9]

TRUST AND RESPECT

These are essential to allow the commitment from the participants and the exchange of strategic information required for a successful long-term collaboration. Reliability and integrity are of paramount importance.

COMMITMENT AT ALL LEVELS

Within all participating organizations this is a prerequisite if the relationship is to succeed, given the time, effort and resources required to partner successfully, without realizing many of the benefits for a long time (12–18 months is normal). Also, no matter how committed management and team participants are, the partnership will not run itself. In order to track, care for and build the process, individuals from each organization must be assigned responsibility for maintaining the momentum of partnering throughout the life of the project and the relationship.

TEAM BUILDING AND TRAINING

These help cooperation, and are encouraged when people perceive a shared fate.[10] Formal team-building activities are required, usually in the shape of facilitated workshops which should include all key personnel. This assists in affecting the necessary culture change (from confrontation to cooperation) to get people working together. The intention is also to increase the understanding of what is required and sow the seeds for the necessity for continuous improvement.

PROBLEM RESOLUTION

These mechanisms should be defined. Escalation is the control and resolution mechanism for dealing with problems, including conflict. This means that personnel must be encouraged to solve problems at their level within a time limit, or they are escalated to the next management level before they impact on the project and consequently the relationship. It is not always possible to resolve disputes internally, hence it is necessary to have in place a process promoting the expeditious settlement of controversies. Alternative Dispute Resolution (ADR) processes such as mediation or mini-trial are recommended.

8.6 Legal and commercial

Contractual relations

Arrangements may be subdivided into two types:

- *Multiple project* The agreement is the main relationship to cover a wide business sector. Individual projects then emerge to be covered by more traditional contract agreements as required. Here, a specific partnering agreement will be drafted.
- *Single project* The concept of partnering is applied under the main contract for a particular project. Here the partnering application will be detailed as part of the project contract document.

There is no current standard legal format for partnering arrangements, and none is advocated. However, simplicity is important to maintain flexibility.

Contractor reimbursement

The main choice of reimbursement falls into two categories:

- *Price related* lump sums, remeasurable, etc.
- *Cost related* reimbursable.

The former must be based on significant design specification which is not always possible in schedule-led projects. Without removal of substantial commercial risk from the contractor, the degree of openness and cooperation sought will not emerge. There are various ways in which a contractor can be reimbursed and controlled, avoiding the previous adversarial approaches. The following may be worth considering:

- Reimburse the contractor against cost schedules, fixing only those elements which may be more accurately calculated, such as site establishment, profit and overheads.
- Provide incentive to act in the client's best interests and minimize wasted effort by sharing savings to an initial realistic budget.
- Do not relate profit to man-hours expended; that is use fixed fee as opposed to percentage addition.
- Impose target man-hours and declared bonuses to concentrate thought on schedules, but ensure they do not cause a disproportionate amount of time away from more constructive thought.
- Apportion liability to the contractor for rework caused by design error, say up to 20 per cent of contract value; that is affecting the contractors profit only.
- Procure long lead items 'for and on behalf of' the client on a man-hour cost rate basis ensuring no encouragement to expend excessive man-hours.
- Adopt fully defined lump sum fabrication and construction contracts, 'for and on behalf of' the client.

However, as most projects these days are market led, it is rare that schedules allow time for formulation of sufficient design prior to construction commencement. Therefore, contracts are generally best formulated on a schedule of work rates basis.

The EU Utilities Directive

It is sometimes said that partnering is contrary to European Law. The relevant directive is the Utilities Directive. The provisions of the Utilities Directive and its implemented regulations are different from the other directives in that they do not just apply to public bodies or undertakings. It covers procurement of both supplies and works by public and private contracting authorities in the Water, Energy, Transport and Telecommunications (WETT) sectors, and was extended to cover procurement of services in 1994. As a general rule the provisions apply to all bodies which exercise one of the 'relevant activities' and (for non-public bodies) if they operate on the basis of special or exclusive rights granted to them by a Member State.

The EU regime requires that contracts are only awarded following an open and competitive tendering process, and on the basis of lowest price or the most economically advantageous offer. If the procurement process is transparent, objectively entered into and is non-discriminatory, the principles of the EU legislation are satisfied. For client conducting a relevant activity to obtain a repetition of works or services from the same contractor, either the original contract notice must specify that this may be required (and the procedure must begin within three years of the original contract), or the actual partnering agreement itself is put out to competition in accordance with the rules.

8.7 Summary

1. Partnering may not be the solution to all situations, and it is recognized that a great deal of work is necessary to reverse the current approaches which put an undue emphasis on the contract wording. However, where some form of partnering is possible, there are numerous gains to be made by all parties concerned.
2. Advantages to the client may include:
   - Less confrontation – problem solving not escalation
   - Sharing of information
   - Reduction in fixed overheads
   - Reduced learning curves for each project
   - Improved productivity
   - Long-term quality programme application
   - Reduced tender analysis costs
   - Improved 'buildability' in design
   - More open communications
   - Regaining the initial expenditure on the instigation of Total Quality Management programmes (TQM)
   - Reduced duplication of roles, such as checking and monitoring.
3. Advantages to the contractor may include:
   - Workload stability
   - Improvement in operating systems
   - Better management of resources
   - Better employee career development
   - Reduced expenditure on tendering process
   - Opportunity to promote capability to a client for work elsewhere
   - Opportunity to learn from others
   - Research and development opportunities
   - Opportunity for long-term development of safety and industrial relations.
4. However, there are also disadvantages. Disadvantages to the client may include:

- Continuous work must sustain partnering core teams
- Continual requirement to avoid contractor complacency
- Reduced market influence on commercial aspects
- Possible adverse affect on non-project staff
- Greater liability for consequences of errors
- Sharing in cost of problem solving.
5. Disadvantages to the contractor may include:
- Possible loss of short term lucrative work elsewhere
- Possible loss of partnering opportunity elsewhere
- Reduced profit margins for each project
- Risk that continuous workload will not be forthcoming
- Loss of opportunity to profit through variations
- Sharing of gains to be made due to in-house expertise.

References

1. Cowan, C., Gray, C. and Larson, E., 'Project partnering', *Project Management Journal*, **22** (4), 1992.
2. Gray, C. and Larson, E., 'Partnering in the construction industry', in *Proceedings of the International Conference Management by Projects in Practice*, Vienna, June 1993, Gareis, R. (ed.), Project Management Austria, 1992.
3. Haydn, S. (ed.), *Collaboration Management: New Project and Partnering Techniques*, Wiley, 1994.
4. Lamming, R., *Beyond Partnership*, Prentice Hall, 1993.
5. Sonnenberg, F.K., 'Partnering: entering the age of co-operation', *Journal of Business Strategy, Marketing*, spring 1992.
6. NEDO, *Partnering: Contracting without conflict*, National Economic Development Office, Partnering Working Party, 1991.
7. Hamel, G., Doz, Y. and Prahaled, C.R., 'Strategic partnership: success or surrender', in *Proceedings of the Joint Research Colloquium of the Wharton School and Rutgers Graduate School of Management on Co-operative Strategies in International Business*, Wharton and Rutgers, 1986.
8. Loraine, R.K., *Partnering in the Public Sector*, The Business Round Table, 1993.
9. Moore, C., Mosley, D. and Slagle, M., 'Partnering: guide-lines for win–win project management', *Project Management Journal*, **23**(1), 1992.
10. Kanter, R.M., *When Giants Learn to Dance*, Simon & Schuster, 1989.

9
Build–own–operate (–transfer), BOO(T)

Peter Morris

9.1 Introduction

BOO(T), build–own–operate(–transfer), is applied to projects which are primarily infrastructure projects, but instead of being financed by the public sector, as is normal practice, they are financed by private promoters who build, and subsequently own and operate the facility. The private promoters obtain their profits not from being paid for the work, but from the revenue streams obtained by charging the public a 'toll' for using the facility. In some situations the government, who must have approved the project (for it would have been undertaken by the public sector unless special permission had been given), may only grant ownership for a certain period – for example 15, 20 or more years. In this case there is a 'transfer' condition attached for the facility, by which it is transferred to the state at the end of the licence period. This condition is obviously important since it limits the amount of profit which may be taken from the project by the private sector promoter.

BOO(T) projects are extremely important for two reasons. First, they reflect a growing trend towards replacing public sector financing with private sector. Second, they encourage the principal participants, most of whom are also involved in the financing of the project, to concentrate on its overall business success. In the past there was a tendency to suboptimize, to push particular interests (such as new technology) and for conflict to arise (for example between client and contractor).[1]

In this chapter we describe the BOO(T) method as a form of project finance involving a partnership between the public and private sectors. We consider the issues raised by the BOO(T) method, and describe its origins and characteristics. We close by identifying the principal risks raised by the BOO(T) method.

9.2 Issues raised by the BOO(T) method

It is unusual for the state to 'let out' its responsibilities for providing infrastructure. However, doing so became somewhat fashionable during the 1980s as part of the 'privatization' philosophy of certain governments, particularly the British Conservative Government. However, it does raise several issues:

1. Issues of macroeconomics, particularly as regards the stimulation of the economy.
2. Issues of planning (see Chapter 16); for example:
   – Who should decide the route of BOO(T) roads?
   – What are the mechanisms for planning approval?
   – What risks do these pose to BOO(T) promoters?
3. Doctrines of competition; for example, if someone comes up with an idea for a BOO(T) scheme, should they immediately have proprietary rights over that idea or will the government (as it does in the UK) want to invite others to tender for the scheme?

In many ways the BOO(T) method is similar, at least technically, to much of the private sector's approach to initiating and executing projects. With BOO(T) and private sector projects, any potential investor will look at the financial attractiveness of a project before making an investment. The approach is almost identical to project finance (Chapter 6). The key point about BOO(T) is that private sector businessmen and women and financiers are being asked to make investment and ownership decisions about projects that essentially lie in the public domain.

9.3 Project finance revisited

Project finance is a method of financing where the lender's financial returns are generated by the project alone. Project finance differs from non-project finance in that the only guarantees that the lender has are those generated by the robustness of the project itself. Most financing for projects is in fact done on a corporate or a sovereign basis; that is, the lending is made directly to a company or a sovereign state (i.e. a country). In these cases the loan is guaranteed by the financial strength of the company or country. With project financing, however, the lender has 'no recourse' to the financial assets of the companies or countries behind the project, and is repaid solely out of the income stream from the project. For this reason, the method is often also known as 'non-recourse lending'. Actually, there are very few projects which are 100 per cent non-recourse – simply because the risk is generally too great and borrowers will not lend on such a basis. We will see shortly that although BOO(T) projects are supposed to be 100 per cent non-recourse, in practice it is often the case that some government guarantees are also required. Since 100 per cent finance is not normally obtained, another frequently used name for the method is limited recourse finance.

9.4 Origins of the BOO(T) method

Project, or limited recourse, financing first appeared in the mining and oil and gas industries. An RTZ project in Bougainville in the late 1960s was financed on this basis. In the southern United States at the same time, a number of owners of oil deposits, who had little in the way of corporate assets, financed the developments of their projects solely on the basis of their anticipated future income stream. With these types of loan, the lender's security comes from the project alone. The principal kind of security is title, either:

- To the assets in the ground – for example through a mortgage arrangement; or
- To 'forward sales' contracts – for example, if the promoter has obtained a contract from someone to buy their minerals at x tonnes per year, then this is real security to the lender who is going to finance the building of the plant which is expected to produce x plus tonnes per year.

During the 1970s limited recourse finance was used for a number of North Sea Oil developments, largely, frankly, as a method of keeping the finance off the developers' balance sheets in order to obtain tax benefits. (Hence the term, 'off-balance sheet financing'). Property/real estate financing was another area where the method was used. Early examples of BOO(T) projects (both often not referred to) were:

- The Hong Kong metro, financed and built by the Japanese on this basis in the 1970s.
- Toll roads, particularly the French and Spanish ones.

In 1984 two dramatic initiatives propelled the BOO(T) idea to the fore. One was the proposal to undertake the Channel Tunnel on this basis. The other was the proposal by Turkey's Prime Minister, Turgat Ozal, to use the method for a number of Turkish infrastructure projects. Ozal used the term BOT. Other terms which have been used include BOO, BRT and BOOST: in fact there are all kinds of acronyms which have sprung up:

- BOT: build, operate, transfer;
- BOO: build, operate, own;

- BRT: build, rent, transfer;
- BOOST: build, own, operate, subsidize, transfer.

Ozal introduced the BOT idea as a way of getting infrastructure spending into his country essentially in an off-balance-sheet manner. He was seeking to get investment into Turkey without increasing his country's national debt, which was already heavy. In fact it has proved enormously difficult to initiate many BOT projects in Turkey, for reasons which will become apparent in a moment.

In the mid-1980s, many people saw the BOO(T) method as a way of stimulating projects in the Third World which, at that time, was deep in the middle of a lending freeze caused by the oil crisis and loss of confidence following Mexico's repayments schedule. The World Bank went some way to encouraging this route, seeking to establish co-financing on this basis (i.e. joint Bank/BOOT financing). Again, however, it would be fair to say that progress has been slower than many both expected and hoped.

In the United Kingdom there was, and still is, considerable interest in the method. The Conservative Government has been seeking BOO(T) schemes for a number of toll roads, but so far the only schemes which have gone ahead are the Dartford Crossing and the Second Severn Bridge, though it is likely there will be others before long. (Note that all the UK ones so far, including the Channel Tunnel, are for water crossings. The reason for this is simply that the traffic revenues can be calculated with greater certainty and hence the projects are easier to finance.) In the United States there have also been a number of attempts to initiate BOO(T) projects, with about the same success as in the United Kingdom, except perhaps in the roads sector where the success rate has been higher. (In the United States, many elements of infrastructure have been traditionally owned by the private sector which in other countries would have been owned by the public sector, for example utilities.)

9.5 Characteristics of BOO(T) projects

Although no two BOO(T) projects are exactly alike, they generally follow similar lines. In this section we consider some essential features of the BOO(T) method which must be addressed when establishing a scheme. The main elements of BOO(T) projects include:

- Host government
- The promoter, the project company
- Local partners
- The construction organization
- Financing.

Host government

Without the wholehearted desire and commitment of the host government a BOO(T) project has no chance of success. Not only must the host government 'liberate' the project from the public into the private sector, it must champion its cause, implicitly or explicitly. It must even be willing to provide certain guarantees (for example, as to expropriation). Special legislation is often required (which, as we have seen once or twice in the United Kingdom, might have to be timed with elections). The terms of the operating, or concession, agreement will have to be agreed with the government. Host country financing may be necessary and in any case economists, whether in central government (as in the UK's Treasury) or lending institutions, will look at the effect the project has both on the overall level of borrowing in the country and on the level of demand for services.

In reality, it is unlikely that BOO(T) projects can be accomplished free of the shackles of government interference. Beware new legislation (particularly following a change in government). This can totally change the basis upon which the project is proceeding. Political and bureaucratic support must be obtained too: without it the project will be enormously harder to realize. Two 'political' issues which have been important in the United Kingdom to date have been planning and competitive bidding:

– Planning is the risk that planning permission might not be obtained after all the development work put in so far.
– Competitive bidding is the Government's insistence that schemes be bid openly even if they have been 'invented' by just one group.

These are typical of the kinds of issues which BOO(T) sponsors will require government action in dealing with. Gauge to what extent the host government has the technical, legal and financial skills at hand and is mentally predisposed for this form privatization.

The liability of the host government to change the basis of its support is known as political risk. Note that political risk may apply at local level as well as at national level. Changes not aimed at the BOO(T) project – for example, on issues of taxation – also count as political risk. Beware of the trap that many fall into: countries which have posed no political risk for some time, may still have high political risk. However, many well intentioned, experienced but intellectually naive people have for years been trying to develop parametrics for measuring political risk.

The promoter: the project company

The project company must be strong: that is, knowledgeable, capable and willing to raise the necessary finance, negotiate contracts and implement the development work. The promoter organization must be willing to spend quite literally millions of pounds in developing the BOO(T) scheme – certainly this has been the scale of effort in most of the large UK and Third World projects so far.

The legal aspects of BOO(T) projects are particularly daunting since essentially the owner organization is being cobbled together solely out of contracts. So be ready for substantial legal fees as well as those of financial advisers, insurers and others.

An important lesson from the Channel Tunnel project is that the owner organization should not reflect too closely the particular interests of any one of the supplier groups. The sponsor must be strong financially, and have real operating expertise. BOO(T) projects are, by definition, contractor initiated but having these contractors negotiate contracts with themselves is a recipe for project disaster.[2] Promoters often form a consortium type organization made up of several of the principal suppliers but also possibly including representatives of the finance groups and possibly the government and others.

The 'owner organization' should be formed at as early a stage as possible. This allows it to begin forming its own character and to move quickly on to issues as they arise. The Channel Tunnel concession was won by a group consisting only of contractors and bankers. You might like to consider what you would expect the first year or two of the owner company's existence to have been like.[2]

Local partners

On 'overseas projects' it is generally advisable to have a strong, well-connected private sector participant among the owner/investor group. Such a participant could be a local supplier or an investor who will ease the way into the local community and should help reduce antagonism towards 'selling off national assets to imperialists' (Chapter 7).

The construction organization

The project financiers will require clear (time and cost) completion guarantees. The construction capability must therefore be excellent! As noted above however, beware of 'letting' construction contracts which are too easy – this will not be in the 'owner's' interest. If possible, employ a local construction company at least to some extent – not only for the reasons mentioned above but also because they will have a better understanding of local construction conditions.

Financing

Host governments will generally want to see some form of long-term financial commitment. This may take several forms: subordinated debt, invested equity, equity in the form of deferred fees, etc. Most BOO(T) schemes have a minimum 10–30 per cent equity element. Some are higher. The ratio of debt to equity essentially reflects the level of risk perceived in the project – as a rule, the higher the risk the higher will be the equity element. (Equity generally earns a higher rate of return than debt; it also reflects a different financial market.)

The proportion of local to foreign currency obviously depends to a significant extent upon the work content of the project and the nature of the country in which it is being built. It is however a critical element, for the difficulties of *repatriation* of foreign currency can be a major factor in getting the BOO(T) established. This is particularly the case in infrastructure projects, which of course most BOO(T) projects are – since the project's output is nearly always sold or measured in local currency. ('Swapping' of blocked local currency, for example in debt–equity swaps, is a technique much favoured by commercial bankers, though less so by central bankers because of its potential inflationary impact.) A further financial risk is that of inflation and devaluation of the local currency. Both these lead to the critical element of currency or foreign exchange risk.

The financing of most BOO(T) projects recognizes that these projects have different risk phases. For example, the Stage I financing of the Channel Tunnel received a higher rate of return than Stage II, which in turn received a higher return than Stage III, since the risks were correspondingly greater in the earlier stages. Similarly, the construction phases require a higher return than the operating (utility) phases.

9.6 Principal BOO(T) risks

All projects entail risks. Some may reasonably be born. Some may reasonably be contracted out. Others can be insured. Those that remain will either have to be absorbed or declined; and if this means the project will not proceed, then so be it – better it does not proceed than you go bankrupt. Typical risks include:

1. *Completion risk* This is the risk that the project will not be completed on time, in budget or to technical specification. It is normally born by the contractor. Evidently it is assumed secondarily by the promoter in so far as they accept the construction contract. Many bilateral and export credit agencies refuse to entertain completion risks and in this case subordinated loans may be required by the host government to

guarantee senior debt service through project completion.

2. *Performance and operating risk* This is the risk that the project will not perform, and is normally carried by warranties issued by the contractor(s) and their suppliers.

3. *Economic risk* The risk that the input costs or output prices may change such that the project revenue stream is substantially disturbed, and rests with the promoting organization. These matters are normally analysed through modelling but can still be a major issue. (Note for instance the 30 per cent plus rise in gas charges made in the United Kingdom in March 1991.) Lenders to BOO(T) projects often insist upon elaborate ESCROW accounts to cover forward debt service and guard against interruptions to cash flow (Chapter 6). Cash flow insurance is also available.

4. *Inflation and foreign exchange risk* Inflation, devaluation and the blocking of foreign currency repatriation are covered here. Long-term supply and purchase contracts may provide some guarantee but ultimately these risks can be so great that they are often not taken by foreign investors. It has therefore often been the case that the host government has been required to cover these risks.

5. *Insurable risk* On a BOO(T) project these will typically include:
   - Casualty risk covering its plant and equipment
   - Third party liability insurance
   - Workmen's compensation insurance
   - Other insurances for commercially insurable risks.

   Depending on the degree of host government support being provided, it may also have insurance to cover items such as:
   - Business interruption
   - Cash flow interruption.

6. *Uninsurable risk* This is basically *force majeure* risk. The insurance markets rarely take these on. The equity investors may; otherwise the host government will be forced to provide some cover.

7. *Political risk* This can generally be insured against, either from the commercial market, export credit agencies, or through the (World Bank's) Multilateral Investment Guarantee Agency, MIGA.

9.7 Summary

1. BOO(T) projects are (usually) infrastructure projects which instead of being financed by the public sector, as is normal practice, are financed by the public sector, which builds, owns and operates the resulting facility.

2. BOO(T) projects are (in theory) financed by 100 per cent non-recourse financing. The lenders are repaid out of the revenue stream only.

3. BOO(T) projects raise issue of:
   - Macroeconomics

- Planning
- Competition
- Ownership.
4. The main elements of BOO(T) projects are:
   - The relationship with the host government
   - The strength of the promoter or host company
   - The use of local partners on overseas projects
   - The excellence of the construction organization
   - Long-term financing commitment.
5. The principal risks of BOO(T) projects include:
   - Completion risk
   - Performance and operating risk
   - Economic risk
   - Inflation and foreign exchange risk
   - Insurable risk
   - Uninsurable risk
   - Political risk.

References

1. Morris, P.G.W., *The Management of Projects*, Thomas Telford, 1994.
2. Turner, J.R., *The Handbook of Project-based Management*, McGraw-Hill, 1993.

Bibliography

1. Augenblick, M. and Custer, S.B., 'The build, operate and transfer approach to infrastructure projects in developing countries', Working Papers – Infrastructure, The World Bank, 1990.
2. Castle, G.R., 'Project financing guidelines for the commercial bankers', *Journal of Commercial Bank Lending*, 1975.
3. Letheridge, N, *New developments in project finance, construction collaboration: private sector interaction in infrastructure development*, Institute for International Research, 1988.
4. Merna, A., Payne, H. and Smith, N.J., 'Benefits of a structured concession agreement of build–own–operate–transfer (BOOT) projects', *International Construction Law Review*, 1993.
5. Merna, A. and Smith, N.J., *Guide to the Preparation and Evaluation of BOOT Project Tenders*, Project Management Group, UMIST, 1993.
6. Tiong, R.L.K., 'Comparative study of BOT projects', *Journal of Management Engineering*, 6(1), 1990.
7. Tiong, R.L.K. and Yeo, K.-T., 'Project financing as a competitive strategy in winning overseas jobs', *International Journal of Project Management*, 11(2), 1993.

PART THREE
SUPPORTERS

Part Three considers the parties who support the owner and sponsors by supplying goods and services in the widest sense. Over the next three chapters we describe contractors, consultants and the providers of financial services. In each chapter, we explain the role of the various supporters on projects, identify the benefits and risks to the owner from their involvement on the project, identify the risks of the relationship to the supporter, and explain how the relationship can be managed to optimize the outcome to both parties.

We do not attempt an exact definition of the difference between contractors and consultants. It is sometimes said that the difference is the former do work on behalf of the owner, and the latter show the owner how better to do it for themselves. However, in reality, the difference is more in the nature of the service provided: contractors undertake artisan labour; whereas consultants provide professional services; and this is what we assume. Even that difference is not exact: in the civil engineering industry designers are called consultants; whereas in the petrochemical industry they are called contractors. In the IT industry both programmers and systems analysts (artisans and designers respectively) are called contractors; it is the prime or managing contractors who describe themselves as consultants.

There is a fourth type of supporter of a project not considered separately, the suppliers of goods. Again, the difference between a contractor and a supplier is not clear. The EU Supplies Directive applies to amounts in excess of 400 000 ECU (£300 000), and the Works Directive (contracts directive) applies to over 5 million ECU (£3.5 million). However, the limits are more to define the scope of the directive, than because there is some precise cut-off. The difference is more in the nature of risk sharing. Suppliers are given precise targets for the performance of their products, and the time and price of its delivery. The risk that they do not meet those targets is entirely theirs. If they meet their targets, then the risk transfers absolutely to the owner. Indeed, the owner or main contractor often assumes a large amount of the risk of consequential loss. If the product is late, or fails in service, then the supplier's risk is limited to the value of the product, sometimes less. The owner or main contractor takes all the consequential loss. With contractors, there is a much greater amount of risk sharing between client and contractor; this is a significant element of the contract strategy (see Part Five). Apart from this element of risk sharing, there is little mileage in differentiating between suppliers and contractors.

In Chapter 10, Ernie Torbet and Norman Dunlop describe contractors, the core providers of services to the owners and sponsors. Contractors undertake work on behalf of the owner, often to construct all or part of the facility, either on- or off-site. Contractors may work directly for the owner, or as subcontractors to another contractor. Norman Dunlop also considers managing or prime contractors. These provide project management and/or design management services to the owner, managing the delivery of the facility and/or its design on their behalf. All other contractors on the project will be subcontractors to the managing or prime contractor. They will often be barred from taking any of the subcontracts, especially on projects financed by development agencies such as the World Bank. The use of managing contractors is gaining wide acceptance because it is seen as a flexible approach to contracting, especially in the sharing of risk between owner, contractors and subcontractors.

In Chapter 11, Ernie Torbet and John Dingle introduce consultants as people who provide specialist services to the owner. Frank Thomas and Malcolm Watkinson then describe issues relating to designers. Mr Thomas describes their relationship with the owner, and their involvement in the delivery of the facility. Mr Watkinson explains the use of *coordinated project information*. Finally, Jeffrey Blum considers a second type of specialist consultant, shippers. It is often necessary to transport materials for a project from overseas, and shippers can arrange for transport from supplier to project site, including road, rail, air and sea transport. Depending on the nature of the contractual arrangements, the shipper may work for the supplier, the managing contractor or the owner.

In Chapter 12, Ashok Jashapara and Rodney Turner introduce financial supporters, and consider the types of organization who finance projects. We recall the three basic types of financial support, equity, subordinate debt, and senior debt, and describe some specialist providers of these. In particular we consider multinational finance agencies, venture capitalists, international investment institutions, export guarantee and the role of government (written by Bian Yong-Qian). Some unconventional sources of finance are also considered. The service provided by the owner's financial adviser is covered.

10

Contractors

Ernie Torbet and Norman Dunlop

10.1 Introduction

In this chapter we consider contractors, the core suppliers of goods and services to a project. In the introduction to Part Three, we have already tried to differentiate between contractors and other kinds of supporter. We assume that the types of services supplied by contractors are to:

- Supply labour and/or materials
- Supply design documents and drawings
- Manage specialist subcontractors
- Assemble parts and supplied items
- Carry risk
- Provide specialist expertise
- Provide finance in terms of cash flow.

A contractor may fulfil more than one of these roles. Indeed, the contractor may provide some of the services associated with other supporters described in the following two chapters. However, there are particular characteristics of contractors not shared with other supporters which would not be transferred to them under any contractual arrangement. These are the provision of labour and the handling of temporary facilities needed for the construction or assembly of all or part of the facility. Furthermore contractors, unlike other supporters, are often appointed to conduct an activity which has already been clearly defined by others. They are therefore less able to influence the owner's requirements as far as their contribution to the project is concerned.

They are, however, of critical importance to, and therefore of major influence on, the project's duration. On some projects where the contractor assumes partial responsibility for other supporters as we have defined them, they may also be able to influence cost and quality. On most projects, cost and quality are controllable or more heavily influenced by other supporters,

141

whether under the management of the contractor or not. In this chapter, we assume the contractor as being the supporter who controls the labour supply, and consequently the *pace* of progress on the project. This is not, of course, to say that other parties to the project cannot influence these matters, but their influence is often indirect or by persuasion. It is therefore seen that risk is potentially high both to the contractor, who is unable to influence the specification of their services, and to the owner, who is not directly able to influence the pace of work.

In this chapter, we explain this vital relationship between the owner and the contractor, and describe how best to manage it to optimize the outcome for both parties. We consider managing contractors, the owner's project manager. We identify the role of project managers on large contracts, explain their relationships with the client and other parties involved in the project, describe their responsibilities on the project and how these are delegated throughout the team, and identify the control tools required to accomplish the project successfully.

10.2 The role of contractors

We suggested above that the particular service offered by contractors compared to other supporters is the supply and control of labour. However, it is clearly an over-simplification to regard this as their only role. Modern projects involve an increasingly complex mix of many technical, financial and managerial parts. In an effort to limit the contractual arrangements to formats which are understandable and manageable, the roles of supporters frequently overlap, or are absorbed by one or another. There are in fact other aspects of projects which can also be part of the contractor's duties, such as the handling of environmental issues and liaison with statutory bodies. Either of these duties can be made the responsibility of any one of several of the supporters. The choice of where to arrange the responsibilities will depend to a large degree on the nature of the project and the nature and maturity of the owner's organization. In deciding whether to allocate responsibility for the provision of services to the contractor or to other supporters, you may consider the following issues:

- The contractor's ability to provide finance
- The contractor's in-house specific expertise or facility
- The owner's investing in a new area of business
- The owner's establishing in a new location
- The time period allowed for the project.

Thus there can be seen to be many factors dictating the choice of role for the contractor and in many cases the sheer complexity, and hence uncertainty, associated with managing the interfaces between many different factors to the project will encourage an owner, especially of a new facility, to reduce his or her own interfaces by grouping supporter roles in one way or another. On the other hand, in simple projects, or where owners already possesses the skills to fulfil certain supporter roles for themselves, the roles of other supporters can be simple and easily defined, and thereby limited to scopes which carry little risk. This discussion of the potentially variable nature of a contractor's role still leaves us concluding that the essential features are related to management and risk, no matter what the nature or scale of the project.

We now consider what dictates the nature of the owner/supporter (contractor) relationship by examining the benefits and disbenefits to each party. At this stage we are not assuming any particular contracting agreements. These are covered in Part Five. Obviously, the contracting agreement is crucial to a successful relationship as this provides the formal basis for allocating risk and motivational incentives.

10.3 The benefits and risks to the owner

Where the contractor is directly involved in the supply and management of labour for the project, the benefits to the owner can be easily appreciated. They may include:

- No recruitment charges
- Better access to appropriate skills
- Less management commitment
- Limitation of risk associated with industrial disputes, weather, downtime, etc.
- More efficient use of labour as a consequence of contractor's ability to balance recruitment for several contracts (thereby reducing costs)
- Flexibility on pace of contract, for example on research or developmental projects.

There may also be some disadvantages to the owner, arising from their inevitable lack of direct control. The risks that this may create include:

- Poor progress
- Poor quality
- Reduced safety (with consequences for the owner's image and on the project's progress).

These advantages and disadvantages for the owner by and large arise with contractors supplying labour. We might also consider what happens when the contractor has a much wider role, associated with some of the other supporters, including, in particular, the supply of much of the material and plant. Clearly the greater the contractor's role, the wider the scope of works, and the greater the risk of the contract becoming less subject to the influence of the owner. However, there are also advantages to the owner, especially in complex multidisciplinary projects. Here the closer control of the contractor over several interfacing aspects of the work can offer distinct time savings.

10.4 The benefits and risks to the contractor

Contractors, like all businesses, exist to make profits. It goes without saying, therefore, that the principal benefits to a contractor are potential profits. There are, of course, others such as prestige, reputation and even satisfaction of the workforce, all of which have to a greater or lesser extent the benefit of more potential business and a better and more efficient workforce. The main disadvantage to the contractor is the element of risk that must be borne, and indeed the sharing of risk is a significant feature of the contract between client and contractor (Chapter 17). The risks to a contractor are also fairly obvious when we remember that the contractor is generally providing a physical item specified by others, on the basis of a contract priced by them in advance and sometimes to a fixed total sum. Risks in general will include:

– Changes of requirement or scope
– Change of project environment
– Change of circumstances or conditions
– Change of assumed performance.

Some change can of course be beneficial either to the progress of the project or to the value of the completed project to the owner. However, here we are concerned with changes which threaten the completion of the project in an adverse sense. Also the impact of certain risks can vary with the stage of the project and could in any case have increased or decreased as compared to its assessment at the outset, or at the time a contractor was appointed. The factors on a particular project will vary considerably depending on the size, nature and duration of a project. Take the example of a recent project to build a light railway in a major city. The project between inception and completion was affected by:

– Varying forecasts of demand which led to:
– Varying scope of the works
– Accidents in the industry which led to:
– Changes in quality requirements

- Unexpected ground conditions
- Special environmental conditions imposed by a local authority
- Discovery of archaeological remains
- Risk of damage to adjacent historic buildings
- Contaminated ground necessitating special working methods
- Consultant delays including statutory undertakers and design
- Contractor delays, including electrical contractor and train fabrication
- System commissioning delays
- Total redesign of major station.

Furthermore, the contractor's exposure to these risks will vary, depending whether it is:

- The civil works contractor
- Part of an electrical/civil contractor team
- Part of a design-build contract group
- Part of a design-build and operate group.

What this illustrates is that, while the contractor may not be at risk to as many of these items as a civil works contractor, the contractor would lose the potential to ensure greater efficiency which a core comprehensive scope would have offered, even if the latter had some attendant risks. This example helps to illustrate the owner's risks and benefits in a similar way. The awareness of the risks to a project and the understanding of their potential effect is important and the management of the respective liabilities of the owner and the contractor is crucial.

10.5 Managing the relationship to optimize the outcome for both

In considering the benefits and risks to the owner and the contractor we have touched on the possible contractual arrangements which might be put in place in an attempt to optimize these for both parties. This subject will be dealt with further in Part Five. No matter what the contract strategy, however, there is a need to *manage* the relationship between owner and contractor in order to help both sides to achieve the objectives which the contract between them is designed to express. Frequently any risks materializing have effects on both owner and contractor, and each party's objectives are adversely influenced. This applies even if any dispute over the liability for the risk is amicably resolved, because the consequences for other aspects of the project may not be fully recoverable, or adequately compensated for.

In the ultimate best interest of the project, it must be sensible to avoid as many risks actually materializing, or to plan suitable action to minimize or eliminate risks wherever possible. Common understanding is the key, for it is in the interests of neither party if, for example, a contractor spends extra money on accelerating progress to recover lost time and ultimately needs to recoup that cost by savings in other aspects of the facility (such as greater reliability) when the lost time was really a potential benefit to the owner as a consequence of changing market conditions. In many cases the owner and the contractor will not have a direct contractual arrangement, the link being provided by, for instance, another supporter. It can often be the case that almost any management arrangement can be made to work if certain key individuals are of the appropriate calibre. But this does not necessarily mean that the management structure is efficient. In order to define the management structure as efficient, it is necessary to consider the purpose of the structure or more particularly in the case we are considering the purpose of the management link between the owner and contractor.

All management links are a route for communication, and in the context of our previous discussion it would seem that the prime purpose here is to enable the parties to review regularly the risks and responsibilities which each has to the project. By doing so, each can ensure that the other is aware of the degree to which their duties under the arrangements may be influenced by the risks which the other is responsible for managing or monitoring. The management link also provides for the owner to be informed of the progress of the project, but it is reasonable to consider this as a subsidiary facility because the contractual arrangements should provide sufficient incentive for the contractor to perform as efficiently as possible. The removal of impediments and the opportunity for discussion of any potential improvements in terms of basic objectives of the project are therefore the essential purpose of the management of the owner/contractor relationship. The project manager should therefore propose a suitable structure to allow timely discussion at appropriate level. In doing so, they will need to consider the frequency of such discussion in relation to the envisaged time span for resolution of any matters to be addressed, and the relationship of the meetings to other meetings which may or may not be the source of necessary information. The nature of these communication links and structures is described in more detail in Chapter 21.

10.6 Managing contractors

We now consider a particular type of contractor, the managing or prime contractor. In the introduction to this part, we considered the difference between contractors and consultants, and between contractors and suppliers. What is the difference between a managing contractor and a prime contractor? Both take the role of project manager on behalf of the owner, and coordinate other suppliers and subcontractors. The difference is mainly one of usage and industry. If a difference does exist, it is that the prime contractor takes a much greater design management responsibility. The managing contractor may manage the designer as a subcontractor, in that the managing contractor will ensure that all time and cost targets are met. However, the managing contractor takes no responsibility for the functionality of the design. The prime contractor is also responsible for ensuring the design works. The prime contractor may also be a key design contractor, whereas the managing contractor is often barred from that role, for reasons of conflict of interest. (One recent project where the prime contractor had little design responsibility was the provision of helicopters to the Royal Navy. IBM were prime contractors, yet most of the design was done by the suppliers of the helicopters, Westland and Angusta.) The management of design is beyond the scope of this book, and so effectively we do not differentiate between managing contractors and prime contractors, and call them both project managers. We consider:

– The role of the project manager
– The project manager's relationship with the client and project team
– The responsibility of the project manager
– The management tools the project manager uses to provide effective control.

When considering these topics, others are identified which influence how the contractor's project team carries out its role. These vary in importance from project to project, depending on the contract basis (Chapter 17) and must be addressed by project managers to ensure completeness of the control of their projects.

The role of the project manager

The project manager is the person or organization appointed by the contractor to ensure the project is executed in accordance with the agreement, specifications, budgets, schedules and other requirements of the contract. They are the day-to-day contact between client and contractor. They must ensure adequate communications between the two organizations are maintained, and by means of these communications satisfy themselves and those working on the project that all participants receive the necessary information to carry out their allocated tasks effectively. They are also responsible for putting in place the required management systems and controls. These provide them and the project management team with the information required to ensure proper control of the project is maintained. In this role as project manager, they have to make certain that the necessary key data such as budgets, milestone planning dates and project execution philosophies are issued to those required to produce the management systems and controls.[1]

In this respect a key document to be issued early in the project is the *Coordination Procedure*. This contains the information used by all groups in the project team to carry out their work. It identifies key members of both client and contractor's organizations, general requirements of the project such as units, drawing sizes and numbers, distribution of documents, archiving of documents for future use and retention, etc. Included are the *Project Execution Philosophies*, which outline the methods by which the project is to be carried out. The section relating to engineering defines:

- Model requirements (plastic or electronic (CAD))
- Piping to be drawn on isometrics by size
- Policy on civil design (concrete or steel structures)
- Procurement policy
- All matters to be taken into account in designs to suit the method of construction.

In the section on procurement, the philosophy must outline the areas for purchase (own country, own continent, selected countries or world-wide), the type of bid to be obtained, shipping requirements and the various stage inspections to be carried out for different types of equipment. For construction, the method of contracting (direct labour or subcontractors), approach to use of heavy lifts or small piece erection, pipe prefabrication and, if subcontracting, the type of contract to be used.

All this information enables a timely, cost-effective start to be made to the project reducing the need for recycle and duplicated effort. Some information may take longer to finalize so that this coordination procedure may require several issues before the complete document is available. Revisions issued during the lifetime of the project keep all parties informed of changes required as the various phases of the project progress. As information, management systems and controls and the other data necessary to set up a project are put in place, the role of the project manager moves into another phase.

This involves the monitoring and control of schedules, expenditures, manpower levels and man-hour recording. This is usually the longest phase of a project as far as the project manager is concerned. They will review progress on all aspects of the project and apply corrective actions to areas of concern. They are expected to maintain a dialogue with the client, keeping the client fully appraised of the progress, the actions being taken to correct trends where required, and to report the successful outcome of previous corrective actions.

The final phase of the project requires a successful completion to time, budget and safety. The project has to be handed over to the client as required by the *Job Specification*, all relevant documentation, records, catalogues, manuals and other deliverables issued in their final form and all necessary payments, claims, invoices agreed and finalized. Any disposals of surplus materials, site establishment and closing of project accounts, etc., should be completed. Final records on costs, allocations and other financial information should be issued as part of the project manager's project report.

The project manager's relationship with the client

The relationships with the client and the team are both complex and formal, but, at the same time, should retain an element of approachability by both sides. The contractual situation with the client means that all written and oral communications can assume a meaning which can be taken to have financial or commercial implications. It is only by building a relationship with the client based on trust, that views can be exchanged, discussions can take place and the various options for resolving areas of concern on the project can be examined without the discussions being bogged down in a contractual jargon. These views can identify and highlight the contractual differences between the client and contractor, but in a satisfactory relationship they can be discussed without attitudes hardening to the point where the only solutions result in a win–lose situation, whereas the aim should be to reach a win–win result.

The relationship should be developed on the basis of mutual respect between the two project managers. Only in non-controversial or previously agreed matters should a formal and contractual position be confirmed. Areas of potential conflict or disagreement should be discussed only after both sides have done their preparatory work and are familiar with the background to the disagreement. While the project manager is responsible for ensuring his or her own company's interests are protected, the client's viewpoints cannot be ignored. Where controversy is reduced the client will usually respond positively to proposals put forward for resolving the problems. When dealing with other members of the client's project team most benefit will be obtained if the project manager is seen to deal through his or her opposite number. This implies and confirms the authority of the client's project manager in all important matters. In dealing with his or her own team, the project manager must know and accept that while authority and responsibility can be delegated to members of the team, the project manager is ultimately responsible for the project to the client and his or her own management. In this light, project managers must therefore convey to their staff their own authority. They should be accessible, be seen to delegate and at the same time be prepared to back up their staff when they are convinced that they are acting correctly and professionally. Respect is earned by the conduct and guidance on the project. Too little involvement is just as much a matter of concern as too much interference. The correct balance should allow their subordinates to carry out their own functions without the feeling that they are on their own with respect to major decisions while at the same time, allowing them to function in their day-to-day activities without hindrance or interference from outside. The most effective management is provided when confidence among members of the team demonstrates that control of the project in all phases is maintained at all times and all members of the team know their job and what is expected of them.

The responsibilities of the project manager

Put simply, the responsibilities of the project manager are to ensure the project is executed to budget and schedule while meeting the job specifications. The wider aspects of such responsibilities take into account the sometimes divergent relationship the project manager has to the client compared with that to his or her own company's chain of responsibility, the requirement to understand and work to different cultural and business practices as required by the client and project locations and the project manager's own need to communicate with the project team and on occasion with that of the client. While taking steps to delegate as much of the workload as is required to ensure they are not overworked, they still retain full and undenied responsibility for the project to the client and their own company. Most contractors carry out projects on a pyramidal organization chart basis with the project manager at the top. This is how they are viewed by others, including the client, that is the principal contact between the client organization and their own company and responsible for communications between the two organizations. This is not only oral communications, but also written, electronic and any other means. Their written communications include letters, telexes and other methods of conveying information to the client, together with reports on progress, costs and technical matters. In addition they must ensure that information from the client and third parties is distributed within the project team.

The project manager's responsibilities for progress on the project requires him or her to ensure that all parties meet the schedule of activities as detailed in the plan. This is done by reviewing progress figures and taking corrective action where necessary. Major milestones are targeted to spread the workload through discipline and work areas. Additional resources are mobilized where necessary to achieve key activities on time. Corrective actions, where implemented, are monitored to check that any slippage or other adverse trends are recovered and the project is brought back to schedule as quickly as possible. The situation with costs and their control is very similar, in that the cost report for the project is carefully reviewed and action taken to correct adverse trends. The review of costs entails the comparison of monthly cost commitments and forecasts in as much detail as is required by the size of the project. It is essential that the project manager understands the changes in the cost report as they are made. Increases of a significant nature must be fully explained as they occur and they must be able to explain them not only to their own management, but to the client. The progress in engineering, materials management and construction are monitored to meet schedules. The project manager is expected to know the actual progress of these activities compared to the planned figures. They must be aware of areas of concern in the project and what actions are implemented to respond to these concerns.

In all areas, the project manager relies heavily on support staff to highlight areas of concern and advise on corrective actions. These staff members are generally the second level of management and are themselves the managers of various groups making up the project team. They are responsible to the project manager for the project execution of areas of the project, such as engineering and construction, and are required to accept and carry out the project manager's delegated responsibilities. This requires that the project manager is involved on a 'need to know' basis, and thus is kept fully informed and so can play a part as required to keep the project on schedule and to budget while meeting the specifications and standards applicable to the project.

The management tools needed to provide effective control

The project manager will be experienced in the use and application of the management tools used in the effective control of the project. Such tools include:

– The planning system and reports
– The cost control system and reports
– The document management system to ensure the timely, correct distribution of project documents
– The material management system to ensure equipment and materials are delivered to site and used for their proper purpose
– The timely award of necessary contracts and their control of progress and cost
– The effective use of labour by allocation to work in the correct skills and at the appropriate time.

This is not an exhaustive list and is meant only to illustrate the areas of project work to which such tools are applied.

The most important of these is the planning methodology. This, in its various levels, identifies the dates during the life of the project when identifiable actions must be part or wholly completed. At the highest level there are perhaps identified only 10–12 key milestone dates, while at the lowest level (or most detailed level) the issue date for an individual drawing or document is identified. Such planning dates find their way into other management tools such as the *Document Control System* to identify the issue dates for documents, the materials management system to identify the *Required On Site* date for materials and equipment. By a cascade system key dates for such controls as a *Manpower Projection System* to identify manpower requirements, for contract placement schedules and for labour schedules are provided. Cost control techniques provide comparison between budgets and commitments, budgets and forecasts, trends – both adverse and favourable, productivities and estimates and, perhaps, most important, the effective control of change. This latter item if not carried out properly can result in both adverse cost conditions and schedule delays adding to additional cost. Trend analysis is of particular importance in providing the project manager with early warning of cost variations to enable any necessary corrective action to be taken.

The more proactive the management tool, the better is the project manager served in the control of the project. Control techniques which can provide overview of the project without upsetting the progress of the job are most efficient, that is controls which are derived from the day-to-day information on the project and which do not require preparation separately from the normal project documentation and data to effectively control the project are best. This means the information used by the project manager and derived by him or or is available to other members of the team and as such can be just as effectively used by them. Visibility into these areas of the project provide the project manager with information on progress, cost and trends allowing him or her to confirm the actions taken by the team to correct any adverse trends or initiate personal action.

10.7 Summary

1. We have considered the contractor as a supporter who supplies labour. They may provide other services, but their unique service is in supplying the labour needed to deliver the facility required by the project. In doing so the contractor is able to influence directly, indeed dictate, the *pace* of progress.
2. Thus the risks inherent in the owner/contractor relationship are related to *time*. In order that both parties can maximize the benefits, while minimizing the risks to the project and thus optimize the benefits to each

other, the management of the relationship must be based on understanding and openness.

3. This is best facilitated by appropriate meetings between those ultimately responsible for the respective obligations on each side (see Chapter 21).

4. The managing or prime contractor manages the project on behalf of the owner.

References

1. Turner, J.R., *The Handbook of Project-based Management*, McGraw-Hill, 1993.

11

Consultants

Ernie Torbet, John Dingle, Frank Thomas, Malcolm Watkinson and Jeffrey Blum

11.1 Introduction

We now consider consultants, the suppliers of professional services to a project. We begin by describing the role of consultants, the risk and benefit of the relationship to the owner and the consultant, and how the relationship should be managed. We then consider designers, the primary type of consultant. We consider their scope of work, typical contractual relationships with designers, and the imposition of design criteria and guarantees. The design and engineering industries are very fragmented, and so it becomes necessary for the owner to achieve consistency between the efforts of different design professions. We explain the use of *Coordinated Project Information* as an approach adopted to attempt to achieve some uniformity. Usually, the owner's headquarters, the designer's offices, the site of the facility and the factories of suppliers are geographically separated, sometimes in different countries. We explain how the use of computer aided design has enabled the designers to communicate their designs to the owner from great distances, to the point where client organizations in Europe and North America reduce their costs by using designers in parts of the world where labour is cheap. Finally, we describe the services provided by shippers to help transport materials, plant and equipment around the world.

11.2 The role of consultants

Consultants are people or organizations who provide specialist skills and knowledge. Consider a project to establish an oil-production facility in a remote and environmentally sensitive area inhabited by a detached indigenous people. In addition to the design expertise, the specialist skills we may require might include:

– Anthropology

- Language expertise
- Botany
- Other environmental specialisms
- Quality control expertise, to ensure fabricated items are exactly to specification before being shipped
- Transportation and shipping expertise.

If we consider projects nearer home, say in urban areas, we might need specialist expertise in:

- Noise
- Urban planning
- Building ergonomics.

We would recognize all of these as consultants. They all have skills in a fairly narrow field. Consultants in these fields will often operate as one-man experts, or small specialist firms. However there are other skills, such as management or design expertise, which may be more general in knowledge terms, but which are specific in relation to a project in its totality. These too are described as consultants. Consultants in these areas are often larger organizations offering a different cultural perspective or focused service to the client. We consider:

- Consultancy as advice
- Consultancy as information
- Consultancy assignments.

Consultancy as advice

Consultancy can be described as follows:

> The service provided by an independent and qualified person or persons in identifying and investigating problems concerned with policy, organization, procedures and methods; recommending appropriate actions and helping to implement these recommendations.
> Institute of Management Consultants

> Someone who borrows your watch to tell you the time.
> Client's folklore.

There is sufficient similarity between these descriptions of what consultancy is for us to be able to see that it covers a wide range of activities. The origins of consultancy go back to soothsaying (which covered everything from high priest to court jester), which simply meant having special expertise or insight enabling one to give a truthful (or at least convincing) account of the future.

Advice comes in various categories. Modern consultants may:

- Provide information which is not easily available
- Interpret information, to provide an impartial, objective, point of view based on their experience
- Provide special knowledge and/or know-how
- Provide management with arguments which justify measures already decided upon
- Supply intensive professional help on a temporary basis.

In all cases, the advisory services which consultants provide are generally to do with 'problem solving'. If the problem is known – or rather, if the structure of the problem is known – problem solving becomes a matter of applying appropriate techniques with relevant judgement. This means that 'competence' combined with 'experience' are necessary attributes of consultants.

There is, however, another kind of problem which is perhaps more frequent and is certainly more difficult to handle: the *unstructured* problem, which requires that consultants are capable of providing *insight*, in addition to competence and experience. By this we mean that it is not enough for consultants to solve their clients' problems. At any rate in the field of unstructured problems, the consultant should aim to show clients how to solve similar problems themselves. To paraphrase the old Chinese proverb:

> If you give people fish, they can eat today. If you teach them how to fish, they can feed themselves for the rest of their lives.

(And if you show them how to make a bouillabaise, you add a little quality to their lives!) An example of a structured problem might be designing a bridge, or some other complex construction, where the methodology is well established, but difficult, or needs specialized training to apply. An example of an unstructured problem might be for developing a new service, such as welfare or disaster management, where there may be little or no established practice.

Consultancy as information

Obviously, a main plank in the provision of advice is information. Consultants provide information in a number of ways:

1. *Published information* This means information which is in the public

domain, but which may not be readily accessible to clients in the time available. Most consultants maintain their own databases, and can link into national and international databases quickly. Perhaps more important than these in areas of specialized information, consultants usually cultivate personal contacts which typically are mobilized to provide the final pieces in the information jigsaw.

2. *Multi-client studies* Many consultants produce multi-client studies which provide data on specialized topics at a lower cost to individual clients than would be possible for a specially commissioned study. Multi-client studies can help client organizations to build their own databases, but they need to be treated with considerable caution. While they provide background information, they evidently contain nothing about any particular client's situation, and consequently may be misleading, especially in the context of market competition. Sometimes, the updating of multi-client studies is patchy, and this adds to the risk of using them in an uncritical way.

3. *Specially commissioned studies* This is by far the best way to get 'insightful' information on any significant problem. The only disadvantage is that specially commissioned studies are expensive. Because it is the small but crucial details which take most time and effort to obtain, clients are always reluctant to spend money on specially commissioned studies when a multi-client study in what is nominally the same field is available. (The chances are that they will have to spend even more to rectify the mistaken decisions they have taken on inadequate information!)

Practically all information for use in the client organization has to be interpreted in the sense that the consultant has to analyse, synthesize and summarize information in the context of the client organization's interests and aims. It is important that the activities of analysis (such as breaking down the data available to discover what is salient, what conditional), synthesis (such as construction of arguments, propositions and alternatives) and summarizing (which includes comparison and appraisal) should not become confused: 'that way madness lies'! It is at the interpretation stage that problems with information become apparent. The main problems are:

- *Insufficiency* The information is incomplete, and provides less basis for development than is necessary.
- *Unsuitability* The information is either irrelevant or simply wrong, so although it appears to be complete, it is flawed.
- *Bias* This is a special case of *wrong* information, in that it is misleading for either accidental or deliberate causes.

Simply reviewing these information problems shows the importance of *independence* in consultancy. Information – and the advice based on it – is quite useless if it is merely what the client wants to hear, or if it disguises a vested interest.

Interpretation has two aspects, which may be likened to the distinct activities of the composer and the performing musician. The composer creates something new from the information (musical notes, conventions and so on) at his or her disposal. The performer also may create something new for the people who listen to the performer's interpretation of the score. Both aspects are valid, and are complementary. The good consultant should aim to combine the two in the search for insight into the client's problems.

Consultancy assignments

Clients use consultants in many ways. In addition to getting and interpreting information, consultants may also be retained to use their interpretations to make recommendations for clients' decisions and actions, and to help implement them. A typical example is the preparation of plans and the formulation of a strategy for development of the client's business. Within this framework, examples of typical assignments include:

- *Marketing research* Where, how, how much, to sell; and to whom; acquisitions, divestments, diversifications
- *Commercial research* Pricing policy, transfer pricing; competitor analysis; contract and license terms analysis
- *Technical development* Technology evaluation; organizational planning; plant revamps and debottlenecking.

The list is far from exhaustive, and it should be clear that the categories mentioned overlap. Thus a typical feasibility study is likely to contain elements from all the items mentioned above, and may include others as diverse as environmental planning and energy conservation.

Considering technical consultancy more specifically related to project management, consultants may be assigned to:

- Perform critical reviews of project feasibility studies.
- Review the availability and reliability of supplies of crucial inputs to the project (such as utilities, special consumables, etc.) and the logistics of disposing of outputs.
- Review technological options in relation to potential obsolescence, concurrency (technological uncertainty + time pressure), human resource availability.
- Review energy use options.

- Plan project organization and contracting strategy in relation to project financing options.
- Short-list contractors, prepare bid specifications and invitations to bid (ITTs).
- Check and compare contractors' bids for inconsistencies, conformity with ITTs, scope changes and general quality.
- Advise owners on commercial terms proposed by contractors, and assist in obtaining final price revisions and contract terms.
- Supervise contractor's design, purchasing, construction and commissioning activities.

Above, when discussing consultancy as advice, we said that 'consultants should aim to show clients how to solve similar problems themselves'. This highlights the very close connection between consultancy as advice, and consultancy as training.

Almost all consultancy involves some element of training. Some assignments are primarily about training, though they may be described in other terms such as 'organizational planning'. Assignments which are primarily training-related are those which aim to improve the performance of the client organization by enhancing the skills of the individuals (and groups of individuals) employed by it, and there are some special features of this kind of consultancy assignment:

- It must come before actual training, because one of its aims is to define training needs. A training programme which does not focus on the real needs of the organization and its people merely wastes money, and time too.
- It will be expensive, because defining training programmes takes time and needs very experienced specialists, and if the consultancy is skimped, the chances are that the training programme will produce 'almost trained' people as a result, which is frustrating for everybody.
- It demands commitment from clients, partly because of the cost mostly because training is not a short-term affair – training involves not only the acquisition of new ideas, ways of thinking and skills, it also involves practice.
- It will continue for some time after the training programme has been implemented, because the effectiveness of the training has to be monitored.

11.3 The benefits and risks to the owner

Owners are not likely to have at their disposal expertise in all aspects of their projects, or at all stages of their projects. Nor do they need to develop or acquire it for long periods. Thus, there are many different specialisms required for relatively short periods, and the role of the consultant will vary as the particular objectives of the owner change. If these specialists are not available permanently in-house, we will need to consider the advantage of acquiring them and the risk involved for both parties. For an owner, a project involving a major change to the business carries numerous dangers which are not always quantifiable. An owner will clearly wish to have a completed project which allows the business to progress but will wish to avoid disruption or at least minimize it. There are many aspects of the organization and implementation of change with which owners are probably not equipped to cope, because of either the nature or the quantity. They will also wish to be reliably informed of the progress and likely outcome of the project. Where aspects of the project are outside their experience they will wish to be convinced of the quality and accuracy of the information being made available to them. This information may be especially confused in an organization subjecting itself to rapid change which is in itself an entirely new experience.

At the same time, owners will not wish to enter into long-term commitment with relatively unknown parties, and, in the initial stages of a project, they will wish to retain flexibility, while the factors affecting the real viability of their project are assessed. Where internal changes are forced by the project, there may be a need for some restriction of awareness of the project in the early stages. In several of these respects, the use of outside consultants offers relief from vested interests, and therefore greater comfort in the impartial nature of advice. As the consultant will clearly not be under consideration as a long-term employee, owners may well gain knowledge of their own organization which may otherwise not become available to them because of the ready access to various parts of the organization which the consultant's specialist role demands. In the case where a project requires the establishment of a changed or entirely new organization, a consultant's specialist observation of different organizations may ensure a smooth start-up within the new facility.

However, the client may also perceive some risks from the use of consultants. As well as the risks of the permanent staff being adversely affected, the owner may have other concerns:

1. They may feel uncomfortable, for instance, in risking becoming over-dependent on a consultant, especially where the consultant is not universally recognized as the ultimate source of knowledge. In such a case, the owner could be facing other specialists with different views, and being in a position of having to make a choice, or needing a further opinion.
2. If the consultancy service is performed by a team of consultants, there is potential for team members to be changed at the behest of the

consultancy company, or for them to be unavailable at certain times. This may lead to a loss of comfort for the owner that continuous quality of service is available. Despite the slow development of telecommuting, few managers have yet learnt how to manage team members who are not reliably present for predetermined fixed times at a fixed location.

3. Inevitably the consultant will have skills and knowledge which are different or seemingly greater than that of the owner and the organization. This could leave the owner feeling uncomfortably ignorant of what the consultant is doing. The owner may be further afraid of encouraging a new industry of information rather than obtaining a usable product (such as clear advice) from the consultant.

4. If the owner finds that the subject of the consultancy prevents a clear, time-limited brief being written, there could be a danger of an open-ended agreement being established, with the client unable to terminate the consultant's work in a clean and tidy fashion.

5. Cultural and attitudinal differences between the owner's organization and the consultant could at least delay the consultant's ability to give practical advice. They can also lead to a feeling within the owner's organization that it is being led by consultants, and this can prevent the building of good team spirit across the whole project. In circumstances where some cultural change is required as a result of the project, such a situation is not constructive.

11.4 The risks to the consultant

The risks for a consultant can be categorized into professional and personal areas. Often the personal abilities of a consultant in being able to deal with members of the owner organization, or outside parties can be crucial to their ability to perform to the owner's satisfaction. This is especially so in the area of management consultancy where cultural changes are required or attitudes are clearly based on different organizational experience. In consultancies providing purely technical expertise, the inter-personal elements are less important because of the clearly recognizable knowledge of the consultant. Consider for example the following two consultancies:

1. A consultant who specializes in the control of noise on railways is appointed by a railway operator to write specifications relating to noise on a proposed extension of the railway.

2. A firm of consultants specializing in project management is appointed by the same railway operator to manage adjustments to operational divisions to operate the new extension.

The risks that these two consultancies face, and their response to them differ because one is a sole operator, and the other is a larger specialist organization. In the first case, the risks faced by the consultant include:

- A risk of under-achieving a deliverable specification – this could lead to over-compensation and
- A risk of over-specifying a costly item of work – these amount to
- A risk of misinterpreting or misunderstanding the owner's requirements.

If any of the above happens there is:

- A risk of loss of reputation – leading to
- A risk of failure to obtain further assignments (although this is of course an ever present risk)
- A risk of forced over-commitment, resulting in lack of time to generate further assignments elsewhere.

In the second case there are also risks related to loss of prestige, misunderstandings and so on, but these risks arise more from either:

- A failure of the owner organization to cope; or
- A failure of the consultant to deal with the personnel aspect (depending on the scope of the brief).

Either way the risk of failure is reduced by the strength of the firm, whereas in the first case all was dependent on the individual. A risk common to any consultant or firm of consultants is that of the owner deciding to employ his or her own staff, or terminating the consultancy at any time for any reason. Such risks can be avoided or managed in a way which eliminates them as 'risks' and we deal with this in the next section.

11.5 Managing the consultant/owner relationship

Most of the discussion in this chapter has emphasized the personal aspect of the relationship between an owner and a consultant. The management of the relationship is consequently going to depend, to a greater extent than is the case with most other project supporters, on a personal understanding and trust even if there is a written brief or agreement.

The existence of a brief will help mainly in the removal of doubts about the other party's objectives and will form the basis against which the progress and success of the consultant's work can be judged. The brief can itself be used as a basis for a quality plan written by the consultant which they can use for self-assessment in the assignment and to assess the assignment itself. (The preparation of the brief is described further in

Chapter 19.) Because the work of the consultant is of a specialized nature, there is almost certainly a disproportionately high ratio of importance to the success of the project against cost of the consultant's work. Therefore, however short-term the assignment is expected to be, the brief and quality plan should be available from the start so as to ensure no mismatch between the objectives and assumptions of the consultant and the intentions of the owner.

In the case of such important work it is also vital that the owner should be aware of the work of the consultant. For this reason a direct line of communication is almost certainly advisable. This may be effected by ensuring that regular consultant's reports are included within the regular project status on management reports, or that at least the current status and action being taken is so included. A wider circulation in the owner organization than would normally be the case may be appropriate, if only to overcome fears or misconceptions over the consultant's role.

Attendance of the consultant at meetings addressing wider issues, rather than only at meetings convened to address their particular area of involvement, will help to integrate them into the project team and will also give them valuable peripheral knowledge. In this way, they will be helped to put their work into the proper context, and to report in the most acceptable way, thus bridging cultural divides.

11.6 Designers

A consultant used on almost all projects is the designer. The designer works in collaboration with the owner to convert a concept in the owner's mind into a completed facility, or going concern, in accordance with the owner's requirements. In this section, we consider the designer, and review:

– Their role and scope of work
– Typical contractual relationships with designers
– The imposition of design criteria
– Guarantees.

The role of the designer

The term designer covers a broad range of professionals supporting the project owner. Traditional engineering design disciplines include:

– Hardware and software
– Civil and structural
– Building and architectural
– Mechanical and electrical

- Instrumentation and control
- Electronic and communication
- Marine
- Aerospace
- Chemical and process
- Nuclear.

In a wider sense they could be extended to include:

- Personnel
- Marketing
- Finance.

You may recall from Chapter 6 that this last item can account for 15 per cent of the cost of the project by commissioning, and 50 per cent over the life of the facility. It is therefore the most critical 'design' job.

Designers can support the owner throughout the entire project life cycle, (Fig. 11.1) and in that time undertake a variety of tasks, including:

- Receive the owner's conceptual design brief, and interpret his or her intentions and criteria.
- Develop feasibility studies and options, and produce interim designs for further development by other specialists.
- Oversee production of detailed, comprehensive designs, working drawings and instructions as required for purchase, manufacture or subcontracting purposes.
- Support field activities, to ensure compliance with the design.
- Inspect/witness acceptance and testing of procured hardware and the completed facility.
- Produce operating and maintenance manuals, oversee production of as-built drawings and other historical records, and provide continuing support to the users or operators of the completed facility.
- Act as a contact point between other external entities including the general public as directed by the owner.

Figure 11.1 Progression of the design through a project

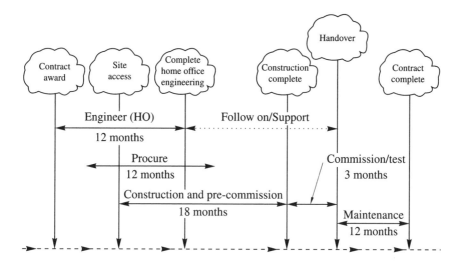

Figure 11.2 Involvement of the designers in an EPC contract for major capital plant in the engineering construction industry

Figure 11.2 illustrates the support of the designer in an engineering, procurement and construction contract (EPC) in the engineering construction industry (ECI).

Contractual relationships with designers

There are several approaches to engaging firms of designers:

1. *In-house design departments* These are kept by large companies as a core team to service ongoing concurrent small projects. Other arrangements such as firms of consultants may still be used on a top-up basis. There is a growing belief that large companies should 'keep to the knitting'. That is, a company like ICI is in business to make and sell chemicals, not design and construct chemical plants, or develop computer systems. Companies are therefore shedding their internal design departments, and employ contract houses on a partnering basis (Chapter 8). This also makes the companies less exposed to cyclical variations in the business cycle. In the area of computer systems development, some organizations are subcontracting all their work to external software houses, and others are floating their internal departments as separate businesses which must compete with others on a commercial basis for the company's work.

2. *Firm of consultants* They are engaged on a strictly as-needed basis and are paid as a flexible service per man-hour used. In this simple

arrangement there is no incentive for the firm to complete on time, and thus it will be the owner's responsibility to progress the work.

3. *Design-and-build contractors* These are used for medium sized projects (installed cost say £5 million). They work to a defined scope of work for a fixed price. Additional work is treated as reimbursable at contract rates.

4. *Managing contractor* They are employed on major projects to take full responsibility (on an EPC basis) for all aspects of the project, including the design from conception to the provision of the as-built drawings after commissioning (Chapter 10). At this level of contracting, several methods of incentive could apply. These will include target cost contracts, with fixed fee (including the profit element) and reimbursed cost of base man-hours (includes overhead). Note, that in this arrangement the incentive lies with the fixed profit element, and hence the percentage profit increases if less is spent.

Procurement of designers and types of contract strategy are considered in more detail in Part Five.

Design criteria

One of the main risks the owner faces is that the facility will not perform to the required level. The owner therefore needs to set the standards or criteria against which the design is to be made. Owners must also put in place guarantees should the design fail to perform. There are two extremes of approach to setting design criteria:

1. The owner specifies the design to a very low level of detail. The design of almost every last nut and bolt is defined. This requires the owner to maintain a large in-house design capability. It also absolves the designer of a lot of risk. If the design fails to perform, then it is easy for the designer to blame the owner.

2. The owner specifies the functionality of the product only, and levels for availability, reliability and maintainability (statistical data). The designer must then produce a design that achieves these levels. That transfers the onus totally on to the designer. However, there is little comfort to the owner if the facility is not used for ten years say (as in the case of a weapons system), and then in the thick of battle the system fails to perform. This approach also gives almost open-ended risk to the contractor. There is a story of a tunnel under the Suez Canal where the supplier had to replace the fans in the ventilation system after ten years because they were designed for the wrong type of sand.

In addition to owner-provided design criteria, design submittals are also regulated by relevant and (usually) mandatory professional standards, specifications and codes of practice. Table 11.1 lists typical criteria and restrictions which should be addressed during the design of a process plant or power station project.

Table 11.1 Typical criteria restrictions on a project in the ECI

Category	Criteria and restrictions
Legal directives	EU Council Directives (Emissions, etc.) Parliamentary consent Local and public authority consent
Standards and codes of practice for compliance	British and American standards Specifications (DoE and DoT) Owner's supplementary in-house standards Process design patents
Physical and environmental considerations	Site location (including physical space limitations) Existing road systems (transport limitations); Landscape and architectural Effluent control limits Noise control limits Air quality control limits Ambient and river cooling water temperature limits Wind velocity limits Seismic conditions limits Ground/soil conditions Weight limits
Feedstock (quantity and quality)	Crude oil Gas/gas condensate Coal Uranium
Product (quantity and quality)	Stabilized oil or gas Refined or treated product Downstream product Electrical power
Interfaces	All perceived interface criteria external to the project envelope

It is worth emphasizing in conclusion that interpretation of the owner's intentions is all important in 'getting it right first time'. The prudent designer will therefore seek detailed clarification and agreement with the owner at periodic stages of design development to avoid the possibility of ambiguity or misunderstanding arising at a late stage when the consequences could be disruptive and costly. (This process is managed through a technique called Configuration Management.)[1] The specification of the design criteria through the design consultant procurement process and the clauses of the contracts is described further in Chapter 17.

Design guarantees

Once the facility is completed, the design must be proved and tested against the typical benchmarks given above. This is usually done by means of objective measurement and statistical performance testing techniques.

We could roughly gauge whether designs are up to scratch by seeking general answers to questions such as:

- Does the completed facility meet the relevant design criteria?
- Is the facility safe and reliable?
- Has design made its proportionate contribution to the overall project goals including cost-effectiveness?

In the simple case of a new house, the purchaser will want tangible proof and a guarantee that it will withstand the elements over a period of time and that the central heating or air conditioning system will maintain a specified room temperature range under varying ambient conditions.

When we are dealing with complex, capital plant or computer systems, the owner will not only demand guarantees and statistical evidence using accepted performance testing methods, but also reinforce the requirement in contract by imposing financial penalties for non-achievement of design predictions. Acceptance of these financial risks could put the unfortunate designer in a very exposed position. The difficulty of proving the design will vary. It is relatively straightforward for a static facility such as a building. However, live, operating plants are a different proposition. Whereas individual plant items such as pumps or electric motors can be proved on a test bed before they are accepted for installation, the overall on-site performance of complex plant can be checked only under commercial operating conditions. Likewise, a subroutine may work on its own, but fail to perform in the overall computer program after system build.

The severity of the potential financial penalties involved in such circumstances can be judged from a recent case where a major international contractor engaged in the design and construction of a power station flue gas desulphurization plant failed to meet the designed chimney emission standards. The company concerned faced crippling bills for:

- The basic financial penalty
- Cost of redesign and subsequent hardware modifications
- Liquidated damages arising from the owner's loss of revenue for power sales during periods of enforced plant shut down.

11.7 Coordinated project information

In terms of risk, the appointment of consultants must be one of the most difficult to measure, yet it is well known that the possibility of change and uncertainty of cost is brought about by both incompleteness of design and failure of consultants to coordinate the design process. We saw above the range of engineering design disciplines that can be involved in a project. It is not uncommon for the designers to be working on different CAD systems. Word processors have helped store a wealth of specification data – a substantial part of it being an historic record of the contentious issues experienced over the years. Neither the drawings nor specification has been properly rationalized/coordinated to ensure it specifically relates to the project. The Coordinating Project Information published by the Committee for Coordinating Project Information, CCPI (a joint working party of RIBA, RICS and BEC), addressed this particularly and it should apply to all modern complex works contracts. All consultants should be appointed on the basis that CPI will be used throughout. In this way, the project manager will be able to measure the performance and ask the right questions relating to the:

– Type of drawing
– Appropriate work section
– Appropriate specification
– Unit of measurement.

This systematic approach coordinates, and uniformly manages, a process bringing together:

– Drawings, for all specialist trades
– Appropriate mechanical and electrical specification based on the national engineering specification system
– Measurement (if required).

While this administration system is peculiar to the 'building' discipline, the techniques recommended can be implemented by other disciplines involving design and build, including:

– Civils
– Mechanical installation
– Telecommunication.

The problem of uncoordinated project information has arisen because the professions have developed their own conventions and working habits. The various members of the industry are not independent; if they are to be fully effective they must act in a more collaborative and coordinated manner. The conventions produced by multidisciplinary effort under the auspices of CCPI provide a clear basis for such action.

The conventions seek to promote coordination by giving recommendations of three main types:

1. *Procedures for producing documents* For example, planning the set of drawings to minimize duplication and maximize use of copy negatives, techniques for coordinating services and drawings, use of libraries of clauses as a systematic way of recording specification decisions.
2. *Technical content of documents* Annotation of drawings, detailed checklists for the content of project specifications, revised rules of measurement.
3. *Arrangement of documents* Structuring of drawn information by type, use of the common arrangement for both specifications and quantities.

Coordinated Project Information has important implications for contractors. More complete, timely, relevant and conveniently arranged information should enable them to estimate, plan and control building work more efficiently to produce buildings of good quality, on time and within cost. At present, the building process can be risky for clients because of uncertainties about the performance of the many individuals involved and their ability to work together effectively. Coordinated project information should significantly reduce the client's risk regardless of type and size of project and regardless of contractual arrangement. Clients may therefore wish to consider specifying compliance with the coordinated conventions when negotiating fees with their professional advisers.

11.8 International working using CAD

While posing a threat from uncoordinated design, CAD enables owner, designer, manager and new facility to be based on separate sites, even in different countries. One major impact is it enables multinational companies to optimize costs through international working. Significant cost and schedule advantages can be gained by:

– Work proceeding concurrently in several countries, even permitting 24 hour working by the design following the sun from Japan to London to California and back to Japan.[2]
– Work moving from one location to another as design develops. This permits early work in the host country, detailed design in a low-cost location, such as India or Korea. Many consultant and contracting

organizations in both the engineering and software industries are finding it cost-effective to undertake design in low cost countries, even for projects being built in Western Europe and North America. The quality is as good as design undertaken in the West, but is achieved at a fraction of the cost.

11.9 Shippers

We now consider those people who arrange for the transportation of goods around the world. Sometimes they are known generically as shippers, although strictly speaking this is a misnomer: a shipper is another word for an exporter, someone whose goods are exported or shipped abroad. However, you should try to avoid the common mistake of referring to shipowners as shippers, despite this error even being perpetrated by maritime publications. There are several functions performed on behalf of shippers in the varied world of shipping by:

– Freight forwarders
– Loading brokers
– Carriers
– Port agents
– Shipbrokers.

Freight forwarders

Freight forwarders (also known as *forwarding agents*) are the link between the exporter (or 'shipper' of goods) and the shipping line. The freight forwarder arranges for collection of the packaged goods, known as *break-bulk* cargo, from an inland factory or warehouse, which may belong to the contractual exporter ('shipper') or may belong to their suppliers, for transportation to the ship's hold at the port of loading (*loadport*). Transportation will be by road haulier, rail, or some combination of the two. The break-bulk cargo may also pass via an *inland clearance depot*, ICD, where the goods are 'stuffed' (loaded) into containers, which are then in turn taken 'in bond' under customs seal to a container collection terminal or direct to the vessel by road or by rail.

Direct transport to the loadport is known as 'through-transport' of break-bulk goods. Transport via the ICD is known as 'multi-modal transport'. If goods are consigned on a site-to-site or warehouse-to-warehouse or depot-to-depot basis, this is known as multi-modal through-transport and is becoming increasingly prevalent. The carriage of the cargo from original inland site to final inland destination is therefore covered by a 'through bill of lading'. The freight forwarder sometimes groups together or 'consolidates' cargo in an ICD, making up less than full container-loads, known as LCLs, or filling an entire container as a full container load, known as FCLs. Such a service to clients is known as 'groupage' or 'consolidation'. This allows small items of cargo to be loaded and sent more economically and speedily by fast container ship than by a conventional break-bulk cargo vessel, which takes longer to load and has greater likelihood of loss or damage to small items of cargo. Thus, although an LCL cargo attracts a higher freight rate than FCL (partly because FCL cargo can be granted a rebate by the shipping line in return for frequent and regular use by an FCL shipper), this mode of transport is still favoured by shippers of small cargo parcels.

After arranging for the inland transportation of goods, the freight forwarder will issue its own 'house bill of lading' to the shipper. This is really only a 'certificate of shipment' (which is another misnomer, since the goods are only legally 'shipped' once they are on board the vessel). Once the goods are on board the vessel, an official bill of lading will be issued by the shipping line, or by the freight forwarder on its behalf, using the shipping line's own bill of lading form. At the port of destination, the local freight forwarder will arrange for the LCL goods to be transported inland to their final destination, if necessary via an ICD, where the container will be 'stripped' (or unloaded).

Freight forwarders are responsible for export (or import) customs clearance, including accurate declaration of the goods according to internationally recognized and used tariff. Each type of goods has its own tariff number, known somewhat grandiosely as 'Brussels Tariff Nomenclature', BTN. Most freight forwarders have their own customs declaration code number allotted, which allows them to make many declarations without having to resort to the time-consuming practice of reporting at a Customs House for approval of each declaration. A freight forwarder would also arrange through the local Chamber of Commerce for an export licence and a certificate of origin, either of which may need to be notarized at a consulate of the country of destination. They may also be asked to arrange for insurance cover for the transportation of the goods.

Loading brokers

A freight forwarder will liaise with a *loading broker*, the local representative of the shipping line in each main port or city where shippers or forwarding agents operate. The loading broker advertises sailings, or changes to scheduled sailings, between a range of ports on the shipping line's routes. They also monitor the centralized system of booking space on board each vessel as each booking is made by a number of forwarding agents and so can advise when each vessel is theoretically full.

Carriers

The shipping line is also known as the *carrier*, which may be:

- A single shipping line operating its own fleet of vessels: this type of carrier is sometimes known as an 'outsider service' if it does not comprise part of a conference line.
- A part of a pool of shipping lines, which are self-regulated by a 'conference' scheme: a conference scheme has some similarities to a cartel, in that they agree on tariff freight rates for all member lines.
- An operator of vessels which it does not own but merely charters as requirements demand: this type of carrier is known as a non-vessel-owning cargo carrier (NVOCC).

Occasionally a regular liner operator will not have sufficient vessels to meet the needs of its sailing schedule and will then charter tramp vessels to make up its fleet, either for a one-off voyage or for a time charter trip or period. This may be as a result of an abnormal increase in demand for cargo space or because one of the regular vessels in the fleet is unavailable through drydocking for routine or abnormal maintenance. This occasional chartering does not of course render a regular operator a NVOCC.

These comments relate mainly to liner shipping. There is a much larger side to shipping, namely tramp shipping. This is when the exporter does not just book space on a vessel through a regular liner service, but hires or charters an entire vessel for his own cargo. This is usually bulk, bagged, baled or bundled homogeneous cargo such as:

- Iron ore and other metal or mineral ores
- Coal
- Grain, rice, or sugar
- Fertilizer
- Cement
- Cotton or hemp
- Metal sheets, rods or pipes
- Liquid or gaseous cargoes shipped by tanker.

These cargoes will be taken between all parts of the world, including certain areas which are recognized ice or war zones – hence the word tramp.

Port agents

Port agents perform various functions, the most important being to act as the shipowner's local eyes and ears before, during and after the vessel's visit to a port. The agent is always appointed by the shipowner, even though the charterer of a tramp vessel may nominate the agent; thus in the first instance the agent's allegiance is to the shipowner. The charterer's nominated agent may not be to the liking of the shipowner because, for example, that agent may have been seen in the past as being biased in favour of cargo interests; the owner nevertheless has to appoint him as port agent but would then appoint another agent in that port specifically to look after the interests of the vessel – this agent is then known as a ship's 'husband' or 'protecting agent'.

In liner shipping, the port agent liaises closely with the line's loading broker and with various local freight forwarders, whereas a tramp ship's agent will liaise with the charterers and often also with the shipbrokers involved in the fixture. The port agent will:

- Organize stevedores, warehousing, and customs clearance.
- Call forward the cargo from the suppliers (who may not necessarily be the shippers).
- Alert the receivers of the impending arrival of the vessel.
- Issue the original bills of lading for or on behalf of the ship's Master at the load port.
- Ensure their accuracy and presence at the discharge port.
- Arrange for any help which the crew may need ashore, including shore passes, visas and passports, crew changes and flights, medical attention and accommodation when the vessel is being fumigated.

Port agents also arrange for the supply of stores, victuals, fresh water, bunkers (fuel and diesel) and spare parts for the ships. They also draw up a full disbursements account of all the moneys outlaid on the owner's behalf from the funds remitted to the agent in advance of the vessel's arrival at that port. That disbursement account may then be allocated in part to the charterers, if they have taken the vessel on time charter.

Another very important function of a port agent is to draw up a statement of facts (SOF) of events during the vessel's stay in the port. This is of particular interest to a shipper who is also the charterer of a tramp vessel, since he and the shipowner will base their timesheets and laytime calculations on the information furnished by the agents in the SOF.

Shipbrokers

The shipper who is also a charterer usually depends on a *shipbroker* to guide him in the search for the right vessel at the right place, date and rate. There are many options and pitfalls, and the marketplace is so vast that a charterer cannot expect to cover all the possible vessels for a particular order. The charterer is therefore well advised to employ the services of a shipbroker's negotiating skills and knowledge of the shipping world, covering:

- Market
- Vessels
- Geography
- Properties of different types of cargo
- Foibles of various shipowners
- Legal terminology which has to be included in the contractually binding charter.

In London, many dry cargo shipbrokers ply their trade on the Baltic Exchange, a unique institution which is both market forum and club. In the other major chartering centres of the world (New York, Sydney, Tokyo, Singapore, Hamburg, Copenhagen, Paris, Athens), contact is by telecommunication, lacking the personal face-to-face aspect of the Baltic. Nevertheless, the representatives of the many shipbrokers and shippers (charterers and shipowners) in those centres outside London cover over 60 per cent of the world's chartering market without any contact with the members of the Baltic.

11.10 Summary

1. There are two basic and different types of consultants:
   - The personal expert, with specialized knowledge and/or skill to accomplish specific tasks which can be clearly defined.
   - The professional firm, with specialized knowledge and/or skill which assists in the management of the project.
2. The skills brought to the project team by these consultants include:
   - Knowledge of facts
   - Knowledge of procedures
   - Skills of a specialist nature
   - Appropriate philosophy and culture
   - Experience in coping with change.
3. The risks to the owner include:
   - Discomfort through ignorance
   - Over-dependence
   - Apparent lack of control
   - Open-ended commitment.
4. These risks are almost mirrored in the risks to the consultant although in some cases they can be an advantage to the consultant.
5. The conclusion is that there is a need for a clear understanding of each

party's objectives and in particular of the possibilities and limitations of the service which the consultant can offer. To achieve this:
- Explain the requirement/service.
- Define the scope/potential/limitation.
- Maintain regular reviews.
- Ensure direct reporting.

These should lead to the *trust*, *quality* and *value* of service.

6. There are four basic forms of contractual relationship with designers, which are achieved by using:
   - In-house design departments
   - Firms of consultants
   - Design and build contractors
   - Managing contractors.

7. There are two approaches to specifying design criteria:
   - Detailed, piece-wise specification
   - Functional specification (cardinal points procurement).

8. Coordinated project information is an approach used to try to reduce the risk of communication failure between different engineering disciplines. It covers:
   - Procedures for producing documents
   - Technical content of documents
   - Arrangement of documents.

9. For people wishing to transport materials overseas, the services of the following are available:
   - Freight forwarders
   - Loading brokers
   - Carriers
   - Port agents
   - Shipbrokers.

References

1. Turner, J.R., *The Handbook of Project-based Management*, McGraw-Hill, 1993.
2. Hutchinson, D.H., 'The specific organisational and design challenges of global engineering design projects', in *International Journal of Project Management*, 12(1), 1994.

12
Financial supporters

Ashok Jashapara, Rodney Turner and Bian Yong-Qian

12.1 Introduction

We end Part Three by considering a third type of supporter: the project financiers. In Chapter 6, we showed that when the facility is commissioned, the finance costs are typically 15 per cent of expenditure, and over the life of the facility they can rise to 40 per cent of total expenditure. They are therefore the most significant element of expenditure on a project, and hence can have greatest impact on success. On a project like the Channel Tunnel, which took seven years to build, at the time of commissioning, the finance cost may have been in excess of one-half of the cost of the tunnel itself, and the servicing of the financing costs is a greater element of the price of travel than the operating costs.

Over the next two sections we briefly describe domestic and multinational financial markets. We then describe various financiers and finance agencies, including venture capitalists, the international investment institutions, export and government guarantee and aid agencies. We close this chapter by describing the support the owner might expect from the financier.

12.2 Domestic financial markets

There are three types of finance available in the domestic market (Chapter 6):

- Equity
- Subordinate debt (or quasi-equity)
- Senior debt (with secured and unsecured loans).

Debt is repaid before equity, and senior debt before subordinate debt. With debt, the amount repaid is the principal lent plus interest. Equity is repaid out of the profits, and so the amount repaid may be greater or less than the amount subscribed. Table 12.1 compares the advantages and disadvantages of these types of domestic finance.

Table 12.1 Comparing the sources of domestic finance

Source of finance	Advantages	Disadvantages
Equity	Collateral for securing debt	High risk
Subordinate debt	Attracts third party lenders	Coordination of parties difficult
Senior debt (secured)	Most popular form of finance for small to medium companies	Need for collateral
Senior debt (unsecured)	Based on financial reputation	Need to be large company with good reputation

1. *Equity* This comprises funds subscribed to a project (or to the parent company of the project) by shareholders from their own funds. This is the highest risk form of finance as there is no guarantee that a dividend will be paid, or that the shareholders will be able to recover their money. However, the upside risk is limitless if the project outperforms its expectations. Equity is the most common source of finance for small, medium and many large projects. For these, equity will often be the only source of finance. However, because of the risk involved, equity is more expensive than debt. Sources of equity finance include:
   - Corporate cash flow generated by existing business operations
   - Corporate or individual investors, or funds raised through the stock markets
   - Joint venture partners
   - Venture capital companies
   - Government subscriptions
   - International investment institutions (Table 12.5).
   The stock market is beyond the scope of this book. A useful description is given by Chapman.[1] Joint venture partners were described in Chapter 7. Venture capitalists are described in Section 12.4, and the international investment institutions in Section 12.5. Government and aid agencies are described in Sections 12.6 and 12.7.
2. *Subordinate debt (or quasi-equity)* This is seen rather like equity, where different parties to a project, such as the owner, suppliers, users or government provide capital for the project to attract greater third party lenders. It can often be treated as equity when calculating debt to equity ratios in negotiations with senior lenders (see below). Providers of subordinate debt are the same as those of equity.
3. *Senior debt* This is borrowing from commercial banks in the form of secured or unsecured loans. Unsecured debt is backed by the general creditworthiness of the borrower established through good reputation with the financial community. Secured loan is debt secured by collateral or assets easily convertible into cash.

Debt is the main form of finance for large to major projects. However, lenders are unlikely to provide finance unless there is a certain amount of equity in the project. This is because equity investors are last in priority for repayment, and can overturn management decisions, or even replace management. They will therefore impose probity on the management. The ratio of debt to equity for a particular project will depend on the negotiations between borrower and senior lender. Banks will also finance small- to medium-sized projects, but usually by lending money to the parent organization rather than directly to the project.

Commercial banks are the main source of debt finance. There is a large choice of banks for companies raising finance, and this has led to intense competition. In London alone, in addition to the large UK clearing banks, there are over 200 branches of North American banks, as well as major Japanese, European, Asian and Australasian banks. The pricing differential between them is small due to the intense competition. Hence the decision as to which bank to use will not be based so much on interest rate as on:

– Size of the bank
– Experience in financing a particular type of project
– Support and working relationships.

For example, a bank specializing in venture capital would provide specialist knowledge to small companies or new ventures. On the other hand, large merchant banks, which are a form of European investment bank, would provide expertise as intermediaries in large projects between the project company and large investors. Other sources of debt are listed in Table 12.2.

Table 12.2 Sources of senior debt

Commercial banks
International lending institutions
Suppliers of equipment and services for the project
Suppliers of raw materials to the project
Buyers of products from the completed project facility
Government export credit and guarantees
Providers of aid

12.3 Multinational financial markets

Multinational financial markets are an important alternative to domestic markets for large, multinational organizations. The most important multinational financial markets are London, Tokyo and New York. As well as acting as domestic financial markets, they also operate as international and off-shore financial markets:

- International markets are where funds flow from domestic/foreign investors to foreign/domestic borrowers.
- Off-shore markets are where funds flow directly from foreign investors to foreign borrowers.

Easy access to foreign sources of funds can be a source of competitive advantage to many firms.[2] Further advantage may result from raising funds in those markets which have an absence of government interference in the form of taxes, reserve requirements, deposit insurance premiums and interest rate regulations. There are many forms of multinational finance, many a variation on a theme.[3] The two major ones are Eurocurrency and Eurobond markets (Table 12.3).

Table 12.3   Comparing the sources of multinational finance

Source of finance	Advantages	Disadvantages
Eurocurrency	Short-term finance Competitive rates	Primarily large organizations
Eurobonds	Most competitive capital market in the world No regulatory interference	Primarily large multinational organizations Based on quality rating

1. *Eurocurrency markets* These are open 24 hours, and are the most efficient markets in the world. They provide smooth movement of funds, with high liquidity and large cash flows, and provide wholesale markets for large multinational organizations. They also exist to avoid government regulation, taxes and certain types of political risk. The Eurocurrency markets serve three valuable purposes:
   - Their deposits are an efficient way of holding excess corporate liquidity.
   - They are a major source of short-term finance.
   - They are useful for arbitrage purposes.[4]
   The most common Eurocurrency is Eurodollar. This is a US dollar time deposit in a bank legally resident outside the United States. The 'Eurobank' may be a foreign bank or an overseas branch of a US bank. There are many other forms of Eurocurrency such as Eurosterling, Euromark and Euroyen. The basic borrowing rate for Eurodollar loans is tied to the London Interbank Offered Rate (LIBOR) which is the deposit rate applicable to inter-bank loans within London. Borrowers pay a premium over the base rate which will depend on their creditworthiness

and the terms of credit. Eurodollars are generally lent for short- and medium-term maturities for a fixed term with no provision for early repayment. The Eurodollar market is primarily accessible to large organizations.[5]

2. *Eurobond markets* They provide promissory notes or bonds which must be issued outside the United States. They are also issued in small denominations making them attractive to the small investor. They also provide anonymity to the investor. They are an attractive source of finance. Interest rates are slightly lower than rates on domestically issued bonds as they are in bearer form and international investors will accept a lower yield in return for anonymity. They can also be issued quickly, in response to favourable market conditions. Issuing organizations with a good reputation are likely to obtain more favourable terms in the form of lower interest rates due to a high quality credit rating.[6] The Eurobond market is the most competitive capital market in the world and exists due to the absence of regulatory interference, less stringent disclosure practices and favourable tax treatment.

12.4 Venture capital companies

A source of domestic finance which found favour during the 1980s is venture capitalists. This arose from the US and UK governments' desire to encourage small businesses in the private sector, and the potential of technology transfer, that is the development of high-technology inventions on a commercial basis. Venture capital is money put into an enterprise which will all be lost if the venture fails. The money is usually put in as an equity stake, and ventures supported may be new business start-ups, a manufacturing buy-out, or a major expansion of a large business. The risks are high, but so are the interest rates or expected returns. Some of the venture capital companies in the United Kingdom are listed in Table 12.4.

Table 12.4 Venture capital companies in the United Kingdom

Investors in Industry (3i group)
Equity Capital for Industry
Venture capital subsidiaries of the clearing banks
Specialist organizations include:
  The Charterhouse Group
  Morecrest Investments
  The Small Business Capital Fund
  The Gresham Trust
  Prutec
  Grosvenor Venture Managers
National Research and Development Corporation

Advantages of venture capital are that it may be the only source of finance to some small businesses. Disadvantages are that the venture capital company will want an equity stake, and that the lender may want to be involved in the management of the company.

12.5 International investment institutions

The World Bank and other area development banks provide debt and equity. They may also be providers of aid (see below). International investment institutions are listed in Table 12.5. Nevitt[3] lists advantages and disadvantages of financing from the international investment institutions.

Table 12.5 International investment institutions

African Development Bank, AfDB
Asian Development Bank, ADB
Commonwealth Development Corporation, CDC
European Development Fund, EDF
European Investment Bank, EIB
European Bank for Reconstruction and Development, EBRD
Inter-American Development Bank, IDB
International Bank for Reconstruction and Development, IBRD, or World Bank
International Development Association, IDA
International Finance Corporation, IFC

Advantages:

– Loans are longer term than other sources.
– Loans have lower interest rates.
– Loans act as an endorsement for credit from other sources.
– Loans act as a basis for co-financing arrangements (Section 12.7).

Disadvantages:

– There is a lengthy approval process;
– The loans are in hard currencies which provide little opportunity for optimizing currency risk.

12.6 Government and export guarantee

Most developed countries face saturated domestic markets which has led firms to seek expansion in international markets, especially developing countries. On their part, developing countries, when pursuing development, desperately need advanced technology. However, lack of capital and restricted access to finance sources constrain their ability to access it. Government agencies are an important source of export finance to support this trade.[2,7] Most OECD countries have an export financial agency or national interest lender (Table 12.6). The UK's Export Credits Guarantee Department (ECGD) illustrates their operation.

Table 12.6   Export finance agencies or national interest lenders

Country	Agency
Australia	Export Finance and Insurance Corporation (EFIC)
Austria	Oesterreichische Kontolbank Aktiengesellschaft (OKB)
Belgium	Office National de Ducroire Creditexport
Brazil	Carteris de Commercio Exterior – Banco do Brazil (CACEX)
	Institutio de Resegguros do Brazil (IRB)
Canada	Export Development Corporation (EDC)
Denmark	Exportkreditradet (EKR)
	Dansk Eksportfinansieringsfond (EF)
France	Compagnie Francaise d'Assurance pour le Commerce Exterieur (COFACE)
	Banque Francaise du Commerce Exterieur (BFCE)
Germany	Hermes Kreditversicherungs AG
	Aus Fuhrkredit–Gesellschaft mbH (AKA)
	Kreditanstalt fur Wiederaufbau (KFW)
Italy	Sezione Speciale per l'Assicurazione del Credito all' Esportazione (SACE)
	Mediocredito Centrale
Japan	Export–Import Bank of Japan
	Ministry of International Trade and Industry (MITI)
Korea	Export–Import Bank of Korea
The Netherlands	Nederlansche Credietverzekering Maatschappij (NCM)
	De Nederlansche Bank (DNB)
New Zealand	Export Guarantee Office (EXGO)
South Africa	Industrial Development Corporation of Africa Ltd (CGIC)
Spain	Compania Espanola de Seguros de Ceditio a la Exportacion (CESCE)
Sweden	Exportkreditnamnden (EKN)
	AB Svenska Export Kredit (SEK)
Switzerland	Exportrisikogarantie (ERG)
Taiwan	The Export–Import Bank of China
United Kingdom	Export Credits Guarantee Department (ECGD)
United States	Export–Import Bank of the United States
	Private Export Funding Corporation (PEFCO)
	Overseas Private Investment Corporation (OPIC)

ECGD's facilities

Responsible to the President of the Board of Trade, ECGD's principal role is to promote UK exports, by providing:

- Access to cheap finance enabling companies to offer competitive terms and win contracts they might otherwise lose.
- Insurance against political, legal, economic and social risk.

SUPPORT FOR EXPORT FINANCE

ECGD does not directly provide finance for export credit, but does provide assistance in the financing of UK exports by the banks. The actual arrangements differ depending on the manner in which the export credit is provided. In the case of 'supplier credit', the exporter sells goods on deferred payment terms, borrowing from a bank in the UK to finance the period from shipment of the goods until payment is made. ECGD can give a guarantee direct to the bank providing the export finance against non-payment by the buyer of up to 100 per cent of the value of bills or notes. Moreover, by arrangement with the UK Government, the bank will lend against the security of the ECGD guarantee at special interest rates, up to a maximum of 5/8 per cent over the base rate for business of up to two years' credit from shipment, and (except for trade with EU countries) at special fixed rates for longer term credit (see below). Normally, the exports which are financed by the bank under the ECGD guarantee should also be insured by ECGD. For major project and capital goods business, including UK goods and services valued at £1 million or more, the exporter may prefer to negotiate on cash terms and arrange a loan from a UK bank direct to the buyer on repayment terms equivalent to the credit they might expect from the supplier credit. Under this arrangement, called 'buyer credit', the exporter receives prompt cash payment from their buyer, who draws on the loan from the UK bank. The loan is then to be repaid by instalments. This loan, up to 85 per cent of the value of the contract, can be made at the same preferential interest rates as the supplier credit. The loan may be in sterling or in approved foreign currencies. ECGD provides guarantee to the bank making the loan against non-payment for up to 100 per cent of capital and interest of the loan.

EXPORT CREDIT INSURANCE

ECGD insures exporters against the risk of not being paid – whether through the default of the buyer or through other causes, such as restrictions on the transfer of currency, cancellation of valid import licences, etc. The export trade is classified into two broad categories:

1. *Repetitive trade* This is in standard or near-standard goods and is normally of short-term nature. Cover on this sort of trade is provided under 'comprehensive' policies designed for insurance of continuous

business. Under these policies, ECGD is liable for 90–95 per cent of the amount insured depending on scope of the risks covered. This type of trade accounts for about 75 per cent of ECGD's business.[8]

2. *Trade in large capital goods* This is of a non-repetitive nature, usually of high value and often involving lengthy credit terms. Such business is not suited to comprehensive treatment and specific policies are negotiated for each contract. These policies cover 90 per cent of the insured loss.

OVERSEAS INVESTMENT INSURANCE

New investment overseas may be insured against the political risks of expropriation, war and restrictions on remittances. Investments are underwritten individually, specific insurance being arranged while the investment itself is being negotiated. In other words, the investor must apply for cover before becoming irrevocably committed to the investment if it is intended to take insurance from ECGD. Once issued, the insurance cover runs for a minimum of three years and a maximum of 15 years at a fixed rate of premium determined at the outset. The maximum percentage of this cover is 90 per cent of the loss insured.

SUPPORT FOR PERFORMANCE BOND

In certain circumstances, ECGD will support the issue of performance bonds. This will be to aid exporters of capital goods or contractors for large overseas projects worth £250 000 or more, where the exports are undertaken on cash or near-cash terms, and are insured by ECGD against the normal pre-credit and credit risks, but where the exporters face particular difficulties. In these circumstances, the bonds may be required by means of an indemnity to banks or surety companies which are willing to issue the bonds. Under its indemnity, ECGD is unconditionally liable to reimburse the bond giver in full for the amount of any bond call. However, any payment by ECGD to the bond holder becomes the subject of a claim by ECGD against the exporter under a related recourse agreement if the bond call is due to the default of the exporter or the contractor under the terms of the contract. In addition to the performance bond, ECGD may also give similar support for the issue of tender, advance payment and retention bonds.

Premium charges of the services

In fixing premium rates at which ECGD charges the exporters for their using its facilities, ECGD must seek to avoid overall loss on its trading account. It is required to operate at no net cost to public funds, but must not aim for surpluses beyond those needed to maintain adequate reserve in the face of growing liabilities. The premium rates for particular classes or items of business are determined on the merits of the risks contained, which are continuously assessed by ECGD on the basis of:

- The buyer's financial position and business reputation
- The political and economic situations in this country where the buyer is located
- The period of cover.

In order to keep premium rates down ECGD also aims to get as much sound business as possible. This has been greatly helped by a continuous and systematic watch on economic and political developments in every overseas country.

Premium for short-term business is paid by an annual, non-refundable (holding) premium and an additional monthly premium on declaration of business. On the other hand, premium rates for medium- and long-term business are determined contract by contract, based upon the length of the period during which ECGD is at risk and ECGD grading of the market with which the business is done. No annual (holding) premium is charged. For the purpose of determining premium for medium- and long-term business, ECGD classifies countries into four categories.

Export credit

Broadly speaking, an export credit arises whenever a foreign buyer of exported goods or services is allowed to defer payment for a period of time. The rationale of the export credit is in response to a market need or a business opportunity, where a firm is to build a facility which will enable it to meet the market need or to take the opportunity. However, the lack of capital may prevent the firm from building this facility. With credit purchase, the firm is able to complete the facility. The production of the facility will hopefully generate enough revenue to cover the production cost and the debt service. If the purchase in this case involves import, then an export credit is required. There are two types of export credit:

- Supplier credit
- Buyer credit.

Supplier credit is defined as:

> A loan to an importer which is guaranteed by the export credit agency of the country of the exporter.[9]

Buyer credit is defined as:

A medium- to long-term loan to the foreign buyer of exported goods. The loan is given by the exporter's bank and usually carries the guarantee of the exporter's national export credit agency.[9]

Supplier and buyer credit are described in Chapter 6. The comparative advantages of the two types of export credit arrangements are as follows:

1. Supplier credit is much simpler and does not involve the buyer in the financial arrangements.
2. Supplier credit allows the parties to contract very much on what terms they are willing to negotiate and ECGD plays no part in these negotiations.
3. Supplier credit leaves the exporter with a residual risk in the event of default by the buyer in payment.
4. Supplier credit means the exporter does not receive payment until goods have been shipped.
5. Buyer credit may allow the exporter to draw on the loan prior to the shipment of goods or during the course of work, under certain terms of contract between the buyer and exporter and the loan agreement between the buyer and the exporter's bank.
6. Buyer credit takes considerably longer to negotiate because there are four agreements involved each of which has to tie in with the other:
   – The trade contract
   – The loan agreement between the exporter's bank and the buyer
   – The guarantee agreement between ECGD and the exporter's bank
   – The premium and recourse agreements between the exporter and ECGD.
   Because of the need for the agreements to mesh together and the fact that ECGD is guaranteeing the whole transaction, ECGD requires to approve both the trade contract and the loan agreement. The negotiations involved can therefore become protracted, and at times a little heated on certain provisions in the contract or the agreement. The lengthy negotiations may cause the delay of the commencement of the contract work or the delay of the shipment of goods and hence the delay of the income produced by the project.
7. Under buyer credit, the financial charges which the buyer is called upon to pay in order to obtain the loan facility are necessarily higher because of the extent to which the UK bank is involved in negotiations.

Whichever method of export credit financing is selected, there are certain disadvantages from the buyer's point of view. These are:

- The credit only applies to goods and services provided by the country offering the credit – so-called 'tied financing', which can be very expensive in the sense that goods and services are purchased without competition or with limited competition.
- Locally incurred costs together with those for the 'front end' need to be covered either by cash or by Eurodollar loans. Since these latter are at commercial rates of interest, most borrowers would prefer to find some alternative.
- The interest rates for export credits and the periods for credit are fixed under 'Consensus'. At present the interest rates for the relatively rich countries are set at a level which approximates to the commercial interest rates for long-term government bond yields and as such are not particularly attractive, especially as the rates are fixed for the period of the loan while commercial rates can float.

Consensus

Buyers naturally seek the best terms of credit they can get. There is thus a constant danger of a 'credit terms race' developing between sellers in different countries in order to secure business. Such a race would be damaging to the balance of payments of all countries. In 1976, in an effort to avoid such a race, members of the Group on Export Credits and Credit Guarantees (ECG) of the OECD Trade Committee reached an informal 'Consensus' that set for most officially supported export credits of two years or more:

- A floor under permitted interest rates
- Ceiling on maturities
- Minimum down payments
- Maximum local-cost financing allowances.

On 1 April 1978, these rules were incorporated into an Arrangement on Guidelines for Officially Supported Export Credits, in which all OECD members except Iceland and Turkey are participants. The Arrangement provides that any participant who intends to offer a credit that exceeds the maximum degree of permitted concessionality (e.g. by a lower interest rate, or a longer maturity) should notify that intention beforehand to other participants, and explain the reason for the intended action. Participants meet at OECD Headquarters for an Annual Review of the functioning of the Arrangement and the appropriateness of its Guidelines.[10] Table 12.7 lists the main contents of the Guidelines.

Table 12.7 OECD Guidelines for Officially Supported Export Credits‡

Country category*	Minimum payments by delivery	Maximum credit periods (years)	Minimum interest rates† 2–5 years	Over 5 years
Relatively rich	15%	5		
Intermediate	15%	8.5		
Relatively poor	15%	10		

Notes * Country categories are classified by GNP per capita.
    † Interest rates are calculated every six months in January and July against interest movements in SDR. These rates are lower than commercial rates prevailing in most capital markets. The gap between the credit rate and the commercial rate is covered by the government subsidy, in the United Kingdom by ECGD.
    ‡ These guidelines are not applicable to exports to other EU countries. While ECGD's unconditional guarantees to financing banks are available for those exports, there is no ECGD support for the interest rate at which finance is provided.

12.7 Aid agencies

Aid is a source of finance available to projects in developing countries.[11] Aid may be:

- Direct from one government to another (Fig. 6.3), via the aid agency of the donor country
- From one of the supranational aid agencies.

Aid agencies in European OECD countries include:

- The UK's Overseas Development Administration, ODA
- France's Direction de Relations Economiques Exterieur, DREE
- Germany's Kredit fur Weideraufbau, KfW.

The aid route to raising finance can be long and time consuming, with no certainty that the contract will be awarded. Many companies have decided that aid finance does not merit the effort. There is a trend among international aid agencies towards blurring the edges between development and commercial lending through soft (low interest rate) loans, aid used to dilute interest payments, and co-financing. The term 'co-financing' refers to any arrangement under which funds from the *World Bank* are associated with funds provided from other sources outside the borrowing country in financing a particular project. Official sources of co-financing include member governments, their agencies and multilateral financing institutions. This source is often referred to as 'donor' financing. There can also be co-financing by private institutions such as banks, insurance companies and other private capital markets outside the country of the borrower.

There are several methods of procurement developed by the World Bank which have been adopted by many other aid agencies. These include:

- International competitive bidding
- Limited international bidding where participation is through invitation
- Local competitive bidding where foreign bidders are unlikely to be interested due to small-scale of work
- Direct purchase where a single source is negotiated
- Force account where the works are unsuitable for bidding such as in remote areas, high risk, maintenance, emergency and training.

For major projects, which are often subject to intense competition, there is a practice of using mixed credits where officially supported credits are combined with an element of government aid. In the United Kingdom, the Projects and Export Policy Division of the DTI has prime responsibility in this area. The support is discretionary and made available through arrangements agreed by Ministers. The project must meet certain industrial and commercial criteria to be supported by this aid. It must also be financially and economically viable and technically sound.

12.8 Support from the financier

Often the project manager, or even his or her parent organization, may have little experience of project financing (Chapter 6.) It is a large part of the expenditure of the project, but least understood by the investors. The borrower may therefore be looking for considerable support from the lender, and this can be provided in many ways,[2] including:

- Conducting the feasibility study
- Planning the project finance
- Arranging the total financial package
- Controlling the financial package
- Assuming risk for the borrower.

Sometimes the borrower will recruit the services of a separate financial consultant to undertake some of these steps.

Conducting the feasibility study

The sponsor may often not have the internal resources or skills to assess the viability of the project. In these cases, the financier may undertake the feasibility on the sponsor's behalf. This often happens with governments investing in infrastructure projects, when the World Bank may support them in the feasibility study. The first three of seven steps in the World Bank's project management life cycle address the feasibility stage of the project.[12] (The conducting of the feasibility study is described by Turner.)[12]

Planning the project finance

Having conducted the feasibility study, the financial consultant will help the sponsor plan the financial package. This will involve the following steps:

1. From the feasibility study, the consultant will have identified the total cost of the facility to be built, and the total amount of money to be borrowed.
2. The consultant will help the sponsor identify sources of finance, and the cost of those sources. They will thereby develop a financial strategy for the project, involving a mixture of loans and equity.
3. The consultant will help the sponsor to schedule the rate of expenditure, and hence to identify the rate at which the loans will be drawn.
4. The total cost of the project can be calculated by adding the raw cost of the facility to the cost of servicing the debt. We saw in Chapter 6, that the cost of servicing the debt can be 60 per cent of the total capital cost of the project, that is it can be one and a half times the money to be borrowed.

Arranging the total financial package

The consultant will then help the sponsor identify and raise additional sources of finance. The consultant will often (usually) be the main supplier of senior debt and will also help the sponsor by:

- Raising equity – a merchant bank will almost certainly assist in this process
- Identifying additional sponsors and suppliers of subordinate debt
- Raising finance through syndicated loans (Eurocurrency) or Eurobonds
- Liaising with Export Credit Guarantee Departments and arranging buyer or supplier credit
- Arranging more sophisticated or less conventional financial packages, as described in Chapter 6.

Controlling the financial package

As the work of the project progresses, then the financial consultant will control progress on the financial arrangements. That will involve monitoring progress against the financial plan, and helping the sponsor to take action to eliminate any deviations from the plan. This may include:

1. *During the construction stage* Ensuring that expenditure follows the predicted rate and that the debt is drawn in accordance with the plan, monitoring the forecast of cost to complete to ensure it remains within the original budget, and arranging additional finance if variations occur.
2. *During the commissioning stage* Monitoring the costs of production to ensure that the financial plan and operating objectives are achieved, and monitoring sales revenues to ensure that income will service the debt and make a profit for the sponsors.
3. *During the operating life of the facility* Helping the sponsor with the management accounting to ensure the facility achieves its optimum profitability, and to provide reports to the lenders to avoid nasty surprises.

Assuming risk for the borrower

Often, through the financial package, the lender will assume risks on behalf of the borrower. These risks may include some of the following:

– Country risk, from political action, nationalization, regulations or sovereign ownership.
– Financial risk, from variations in exchange rates, interest rates or inflation.
– Feasibility risk, that the facility will not perform as expected from lack of capacity, operating inefficiency, price or take-up of product – energy banks in the United States have shared the risk that an oil or gas reservoir will not have the predicted reserves.
– Contractual risk, including price or availability of raw materials, permits and licences, sale of the product, or *force majeur*.
– Refinancing risk.
– Completion risk.

12.9 Summary

1. There are three forms of domestic finance to projects:
   – Equity, the riskiest for the investor and therefore the most expensive
   – Subordinate debt
   – Senior debt, consisting of both secured and unsecured loans.
2. There are two main forms of multinational finance:
   – Eurocurrency
   – Eurobonds.
3. Venture capital companies are a significant source of finance to small projects.

4. Advantages of using international investment institutions are:
   - Longer term loans
   - Lower interest rates
   - Endorsement for credit from other sources
   - They can lead to co-financing arrangements.

   The disadvantages are:
   - Lengthy approval process
   - Loans in hard currencies which provide little opportunity for optimizing currency risk.

5. Services provided by export credit guarantee are:
   - Support for export finance
   - Export credit insurance
   - Overseas investment insurance
   - Support for performance bonds.

6. Support provided by the project's financier may include:
   - Conducting the feasibility study
   - Planning the project finance
   - Arranging the total financial package
   - Controlling the financial package
   - Assuming risk for the borrower.

References

1. Chapman, C., *How the Stock Market Works*, 4th Edition, Century Business, 1991.
2. Eiteman, D. and Stonehill, A., *Multinational Business Finance*, Addison-Wesley, 1989.
3. Nevitt, P., *Project Financing*, Euromoney Publications, 1989.
4. Gunter, D. and Giddy, I.H., *The International Money Market*, Prentice-Hall, 1978.
5. Kemp, L., *Wardley Guide to World Money and Securities Markets*, Euromoney Publications, 1986.
6. Watson, M., *International Capital Markets*, Ballinger Publishing, 1987.
7. Dun, A. and Knight, M., *Export Finance*, Euromoney Publications, 1982.
8. Central Office of Information, *ECGD Services*, Central Office of Information, 1985.
9. Hindle, T., *The Economist Pocket Banker*, The Economist and Blackwell, 1985
10. OECD, *The Export Credit Financing Systems in OECD Member Countries*, OECD, 1992.
11. Weigand, R., *International Trade Without Money*, Harvard Business Review, November/December, 1977.
12. Turner, J.R., *The Handbook of Project-based Management*, McGraw-Hill, 1993.

PART FOUR
STAKEHOLDERS

Part Four looks at the impact of projects on the environment, and how that impact must be managed as part of the decision to invest in the project. The strategy for managing the impact may be to reduce it. Often the impact can be reduced without reducing the performance of the project or its profitability. Indeed, if we put a value on the environment, then reducing the impact can make the project overall more profitable. Alternatively, our strategy may be to manage the expectations of the local stakeholders, to demonstrate the project is beneficial to them, to show the impact of the project is small and everything is being done to minimize it.

In Chapter 13, David Topping describes the relationship between projects and the environment. He introduces modern environmental principles as they apply to projects, and considers the different effects that projects can have on the environment and how they can be managed.

In Chapter 14, Stuart Calvert explains how to develop a strategy for managing the stakeholders. He identifies the need, and introduces tools for analysing the impact of the project and identifying the relevant stakeholders. He then explains how to communicate with the stakeholders before describing techniques for developing a stakeholder management strategy.

In Chapter 15, Dennis Burningham considers environmental impact assessment, and the process of greening projects, that is making them more environmentally friendly. He describes how to conduct an environmental impact assessment.

In Chapter 16, John Stringer describes the planning and inquiry process. An inquiry can be an essential, even a mandatory, part of some major projects, especially in the public sector. The inquiry must be managed like any other stage of the project, and yet so often proper project management techniques are not applied.

All four authors draw on their experience of the construction of infrastructure projects. This is the industry which has the greatest experience of environmental impact. However, increasingly, the principles are being applied in other areas. For instance, the computer control system was a key issue in the planning and inquiry process for the Sizewell B Nuclear Power Station. Many of the issues discussed are easily extrapolated to other industries.

land ever return to agriculture? Roads also need large quantities of quarried aggregates and although research into reuse of industrial waste as an alternative is being undertaken,[4] very large areas of agricultural land will be mined for suitable road building and other construction materials. Land is often returned to agricultural use after quarrying is completed. Between 1982 and 1988, some 20 000 hectares of land were reclaimed – but only 63 per cent of it for agriculture and forestry and the demand for aggregates for road building and other activities continues to grow. Almost 40 per cent of land subject to quarrying activities is therefore lost for good as a result of construction. By 1988, there were some 96 000 ha of land with outstanding mineral working permits.[5] (The environmental effects of transport projects are considered further in Section 13.3.)

The precautionary principle

The precautionary principle states that where an activity has unknown consequences for the environment, we should take steps to limit or if possible avoid it. For example, the group of chemicals known as PCBs (polychlorinated biphenyls), used in electrical components is man made, is not broken down into natural compounds by natural processes when disposed of, and is taken up in the food chain. Although we do not yet have absolute proof that build-up of PCBs in the seal population of the North Sea is a significant contributor to their sudden decline in recent years, there is strong evidence that this is the case and therefore the principle implies, we should take steps to eliminate that possibility. This is one example where international action has been taken, but there will remain huge quantities of PCBs in the environment for decades to come.

The alternative approach, fast losing its power as an objective argument, with too many questions without satisfactory answers, is that we should take no action until the consequences of activities are formally proven. As an example, those who support this 'technical fix' approach would wait until all meteorologists are agreed upon the existence, the causes and the extent of global warming before we take any steps to limit carbon dioxide emissions, by which time it may be too late to reverse.

BPEO, BATNEEC and IPC

The concepts of Best Practical Environmental Option (BPEO) and Best Available Technique Not Entailing Excessive Cost (BATNEEC) are defined within the Environmental Protection Act 1990.

1. BPEO concerns high-level decision making at governmental or project level, for example in waste disposal. Is it better to incinerate a particular

substance or to bury it in a landfill waste tip? BPEO takes no account of economic comparisons. In transportation, it may be seen as the choice between road and rail transport, whether at national policy level or for a particular route. 'Practical' generally means feasible using currently available technology, and in legal and planning terms.

2. BATNEEC then applies at project-specific level, and has regard to the relative costs of the various options for carrying out an activity. Effectively, commercial decisions will be made with cost as the main determinant. However, cost is influenced by the need to satisfy evermore stringent regulations, for example in pollution control and waste disposal; and the penalties of failing to meet them.

Within the Act, these concepts are discussed chiefly in terms of Integrated Pollution Control (IPC), also defined by the Act. The main objectives of IPC are:

- To prevent or minimize the release of prescribed substances and to render harmless any such substances which are released.
- To develop an approach to pollution control that considers discharges from industrial processes to all media in the context of the effect on the environment as a whole.

Its general purpose is to control disposal of pollutants and waste. This recent development gives teeth to the principle set out in the Fifth Report of the Royal Commission on Environmental Pollution,[6] which proposed that polluting releases should be directed to the environmental medium (air, land or water) where the least environmental damage would be done. The Environmental Protection Act is the United Kingdom's centrepiece of environmental legislation, and acts as a framework for implementing both United Kingdom and European legislation by bestowing powers on Ministers to introduce regulations under the Act which are being developed or likely to be developed in future. A *Practical Guide*[7] explains fully the workings of IPC – and gives the timetable for its statutory implementation in a number of sectors. These include fuel and power, waste disposal, mineral, chemical, metal and other industries. Of particular relevance to construction are the manufacture of cement, iron and steel, tar and bitumen, timber and glass – major components of infrastructure projects.

The polluter pays

Government policy confirms this principle in theory but its practical application is far from complete. The Environmental Protection Act embodies the principle. An example, one of the major infrastructure debates currently taking place, concerns transportation policy. The rail industry and its supporters have long protested that road projects are justified by an investment appraisal methodology which favours road over rail, and also fails to take into account environmental costs in full.

> There is a need to assess investment proposals for the various transport modes on a common basis.[8]

This is a serious issue which the government, despite its rhetoric, has so far failed to address. The ICE argues that a level playing field would favour rail investment above road for many routes, thereby relieving congestion and reducing the need for road building. Two environmental disbenefits of road building were mentioned earlier in this section and Section 13.3 describes further disbenefits.

In another example from the United Kingdom, water and sewerage household bills have risen since privatization of the water industry, because of the stricter standards for drinking water quality, imposed by the EU, and the stricter standards for treated effluent discharging to rivers, imposed by our National Rivers Authority. The Water Utilities, which treat sewage and industrial water-borne wastes on our behalf, are the polluters in this example. We as individual householders or as industrial operators have been presented with the full costs of complying with the new standards. The improvement in drinking water and effluent discharge standards has created a ten year, £30 billion, investment programme involving many major projects.

Environmental accounting and costing

Environmental accounting may influence projects in two ways. Firstly, more and more companies are including an environmental statement in their annual reports to demonstrate the effects of their policies and projects upon the environment. For example, a company may invest in a water recycling plant, atmospheric emission controls or office and plant energy efficiency devices. They will of course make these investments only if economically justified, or they are obliged to do so by regulations. However, there is a benefit in describing these initiatives as environmental improvements for publicity purposes and in many cases they will be genuine claims. The second form of environmental accounting is at government level and done for much the same reason – to demonstrate publicly a commitment to the environment. We see the United Kingdom, Germany and Belgium, now putting monetary values on the cost of their environmental programmes, and increasingly, the monetary value of the subsequent improvements.

This leads to the increasing use of environmental costing techniques. How much is a panoramic view of the countryside worth, for example, and what would be the cost to the nation of its partial loss if a power station were built within it, or a pylon line strung across it? What is the value of improving the quality of water in a particular watercourse? How should we place a monetary value on reduced CO_2 emissions? After all, government economists do like to see a return for their expenditure – and feel a need to demonstrate that the cost of policies is outweighed by the value of their implementation.

Project managers will increasingly be asked to provide answers to these questions when carrying out infrastructure projects. Here is a brief summary of methods which may be used:

1. *The contingent valuation method* This involves asking individuals what they would pay for an environmental improvement, or accept as compensation for a disbenefit (for example the loss of a view, the improvement of a river's quality).
2. *The travel cost method* For national parks, other public amenities, heritage sites and buildings, we can carry out surveys to find out how many people visit in a year, and the time and cost of travelling there. The estimated value of people's leisure time and cost of visiting provides an intrinsic value over and above the value of land, bricks and mortar.
3. *The hedonic pricing method* This is best explained using house prices as an example. The difference between the price of houses which either enjoy a local benefit, or suffer a disbenefit, compared to other substantially similar houses which are not affected in the same way, gives a cost. This is typified by the established practice of compensating householders who may be affected by the construction of a new road – or the proposed high speed Channel Tunnel rail link, where different levels of compensation are paid depending upon distance from the route.
4. *The least cost alternative method* This is the method with which project managers may be most familiar. Alternative projects are considered which satisfy the same business objectives, and the difference between the cheapest and the chosen project implies the value of its environmental benefits.

These methods are summarized from Ramchandani,[9] who has explored their potential use in water quality improvement projects.

13.3 Environmental effects

The effects of construction and infrastructure projects fall broadly into two phases (construction and operation) and seven, interrelated categories:[4,10]

- Energy
- Construction waste
- Pollution
- Transport
- Noise
- Land use and waste disposal
- Internal building environment.

Two additional phases may be identified when considering life cycle analysis of projects. These are the production of materials and components used in construction projects, and the disposal of materials at the end of the project life, when demolition takes place. The first phase would include, for example, extractive industries such as quarrying for aggregates. The final phase is of growing importance in consideration of recycling and reuse of construction materials, particularly as the life cycles of many types of project are becoming increasingly shorter.[11]

Energy

The common currency of environmental life cycle analysis is energy; that is the energy used to extract, transport and manufacture primary materials such as steel and cement; that used in producing the project, for example mixing concrete and rolling steel sections (embodied energy); and that used in heating, lighting and powering buildings and the processes within them during the project's operational life. Thus, for example, it is found that timber requires considerably less total energy to be used in the process from extraction to incorporation into a building than do either steel or concrete structural elements, or other forms of internal cladding such as gypsum-based partition walls. Additional advantage is provided by timber's thermal insulation properties. Table 13.1 shows the importance of considering the use of energy during the operation of buildings.

The construction industry plays the primary role in determining the energy efficiency and hence consumption of buildings. Design and

Table 13.1   Energy usages in the United Kingdom

Usage	Ratio (%)
Buildings	47 (of which 60% domestic)
Industry	23
Transport	29
Agriculture	1

After Shorrock and Henderson.[12]

construction to minimize the need for heating and air conditioning, and also to maximize the use of natural daylight, will play a significant role in energy reduction in building use. Implementation of all the most energy efficient forms of construction currently available would reduce building energy consumption by 35 per cent, while implementing only those which are currently economic would reduce consumption by 25 per cent, or 12–17 per cent of total national energy consumption.

To these savings may be added those attributable to innovative power generation systems. In particular, project managers should note that efficiency combined heat and power (CHP) gas systems, in which the heat from combustion is reused to heat offices or provide heat for industrial processes, can be as high as 85 per cent. For certain applications, CHP can be an economic alternative to electricity from the national grid, on installations as small as 750 kW. However, before project managers get too excited, they should note that British Petroleum put the world's petroleum and known gas reserves at no more than 40 years at current consumption rates, while there are at least 200 years of coal reserves.

Construction waste

It will surprise most project managers to find that the United Kingdom construction industry is responsible for taking up almost 50 per cent of available, licensed landfill volumes with construction waste (24 million tonnes annually). This is largely from demolition and excess earthworks as well as mineral wastes. However, the industry also wastes 10 per cent of all materials delivered to construction sites, at an annual cost of £2 billion to the United Kingdom economy.[4] The CIEC Task Force has recommended that landfilled construction waste be reduced through various measures by 50 per cent by the year 2000. Pollution from construction includes hazardous materials such as asbestos which is rapidly being phased out. There are now alternatives to ozone depleting chlorofluorocarbon (CFC) filled air conditioning systems for offices, and alternative foaming agents for insulants. During construction, mud on roads and dust in the air can cause significant local aggravation particularly during urban redevelopments. Another area in which the industry has a poor performance record is in the quantity of materials used for packaging and palletizing building materials and components. It is here that the building material producers must play a role in either developing less wasteful packaging or making it recyclable/reusable.

Recycling of construction materials has already been mentioned. There is scope for considerably increasing their use. Unfortunately, standard construction specifications often preclude the use of recycled materials, often because their use in new construction has not yet been proven.

However, project managers should make it their business to enquire of specifiers and designers not only how the project may be designed to generate minimal waste, but also to what extent it may be possible to reuse waste material such as crushed concrete and building rubble, minestone (where it is locally available) and pulverized fuel ash (PFA). The last named is a good example, as it can be used as a partial replacement for cement in concrete, to make lightweight blocks with good insulation properties and as a stable, inert and lightweight general fill material. It has been actively marketed and used for these purposes for many years.

Pollution

In Section 13.2 we introduced the concept of Integrated Pollution Control which is now embodied in statutory regulations, most of them made under various provisions of the Control of Pollution Act 1974, Environmental Protection Act 1990 and, for discharges to the water environment, Water Resources Act 1991. The agencies responsible for implementing the provisions of these statutes are:

- *Her Majesty's Inspectorate of Pollution, HMIP* For all discharges to the air and for discharges of substances prescribed under the EPA ('red list' substances) to water.
- *National Rivers Authority, NRA* For all discharges to controlled waters (watercourses, rivers, lakes, estuaries and, importantly, groundwater) – except those scheduled substances controlled by HMIP.
- *Waste Regulatory Authorities* For all disposal of solid waste, whether 'special waste', 'controlled waste' or simply inert building material waste, for example.

These agencies are to be amalgamated into a single Environment Agency in 1995, and they already have a major influence upon the choice of sites for infrastructure and building projects, the method of construction and their operation. Project managers with experience of dealing with the US Environmental Protection Agency (upon which the United Kingdom version is largely modelled), will appreciate how significant the influence of these regulatory stakeholders is upon major projects.

All projects, particularly any manufacturing process project should therefore be rigorously audited at feasibility study and detailed design stage to assess the impact of environmental legislation on operational requirements during the lifetime of the project. In this context, the guidance note on Integrated Pollution Control,[7] is essential reading.

Transport

Transportation infrastructure schemes are major projects in their own right, exemplified by the Channel Tunnel, Motorway Widening Programme (well underway), the Jubilee Line Extension (just started), and Heathrow Fifth Terminal proposals. It is important in the context of the wider project environment to recognize certain strategic influences.

Firstly, transportation is a service industry and exists to serve the needs of society primarily in the form of the manufacturing, leisure and other service sectors. In the short term the transportation needs of these sectors are unlikely to change significantly in character, while planning periods for transportation infrastructure are considerable. Those for the projects mentioned above all exceed ten years. This means that the basis upon which initial decisions are made for each project may be partly invalid by the time the projects are implemented. The classic United Kingdom example is the M25 orbital motorway which was of inadequate capacity from the day it was completed. During such long periods, environmental regulations change and may significantly alter the basis of earlier decisions.

Secondly, transportation carries with it significant environmental disbenefits. Most people are aware of the increasingly influential public debate in the United Kingdom regarding the use of road and rail transport, in the run-up to the government's controversial rail privatization programme. Promoters of road schemes point to the ever-increasing forecasts for transportation needs, and the inability of the rail system to supply additional capacity. This has much to do with the fact that the rail system is still a government-run business. However, even if rail capacity were doubled in the next ten years, this would not adequately satisfy increasing transportation needs. The United Kingdom is not alone in this dilemma. European networks are held up as role models but the cost to governments in Germany and France, for example, is enormous, and many regional networks are no improvement upon their much maligned British equivalent. It is perhaps worth considering the main environmental effects of road transportation:

- Atmospheric emissions of CO_2, lead and NOX
- Noise from roads
- Land lost to road construction aggregate quarrying
- Road surface drainage carrying pollutants to the natural water environment
- Congestion, which affects the health and productivity of people and increases exhaust emissions.

The debate over strategies for transportation planning in the United Kingdom will run for some time yet, but there is growing public dissatisfaction with road building and there are powerful voices within the industry calling for a change of emphasis. The government's response is that rail investment has increased substantially, worth £1.2 million in 1992 (up by 50 per cent compared with 1980), and that rail privatization will enable the rail sector to flourish once again.[13] Already there are consortia putting together proposals which, if successful, could transfer up to 30 per cent of intercontinental freight transport from road to rail once the Channel Tunnel is operating.

The Government's Planning Policy Guidance Note 13, Highway Considerations in Development Control, has recently been amended to emphasize the need to consider transportation infrastructure in strategic development plans, and to attempt to plan new developments to minimize the need for transport.[5] Major employment-generating projects will be assessed by planning authorities with this in mind.

Noise

Noise has been considered as an environmental impact by the United Kingdom Government,[5] and the construction industry.[4,10] The three key areas of concern are:

- Noise generated during construction operations
- Transmission of noise, both within buildings and from buildings to the outside world
- Noise created by the use of construction projects (in particular, transportation projects).

Noise emissions are dealt with through a comprehensive regulatory regime, principally the Health and Safety at Work Act, Control of Pollution Act and Environmental Protection Act. Noise should be considered under all three headings during project development. Its amelioration is fundamental to major project planning, detailed building design and choice of operational equipment. EU Noise Limit Directives are now in force, and attenuation of noise from plant is also required under the EU Construction Products Directive.

Dealing first with noise generated during construction, CIEC[4] attributes unnecessarily high noise levels to poor planning, insensitive location of plant and a lack of understanding on the part of plant operators. All this can and should be reduced by careful planning of operations, and choice of appropriate construction methods. The location of the site will also have a strong influence on how sensitive the noise issue will be. Limitations on working hours are often imposed by environmental health officers to limit construction noise to the normal working day, with Saturday afternoon and Sunday working banned. As a result, the construction industry has invested considerably in 'silent' pile driving techniques, compressor insulation and quieter demolition equipment, for example. Use of ear protectors by construction workers is mandatory for many types of equipment. While the critical issue for them is the level of noise and the fact that they will be exposed to it over many years, for the general public it is often the type of noise, its frequency and pattern which are more important, the level having been reduced to an acceptable volume beyond the construction site.

With regard to the second issue, noise insulation is now an important component of building regulations approval for new buildings, implemented by local planning authority environmental health departments. Internal building noise causes severe social problems in many older buildings, for example the 1960s style residential tower blocks. Laws in Switzerland and parts of Scandinavia now effectively enforce an urban curfew in residential areas of densely populated cities. Complaints about noise in 1989/90 in the United Kingdom were made up as shown in Table 13.2. Note, 13 per cent is attributable to the construction and operation of infrastructure projects.

Table 13.2   Complaint of noise in the United Kingdom in 1989/90

Source	Ratio (%)
Domestic premises	60
Industrial and commercial premises	27
Roadworks, construction and demolition	7
Other (including road and air traffic)	6

As far as the government is concerned, noise is best dealt with at source and this principle runs throughout environmental policy where discharges and emissions of any kind are concerned. Careful planning of construction activities, labelling of noise emitting equipment, and building control regulations, are the principal methods of achieving reduction of construction-related noise.

Land use and waste disposal

Major projects have a significant impact on land use, and are influenced by land use planning policies and regulations throughout Europe. These policy decisions are made at national, regional and local levels by various government institutions. One effect of the European Union has been to add an international dimension to company strategic investment planning which must assess land use planning policy as well as locations of markets and raw materials. Land use planning must balance the needs of economic development with those of environmental protection. The UK Government has identified some 60 000 hectares of vacant land within existing urban developed land, of which 25 000 hectares have previously been used for some type of development. It is therefore actively promoting the redevelopment of derelict sites, and in some cases will award Derelict Land Grants to help develop these, rather than previously undeveloped, 'green field' sites. To this end, and to help solve unemployment problems, 12 urban development corporations, set up since 1981, are actively promoting redevelopment in the country's dereliction and unemployment blackspots.

A major issue for development projects is the possibility that land previously used for commercial purposes is contaminated. Land which has previously been subject to use as a site for many industrial processes may be contaminated with hazardous substances which must be contained, neutralized or removed to a safe disposal site prior to redevelopment for new uses. Contamination and the costs of its removal or containment, are often major issues, for example in the redevelopment of gas works, scrap yards, waste disposal facilities, petrochemical works and abattoirs. Mineral workings, many of them needed to provide raw materials for construction, and mineral waste disposal areas, account for 116 000 hectares in England. These areas also play an important role in disposal of wastes other than mineral, as 85 per cent of UK waste of all kinds goes to landfill sites which are mainly worked-out mineral workings. They are then sealed and landscaped, and either returned to agriculture or put to some other use.

Table 13.3 shows how waste is generated from various industries and activities in the United Kingdom. Note, construction-related sources account for 46 per cent. A proportion of industrial and commercial waste can also be attributed to the construction industry which is why CIEC[4] estimates a total of 50 per cent of landfill sites are occupied by construction-related waste.

Table 13.3 Generation of waste by various industries and activities

Source	Ratio (%)
Agriculture	20
Sewage sludge	8
Household waste	5
Commercial	4
Industrial	17
Demolition and construction	8
Quarry mining and dredged materials	38

Source: Brown.[14]

There is therefore a need for project managers to consider the following:

- The reuse of previously developed or derelict sites for the siting of new projects.
- Minimizing the need for major land forming in the design of the project so that minimal off-site disposal of excavated material in landfill sites is required.
- Reuse of mineral wastes as low-grade infill in foundations, and use of construction materials which are made from recycled mineral or other waste products.

Internal building environment

The final topic is the effect of the internal environment upon people working it. Under 'Noise' above, the need to consider noise within buildings was discussed. In addition, lighting and air quality are important issues. We are now aware that Legionnaire's disease, which is often fatal, arises from inappropriately designed and inadequately maintained wet ventilation systems. We are less sure about the precise causes of Sick Building Syndrome, but it appears to arise from a combination of internal environmental defects. Poor lighting, whether because of its intensity or frequency composition, causes stress and fatigue. Air quality is artificially maintained in many office blocks and other workplaces, whether by mechanical ventilation systems or air conditioning. Air conditioning is a highly detrimental development, requiring considerable energy and the use of CFCs as the refrigeration liquid. Although CFCs are being phased out, the alternatives also have ozone depleting effects and the energy requirement remains. Architects are beginning to consider seriously these issues at the earliest stages of building design, in order to maximize the use of natural ventilation and lighting.

A recent report commissioned by two of the UK's leading private estate developers found that air conditioning systems were in fact considerably over-designed, based upon maximum building energy usages (and therefore heat dissipation rates) of 45 watts/m^2 rather than the average 25 watts/m^2 which are normally found in practice in an office environment. The implications for the design and specification of air conditioning are obvious. This aspect of design of new office buildings is addressed within the Environmental Audit Method for New Offices developed by the Building Research Establishment (BRE).[15] The Method comprehensively addresses environmental issues and its objectives are summarized as follows:

- To provide recognition for buildings which are friendlier to the global environment than normal practice, so to stimulate a market for them.

– To improve internal environmental quality and occupant health.
– To raise awareness of the dominant role which the use of energy in buildings plays in global warming through the greenhouse effect, and in production of acid rain and depletion of the ozone layer.
– To reduce the long term impact buildings have on the global environment.
– To provide a common set of standards so that false claims of environmental friendliness are avoided.
– To encourage designers to achieve environmentally sensitive buildings.

The assessment is carried out at the design stage, based on readily available information. Many issues are related to internal environment, and thus human health: but issues of noise, land use, global impact, energy efficiency and many more are accommodated. The BRE has also produced assessment methods for major retail stores and residential developments. It is not only offices which suffer internal environmental problems. For example, there remain some 3.5 million homes in England which are affected by damp, causing many direct and indirect health problems.

13.4 Concluding remarks

Finally, we mention BS 7750, Environmental Management Systems. This standard provides a broad framework which may be used throughout a business organization, or for any project. Its introduction as a pilot standard in 1992 has led to its use in approximately a dozen projects, and at least twenty construction-related businesses are aiming to achieve certification to the standard in 1994. It has been drafted to operate within business cultures and management systems similar to those introduced to implement BS 5750, Quality Systems. Although the construction industry was slow to accept BS 5750, it is now being implemented by many consultants and contractors and it seems likely that they will also progress to BS 7750 in due course.

Various references are provided of both a general and particular nature which are readily available to interested readers. While this chapter and the references appear to focus on issues arising in the United Kingdom, the same issues will be faced across Europe and the United States, and increasingly in developing countries where aid-funded projects require environmental issues to be considered.

13.5 Summary

1. There are five principles of environmental management:
   – Sustainable development
   – The precautionary principle
   – BPEO, BATNEEC and IPC

- The polluter pays
- Environmental accounting and costing.

2. Sustainable development is: 'development which meets the needs of the present generation without compromising the ability of future generations to meet their own needs'.[2]

3. The precautionary principle states that if we do not know what impact an activity will have on the environment, we should limit or even avoid that activity.

4. BPEO: Best Practical Environmental Option.
BATNEEC: Best Available Technique Not Entailing Excessive Cost.
IPC: Integrated Pollution Control.

5. Environmental accounting and costing gives the environment some value, and includes the loss of that value in the investment appraisal of the project. There are four methods:
- The contingent valuation method
- The travel cost method
- The hedonic pricing method
- The least cost alternative method.

6. There are seven significant environmental impacts which need to be managed:
- Energy
- Construction waste
- Pollution
- Transport
- Noise
- Land use and waste disposal
- Internal building environment.

References

1. Hutchinson, C., *Business and the Environmental Challenge*, The Conservation Trust, 1991.
2. WCED, *Our Common Future*, World Commission on Environment and Development (The Bruntland Commission), 1987.
3. Department of Transport, *Roads for Prosperity*, HMSO, 1988.
4. CIEC, *Construction and the Environment: Report of the Environment Task Force of the Construction Industry Employers Council*, Building Employers Confederation, 1992.
5. Department of the Environment, *This Common Inheritance: Britain's environmental strategy*, DoE Communication 1200, HMSO 1990.
6. Department of the Environment, *Fifth Report on the Royal Commission on Environmental Pollution*, HMSO, 1976.
7. Department of the Environment and the Welsh Office, *Integrated Pollution Control: a practical guide*, HMSO, 1990.

8. Institution of Civil Engineers, *Congestion: Report of the Infrastructure Planning Group of the Institution of Civil Engineers*, Thomas Telford, 1989.
9. Ramchandani, R., 'Valuing water quality improvements' in *Water Research Centre in the European Environment*, 2(2), April 1992.
10. CIC, *Our Land for Our Children: An environmental policy for construction professionals*, Construction Industry Council, 1992.
11. Turner, J.R., *The Handbook of Project-based Management*, McGraw-Hill, 1993.
12. Shorrock, L.D. and Henderson, G., *Energy Use in Buildings and Carbon Dioxide Emissions*, Building Research Establishment, 1990.
13. Institution of Civil Engineers, *Rail Privatization: Deregulation and open access*, Thomas Telford, 1992.
14. Brown, A. (ed.), *The UK Environment*, Department of the Environment and Government Statistical Service publication, HMSO, 1992.
15. Building Research Establishment, *Environmental Assessment for New Office Designs*, BRE, 1990.

14
Managing stakeholders

Stuart Calvert

14.1 Introduction

A project's stakeholders can be defined as:

> all the people or groups whose lives or environment are affected by the project, but who receive no direct benefit from it. These can include the project team's families, people made redundant by the changes introduced, people who buy the product produced by the facility, and the local community.[1]

Stakeholders are also those people or groups who believe they are affected by the project or who have an opinion on the project or the changes that the project will create. It is important to recognize that stakeholders are all the parties that may be affected by the project and not just the easily identified parties with direct involvement in the project. Although appearing as indirect players in the project environment, stakeholders can have a major impact on project success. Failure to recognize their existence and their potential power at a project's strategic level may lead to serious problems at the advanced stages of project planning and implementation. The campaign mounted by some residents in Kent against the proposed high speed rail link between London and the Channel Tunnel illustrates this point. The strength of this campaign caused serious problems for the project's supporters and managers and brought into question the project's viability.

In this chapter we identify the importance of knowing and managing a project's environment and its stakeholders. We then describe the process of analysing a project's environment and identifying the stakeholders and identify the importance of communication within the project environment and to describe the methods of communication. Finally we explain what processes are involved in the adoption of a formalized stakeholder management strategy.

14.2 The need to manage stakeholders

The high speed rail link between London and the Channel Tunnel is just one of many projects where stakeholder issues have been shown to have a significant effect on the project's success. Projects such as new railways, motorways, and nuclear power stations have a very significant effect on the environment. It is not surprising that they cause so much interest with many groups of stakeholders. The need for the project managers and sponsors to manage in the face of skilfully organized opposition is well documented through national and international news coverage. However, stakeholders exist for even the smallest of projects and can have an equally significant effect on the success of these projects as they have on the major projects.

For example, seemingly simple projects such as renewing office furniture can create dreadful problems for the project manager if the effects on both those receiving the furniture, and those who are not, are not well thought out. Those receiving new furniture may think that it is not as good as what they had before, while those not receiving it will be jealous of the treatment given to others. Meanwhile customers and shareholders believe the money would be better spent elsewhere!

In both the major and minor project scenarios described above, identifying, communicating with, and managing the stakeholders are essential tasks to be completed alongside the traditional management of the physical works to ensure complete project success. Failure to understand the project environment and to manage it effectively may result in the project becoming less viable due to increased costs, project delays, or reduced revenue. Carrying out an appraisal of the environment as described below, and assessing the likelihood of various project outcomes as part of a full project risk analysis gives quantitative information to allow reasoned decisions to be made to best manage the situation.

14.3 Understanding the project environment

The project environment consists of two main groups: those 'internal' to the project with direct responsibility; and those 'external' who are affected by the project or have an interest but are not part of the main project team. Table 14.1 gives examples of some the members of these two groups. The behaviour and performance of the 'internal' members are, theoretically, controlled and predictable. However, the members of the 'external' group, the project stakeholders, are free to behave in any way they choose with no regard for the project. To understand how these stakeholders will behave it is necessary to fully appraise the project environment.

Table 14.1 Members of the internal and external groups

Internal group	External group
Sponsor	Press
Owners	Government agencies
Champion	Unions
Project manager	Financiers
Project team	Pressure groups
	Suppliers
	Contractors
	User groups
	Competitors
	Neighbours

The first step in the appraisal is to draw up a list of the stakeholders. This can be achieved easily by the project team using a 'brain-storming session'. The list should also identify what 'stake' these groups have in the project, that is why are they interested in the project? The stakeholders are likely to behave in one of three ways towards the project:

– They will show no interest in the project.
– They have the potential to and may work against the project.
– They have the potential to and may support the project.

Their behaviour will be influenced by many external factors which exist in the project environment. One method of assessing these influences would be to use a PEST analysis. Using this method the project team will identify what circumstances surround the project and will categorize them under the four headings, Political, Economic, Socio-cultural and Technological. Figure 14.1 shows a PEST matrix with some of the categories that may be identified under each heading. The project team is now equipped with information describing who or what exists in the project environment, and what forces are present to influence their actions.

14.4 Communicating with the project environment

Many of the problems experienced in projects, caused by stakeholders, have occurred because of poor communication from the project team. This can allow misinformation or no information at all to fuel the imagination of those with an interest. Research[2,3] has shown that communication is perceived as a vital ingredient for project success. It has been calculated as being second only to technical performance in importance. The project manager and team need to draw on the full range of communication

Political Environmental protection laws Taxation policy Foreign trade regulations Employment law Local government	Socio-cultural Population demographics Social mobility Attitudes to work and leisure Education
Interest rates Inflation Disposable income Labour costs Material costs **Economic**	Rate of obsolescence Speed of technology transfer New discoveries Research **Technological**

Figure 14.1 PEST analysis

methods and media to communicate successfully with both the internal and external members of the project environment. Table 14.2 shows some of the communication methods and media open to project managers.

Table 14.2 Methods and media of communication

Methods	*Media*
Written	Meetings
Spoken	Radio
Drawn	Television
Other audio	Minutes
Other visual	Posters
	Newspapers
	Letters
	Telephone
	Facsimile
	Electronic mail
	Engineering drawings

Within the project team it is common practice to use drawings, bar charts, work breakdown structures, organization breakdown structures, network diagrams, meeting minutes, memos, etc. to communicate information. Control of this information flow is usually formalized and agreed between team members using drawing issue sheets, project responsibility charts, communication plans and meeting schedules. However, control of information to external stakeholders is rarely so well organized.

Communication with external parties can be planned and unplanned. Table 14.3 shows examples of typical project communication that may occur in either of these categories. Communication to external parties must be controlled by the project team to ensure suitable information is given at the most advantageous time for the project and to reduce rumour and hearsay. To achieve this a communication plan must be formalized which will make best use of planned communications to reduce unwanted or unplanned communication. The project's external communication plan can be formulated by considering the stakeholders and environmental influences that were identified using the process described in the previous section. In all cases it is likely to be beneficial to contact supporters and opinion formers to advise them of the project's aims and benefits. The plan should include contingencies for dealing with possible detractors so that communication is managed as proactively as possible. Consideration should be given to using any of the communication methods and media identified above. Proactive communication of information is cheap compared with reactive responses to misinformation.

Table 14.3 Communication with external parties

Planned	Unplanned
Letters	Public meetings
Mail shot	'Looking over the fence'
Presentations	Government Select Committee
Personal calls	Government agencies
Public meetings	– Environmental protection
Meeting decision makers	– Health and safety
Meeting opinion formers	Media coverage
Advertising through:	– Newspapers
– Site hoardings	– Radio
– Newspapers	– Television
– Television	
– Posters	
– Radio	

A simple communication plan can be produced showing target audience, type of information, method and media, timing and responsibility. Figure 14.2 shows an example. Failure to communicate effectively with the external environment can result in the project team losing control of the information flow. Potentially, this will lead to a loss of credibility for the project and those associated with it.

Project: Redwings Supermarket			Project Manager: P. Smith		
Audience	*Information*	*Timing*	*Method*	*Media*	*Responsibility*
Local residents	Brief on project	Start of site work	Press release	Newspaper	Project manager
Close neighbours	Noise of foundation work	ditto	Letter	Mail shot	Site engineer
Local residents	Completion of work	4 weeks before opening	Interview	Radio	Store manager
Etc.					

Figure 14.2   Example of a communication plan

14.5 Adopting a project stakeholder management strategy

The objective of adopting a project stakeholder management (PSM) strategy is to curtail adverse stakeholder response while encouraging positive stakeholder response. This will help the project team to develop the best strategy for dealing with stakeholders by allowing decision making to be based on real information and not hearsay. Formalizing the process will also ensure that stakeholder information will be retained within the project while manpower and other cultural changes may take place. This is particularly important on large and complex projects. There are seven steps in the process of producing a PSM strategy, summarized in Table 14.4.

Step 1 Identify all the stakeholders who may be affected by the project. This may be done as described in Section 14.3 by holding a brain-storming session with the project team.

Step 2 Gather information on all the stakeholders in terms of their resources, power, past record, motives, etc. This can be done by consulting user groups or professional associations. Information may also be gathered from the local press or trade press and from annual reports.

Step 3 With this information, appraise each stakeholder's mission. Stakeholders can be appraised as being supportive, adverse, or disinterested.

Step 4 Carry out a SWOT analysis on each stakeholder. This analysis will provide information describing the strengths and weaknesses, opportunities

Table 14.4   Developing a project stakeholder management strategy

Step	Process	Main questions/issues
1	Identify stakeholders	Who are the stakeholders?
		What are their stakes?
2	Investigate stakeholders	Gather information on all stakeholders
3	Identify mission	Are stakeholders likely to be supportive?
		Are stakeholders likely to be opponents?
4	SWOT stakeholders	What are stakeholders' strengths?
		What are stakeholders' weaknesses?
5	Predict behaviour	What will stakeholders do?
6	Make action plans	Formulate plans and procedures
		Maintain contact with key stakeholders
7	Implement PSM strategy	Make PSM a project policy
		Make PSM part of project review
		Make PSM part of change control

and threats open to each. The appraisal should consider the resources that are available to the stakeholders and what political and public support they possess. It should also evaluate how well organized they are, their ability and dedication.

Step 5 Predict the strategy of each stakeholder by considering information gathered in the previous steps and deciding what they will do, when they will do it, why they will do it, how they will do it and where they will do it.

Step 6 Produce action plans, and agree how stakeholders will be managed and to show what actions will be taken under certain specified contingencies. These plans include the communication plan discussed in Section 14.4. Where necessary, the main project strategy and plans may require modification as a result of this analysis of stakeholder behaviour. Stakeholder information and PSM contingency action plans should be included in a PSM strategy document to be filed with the project's key documents. Examples of a typical PSM stakeholder information sheet and a contingency action plan are shown in Figs 14.3 and 14.4.

Step 7 Implement the PSM strategy. To achieve this it is essential to make it a company or project policy to manage stakeholders. The need to do this can be emphasised by clearly highlighting the risks associated with not doing it The PSM strategy document should be a key project document and should be re-appraised at project review meetings. Also, it is important that stakeholder assessment becomes part of the change control procedure.

It is important to remember that the information that is gained as part of the PSM process can be confidential and highly sensitive. Security of all of the PSM information should be guaranteed by the project team.

STAKEHOLDER INFORMATION SHEET	
Project:	**Project Manager:**
Stakeholder:	Supportive/Adverse
Useful information:	
Strengths:	Weaknesses:
Opportunities:	Threats:
Likely strategy:	

Figure 14.3   Stakeholder information sheet

PSM CONTINGENCY ACTION PLAN	
Project:	**Project Manager:**
Contingency in case of following action:	
By:	
Action to be taken:	
Responsibility:	
Persons to be advised:	

Figure 14.4   PSM contingency action plan

14.6 Summary

1. Stakeholders have the potential to disrupt projects. In the extreme they can make projects uneconomic and no longer practicable. This can cause a loss of credibility for those involved in the project and a loss of market for those who depend on the project's outcome. Failure to manage a project's stakeholders and to predict and prepare for their behaviour will increase the risk of these problems occurring.
2. To manage a project's stakeholders it is necessary to identify those stakeholders that exist and to understand the environmental forces that may influence them.
3. Good project communication is essential to ensure project success. External communications must be managed proactively to ensure that the project team has control of the information flow. An external communication plan can be prepared to formalize the communication methods. The project team should communicate with supporters and opinion formers and must be proactive in promulgating the information it considers to be important as and when it needs to.
4. Adoption of a project stakeholder management strategy will formalize the process of identifying stakeholders, evaluating likely behaviour and preparing contingency action plans. This process allows the project team to act on real information and not just on rumour and will operate across changes in manpower to ensure continuity.

References

1. Turner, J.R., *The Handbook of Project-based Management*, McGraw-Hill, 1993.
2. Baker, B. and Murphy, D., 'Factors affecting project success', in *The Project Management Handbook*, 2nd edition, Cleland, D.I., and King, W.R. (eds), Van Nostrand Reinhold, 1988.
3. Wilemon, D. and Baker, B., 'Some major research findings regarding the human element in project management', in *The Project Management Handbook*, 2nd edition, Cleland, D.I. and King, W.R. (eds), Van Nostrand Reinhold, 1988.

Bibliography

1. Cleland, D.I., 'Project stakeholder management', in *The Project Management Handbook*, 2nd edition, Cleland, D.I. and King, W.R. (eds), Van Nostrand Reinhold, 1988.
2. Johnson, G. and Scholes, K., *Exploring Corporate Strategy*, Prentice-Hall, 1988.
3. Kliem, R.L. and Ludin, I.S., *The People Side of Project Management*, Gower, 1992.
4. Minton, P., 'Marketing your project', *Project*, **5**(4), 19–25, 1991.

15

Environmental impact analysis

Dennis Burningham

15.1 Introduction

As the environmental problems brought about by industrial development continue to grow, legislation and public pressure require project developers to analyse and control the impact that their projects may have on the environment. In order to do this, it is necessary to understand the various aspects of the environment which can be affected, and then to consider systematically how project activities will affect each of them. This process, called *environmental impact assessment*, provides the project manager with a useful structure for doing this.

In this chapter we will examine the several different aspects of the environment that are affected by projects, and then review why, when and how to conduct an environmental impact assessment. We identify the ways in which projects can affect the environment, and describe environmental impact assessment as a tool for managing that impact.

15.2 Projects and the environment

We introduce the term 'the greening of a project', to describe the intent to reduce the impact of a project on the environment, to ensure that it has a minimum adverse affect. In this section, we consider what we mean by the environment, its relationship to projects and the greening of projects.

The environment

In simple terms, it is appropriate that we should try to reduce the adverse effect of projects on the environment, but we need to define what we mean by the environment, and when we try to do that we find that there are quite a number of 'environments'. The term means different things to different people, depending on their point of view and the purpose for which they are defining it.

For the environmentalist, it means the natural environment made up of the air, earth, waters and the myriad of creatures and organisms that occupy the natural world. For the planning authority, it may mean the social environment, the community with all its interdependent human groups. For shop stewards it may means the working environment in which their union members carry out their jobs. For the economist it may mean the economic environment upon which the nation's GNP is dependent.

The meaning we attach to the word 'environment' and our response to it has tended to change as our perception of problems has changed. In the past it was used in relation to the working environment and the origin of many of our regulations regarding health and safety in the workplace came from the early concerns about this environment. The original requirements for safety and health in mines and smelters came as a result of workers demanding better and safer conditions to reduce work-related accidents and illnesses. (The requirements of current legislation such as the Health and Safety at Work Act 1974 exert a strong 'greening' influence on projects.) The focus subsequently widened as communities adjacent to industrial works became concerned about the effects of toxic fumes. Legislation such as the Alkali Act was passed to control air and water pollution in the local environment. COSHH regulations are the result of concern about dangerous substances which are transported and distributed through our cities and towns. (Again these and other current regulations like the Control of Industrial Major Accident Hazard Regulations 1984 provide a strong 'greening' effect.)

The regional effects of air and water pollution on the natural environment have been recognized and regulations have been developed by the European Union to control cross-border pollution. Pollution of the world's oceans by oil from marine tankers resulted in international agreements in the 1960s and 1970s. In recent years, global warming and ozone layer depletion have prompted international accords aimed at controlling pollution of the global environment. (Finally, these more recent moves have been prompted primarily by a concern for the state of the natural environment.)

Currently, 'environment' tends to mean the air/water/land that humans view as an important element of their quality of life. For the deeper 'Greens' it means the air, the water, the soil, the geochemistry that the global ecosystem comprising all species, man included, depend on for survival.

An indication of the increasing acceptance of this wider interpretation of the environment is contained in the EU directive regarding environmental impact assessment which requires that:

the effects of a project on the environment must be assessed in order to take account of concerns to protect human health, to contribute by means of a better environment to the quality of life, to ensure maintenance of the diversity of species and to maintain the reproductive capacity of the ecosystem as a resource for life.

Relation to projects

It is increasingly the case that without proper care and regard for the environment, projects will not be granted approval to go ahead. We therefore need to focus on the 'greening' of projects as a means of facilitating project development. The environmental impact assessment procedure therefore becomes an essential tool to assist in obtaining the necessary planning permission for a project. Projects affect various groups in various ways in the major phases of project existence. A 'green' project ensures that the effect on all of these groups is within acceptable limits.

During the construction phase, that is in the short term, a project will affect staff, local residents, and even other species, by noise, vibration, dust, light, visual intrusion, etc. The effect on staff and on local residents is subject to control within specified limits set by local ordinances, national laws and standards, company and industry practice, etc. (The effect on other species is not generally specified by law except in the case of endangered species where, in a last ditch effort, we are trying to safeguard the few habitats that remain.)

In the long term, that is when the project is complete and the facility is in operation, the effects on staff, local residents and other species will be different and more enduring. There may also be regional and global implications depending on the nature of the project, the raw materials, the intermediate compounds and the final products, by-products and wastes generated. These operating effects are subject to control by additional standards and regulations which generally reflect concern for the impact on human welfare locally, regionally and globally.

And finally when the facility reaches the end of its useful life, its ultimate disposal and the effects of that operation on the environment must be considered.

Of the various affected groups, the ones most in need of reassurance that a project will not be unacceptably damaging to their 'environment' are the local residents and the 'environmentalists'. Under their increasingly critical and watchful eyes, project development must evaluate and mitigate the impact it will make on local residents and other species.

Greening

'Greening', therefore, does not just consist of merely hiring a landscape architect to design screening bunds and belts of trees and shrubs to conceal the facility. It demands a comprehensive and imaginative survey of the potential impact of the project, consultation with all concerned parties and then a well thought out plan to deal with their legitimate concerns and to minimize the adverse impact of the project on the various 'environments' that these groups see.

15.3 Environmental impact analysis

The tool which assists the project manager to do this is environmental impact assessment, EIA. This is a technique by which information about the environmental effects of a project is collected by the developer so that it can be taken into account by the planning authority in forming a judgement on whether the development should go ahead.

It helps everyone involved. For the project manager it provides a framework within which the environmental considerations and the design development can interact to reduce the impact of the development on the environment. Early environmental analysis will indicate ways in which the project can be modified to eliminate or reduce adverse effects perhaps through better environmental options or an alternative process.

It also provides a disciplined format in which to describe the project's environmental effects, a format which identifies problems and enables consultation and modifications to take place in the atmosphere of objective and comprehensive evaluation. It sets the scene for better decision making for the project designer, the local pressure groups and the planning authority. We consider:

– When to prepare an EIA
– What format should be adopted
– The sources of detailed information
– The contents of an EIA
– Other information that might be included.

When to prepare EIA

A booklet has been produced by the Department of the Environment entitled *Environmental Assessment – a Guide to the Procedures*,[1] which spells out when and how to carry out such an assessment under the Town and Country Planning (Assessment of Environmental Effect) Regulations 1988. In general an environmental assessment is required for any project that will make a significant impact on the environment. One is always required for major oil, gas and chemical works, power stations, large transportation projects such as special roads, rail routes, airports, ports and inland waterways, toxic waste disposal or incineration facilities.

In addition other projects which are likely to have significant effects on the environment by virtue of nature, size or location will require an environmental impact assessment, either as a requirement of the planning system or as a special requirement for projects not subject to planning control. A comprehensive listing is given in the appendix to the DoE booklet. A ruling can be obtained from the planning authority if a project manager is unsure of the requirement to prepare an EIA for a particular project.

What format?

There is no specified form of EIA statement. Its preparation should be a collaborative exercise involving the project manager, the planning authority, statutory consultative bodies and other interested parties. The aim is to provide as systematic and objective an account as is possible of the significant environmental effects of the project.

The main emphasis is on full and early consultation with all the concerned bodies to unearth all the potential areas of concern. EIA should start at site selection and in the case of process and energy projects at the time of process selection so that the environmental effects or merits of alternative sites and processes can be evaluated before crucial design parameters are fixed. Involving local authorities and interest groups early will gain access to local knowledge, local conditions and local feelings about the project. The scope of the EA should be agreed with the planning authority before beginning its preparation. This sounds like common sense but it is not unusual for project managers to rush off with the guide in hand and fail to agree with the planning authority the scope required. The guide contains a rather complete checklist which can be useful in the definition of scope between project manager and planning authority.

The project manager is responsible for the final contents of the EIA but he or she is wise to agree the items that the planning authority expects to have covered in the environmental statement. Where the EIA is obligatory, statutory bodies are advised of the development and then they are obliged to provide information to the developer. Statutory consultees include those required by law such as the Nature Conservancy Council, the National Rivers Authority, Her Majesty's Inspectorate of Pollution, Health and Safety Executive, etc., where the project will impinge on areas within their jurisdiction. The guide indicates when they must be involved.

Non-statutory bodies, sometimes referred to as non-governmental bodies

(NGOs), which are frequently involved include national groups such as the Royal Society for the Protection of Birds, The Royal Society for Nature Conservation and the National Trust and local groups such as conservation and civic societies. These NGOs can be helpful or obstructive depending on the relationships established with them. Early consultation will establish their concerns about the project and should encourage joint efforts towards finding alternative sites, designs and procedures to minimize environmental impact.

While there may be a temptation to adopt a confrontational stance with NGOs, it is essential that the project manager exercise patience and tact to ensure that a mutually acceptable compromise is reached which will enable the project to go forward with general acceptance by the local pressure groups. NGOs generally have extensive local knowledge which can be helpful or alternatively damaging to a project manager's plans.

Sources of detailed information

While it is not normally necessary to carry out original scientific research for an EA, careful study of the site will be necessary including environmental survey information. 'Base line' surveys to establish the flora and fauna present on the site and in adjacent areas is a useful starting point in defining how sensitive a location will be to disturbance during construction and to the results of continuous operations. Local county wildlife trusts, natural history societies, universities and polytechnics, county environmental survey centres can provide this type of survey information quite inexpensively and often from existing files. In addition to its immediate value in the EA, this 'base line' survey data can provide the basis for an ongoing monitoring system to determine how the project is affecting the local environment throughout its life.

Contents

An environmental statement must contain the following:

- A description of the development including information about the site, the design, size, scale, etc.
- Data needed to identify and assess the main effects on the environment.
- A description of the likely significant effects on the environment explained by reference to its impact on human beings, flora, fauna, soil, water, air, climate, the landscape, the interaction between the foregoing, material assets, the cultural heritage, etc.
- Where significant effects are identified, a description of measures to avoid, reduce or remedy them.

– A summary in non-technical terms of the above information for the layman.

Further information

Further specialized information may be needed to explain or amplify the above information, such as:

– Land use during the construction and operation, including access and transportation arrangements.
– Main characteristics of production processes including nature and quantities of raw materials, energy and natural resources used.
– Estimated types, quantities, compositions and strengths of emissions and waste products.
– Main alternatives investigated with indications of why the proposed design is environmentally superior.
– The likely significant direct and indirect effects on the environment from the natural resources used and the emissions and wastes created.
– Forecasting methods used to predict these effects.
– Technical deficiencies encountered in compiling information on environmental effects.
– A summary in layman's terms of the above special information.

Checklist

The DoE booklet,[1] contains a checklist of subjects that need to be considered in preparing an EIA. Effects during construction, during operations and during/after dismantling must be considered separately as different phases of the project.

15.4 Summary

1. The 'greening' of projects requires the careful attention of project managers and developers beginning at the earliest possible time in the project's life.
2. Existing regulations and standards for health and safety and pollution control provide 'green' influences on the project. Energy conservation considerations in design and the selection of materials of construction which are least environmentally damaging are two areas in which the project managers can exert a 'green' influence on their projects.
3. Additional specialized advice should be sought from statutory and non-governmental bodies regarding the environmental impact of a project. 'Base line' surveys will establish the species and habitats which the project

will impinge upon. Care must be taken to ensure that endangered species and habitats are protected and that the long-term effects of the project do not result in degradation of the local ecosystems.

4. The environmental impact assessment procedure provides a useful tool for the collection, analysis and use of environmental impact information from all sources. Properly used, the EIA will ensure that a project is truly 'Green' and that all concerned parties have had an opportunity to contribute to the 'greening' process.

References

1. DoE, *Environmental Assessment – a Guide to the Procedures*, HMSO, 1989.

Bibliography

1. Brundtland, H.G. (ed.), *Our Common Future*, Oxford University Press, 1987.
2. Morris, P.G.W. (ed.), 'Major Projects and the Environment', *Proceedings of the Royal Geographical Society/Major Projects Association Conference*, London, November 1988, The Major Projects Association, Technical Paper No. 8, 1989.

16
The planning and inquiry process

John Stringer

16.1 Introduction – 'externalities'

Projects have effects that are not reflected in the internal financial calculations of their owners and associates. The planning and inquiry process brings these 'externalities' to light and, if they are judged to be against the public interest, consent may be refused. What 'public interest' means is controversial, of course, so the process is of a political nature. The most complex issues arise from changes in the way land is used, which is the concern of the *planning system*. A project needs public consent both in the formal sense that there are legal requirements for planning permissions, and other forms of licence in some instances, and in an informal sense. A project which upsets the interests of third parties is less likely to succeed than one which is seen as benign.

This chapter describes the planning and inquiry process in the United Kingdom, the need to obtain consents, the costs and risks involved, and how to manage the process. We show that *consent management* is an integral part of project development and implementation and analyse the nature of the consent management task. We also describe the planning system in the United Kingdom from the project manager's viewpoint, as an illustration of requirements that projects have to meet.

16.2 The planning system in the United Kingdom

Any 'development', defined as:

> the carrying out of building, engineering, mining, or other operations in, on, over or under land, or the making of any material change in the use of any buildings or other land,

requires planning permission, although exempt categories are laid down from time to time and simpler rules apply in some instances. The District Council, as Local Planning Authority (LPA), normally makes the consent decision but, if issues of more than local importance are involved, the Secretary of State for the Environment (SoSE) may 'call-in' the application. Also, an applicant can appeal to SoSE against a rejection by the LPA. For appeals and call-ins, a public inquiry is held under an inspector, before the SoSE decides.

An applicant need not own the land and there could be several concurrent applications about the same site. There is no obligation to proceed with a permitted development. 'Outline' permission can be applied for, giving indication of conditions under which a full application would succeed. In 'sensitive' areas, such as Green Belts and National Nature Reserves, there is *presumption in favour of conservation*. This is an exception to the *presumption in favour of development* which is the general tenor of government policy. The aim of this policy has been to reduce delay by imposing time limits on LPA decisions and on public inquiries; and seeing that development plans, indicating what types of project will be acceptable and where, are in place and up to date. Since the system was set up in 1947, such plans have not always been available, and the resulting uncertainty has led to many appeals and public inquiries. This may have contributed to a belief that public inquiry is the norm for big projects, whereas it is supposed to be the exception.

Presumption in favour of development is balanced by a principle that objectors get a fair hearing. Proposals are liable to be treated with suspicion by local people and by amenity and environmental bodies (e.g. the Council for the Protection of Rural England and the Royal Society for the Protection of Birds are active in general planning policy and in specific instances), which monitor applications and organize objections where they consider it necessary. Even projects widely recognised as needed, nevertheless meet NIMBY ('Not In My Back Yard') objections.

An LPA can only implement its development plan indirectly, that is by the signals it gives to developers and by its decisions on planning applications. It may impose conditions, such as about suppression of noise and dust, or seek 'Planning Gain', that is amenities provided by the developer for the benefit of the locality but lying beyond the development itself.

It is not the function of the planning system to compensate affected property owners, but anxiety about compensation motivates objectors and desire for compensation may hide as 'environmental' objection. Generous and speedy resolution of compensation issues may reduce risks of delay or rejection.

There are special consent procedures for certain categories (such as power stations; pipelines; trunk roads) but where existing legislation does not cover the case (railways are the prime example) an Act of Parliament is required. A Private Bill may only be introduced to Parliament in November each year, and the outcome is known about 14 months later. There is no appeal. If government also has to obtain powers relating to the project, as for the Channel Tunnel, then the Bill is a hybrid and can be introduced at any time with government support.

The total 'consent system', comprising Town and Country Planning, Special Category legislation, Parliament, and also regulations about Health and Safety, Pollution, etc., is complex. It is continually evolving and up-to-date advice needs to be obtained on consents required for the project under consideration. As an example of evolution, special rules were introduced in 1988 for a new class of *major* planning inquiries, where:

> the development proposal is of major public interest because of its national or regional implications, or the extent or complexity of the environmental, safety, technical or scientific issues involved, and where for these reasons there are a number of third parties involved as well as the applicant and the LPA.

These rules emphasize pre-inquiry consultation between the parties and with the inspector to identify the critical issues and set a timetable for the inquiry. Parties are expected to be ready in time, and 'surprise' or 'delay' tactics are frowned upon. The main parties are usually represented by legal counsel but the inspector will normally allow anyone to appear who has a point to make. Issues examined in major inquiries include:

1. *Need* Objectors argue that the need for the project is insufficient to outweigh the damage to the interests of those affected, or to the environment.
2. *Alternatives* Arguments that the need can be met in better ways or the location, scale, or timing of the project improved.
3. *Safety issues* Especially for energy and chemical plants, include the health and safety of workers and residents and also the risk of fire and explosion. The fact that health and safety is covered by specific regulations does not reduce its prominence in a planning inquiry.
4. *Environment* This covers issues of local concern, such as noise, dust, and visual intrusion, plus, increasingly, issues of wider concern, such as wildlife habitats, acid rain and the greenhouse effect.
5. *Methodology* The methodology used for forecasting, for assessment of catastrophe risks, and for handling multiple criteria is often challenged.

As another example of evolution, following a European Union Directive, planning applications for certain categories of project have, since 1987, required an environmental statement describing the project and its likely impacts on the natural and social environment, and some require an environmental assessment, which adds up the combined effect of these impacts. Weighting impacts of different kinds involves subjective, and therefore political, judgements, so the assessment is supposed to be made by the LPA but since it may not have the resources, or the will, it can be in the applicant's interest to offer an assessment.

Consent systems in other countries have similar aims and are tending to converge (as over environmental assessment). In some places each aspect (land-use zoning; pollution; health and safety, etc.) is taken separately, at hearings held by different agencies, whereas UK practice favours the single comprehensive inquiry. There are differences, too, in the powers and political will of governments to force through developments they favour. In some places, custom and practice require distribution of largesse to officials and politicians, in others this would be regarded as corrupt and quite unacceptable. When in Rome ...?

16.3 Consent, costs and risks

The consent system imposes costs on a project, partly because it introduces uncertainty and delay (ranging from six weeks for a straightforward planning application, to several years for a controversial project subjected to public inquiry). The need to obtain planning and other consents can and does add to the cost of a project. However, although the consent process is concerned with the public interest, there can be benefits *from the owner's point of view*. The following can contribute to the increased cost:

- Drawing up the statement of case and supporting evidence for an inquiry; preparing an environmental statement; legal fees; attendance at an inquiry; costs of the inspector, his or her secretariat, the inquiry venue, etc.
- Since the project must be well defined before application, critical features are decided early and perhaps prematurely. The project team builds up rapidly and then 'marks time' during the inquiry stage, whereas the ideal would be a steady build-up over the whole period of project definition. When a project team expands (or contracts) rapidly, communications suffer and mistakes are made.
- Conditions attached to the consent (or costs incurred in anticipation of such conditions being imposed).
- 'Mitigators' (features such as community facilities not essential to the project) are included to improve its chances of acceptance.
- Anything not in the original application which later turns out to be necessary could mean a fresh application, and further delay.

- Choice of 'acceptable' technology or location, instead of a more economic alternative, because of the risk that unfamiliarity of the latter would provoke objections.
- Lost commercial value of information that has to be disclosed in the course of public inquiry.
- Delayed return on initial investment. Moreover, the longer the time-horizon over which market and other forecasts have to be made, the larger the margin needed to cover forecasting errors.
- If the consent process takes longer than allowed for, costs are carried over a longer period and there may be lost markets, lost profit, costs of retaining old plant in service, or costly attempts to catch up lost time.
- If, finally, consent is refused or the owner decides not to proceed, the effort put into the project is wasted.

On the other hand, the fact that the project is scrutinized from a variety of different viewpoints can result in a more robust, and ultimately successful, scheme than would otherwise have been the case.

16.4 Managing consent

We may contrast two extreme styles which a project's sponsor might adopt:

1. *Define and inquire* In which formulation of the project proceeds entirely within the sponsor organization, only being made public knowledge when consent is applied for.
2. *Consult and refine* In which consultation with affected interests begins early, while significant options are still open.

The planning system in the United Kingdom tends to be *reactive*, since many projects are not provided for in existing development plans. In the absence of prior signals that a project of such-and-such characteristics will be consented to, the 'consult and refine' style is the more suitable. Early consultation, with official bodies and with interest groups, can contribute ideas as well as giving early warning of the nature and strength of possible objections, but it is counter-productive to open up too many options for public debate which can become inconclusive and raise unnecessary anxieties. It is the developer's job to establish the main parameters of the project for which consent is being sought. The aim of consultation is to resolve conflicts between the project and the interests of affected parties at the design stage rather than by later confrontation and legal manoeuvrings. There are many cases, however, where developers have adopted a 'define and inquire' style.

Direct costs of consent are minor compared with those arising from delay, uncertainty as to how long the process will take, possibility of final rejection and onerous attaching conditions. Thus the aims of managing the consent process are:

- Minimizing the total of all the costs associated with consent; which in turn involves
- Minimizing both the time the process can be expected to take, if all goes reasonably well, and the risk of it taking significantly longer; and also
- Minimizing the risk that, having gone all through the consent process, the project is abandoned whether because consent was refused *or for any other reason.*

Mention of *risk* is a reminder that much of the consent process is outside the proponent's direct control, and that consent management is a form of risk management (see Chapter 4), which involves:

- Identifying sources of risk, and their possible effects; and for each source
- Eliminating it; or failing that
- Reducing the magnitude of the risk; and/or
- Shifting it onto broader shoulders; then
- Considering secondary risks, arising from the actions to deal with primary ones; and finally
- Consciously accepting, and making provision for, those risks that are unavoidable.

Applying a risk management approach to a number of consent examples leads to some general observations:

1. *Eliminating* a source of risk is only possible while the definition of the project (such as choice of site, alternative technological options) can still be altered, that is early in the project definition phase.
2. *Reducing* a risk is mainly a matter of careful management of detail, timely and effective consultation, control of information, and wise deployment of 'planning gain' and other 'mitigators'.
3. *Distributing* risks to others is rarely possible. (This contrasts with other phases of a project where allocation of risks between owner, financiers, and contractors is central.)
4. *Choice* between alternative ways of reducing a risk may turn on *secondary risks*, for example withholding information to reduce risk of its being used by opponents, may contribute to a loss of trust in the proponent.
5. In many cases, the only action possible is to reduce a risk as far as practicable, and *accept* what remains. The further implication is that provision must be made financially and in the schedule, and with the

possibility of failure to gain consent, the fallback position evaluated.
6. Risks, and perceptions of them, will change as the project progresses so provide for continuous updating of the analysis.

Careful control and attention to detail have been stressed. At the consultation and inquiry stages, when external relationships are involved, significant matters of policy may get settled 'on the run'. To avoid the problems this can cause a strategy document should be prepared, and updated as necessary, covering:

– Consents required and, where options exist, the avenues to be used. (It may be possible to define the project so that an Act of Parliament (which will include deemed planning consent) is required, thereby avoiding a public inquiry.)
– Policies on consultation with local residents; with planning and other authorities; with adjoining landowners and industrial establishments; environmental and other interest groups. As a first step, these need to be identified and listed.
– Strategy towards opposition stemming from competitors.
– Policy on the release of information, including timing and to whom access is to be given.
– Identification of contentious issues, and stance in relation to them.
– Alternatives to be mentioned in the application.
– Tactics for handling proposals for attaching conditions.
– Stance on compensation.
– Policy on providing benefits to local communities and other 'mitigators'.
– Style and coverage of environmental statement.
– Allocation of responsibilities and authority for action on consent matters.

Management of the consent process falls naturally into two stages:

Stage 1 Actions during the formulation of the project, up to the decision to make application for consent. These will be mainly concerned with ensuring the project is defined in such a way as to minimize consent costs and risks.
Stage 2 Actions from the decision to apply for consent until the way is clear for the project to go ahead (or it has been abandoned). These are mainly concerned with managing external relationships.

Although it is convenient to make this separation, it cannot be total since consideration of consent risks logically involves anticipating how the inquiry stage will be managed.

In the formulation phase, the main task is to see that consent implications are taken into account in decisions on scope, location, design and implementation of the project. Formulation is an iterative process and the consent aspect of it is depicted in Fig. 16.1. It starts with the current definition of the project, which term is meant to include both the documented description and a forward projection based on how the project team expects the more detailed definition to evolve.

The definition is scrutinized to *identify consent factors*, that is anything which might affect the costs and risks in obtaining consent. At the same time, parallel work will be carried out on *all other factors* on the engineering, financial and other sides. The next step is to *assess consent risks*, seeking ways to eliminate or reduce them or consciously deciding to accept them. At the same time, efforts can be made to *identify mitigators*, that is measures that might be taken to ease the consent problems. It should now be possible to formulate the *consent strategy* (see above). It is essential that the various

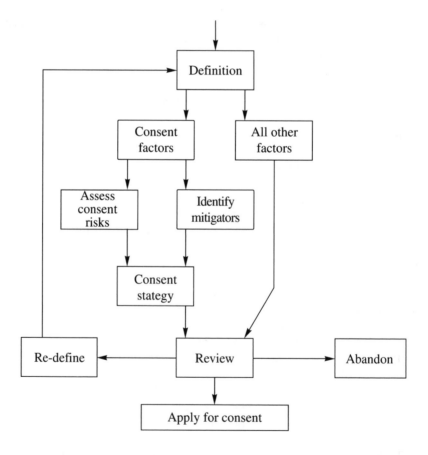

Figure 16.1   Decisions before consent application

analyses be brought together in a thorough and dispassionate *strategic review*, which will lead to one of three outcomes:

1. A decision that the project is now sufficiently well defined, and has sufficiently favourable prospects to proceed to the stage of *applying for consent*. (Detailed design work will presumably continue, the essence of the judgement to be made is that changes introduced from now on will not upset the basis for the application.)
2. A decision to continue iterating, and to authorize *further definition* work, either to incorporate significant modifications, or to proceed to the next level of detail.
3. A decision to *abandon* the project. Recognizing the high costs of project development, if the project will be abandoned eventually, the sooner this can be recognized, the better.

From the point where the decision has been made to proceed and apply for the necessary consents, the iterative decision process just described is replaced by a linear one, as depicted in Fig. 16.2, which is largely self-explanatory. *Preparing for the inquiry* involves preparing documentation and arguments, and building a multi-professional team who understand the project and each other's roles and language. Meticulous care should continue while *managing the inquiry stage*, such as over rebuttal of objectors' arguments, dealing with the media, etc. *GO* does not follow automatically from grant of consent, since circumstances may have altered.

16.5 Summary

1. Obtaining public consent exposes a project to varied scrutiny.
2. The planning system in the United Kingdom has been described. Its implications for project management are typical of other consent systems.
3. A recommended approach to managing the consent process involves use of risk management procedures from the outset of project formulation, with explicit assessment of consent risks including those of delay or rejection.
4. An explicit consent strategy, with clear responsibilities for managing the consent process, is necessary, and regular and rigorous strategic review is vital.

Bibliography

For up-to-date information on the planning system, see the series of Planning Policy Guidelines (PPG) and Minerals Policy Guidelines (MPG) circulars issued by the Department of the Environment.

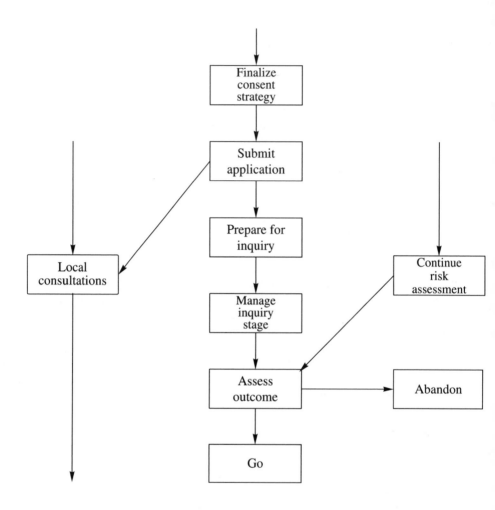

Figure 16.2 The inquiry stage

1. Salt, A. and Brown, H., *Planning Applications – The RMJM Guide*, BSP Professional Books, 1987.
2. Stringer, J., *Gaining Consent: Guidelines for managing the planning and inquiry stage of project development*, Major Projects Association, Technical Paper No. 9, Major Projects Association, 1991.
3. Wathern, P., *Environmental Impact Analysis, Theory and Practice*, Unwin Hyman, 1988.

PART FIVE
CONTRACT
MANAGEMENT

It is quite typical for between 60 and 100 per cent of the cost of a project to be spent through outside agencies. Hence, the procurement function, and the letting of contracts, is the most significant area for saving or wasting money. Part Five describes the contract and procurement process from the client's and contractor's viewpoint. We describe contracts and their forms and types, we explain the procurement process and how to choose contractors and consultants, and we describe how to bid for and win contracts. Contracts have to be set in the context of a legal system. We assume the English system. This is constraining in that it is limited to part of one country. However, the English system is the basis of those of many countries throughout the world, mainly former colonies and empire – including the United States of America. Hence, it is illustrative. We describe the English legal system and give an overview of the law of contracts. We also explain the increasing influence of European legislation. We close by describing how to administer contracts, and resolve disputes.

In Chapter 17, John Dingle describes the fundamentals of procurement and contract strategy, with contributions by David Topping and Malcolm Watkinson. They identify what we mean by a contract, and different types of contract, categorized by scope of supply and terms of payment. They describe the relationship between contracts and risk management, and the use of standard forms.

In Chapter 18, Paul Kersey and Rodney Turner explain contract law. They give an overview of English law, and explain the law of contracts. Malcolm Watkinson explains the impact of European law, with contributions by Rodney Turner and Steve Tonks.

In Chapter 19, Rodney Turner, David Topping, Malcolm Watkinson, and John Dingle describe the procurement process. They describe how to identify roles and responsibilities on a contract, and to select the types and forms of contract. They then describe how to select contractors and consultants.

In Chapter 20, Bart Bernink describes how contractors win tenders. He describes a three stage process, including pre-receipt of ITT, tender preparation and submission and contract negotiation.

In Chapter 21, Geoff Quaife and Rodney Turner describe the administration of contracts. They describe how to establish relationships between the client and contractor, how to monitor and measure progress, variations and changes, and the completion and close-out process.

In Chapter 22, Frank Thomas describes dispute resolution procedures. Tim Adams describes alternative dispute resolution (ADR), a specific approach gaining wide acceptance.

17

Procurement and contract strategy

John Dingle, David Topping and Malcolm Watkinson

17.1 Introduction

There are many instruments which govern the way the parties involved in a project work together, called variously: agreement, licence, contract. We refer to them all as 'contracts', because that is their *functional* purpose. In general, the terms of these instruments – contracts – are established by negotiation. This is a process by which we suppose (idealistically) that the parties will seek to optimize, by reciprocal concession and compromise, the procedures by which they will work together. In as much as they intend the instrument to be legal and enforceable, it has the formal characteristics of a contract, but it will also apportion obligations and liabilities, risks and rewards, so it has also the characteristics of a means of motivating the parties. The concept of establishing the terms of a contract by 'reciprocal concession and compromise' is an attractive generality. However, it is difficult to achieve in reality because one party is more powerful than the other. That may be the case in the following circumstances:

- Contracts between parties of different commercial muscle, 'Big Oil' and small specialized contractors.
- Contracts negotiated between parties of widely different technical competence, such as high technology projects in developing countries.
- Contracts negotiated between parties of widely different business cultures.

It is often said that the function of a contract is to assign risks to the party best able to manage them;[1] this is a platitude sufficiently bland to soothe the self-esteem of any cowboy jerry-builder, yet containing enough truth to give the flavour of good sense. We need to think how to employ this good sense in the management of our projects. We need to evolve a contract philosophy

244 THE COMMERCIAL PROJECT MANAGER

too, for this will guide the negotiations by which we establish the legal framework for our technical and commercial work on the project.

In this chapter, we set out the main features of a contract philosophy: not as lawyers, but as managers recognizing that contracts are the means through which 'fitness for purpose and economic use of resources' is actually carried out, in the context of managing a project. We identify what we mean by a contract, describe typical types of contract and their features, categorized by scope of supply or terms of payment, and identify atypical aspects which can create pitfalls for the project manager. We explain the relationship between contracts and project risk, and discuss standard forms of contract.

17.2 What is a contract?

A contract is 'a promise or set of promises between parties, which the law will enforce'. This is an elementary definition, to which we need to add some additional concepts:

1. *Parties* The parties to a contract have to intend to enter into a legal relationship.
2. *Agreement* The contract must be in the form of an offer (the 'promise') which has been duly accepted. The promise in such a form sets out the obligations of the promisor, and hence, in effect, of the parties.
3. *Consideration* The promise is supported by a consideration, being some benefit conferred on the promisor (or detriment suffered by the promisee) such as the price.
4. *Date of coming into effect* It is useful to state the date when the contract comes into effect.
5. *Conditions precedent* The date on which a contract comes into effect is often specified by reference to some previous event(s), sometimes called 'conditions precedent'. Examples may be:
   - Payment of a proportion of the contract price (to the contractor or supplier, as a 'down payment')
   - Completion of preliminary work (by a third party, so that the main project work can begin)
   - Receipt of authority, for example from a government department, to proceed with the project.
6. *Proper law* Again it is useful – some would say very important – to state the legal code under which the contract will be interpreted, should any dispute arise. We have said that in this part, everything is said in the context of English law. Case precedents are important in English law, and examples can often be found where cases contradict the obvious interpretation. (For example the date of coming into effect of a contract

has been held to be the date of posting the letter of acceptance, even though that letter never arrived. This kind of situation provides bread – and jam too – for lawyers.) Evidently, other codes may lead to other interpretations, which may be very important factors in a contract strategy, though the basic concepts in setting up a strategy seem to be international in character.

In a project environment, the parties to a contract consist of the *buyer* (the owner, sponsor, licensee, etc.), and the *seller*(s), (the supporters, contractors, consultants, material suppliers, licensors, etc.). The promise is to supply goods or services such as designs, technology, plant, a complete installation, etc. The consideration may be money, goods, reciprocal services (as in cross-licensing), etc. Contracts can be categorized by the type of goods or service to be supplied, and by the form of the consideration. These ideas on the law, and the legal status of contracts are described further in the next chapter.

17.3 Types of contract – goods and services supplied

There are different categories of contract, depending on the scope of supply, including:

– Supply of materials, equipment or artisan labour
– Professional or consultancy services
– Complete plant, 'turnkey', supply, or design and build
– Management contracts.

Supply of materials, equipment or artisan labour

These are the simplest type of contract, and form a model for all others. Typical clauses contained in a contract of this type are given in Table 17.1. Materials are often offered under seller's 'standard conditions of sale'. Many buyers issue 'standard conditions of purchase'. These 'standard' conditions very rarely match, especially when the parties are of different nationality. The United Nations has attempted to produce and popularize General Conditions, but without – it seems – very great success.

Professional or consultancy services

The supply of professional or consultancy services has the characteristic that such services have no intrinsic value except for the particular buyer in relation to a particular project. Consider for example:

Table 17.1 Typical clauses in a material supply contract

Typical clauses	Sub-clauses	Qualifications
Definitions	Buyer Seller Documents making up the contract Contract works	
Scope of supply	What the seller will supply Spares and replacements	Beware inclusions and exclusions
Timing	Earliest/latest delivery	Delivery location
Delivery stipulations	Inspection and testing Marking Protection and packaging for delivery	
Ownership of goods		Defines when responsibility passes from seller to buyer
Installation	Codes of practice and/or regulations to be observed Stipulations for carrying out site work Issue of materials for installation	
Changes	Responsibilities for corrections to documentation Procedures for modifications or variations in work	
Liability for defects	Maximum liability	Period of liability
Terms of payment	Amounts Timing Methods of effecting payment	
Confidentiality	Responsibilities for protecting confidential information Patent rights	
Miscellaneous	Extension of schedule Assignment and sub-letting *Force majeure* Resolution of disputes Termination and cancellation Seller's default Bankruptcy or liquidation Addresses Proper law	

1. *A design package* This consists of a specified collection of specification sheets, calculations, manuals, functional and systems specifications, drawings and similar documentation. While the scope of supply is easy to specify, the quality of information contained in each type of document may be difficult to define (although this may be done through conditions and guarantees, Chapter 11). The design package is, in practice, defined by reference to the design basis and operating philosophy for the facility, its context, the extent of information to be provided in each document type and the delivery programme. Table 17.2 contains a list of typical clauses used on a design contract.
2. *Technical assistance* This may be described, but is largely undefinable except in terms of commitment of specified personnel, for example: numbers and types of specialists; duration of commitment, and timing, for each type; rate per day; allowable expenses. A technical assistance contract will also contain clauses regulating such things as reasons for withdrawing and replacing specialists, facilitating their travel, providing working and welfare facilities. Definition, and therefore control of cost-effectiveness, is helped by setting out, for example, the limits of a specialist's responsibility (and authority); normal/abnormal work and rates; the working conditions required – and which party provides them. Technical assistance, especially that involving training of local personnel, often falls within a technology licensing agreement although it may be governed by a separate contract.

Table 17.2   Core clauses and options used on design contracts

Core clauses	Options
The brief	Feasibility
The service	Scheme design
The parties	Detail design
Time	Tender list
Quality	Admin/Project manager
Payment fees	Construction supervision
Variation	Inspection and approval
Interim	Third party audit
Expenses	Cost plan
Records	Specific negotiation
Compensation	Design co-ordination
Professional indemnity	Maintenance manual
As-built drawings	Copyright
Disputes and termination	VAT

Complete plant 'turnkey' supply, or design and build

A 'turnkey' contract is one in which the client hands over complete responsibility to the contractor for design, procurement and construction, and perhaps commissioning. It may also include financing up to completion, when payment occurs. The client has effectively no involvement in the work until given the keys to the completed plant, which it should be possible to just start up and run, that is just 'turn the ignition key'. Complete plant turnkey supply will include provisions for both equipment supply (including construction equipment and tools, and special materials such as catalysts) and engineering services (including technology and technical support). The contract philosophy has to be consistent: it is important to avoid the possibility of contradictory positions evolving for different elements of the supply.

The basic instruments of definition for all these supplies, which typically form the Technical Annexes to the contract, are:

- The definition of the context of the facility
- Equipment, materials and labour supply lists
- Technical services supply lists
- Schedules for delivery, construction and commissioning
- Performance guarantees.

Technical services will include the various process and functional disciplines, procurement, expediting, inspection, quality assurance, project management, supervision of erection and commissioning. Even with a turnkey contract, the buyer will often assign personnel to take part in these activities. It is important that their participation is regulated by the contract in such ways that the project as a whole benefits. Other technical services will be supplied in which buyer's personnel are not usually involved, in the sense of being assigned to work within the seller's activities. These include commercial management of shipping, insurance, finance, training, product marketing and project accounting.

Management contracts

Under a management contract, the *manager* (who may be an individual or a firm) assumes responsibility for the management of an operation, which remains owned and financed by the *owner*. Under the contract, the manager is usually paid a fee for management skills. Sometimes the manager may have separate financial interests in the operation. However, the key feature of a management contract is that the manager is given authority to manage, not just to provide advice or consultancy services. Sometimes, project development contracts have some of the characteristics of a management contract. The owner of a complex project retains a specialist (individual or firm) to manage and coordinate design, procurement and/or construction. Often, the manager lets subcontracts for these activities to other parties (and indeed often managers are barred from doing them themselves). Note, under the arrangements described, the specialist is responsible only for the physical development of the project, not for the management of the business which the project is intended to support. In some cases, however, the specialist may also be made responsible for training local personnel, for commissioning, and even for running the plant, marketing products and generally conducting the business for a certain number of years. In such cases, the arrangement becomes a fully-fledged management contract.

Usually, management contracts are adapted to each particular situation, but it has been suggested that there are four general factors which are crucial for success:

1. The 'external environment' (including government policies, general market behaviour – factors outside the control of the management, which none the less affect the organization) should be supportive.
2. The contractor must be fundamentally viable.
3. The owner must be enthusiastically behind the management contract concept.
4. The manager must be given full authority and control of the organization so as to be able to meet the aims of the contract.

If these factors are missing, the management contract will probably fail.

Management contracts are often politically sensitive, difficult to structure and operate in a volatile situation. Consequently, the scope of work of the contract should be defined with care, especially with respect to objectives and performance criteria. The choice of the management team is also important. A checklist of strategic items to be considered when planning work under a management contract would probably give high priority to the following, as main contributions to building a satisfactory relationship between manager and owner:

- Clear definition of each party's responsibilities.
- The scope of the manager's authority and control.
- What facilities, services, etc., are to be supplied by the owner.
- Processes and procedures for communication, decision making, monitoring and control.
- Personnel, training and transfer of technology and know-how.
- Financing including compensation (such as counter-trade, buyback, etc).

Some people may differentiate between a management contract and a construction management contract. The major difference between the two forms is that although the client engages the designers and the managing contractor separately in both forms, with construction management the managing contractor provides only a professional project management service, and the client enters into contracts directly with works contractors who actually carry out the construction.

In the management contracting form, the client engages a major contractor as main contractor who provides a professional project management service but who also enters into contracts with works contractors. This is illustrated in Fig. 17.1 where the contractual and organizational relationships are illustrated.[2] This report also summarizes the management functions and responsibilities in traditional building and civil engineering contracts, and in management contracts. Developed originally for the building industry, the method is now being used for civil works.

The strengths of management contracting are:

- Extensive concurrency of design and construction is possible.
- Cost savings may be achieved over other methods by better control of design (designer and management contractor working together with the client).
- Improved buildability may be achieved through direct involvement of contractors in the design.
- Improved planning of design and construction into packages for individual tendering to works subcontractors (separate works contractors in the construction management method) can increase the effects of competition in minimizing costs.
- Better packaging of work elements is possible to suit specialist contractors' capabilities.

The weaknesses are:

- The client may be exposed to increased financial risk from the works contractors because of the absence of a direct contractual link (supporters argue that this is overcome by the construction management approach).
- Difficulties may arise in defining and identifying risks and liabilities between the client, managing contractor and subcontractors.
- There may be a tendency to increase administrative system and supervision.
- Problems have arisen in projects with high mechanical and electrical service content because the management contractor lacked specialist knowledge in these areas.

The Management Contracting Contract

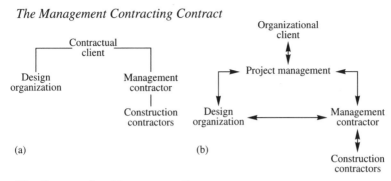

(a)   (b)

The Construction Management Contract

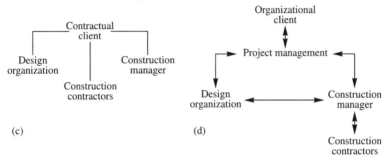

(c)   (d)

The Design and Management Contract

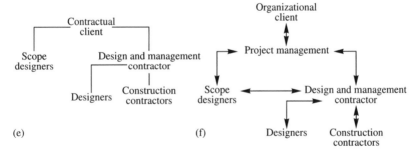

(e)   (f)

Figure 17.1 Contractual and organizational relationships, (after CIRIA 100[2]).

17.4 Types of contract – terms of payment

There are essentially three methods of payment for contracts:

1. *Price* The contractor is paid a price for doing the work. These can
   include:
   – Lump sum, or fixed price

- Work package
- Time rate or daywork.
2. *Measurement* The work is measured and the contractor is paid an agreed rate for the work done. These can include:
- Bill of quantities
- Schedule of rates.
3. *Costs* The contractor has costs refunded, and an agreed mark-up is paid. These can include:
- Contractor incentive, such as target cost or milestone payments
- Cost plus fixed fee
- Cost plus percentage fee.

As you move down this list, the contractor's risk decreases, and the client's risk increases, (Table 17.3, p. 269). We discuss the contract types in turn.

Lump sum contracts

A firm price is given for the work, with provisions for contract price adjustment due to increases in labour and materials costs. Changes should, where possible, be priced as lump sum.

1. *Advantages* The advantages of lump sum contracts are:
- The contract cost is known at the outset.
- The contractor assumes greatest risk, and the owner assumes least risk.
- This gives the strongest motivation of the contractor due to their commitment on time and cost.
- The high degree of contractor responsibility means simpler contract control by the owner.
- There is more opportunity to select the best contractor because of firm price quotations and precise planning.
- There is usually lower investment cost.
- The contractor will tend to use the best staff on this type of contract because performance has a large effect on profit.
2. *Requirements* The requirements of a lump sum contract are:
- Precise definition of the work scope.
- Reasonable financial risk to the contractor.
- Stable market conditions and absence of major economic or political uncertainty.
- Close control of changes.
3. *Disadvantages* The disadvantages of the lump sum contract are:
- The contract award may be delayed later than with other types because of the need to define work fully, so that the tender period will be longer.

- The owner's ability to influence performance within the terms of the contract is reduced because of the extent of the contractor's responsibility especially as regards cost.
4. *Owner's manpower commitment* The owner's manpower commitment is at a minimum. The contractor exercises control of the work. The owner's role is essentially to monitor the contractor's performance, but the owner must also ensure quality because the extent of the contractor's responsibility carries the risk that quality may suffer under pressure to maximize or retain profit. The owner must closely monitor changes through clearly established procedures. The effect of proposed changes on time and cost must be evaluated throughout the whole programme.

Work package

A fixed price is paid for the work in each work package. The initial work package would constitute the basic contract to which successive packages would be attached.

1. *Advantages* The advantages of work package contracts are similar to lump sum, but as the definition of all the work is not required at the outset, the contract award may be advanced.
2. *Requirements* The requirements of a work package contract are similar to lump sum contracts. The first work package must contain the basis for pricing and scheduling the later, negotiated packages. Each work package must be discrete, with minimal and well defined effects on other work packages.
3. *Disadvantages* The disadvantages of the work package contract are similar to lump sum, except a greater commitment is required from the owner to control interfaces between packages. Successive packages would in principle be negotiated with the original contractor rather than put to competitive tender. Where work packages are let to different contractors they become separate contracts.

Time rate or daywork

This is a series of time-based fixed prices for units of work input.

1. *Advantages* The advantages of these contracts are similar to reimbursible type, but as the contractor quotes fixed rates they assume risks related to labour compensation and equipment operating costs.
2. *Requirements* A precise definition of work scope is not required for a time rate or daywork contract.
3. *Disadvantages* The disadvantages of the time rate or daywork contract

are similar to reimbursible, with the owner taking risks related to effective performance or productivity.

4. *Owner's manpower commitment* This is similar to reimbursible contracts.

Measurement

A schedule of rates is a series of fixed prices or rates for units of work output set forth as an itemized list. Quantities are either not given against the schedule of rates, or are only approximate. The bill of quantities type is similar to schedule of rates, except that the quantities are accurately specified. A bill of quantities contract is close to a lump sum contract, whereas a schedule of rates is similar to a cost plus contract.

1. *Advantages* The advantages of schedule of rates contracts are similar to lump sum, except the owner assumes risks related to determining the quantities. The advantages of lump sum are therefore present, though to a lesser degree. The contract cost is not clearly defined as in lump sum. Change control can be somewhat simpler than lump sum, as changes in quantities can be picked up in measurement.
2. *Requirements* The requirements of a schedule of rates contract are similar to lump sum, except accurate definition of the extent of work is not necessary. However, where no quantities are given the contractor needs some indication of the scope of the work, because this may affect the rates. All work must be covered by the rates quoted.
3. *Disadvantages* The disadvantages of the schedule of rates contract are similar to those for lump sum, except greater control by the owner is called for, as there is not such complete definition of the work scope. On bill of quantities, the definition of the material work scope is closer to that needed for lump sum. The final cost is not well defined. This type is more suitable for contracts such as fabrication, erection and pipework than for plant supply and installation.

Reimbursible contracts

The contractor is paid costs for the work, plus a profit. The profit component may be a fixed fee, or a rate related to time, or a percentage of the cost. There is a slightly stronger motivation of the contractor on a cost plus fixed fee type, than on a simple cost plus contract.

1. *Advantages* The advantages of reimbursible contracts are:
   - The owner's ability to influence performance is greatest.
   - The contract award may be earlier than with other types because the work scope does not have to be well defined, so the tender period is shorter.

- Change control is simpler.
2. *Requirements* The requirements of a reimbursible contract are minimal due to the high risk assumed by the owner, and lack of clear definition of the work scope. Where the add-on element is a fixed fee the work must be defined sufficiently for the contractor to be able to estimate the extent of the services that must be supplied.
3. *Disadvantages* The disadvantages of the reimbursible contract are:
   - The cost is unknown until the end of the contract.
   - The owner retains greatest risk.
   - The contractor is not required to apply direct control.
   - Identification of the best contractor may be difficult.
   - Control of work by the owner demands considerable effort.
4. *Owner's manpower commitment* The owner's manpower commitment is at a maximum. The owner must assume active control and direction of the work. This requires an appropriate organization to cover all control elements. The contractor is essentially responsible for technical super-vision, labour and labour relations.

If clients are able to accept a reduced level of flexibility they may increase their control of costs through what are known as target cost reimbursable contract forms. Many variations have been used with varying degrees of success but the principle involves defining the work with sufficient accuracy that either a negotiated or tendered 'target' may be set for the cost of the works. A target fee or fixed fee may be stated to cover contractor's overheads. The client will pay the cost of works and fee within a stated range of the target. Beyond this, a share formula operates to distribute savings between the two parties if the actual cost is less, or expenses if the cost increases. The client may accept a larger range in order to secure a fixed maximum as an alternative but still providing the share mechanism on savings to provide incentive. CIRIA 85[3] illustrates such a system.

Contractual incentives

Incentives are used on contracts to motivate contractors towards reducing the time or the cost of the work. They are features added to other contract types, rather than being a separate type in their own right. Incentives relate either to the magnitude of payments made to the contractor or to their timing.

1. *Advantages* The advantages of contractual incentives are higher motiva-tion of the contractor either because improved achievement means more profit, or payment is linked to completion of physical stages of the work.
2. *Requirements* The different types of incentive arrangements have different requirements. A common form is to set the duration of the

contract and to make predetermined payments for early completion. The incentive is more money for an advanced end date. Such arrangements should be included in the main contract. This form applies to lump sum and related types of contract. Milestone payment terms may be used as an incentive. Milestones are set for physical completion of stages or sections of the work, and payment is linked to achievement of each milestone. This only affects the timing of payments, and does not involve extra money. Target cost incentives can be used with reimbursible or related types of contract. A target cost is set and any savings or losses on the target are split in a predetermined proportion between the contractor and the owner.

3. *Disadvantages* Although incentives are intended to confer specific advantages, a disadvantage may be the potentially disruptive effect of changes on the incentive provisions. Incentives may also have an unsettling effect on the labour force, if workers feel they are not sharing in the benefits.

4. *Owner's manpower commitment* The use of incentives usually means additional effort from the owner as regards change control. The effect of changes on incentive provisions has to be determined and suitable adjustments made to ensure that the incentives are not weakened. Some additional effort will also be needed to calculate the incentive payments to the contractor.

17.5 Contracts and risk management

A contract is an instrument for *balancing* risks and motivations. We stress the word 'balancing', for both parties should carry some of the risks in a project. If a contract transferred all the risks in a project from party A to party B, only B will be motivated to manage the risks so as to achieve project success. Projects are inherently risky, being complex, unique and novel. Whether initially of a technical nature (untried technology, inadequate design or faulty materials) or financial (insolvent contractor, adverse exchange or interest rate movements, operation of CPFC – contract price fluctuation clauses, or inflation), ultimately the risk is a financial risk to the client. Even a delay in commissioning in itself not costing additional expenditure (though this is rare), results in the client's revenue stream being delayed – in extreme cases to the point where the entire viability of the project may be jeopardized. (It is said that the delay to the commissioning of the Channel Tunnel means its viability is on a knife edge.)

There are four principal ways of dealing with risk:

- Avoid it by choosing alternatives (avoidance).
- Reduce it to an acceptable level (partial avoidance).

- Transfer to another party via contract conditions or insurance (deflection).
- Absorb it and allow for it in the project cost estimates (contingency).

Hence risk management is an essential part of contract strategy. In this context, we should recognize:

- All projects entail risks which affect, to a greater or less extent, both parties to a contract.
- None the less, both parties intend that the project will succeed, and both should be motivated to achieve that end.
- Ideally, through the contract, risk should be assigned to the party best able and motivated to deal with it.
- If it is assigned to a party not able to manage it, such a party should be appropriately rewarded.
- If losses are incurred, they are not likely to be offset by any penalty payment.
- While *penalties* may act like a stick to drive the parties on, their motivations are just as likely (some would say, more likely) to be strengthened by *incentives*, which act like the proverbial carrot.

Contract strategy for successful risk management should focus upon the choice of contract form, the number and interrelationship of contracts where more than one is required, how the contractor is to be selected and the allocation of contractual responsibilities. CIRIA 85[3] gives a checklist summarizing the main considerations which must be taken into account in selecting contract types to meet the strategy. When considering the allocation of risk, it is necessary to consider which party is best placed to control events leading to the risk occurring, which may best manage it if it occurs and who should carry the cost of the risk. If risk is to be transferred, particularly to the contractor, is the contractor financially capable of sustaining it – particularly if competitive tendering in a tight market has led contractors to under-assess and under-price the risk?

Ingenious people will seek to find ways of avoiding penalties, and other ingenious people will seek to find ways of frustrating the first group. Hence the tortuous complexity of penalty clauses in many contracts.

Some clients, particularly highly risk-averse public bodies whose core business is operational rather than project based, are also both inexperienced and fearful of cost over-runs. Their attitude to risk can be unreasonable and they may insist on unnecessary and ineffective measures being taken to minimize risk. This usually results in attempting to complete all aspects of design and specification prior to commencing construction, which can considerably lengthen the total project duration. More unfortunately, they may amend standard forms of contract to place more risk on contractors and this should be resisted. Standard forms of contract attempt to strike a balance of risk between client and contractor which is reflected in the contract as a whole rather than individual clauses. It therefore follows that risk allocation should be equitable and the form of contract should be chosen with the management of risk in mind. Clients who require a flexible form of contract in order to allow them to vary the works during the contract cannot then expect to operate a fixed price form of contract successfully. Dispute and litigation will surely follow.

There are some clients who believe that contractors who demonstrate adherence to quality assurance procedures do not require supervision in the traditional sense of the word. A much cheaper and less intrusive audit can, they believe, be carried out by the engineer or project manager simply to ensure that the quality assurance procedure is being adhered to. This philosophy is flawed for two reasons. Firstly, no quality assurance system *guarantees* that work has been carried out correctly, merely that a system of checking and recording has been followed. Secondly, the commercial pressures on contractors particularly working under price-based contracts competitively tendered, are extreme. The temptation to cut corners is high when the likelihood of being discovered is small, and the risk to the client of taking over latent defects in the completed works, not worth accepting.

The form of contract chosen to reflect the risk allocation will be either price based or cost based. Price-based contracts,[1,4,5,6] may be lump sum or admeasurement types where the contractor prices detailed schedules and bills of quantities provided by the client or the designer. The contractor includes most risk in the pricing but more work is required by the designer to detail adequately the work beforehand. Cost-based contracts such as target cost or cost-reimbursable types,[1,2,3,7] may allow for 'open book' accounting and guaranteed payment of costs incurred by the contractor whatever they may be. These effectively return the risk to the client in exchange for flexibility, in recognition that the client rather than the contractor is best placed to accept the risks of incomplete design, new technology or complex construction sequences. Table 17.3 shows how risk assessment can influence the choice of contract form. Figure 17.2 is another way of representing this. Each type effects a different balance between the risk accepted by the buyer (or owner) and the information available or needed to control the project. In essence, a lump sum type of contract minimizes the owner's risk, but requires a lot of information in order fully to define the work. A reimbursable contract type requires little information to define the scope of work, but exposes the owner to considerable risk. It will be obvious that situations arise where this is unavoidable, but should not be allowed to continue for very long, so there is need for a mechanism for converting from a reimbursable to a lump sum contract type.

Table 17.3 Matching risk assessment to contract form

Risk assessment	Price	Measurement	Incentive	Cost
Contract discipline	High	Medium	Medium	Low
Contract incentive	High	Medium	Medium	Low
Employer risk	Low	Medium	Medium	High
Employer flexibility	Low	Medium	Medium	High
Financial objectives of client/contractor	Different/ independent	Different/ in conflict	Mutual	In conflict
Flexibility for design change/variations	Limited	Some	Extensive	Unlimited
Overlap of design/construction	None	Limited	Extensive	Unlimited
Contractor involvement in design	Excluded	Excluded	Encouraged	Desirable
Client involvement in construction management	Excluded	Ex works	Desirable	Active
Payment for risk	Undisclosed contingency	Undisclosed contingency	Payment if it occurs	Payment of actual cost
Claims resolution	Difficult	Difficult	Easy	Unnecessary
Knowledge of final price at tender	Known variations	Uncertain	Uncertain	Unknown

After Hayes et al.[8]

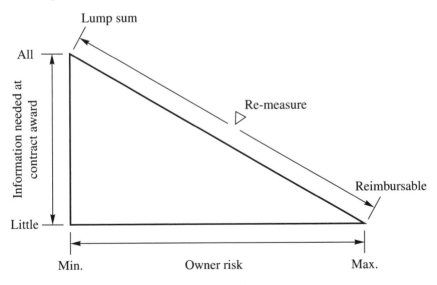

Figure 17.2 Contract type versus risk allocation

17.6 Standard forms of contract

A number of standard forms of contract have been developed by the professional engineering institutions (in Britain; Table 17.4), FIDIC (for consulting engineers operating internationally), the World Bank (for suppliers of goods or services under WB aid programmes) and others. Many large operating companies, such as the oil and chemical majors, use their own standard forms. So, of course, do government departments. Wright[9] gives a good guide to standard forms in the process industries.

The basic justification for standard forms of contract is simply to facilitate the conduct of trade, especially where the objects of trade are technically and commercially complex, as in engineering projects, while the parties work frequently together and have established a common business 'culture'. But we cannot assume that standard conditions, even when used to regulate contracts under these fairly ideal conditions, operate to apportion risk and reward fairly and equitably between the parties. On the contrary, they may be used by powerful buyers to oppress relatively weaker sellers (as when highly complex consultancy services are demanded under terms designed for straightforward construction contracts), or by knowledgeable sellers to mislead relatively inexperienced buyers (as in some 'technology transfer' projects for the Third World).

The building and engineering industries make extensive use of standard forms, though often as 'models' on which to base negotiated contracts. An interesting observation by lawyers is, that while the standard forms in use in both industries are quite similar, they result in considerable litigation in building, and very little in engineering. The reasons for this are not clear.

Table 17.4 Standard forms of contract produced by the engineering professions in the United Kingdom

Industry	Institution(s)	Standard forms of contract	Type of contract
Building	RIBA, RICS	JCT63 and JCT80[10]	Price
	RICS	Project Management[11]	Management
	CIRIA	CIRIA 85[3]	Target cost
		CIRIA 100[2]	Management
Process	IChemE	Red Book[6]	Price
		Green Book[7]	Cost
		Yellow Book[12]	Subcontracts
Civil engineering	ICE	ICE 5th and 6th[5]	Price/remeasurement
		New engineering contract[1]	Variable
M&E	IMechE, IEE	MFI[13]	Price
IT	BCS	None as yet	

Suggestions include: greater potential for on-site disputes in building; builders' clients (such as local authorities) are more litigation-minded and consequently more likely to seek a resolution of contractual problems through the courts. Perhaps it is also the case that building contracts are more open to misinterpretation: it has been said that the standard form of building contract 'works very well in practice so long as it is not read'.[14]

From the point of view of the project manager considering how to run a project efficiently under a proposed standard form of contract, probably the most important issue is to identify where the standard form imposes inefficiency. For example, if the standard form requires the project to be run under a lump-sum price regime, it should be sufficient for the project manager to provide only *time* auditing information to the client (except for engineering or site changes, which need both time- and money-expenditure data). This sort of problem arises especially when a change from one price regime (say, 'reimbursible cost + fee') to another (say, 'firm price') is envisaged, as the project moves from an early phase to a later one. Because of the inherent complexity of engineering operations, engineering contracts tend to be very much concerned with establishing the parties' rights to be indemnified against losses. This extends to third parties, and notably to the chain – which is often composed of several links – of subcontractors. It is often in this area that a standard form becomes potentially oppressive, as where a powerful buyer seeks to establish the right to recover from the seller any loss, from whatever third parties, arising from performance of the contract.

It seems fair to say, in summary, that the benefits of standard forms of contract accrue to the (corporate) parties, while the concomitant problems accrue to the manager of the project. The project is, of course, non-standard. Part of the project manager's contract strategy will therefore be to determine to what extent acceptance of standard forms is justified in the context of the particular project being considered.

The new engineering contract

Until recently, standard forms of contract for management contracting and construction management did not exist. Forms for target and cost reimbursable forms of contract exist but are based upon the traditional forms of fixed price contract such as the ICE 5th and 6th editions.[5] A recent initiative by the Institution of Civil Engineers may, however, overcome many of the problems associated with the proliferation of forms and models. In 1985, recognizing the growing need for forms of contract which addressed the changing requirements of the construction industry, the ICE set up a working party to investigate, consult and draw up recommendations for a new form. The result is the new engineering contract.[1] The NEC was drawn up from scratch by a team led by Dr Martin Barnes of Coopers & Lybrand. The team included construction professionals, legal experts and members from the contracting side of the industry. The objectives underlying the NEC are as follows:

- To achieve a contract form which is flexible enough to accommodate all types of work found in construction and the full range of risk allocation and cost control from design and build to management contracting forms.
- To be written in simple, clear English rather than legal terms.
- To achieve flexibility through modular form whereby a core of clauses common to any contract may be added to with clauses achieving one of the six basic types of contract hitherto discussed.
- To stimulate good management through cooperative interaction between parties rather than the adversarial relationship which arose from many previous forms, and through appropriate risk sharing.

The new engineering contract recognizes up to eight parties to a contract, with a leading role played by the project manager:

- Employer/client
- Project manager
- Supervisor of construction (may be a quantity surveyor; may be the same as the project manager)
- Contractor
- Subcontractor (if used)
- Supplier (of plant and materials)
- Adjudicator (to settle disputes quickly and simply between project manager and contractor or employer)
- Arbitrator (to settle disputes if adjudication fails).

Some roles may be combined, for instance that of project manager and supervisor particularly on smaller and more straightforward projects. Note the absence of the designer explicitly, who may be employed directly and not party to the contract. Alternatively, as with other forms, some or all of the design may be carried out by the main contractor or subcontractor and this requirement is clearly set out in the works information which replaces traditional conditions of contract clauses in this area.

The modular form of the contract is as follows:

- Core contract conditions
- Option Form A Conventional contract with activity schedule
- Option Form B Conventional contract with bill of quantities
- Option Form C Target contract with activity schedule

- Option Form D Target contract with bill of quantities
- Option Form E Cost reimbursable contract
- Option Form F Management contract

Plus a standard form of subcontract written in complementary form.
For simple contracts, the core contract conditions can be used alone, supported by the works information. A further set of 14 optional clauses is available to modify some main options to achieve the diverse purposes of existing forms of contract.

The contract, whatever the options chosen, falls logically into the following sections:

Section 1 General information such as who the parties are, the works and site location, which options are to be used.
Section 2 The contractor's responsibilities, generally and in respect of the chosen options, for example with respect to responsibility for design, approvals required and limitations on assigning or subcontracting parts of the contract.
Section 3 Time: completion date, contractor's programme, periods when the construction site is available, how requests to accelerate the work are dealt with.
Section 4 Quality: testing, correcting defects.
Section 5 Payment: certificates, 'actual costs', when payment is made.
Section 6 Compensation events: this unusual terminology covers 17 forms of 'risk' including changes in client's requirements, unforeseeable ground conditions and unusual weather conditions. When one of these occurs, a procedure for establishing the additional cost is clearly set out.
Section 7 Property: who owns what during the contract.
Section 8 Risks and insurance: allocation, employer's risks (*force majeure*), liabilities for damage and personal injury.
Section 9 Disputes and termination, including adjudication and arbitration procedures.

The majority of these clauses can be traced to origins in traditional forms such as the ICE 6th edition.[5] What makes the NEC different is that procedures are more clearly defined, the way in which variation costs are to be made up are explicitly stated, and most eventualities which experience has shown to cause contractual and management problems, are taken into account. This approach is supported by a volume of some 50 flow charts which clarify the intended operation of the text in certain circumstances. This unique development in itself should help to avoid many of the disputes surrounding interpretation in other forms regarding who does what and when, in the event of changed requirements or problems arising. This development goes to the heart of good project management, providing clear definition and stimulation of cooperative communication rather than relying on *ad hoc* and usually adversarial interpretation by the different parties when problems arise.

It remains to be seen how well the new engineering contract will be received, but it deserves to succeed and it is to be hoped that clients, project managers and users of traditional forms in construction will take the trouble to understand it and learn how to use it to best effect. If its objectives are realized in practice, all parties to the construction procurement process stand to benefit. The NEC was highly recommended by the Latham report into contracting in the construction industry, published in 1994.[14]

17.7 Atypical aspects

While it is normal – typical – to adapt standard forms of contract to suit particular projects, the project manager sometimes comes across aspects of proposed contractual relationships which, being atypical, are potential pitfalls for the unwary. Three of these are described below. These by no means exhaust untypical aspects (or pitfalls), but they are useful examples of what should trigger alarm bells in the mind of the project manager.

Letters of intent

It happens quite often, in connection with major projects in the engineering industries, that the parties agree to begin work before a formal contract comes into effect. This work may be undertaken under a 'letter of intent' – a document stating that the writer (usually the project owner) *intends* to enter into a contract with the addressee (usually the contractor).

Beginning work on the strength of a letter of intent enables the contractor to gain time in what may otherwise be an extremely tight schedule, and he may have other reasons for making an act of faith in the owner's intentions. The contractor is evidently put in a position of some vulnerability, for the (English) courts normally consider a letter of intent in the same light as an agreement entered into 'subject to contract', i.e., no binding obligation has been created unless and until the contract comes into effect.

However, the courts have been known to deem such a contract to have come into effect from the date of the letter of intent, that is, to have retrospective effect. Then, even if no contract is ever entered into, it may be possible for a contractor to recover a reasonable rate for work done and accepted under a letter of intent. In such a case, the court will decide what is reasonable, on the basis of *quantum meruit*, the amount merited. The court's view is unlikely to match the contractor's expectations.

The situation arising from a letter of intent is an example of the grey area which exists between contract law, with its apparently clear-cut inflexible rules governing the formation of contractual agreements, and actual practice where the pressures of business and the marketplace make it impossible – or infeasible – always to hold to the strict letter of the law. If a dispute does arise, the courts are likely to try to infer practice from precedents of regular patterns of business dealings in the past. However, even where such precedents exist, there appear to have been very many alternative interpretations of the obligations created by letters of intent. Where there is little previous experience to guide a court, the outcome of a dispute is likely to be little different from a lottery.

Letters of comfort

An even more unsatisfactory situation arises from 'letters of comfort'. These purport to confirm the policy of a parent company to support fully a subsidiary, for instance, in the case where the subsidiary is a party with others to 'joint-and-several' liability in respect of obligations undertaken in a contract with another party. The latter is thereby 'comforted' that, should the liabilities fall due to be settled by the subsidiary, the resources of the parent will be available to support the subsidiary. The (English) High Court, however, has recently decided that a letter of comfort is not equivalent to a guarantee (in connection with joint and several liability for the costs of abandoning an oil rig).

Collateral warranties

The intention of a collateral warranty is to pass the obligation (and cost) of rectifying defects to another party, which may have no direct contractual relationship with the parties to the project contract (or sometimes, which are already in a contractual relationship which is however extended or modified by the collateral warranty). A typical application is to give to a developer, financier (or even tenant of a building) the right to recover losses directly from any party alleged to be responsible for a defect causing them loss – such as the designer, constructor or project manager. In some cases, acceptance of collateral warranties is made a condition of the appointment of such (professional) parties. Since the warranties are usually drafted by lawyers retained by the developers, they are drawn to cover all the possibilities of loss against all likely parties. Furthermore, because collateral warranties are considered likely to affect others to whom the obligations may be assigned (thereby creating an apparently infinite scope for claims), professional indemnity insurance is difficult, i.e. expensive, when such warranties are involved. Collateral warranties are a recent phenomenon in the United Kingdom, and their impact in practice has not really been tested in the courts. In the EU however, single project insurance obviates the need for collateral warranties.

17.8 Summary

1. A contract is a promise between parties which the law will enforce, and has as its essential features:
   - Parties
   - Agreement
   - Consideration
   - Date of coming into effect
   - Conditions precedent
   - Proper law.
2. Contracts can be categorized by:
   - Scope of supply
   - Terms of payment.
3. Scope of supply can be:
   - Equipment and material
   - Professional services
   - Labour
   - Turnkey
   - Management.
4. Terms of payment, of increasing risk to the owner, may be:
   - Price: including lump-sum, work package, or day rates
   - Measurement: including bill of quantities or schedule of rates
   - Cost: including target cost, fixed fee or percentage fee.
5. The contract is a tool for balancing risk between client and contractor.
6. Standard forms of contract have been developed to facilitate the conducting of trade.
7. The new engineering contract is an attempt to rationalize the standard forms used in the civil engineering industry, which have become somewhat diffuse over the six editions.
8. Untypical aspects of contracts include:
   - Letters of intent
   - Letters of comfort
   - Collateral warranties.

References

1. Institution of Civil Engineers, *New Style Engineering Contract*, Thomas Telford, 1992.
2. CIRIA 100, *Management Contracting*, Construction Industry Research and Information Association, Report No. 100, 1983.
3. CIRIA 85, *Target and Cost Reimbursable Construction Contracts*, Construction Industry Research and Information Association, Report No. 85, 1982.
4. Sawyer, J.G. and Gillott, C.A., *The FIDIC Digest: Contractual relationships, responsibilities and claims under the fourth edition of the FIDIC conditions,*

Federation Internationale des Ingenieurs Conseils, Thomas Telford, 1990.
5. Institution of Civil Engineers, *Conditions of Contract and Forms of Tenders, Agreement and Bond (6th Edition) for use in Connection with Works of Civil Engineering Construction*, Thomas Telford, 1991.
6. Institution of Chemical Engineers, *Model Form of Conditions of Contract for Process Plants: Lump-sum Contracts (Red Book)*, 2nd edition, Institution of Chemical Engineers, 1981.
7. Institution of Chemical Engineers, *Model Form of Conditions of Contract for Process Plants: Reimbursable Contracts (Green Book)*, 2nd edition, Institution of Chemical Engineers, 1992.
8. Hayes, R.W. *et al.*, *Risk Management in Engineering Construction*, University of Manchester Institute of Science and Technology, Project Management Group, Thomas Telford, 1987.
9. Wright, D., *Model Forms of Conditions of Contract for Process Plants: an engineer's guide*, Institution of Chemical Engineers, 1993.
10. JCT 63, *Joint Construction Tribunal Standard Forms of Contract*, Royal Institute of British Architects, 1963.
 JCT 80, *Joint Construction Tribunal Standard Forms of Contract*, 2nd edition, Royal Institute of British Architects, 1980.
11. Royal Institute of Chartered Surveyors, *Project Management Agreement and Conditions of Engagement*, 2nd edition, Royal Institute of Chartered Surveyors, 1992.
12. Institution of Chemical Engineers, *Model Form of Conditions of Contract for Process Plants: Subcontracts (Yellow Book)*, Institution of Chemical Engineers, 1992.
12. MF1, *Model Forms of Contract*, Institution of Mechanical Engineers, 1992.
13. Tillotson, J, *Contract Law in Perspective*, 2nd edition, Butterworth, 1985.
14. Latham, M., *Constructing the Team: Final Report of the Joint Government/ Industry Review of Procurement and Contractual Arrangement in the United Kingdom Construction Industry*, HMSO, 1994

Bibliography

1. DLE, *Contracts in Use*, Davis Langdon Everest and the Royal Institute of Chartered Surveyors, 1992.
2. Griffiths, F., 'Contract strategy' in *Perspectives on Project Management*, Burbridge, R.N.G. (ed.), Peter Peregrinus Ltd for the Institution of Electrical Engineers, 1988.
3. Griffiths, F., 'Project contract strategy for 1992 and beyond', *International Journal of Project Management*, 7(2), 69–83, 1989.
4. Hegstad, S.O., *Management Contracts: Main features and design issues*, Technical Paper No. 65, The World Bank, 1987.
5. Latham, M, *Trust and Money: Interim Report of the Joint Government/Industry Review of Procurement and Contractual Arrangement in the United Kingdom Construction Industry*, HMSO, 1993.
6. NEDO, *Contract Strategy – A Report on Client Strategies When Letting Construction Contracts*, National Economic Development Office, 1985.

18

Contract law

Paul Kersey, Rodney Turner, Malcolm Watkinson and Steve Tonks

18.1 Introduction

Contracts are essential to modern economic life; without them, nothing can be bought or sold, and if things cannot be bought or sold easily, a free market economy simply cannot function. Hence the law of contracts must be simple. Wright[1] sums up the law of contracts in a single sentence:

> In the commercial world, you are free to make any bargain you wish, provided that it does not conflict with the public interest, but when you have made your bargain, you must carry it out or compensate the other party for the bargain they have lost.

Within the context of project management the law seeks to ensure the rights of parties engaging in contracts and those affected by the activity are supported. A contract is defined as a promise or set of promises between parties which the law will enforce.

Problems typically arise because contracts are written by busy business people, not lawyers or people expert in the use of English, and this can lead to disparity in the perception of the client and the contractor. In reality every deliverable on a project is a mix of gains or losses for both the contractor and the client. This produces an attitude, which determines the client's or contractor's motivation to: perform, pay, litigate or amend. The contract serves to establish the integrity of the process and to define the qualitative and quantitative characteristics of the deliverables. The law acts as a referee for the process, ensuring open and honest play. (It does not need to be fair play – the consideration just has to exist, it does not have to be reasonable to either party, and both parties must know what they are committing themselves to.)

In this chapter we describe the law of contracts. We start by giving a brief overview of English law. Contracts only have a legal basis with respect to a given legal system. When both parties to contract are based in the same country, it is assumed that the contract is subject to the law of that country. Where the two parties, or the work of the contract, are in different countries, then the contract must state under which country's law any disputes will be adjudicated. English law is often used. Furthermore, English law provides a model of the legal systems of many countries. Next, we describe contract law, and finish this chapter by describing elements of European law relating to contract and project management.

18.2 The English legal system

English law, like many of its counterparts, seeks to make itself compulsory by imposing penalties and sanctions against those contravening it. The scope of law has changed over the centuries, expanding from just the safeguarding of rights of property and the upholding of public order. Subsequent laws have been developed to address issues in the national economic interest and to increase social responsibilities. To ensure the legal system is both relevant and dynamic, laws which are outdated have been repealed. We consider:

– Types of law
– Sources of law
– The courts with jurisdiction over contract law.

Types of law

English law is divided into two empirical elements:

– Civil law
– Criminal law.

Civil law has two elements: the law of contracts and the law of torts. The former seeks to regulate the agreed, formal relationships between people. The latter imposes a duty of care not to infringe the rights of all people, even those with whom we do not have formal relationships. For example, a contractor, not adhering to statutory health and safety regulations, who injures an innocent party, may be subject to the following charges:

– *Crime* The contractor may have committed criminal negligence under the Health and Safety at Work Act (1974) and other safety legislation, prosecuted by the Crown Prosecution service in a criminal court.
– *Breach of contract* The contract with the client may require adherence to statutory regulations, and so the client may sue the contractor in a civil court to recover compensation for losses incurred.

– *Negligence* The injured third party may sue the contractor as the contractor owes a duty of care to the general public in carrying out his or her activities – this a liability under the law of torts.

Sources of law

Many legal systems are based on the principles of Roman law. English law is case driven, that is it is derived from decisions made by courts. The legal systems of some other countries are also case driven, but English law more so than any other. English law is derived from a number of sources, including:

1. *Common law* This is the primary element of English law and is developed by previous judgements, or case precedent, including decisions on statutory law.
2. *Equity* This is a system developed as a result of the inadequacies of common law, which frequently frustrates plaintiffs with minor technicalities in wording, corruption, or procrastination. Equity is an updating mechanism administered by the Chancellor in the Court of Chancery. The Chancellor reviews petitions to establish the truth of the matter, and then imposes a just solution without undue regard for technicalities or legal points. Equity adds to common law through new rights, better procedure and better remedies.
3. *Judicial precedent* Common law and equity are both the product of decisions made in courts. Where a matter of principle has been decided by one of the higher courts it becomes a precedent. In later cases the same principles should be applied; this is known as *stare decisis* or following a precedent. Judicial precedent has several components, including:
   – *Law reports* These record previous precedent. It is essential that they are comprehensive and accurate.
   – *Legal principle* This is new law created by judges applying certain rules and principles, where there is an absence of both precedent and statute. The judge describes the facts relevant to the case, and reviews previous precedents and alternative theories. The judge then makes statements of law applicable to the legal problems raised by the material facts. The rule applied to the case which forms the principal step in making the decision is known as the *ratio decidendi.* The statements of rules which do not form part of the *ratio decidendi* are known as *obiter dicta* (or 'by the way statements').
   – *Binding precedents* A further factor to be taken into account is the relationship of the court which expressed the relevant *ratio decidendi.* Under this principle, judges in lower courts are bound by decisions taken in higher courts, but not vice versa. A higher court is not only

free to disregard the decision of a lower court, but may deprive it of authority and expressly overrule it. There are some grounds for not following a binding precedent, if it can be shown that:
- The precedents are factually distinguishable.
- The *ratio decidendi* is obscure.
- Previous precedent omitted some essential point of law.
- The previous decision has been overruled by a higher court or statute.
4. *Statute law* This is made by Parliament. Parliament is not governed by previous statute, but may make new law as it sees fit, and can repeal previous statutes, overrule case law developed by the courts or make new laws in new areas. The only constraint that Parliament has is the regulations and directives developed by the European Union. This is in marked contrast to countries such as the United States, where the ability to challenge statutes in the courts is written into the constitution.

Statutes are binding upon courts no matter how unjust it may appear. The applicability of a statute has to be determined by the judge whose ruling may interpret the statute in a way that parliament never initially intended. Statutes are submitted to either the House of Commons or the House of Lords in the form of a draft statute, or bill. These are subsequently submitted to the other House to be passed. The bill is finally made a statute, or act, when it is approved by the Lord Chancellor.
5. *Other sources* Other historical sources include:
- *Custom* where an activity has existed since time immemorial, that is since records began.
- *Law merchant* An ancient law which has subsequently been absorbed into common law.
- *Roman law* Of limited use in the English legal system and is mostly confined to ecclesiastical courts (which were in themselves sources of law) and wills.
Other legal sources include:
- *EU law* Directives issued by the European Commission are passed into English law by statute.
- *Canon law* Law is also made by the Church of England, based to a greater extent on Roman law.

Structure of the courts

There are several courts which have jurisdiction over civil law:

1. *County Courts* County Courts deal with almost every kind of civil case generally relating to the area in which the court has jurisdiction. The County Court has the following limitations:

- Contract and tort claims of up to £5000 unless the limit is waived by the parties involved.
- Equitable matters arising from trusts, mortgages and partnership dissolution, up to £30 000.
- Disputes concerning land of up to £30 000.
- Probate matters (disputes concerning the grant of authority to personal representatives) where the estate of the individual amounts to less than £30 000.
- Miscellaneous matters conferred by various statute, such as the Consumer Credit Act (1974).

2. *Crown Court* This is part of the Supreme Court comprising local courts in large towns. It deals with only a few civil cases.
3. *High Court* This is empowered to deal with any civil matter unless there are other special courts that have exclusive jurisdiction. Cases may be heard by one judge sitting alone, although there may occasionally be a jury. Appeals may be heard by a divisional court where two or more high court judges attend the hearing. The High Court is divided into several divisions, of which those dealing with contract law include: Queen's Bench Division; Chancery Division; Restrictive Practices Court; and Court of Appeal.
   - *Queen's Bench Division* This is the modern equivalent to the common law court and mainly deals with common law matters such as contract and tort. This division has a number of dedicated separate courts dealing with shipping and commercial cases. The Queen's Bench Division also hears appeals on civil matters from Crown Courts.
   - *Chancery Division* Deals with traditional equity issues such as trusts, mortgages and bankruptcies within the City of London.
   - *Restrictive Practices Court* This investigates agreements registered under the Restrictive Trade Practices Act and the Resale Prices Act. It is required to have regard for EU law.
   - *Court of Appeal Civil Division* This court hears appeals from the High Court, the Restrictive Practices Court, the County Court and the Employment Appeal Tribunal. The court reviews the records of the lower court and may:
       Uphold the decision made by the previous court
       Reverse the decision made by the inferior court
       Order a new trial.
   The judicial configuration is the Master of the Rolls and Lords Justices of Appeal comprising three judges.
4. *Judicial Committee of the House of Lords* This lies within the City of London, and constitutes the highest court of appeal in the English legal system apart from the limited jurisdiction of the European Court. It hears appeals from the Court of Appeal and occasionally cases direct from the

High Court. The judicial configuration is made up of Law Lords from the House of Lords where the Lord Chancellor may preside with a total of five judges sitting. The decision is based on a majority.

5. *European Court of Justice* This court consists of 16 judges sitting for a period of six years on recommendation of Member States, distinguished judges and legal experts. The jurisdiction of the European Court is in the following two areas:
   − Legal matters arising from the acts or omissions of Member States.
   − Rulings on matters which arise from EU law.
   In the latter case the judicial committee of the House of Lords upon hearing such a case is required to refer the decisions to the European court indeed any lower court or tribunal may do the same.

6. *Tribunals* They are judicial decision-making bodies other than courts or arbitration. They bear similarity to courts but do not operate within the decision framework, that is a rigid procedural and evidential structure. They are based on expert knowledge and decision making resulting in cheaper and quicker outcomes. Rulings from tribunals are generally only referred to appeal courts on questions of law. In many cases the right to appeal is very limited.

7. *Arbitration* This is often used as an alternative to court proceedings but may be used as a stage in court proceedings. It is defined as the determination of a dispute by one or more independent parties rather than a court. Arbitration works by both parties agreeing to appoint an independent arbitrator such as the Court of Arbitration from the International Chamber of Commerce or the Court of Arbitration of the London Arbitration Centre. Where there are two arbitrators, they will appoint an umpire in the event of both arbitrators failing to agree. Arbitrators are appointed by the parties in accordance with the arbitration agreement. The latter is a contractual agreement to refer an existing dispute or one that may arise in the future to arbitration. Often a commercial contract may have an arbitration clause which may automatically refer dispute arising out of the contract to arbitration. An arbitrator is bound by the law but may apply whatever procedure he or she chooses to and is not bound by the exclusionary rules of the law of evidence but must conform to the rules of natural justice (fair play, unbiased). Arbitration is very closely controlled and monitored by the courts to ensure the correct application of law by the arbitrators.

8. *Privy Council* This is the highest court of appeal in some Commonwealth countries.

18.3 The law of contract

A contract is a bargain by which goods are bought and sold. It is an agreement, freely entered into, which arises as the result of an offer and an acceptance, but once entered into it is legally binding. Hence, once you have reached your bargain, you must fulfil your side of it, no matter how inadequate the price, or consideration, agreed. If a party fails to fulfil their agreement, then the other can seek compensation. We consider:

– Offer and acceptance
– The consideration
– Functions of a contract
– Validity of a contract
– The sources of mistakes in contracts
– Duress and undue influence
– Terms and representations
– Termination of obligations
– Remedies.

Offer and acceptance

A contract results from an offer and acceptance. In establishing a contract it is essential to identify the point at which one party (the offeror) proposes that a contract be made (the offer) and the other party (the offeree) expresses agreement (the acceptance). The following conditions apply:

– An offer or acceptance made by letter is valid from the moment it is posted, but if made by any other means, from when it is received (see Case 18.1).
– The offeror may revoke the offer any time prior to acceptance (Case 18.1).
– An offer is rejected if the offeree makes a counter offer.
– Once acceptance is made, no new terms and conditions can be introduced unless mutually agreed.
– The terms and conditions are as stated in the offer and acceptance rather than the unexpressed intentions of both parties.
– Until there is an agreement either party may withdraw from the incompletely formed transaction.

Special types of offer and acceptance include the following:

TENDERS

A tender is an offer to supply or purchase, goods or services. The process of tendering does not constitute an offer to proceed to the acceptance of any tenders. Submitting a tender cannot compel the person seeking a tender to accept it or any other tender. Generally it falls to the person submitting the tender to make the offer and the person issuing the tender to accept it. The only exception to this is where those parties issuing the tender state that the lowest (or highest) tender will be accepted.

BIDS

The law surrounding bids is similar to that of tenders except that the term bid relates to the process of auction. Where parties are invited to make offers (bids) competitively. Where the auction states that there is no reserve, the highest offer is bound to be accepted. An offer may be extended for a reasonable period of time if there is not a limit expressed for acceptance. What is reasonable depends on the context of the case.

UNILATERAL CONTRACTS

Also known as 'IF' contracts. The offeror is deemed to have included in the offer a term providing that the described performance by the offeree will be a sufficient acceptance and communication is not necessary. The offeror is bound when the offeree performs whatever act is required of him or her according to the terms of the offer.

LETTERS OF INTENT

These are often used to set out the terms of agreement as negotiated. The decision as to whether a binding contract has been made is very much determined by the intentions indicated by the words and phrases used and other relevant background information. Courts will readily imply a term into the later contract where a party commences work outlined in the letter of intent making the later formal contract retroactive. However, there are obvious risks associated with undertaking work before the formal contract has been executed as there is a risk it may never be executed and therefore there is no binding contract.

Consideration

A contract must involve a consideration, or payment. A consideration is rather awkwardly defined as:

> an act, forbearance, or promise by one party with another that constitutes the price for which they buy the promise of the other.

A contract without consideration is said to be *nudum pactum*, or naked contract, and is invalid (see Cases 18.2 and 18.3). Consideration is governed by three main elements:

Case 18.1 Quernerduaine v. Cole (1883)

Q made an offer to C by post. C made a counter offer by telegraph. Q immediately posted a letter accepting the counter offer, but by the time it reached C he no longer wished to enter the contract. Q claimed that a contract had been made.
Held The fact that the counter offer had been made by telegraph indicated an implied condition that prompt acceptance was required. The purported acceptance by letter reached C after the counter offer had lapsed. No contract was made.

Case 18.2 Foulkes v. Beer (1884)

B was owed money obtained under a court judgment against F. She agreed to accept payment by instalments on the agreement she would take no further proceedings. Although interest is accrued on the debt from the time of the judgment until it has been paid, the agreement made no reference to the payment of interest. F paid the debt of £2090 but pleaded consideration when B commenced proceedings to recover the interest payable on the debt.
Held B was entitled to take proceedings for the interest. No consideration had be given by F for the promise by B to waive her rights against him. Therefore there was no binding promise on her.

Case 18.3 William v. Roffey Bros (1990)

The defendant, a building contractor, contracted with the plaintiff to undertake refurbishment of a block of flats for £20 000. Interim payments were agreed and paid, but the plaintiff had under-priced the work and failed to supervise his men properly. As the contractors were liable for liquidated damages if the work was not finished on time they agreed to pay the plaintiff an extra £10 300 to ensure that he continued with the work and completed it on time. The plaintiff wanted interim payments on the additional amount.
Held The plaintiff was entitled to interim payments on the flats in which he completed work after this second agreement and the defendants appealed on the ground that there was no consideration for it. The Court of Appeal held that in the absence of fraud or economic duress, one contracting party had agreed to make a payment to the other over and above the contract price in order to obtain a benefit (viz. the completion of the contract on time and thereby the avoidance of having to pay liquidated damages – curiously called a penalty clause in the report of the case – to a third party). There was consideration for the benefit received. The defendants hoped, by making the additional payment, that they would avoid the penalty payment due under the main contract and would not be put to the inconvenience of hiring a new subcontractor. This amounted to consideration even though the plaintiff was not required to undertake any further work than he had been originally required to do.

1. *Valuable consideration* The act, forbearance or promise must have some economic value. Good consideration (such as moral duty) is not sufficient to render a promise enforceable.
2. *Sufficient consideration* Consideration must be sufficient but need not be adequate. This means that there must be some economic value, but it need not be realistic.
3. *Movement of consideration* Consideration must move from the promisee. For example, if X promises to give Y £5000 in return for Y placing a contract with Z, Z cannot enforce Y's promise as Z has supplied no consideration for it.

Functions of a contract

Wright[1] says a contract should fulfil three functions:

1. *Normal performance* A contract should define what is expected from each party, and how their performance may be allowed to vary under certain circumstances within the contract.
2. *Sharing of risk* As we have seen, contracts involve risk. The seller, especially, is exposed to considerable risk. A contract should define how risk is to be shared between the parties.
3. *Coping with problems* We hope that our contracts will work perfectly, but they often involve problems. The contract should define how the more predictable problems are to be dealt with.

Validity of the contract

For a contract to be valid:

- There must be an intention to create legal relationships.
- The contract must be legal.
- It must not be contrary to public interest.
- It may be written or verbal.
- It may be signed or sealed.
- The parties must have the capacity to contract.

INTENTION TO CREATE LEGAL RELATIONS

There must be an intention to create legal relations. In most commercial arrangements this is evident. This differs from a family environment where there is a presumption that there was no intention to create legal relations. This intention is tested by whether a reasonable man would consider that the parties intended to create legal relations.

LEGALITY OF THE CONTRACT

The agreement must be legal. It must conform to legal requirements to enforce the contract, that is oral, part written, written or in certain circumstances by deed. The agreement must not be rendered void by some common law, statutory rule or defect such as a misunderstanding about a fundamental aspect of the contract. Furthermore, other factors such as the exercising of undue influence (blackmail) will void the contract.

CONTRARY TO PUBLIC INTEREST

Some contracts while not being illegal are considered to be against public policy. For instance they might:

– Oust the courts from their jurisdiction
– Strike at the institution of marriage
– Impede parental duties
– Restrain trade.

The contracts are void only so far as public policy is contravened. Contracts of this type are binding, excluding those clauses that contravene public policy. Typical restraint clauses relate to the protection of confidential information or proprietary rights. An employer is entitled to apply such a restraint clause on a former employee. However, a restraint clause that seeks to restrict an employee from using his or her skill in competition is always void. On the other hand, courts in general are more likely to uphold a restraint clause where a vendor of the goodwill of a business undertakes not to compete with the purchaser. However, restraints of this type are generally void unless there is a definite proprietary interest. For restraint clauses imposed as part of trading agreements, the guiding principle is that agreements between merchants, manufacturers and others will not be regarded as reasonable unless each party derives some advantage from them.

WRITTEN VERSUS VERBAL

In theory, there is no difference between written and verbal contracts. In practice, however, it is easier to prove the agreed terms and conditions in a written contract. If you make a verbal contract, you should therefore try to agree the terms in writing as quickly as possible.

A written contract can be made under signature, or under seal. The only difference is in the event of breach; in the second case damages can be sought for up to 12 years later, whereas in the first only six years.

ABILITY TO CONTRACT

The parties must have the capacity to contract. Corporations formed by Royal Charter have the full capacity to contract. A statutory corporation only has the power to contract for the services for which it was incorporated. In most cases, any person has the legal capacity to enter into a contract except a person who is insane, drunk, a minor or a corporation. Contracts with minors are governed by Acts of Parliament. The Infants Relief Act protected minors from entering into an unwise or binding agreement. This Act was recently repealed and replaced by the Minor's Contracts Act (1987) which moved in favour of those contracting with minors and away from protecting the minors. Corporations are limited by the Companies Act (1985) to entering into contracts within their Articles of Association. Contracts falling outside any of these areas are known as *ultra vires*. The Act protects third parties in their dealings with companies, but only where the transaction is decided on by a director.

Mistakes in contract

Lord Denning defined mistakes in two forms:

– Mistakes which render the contract void (which is the kind of mistake that was dealt by the courts of common law).
– Mistakes which render the contract not void but voidable (that is likely to be set aside and dealt with by the court of equity).

There are two major types of mistake: common mistake; and operative mistake.

COMMON MISTAKE

Where both parties are under the same misapprehension of offer and acceptance. Common mistake is applicable only where the mistake affects the validity of the contracts:

– Mutual mistake occurs where both parties have negotiated at cross-purposes.

– Unilateral mistake occurs when one party is mistaken and the other party is deemed to have known about the mistake. For example, A makes an offer to B. The offer is then accepted by C. In this situation where the offer does not correspond to the acceptance consequently the contract is highly dubious.

OPERATIVE MISTAKE

This constitutes a mistake of fact which prevents the formation of the contract and one which any court of law will declare as void. Types of operative mistake include:

– Non-existence of the subject matter of the contract.
– Fact fundamental to the agreement.
– Mutual mistake as to the identity of the subject matter of the contract.
– Unilateral mistake in the offeror expressing his or her intention, with the mistake being known to the offeree.
– Unilateral mistake as to the nature of the a document signed or sealed.

Duress and undue influence

Duress occurs in common law where a party enters a contract under violence or threatened violence, dishonour or false imprisonment to themselves or their family. Coercion of this type is classified as legal duress and typically applies when it is exercised by another party with the knowledge of the party. Undue influence in Equity occurs where a party enters under any kind of contract that prevents him or her from exercising a free and independent judgement. This requires the plaintiff to demonstrate that the influence was exerted by the other party or his or her agent. There are two forms of influence:

1. *Presumed influence* This arises where the relationship of the parties is such that one relies on the confidential advice of the other, and thus the second party can dominate the first. Examples are the relationship between a doctor and a patient, or a religious leader and a member of that faith. In countering a case of presumption, the defendant must show:
   – Consideration moving from the dominant party was at least adequate.
   – The plaintiff had the benefit of competent, comprehensive independent advice (full disclosure of all the material facts).
   – In the case of gift by deed, the gift was made spontaneously.
2. *Economic duress* This falls within the context of undue influence. Lord Scarman stated that:

There is nothing contrary to render a contract voidable, provided always that the basis of such recognition is such that it must always amount to coercion of will which vitiates consent.

In bringing a case of economic duress a plaintiff is required to show that:
- He or she entered the transaction unwillingly with no real alternative but to submit to the defendant's demand.
- Consent to the transaction was exacted by the defendants' coercive acts.
- The transaction was repudiated as soon as the pressure on him or her was released.

Case 18.4 North Ocean Shipping Co. v. Hyundai Construction Co.

HCC agreed to build a tanker for NOSC for US$30 950 payable in five instalments. The contract required the builders to open a letter of credit for the repayment of the instalments in the event of their default in performance. After the payment of the first instalment, HCC claimed an increase in of 10 per cent on the remaining instalments. There was no legal basis for the claim and NOSC rejected it. However, NOSC later agreed to pay the extra 10 per cent in return for which HCC would increase its letter of credit by the corresponding amount. All further instalments were paid as agreed. There was no protest regarding the additional 10 per cent until six months after the delivery of the ship. NOSC argued the agreement to pay the additional money was void for the lack of consideration and that the 10 per cent was recoverable as money had been received or, alternatively, that the agreement to pay was under economic duress and, thus, voidable.
Held The agreement to pay the additional 10 per cent was binding since it was supported by the HCC letter of credit. Further, although the agreement to pay the additional money might have been voidable under economic duress, NOSC'S failure to protest against the requirement for six months after the delivery amounted to an agreement. The shipping company was not therefore entitled to the return of the 10 per cent.

Case 18.4 in particular demonstrates the situation where a more proactive approach to law could have provided a way out for the plaintiff. If NOSC had not required HCC to alter its letter of credit making the contract voidable for the lack of consideration, and if the company had protested immediately on completion, the increase may have been voidable as a result of undue influence.

Terms and conditions

The terms of a contract determine the extent of involvement for the parties contracted. In a breach of primary obligations these may be substituted by secondary obligations, such as paying financial compensation for the breach. The terms of a contract must not be vague. A vague contract will fail, and meaningless terms will in general be ignored. A court will construe a contract as follows:

- Words have their ordinary literal meaning except in the case of legal terms which will have their technical meaning.
- Where a contract is sufficiently ambiguous to have a legal and an illegal meaning the legal meaning will be preferred.
- Where the meaning of the words is not clear, or where two terms cannot be reconciled, the intention of the parties will prevail in the interpretation of the terms – this can be to the extent where an oral term prevails over a written term if the intention supports the oral term.
- Where a contract has two conflicting ambiguous meanings the court will rule against the party that drew the contract up, *contra preferentum*.
- In construing written terms of a contract intentions of parties prior and during negotiation are not receivable during proceedings, but factual background known to the parties at or before the date of the contract is receivable.

Terms may be: express terms; implied terms; and conditions or warranties.

EXPRESS TERMS

Express terms are statements by which the parties intend to be bound. These can be material statements made during the negotiation process, and can be divided into:

- Statements made which were intended to be binding.
- Statements made which were not intended to be binding.

IMPLIED TERMS

There are certain circumstances where terms that have not been expressed by parties are inferred by law. An implied term is binding to the same extent as an express term. An implied term can be:

- To give effect to the presumed but unexpressed intentions of both parties; to assess the unexpressed but presumed intentions the court may examine the trade customs, the conduct of the parties and the desire of parties for the contract to succeed (business efficacy).
- Imposed by statute, such as the Sale of Goods Act (1979), the supply of

Goods and Services Act (1982), and relevant EU directives.
- A consideration is given where none is specified – in this case it must be realistic.

Implied terms may be excluded as express terms.

CONDITIONS OR WARRANTIES

A term which goes to the essence of the contract is regarded traditionally as a condition. All other forms of term are regarded as warranty. This status is significant in determining a breach of contract. Traditionally, breaking a condition of a contract allowed the other party to be discharged from all contractual obligations and sue for damages. However, the more modern approach considers the nature of the events to which the breach gives rise.

Termination of obligations

Termination of obligations or discharge of contract takes place by:

- Performing the contract
- Expressing agreement which may involve either bilateral discharge or unilateral discharge
- Frustration of contract
- Breach of contract.

DISCHARGE BY PERFORMANCE

The carrying out of obligations under a contract discharges the contract completely. Performance by one party discharges that party alone. The rules relating to this doctrine distinguish between a divisible contract and an indivisible contract. In a divisible contract the obligations of each individual party are independent of the obligations of each other. However, the majority of contracts are indivisible, that is the contractual obligations are interdependent. In such situations, neither party can demand payment unless they have performed their obligations or are prepared to do so. In its common law form, this law could render a party, which was short of the contractual obligations even in some slight defect, ineffective in claiming for work carried out until the contractual obligations were completed in full. However, this position was revised by the inclusion of the doctrine of substantial performance, which allows a party which has discharged the substantial amount of his or her duty to demand payment.

Discharge by agreement occurs in one of three ways:

1. *Discharge by subsequent binding contract* This can be in the following forms:
   - Where the contract is wholly executory, that is neither party has completed the undertaking.
   - Waiver where a contract may be discharged by mutual waiver – that is there is a new contract under which each party agrees to waive the rights of the old contract in consideration of being released from their obligations of the old contract.

   Where a contract is partly executory, that is one party has completely fulfilled his or her contractual obligations and something remains to be done about the other party that has not, then the first party may waive the rights in one of two ways:
   - *Release* The party to whom the obligation is owed may release the other party under seal as the release is given for no consideration.
   - *Accord and satisfaction* The party to whom the obligation is owed may accept something different in lieu. Where the party owed the obligation consents to accept something in lieu but with the threat of getting nothing at all there is no true accord. The guiding principle is unless there is a new consideration there can be no satisfaction.
2. *Discharge by operation of the contractual terms themselves* Contracts may contain a condition precedent which must be satisfied before any rights must come into existence. Determination clauses are used to enable one of the parties to bring the contract to a close before completion. These types of clauses allow one party to terminate the contract on the serious default of another.

The principle of *estoppel* stops one party unilaterally releasing the other from the agreement, while expecting to be released from their obligations. The reason is the second party may have contracted with a third on the basis of the original contract, and will suffer damage if the first contract is not fulfilled. For instance, Y may promise to pay X £x for an item, and then agree to sell it on to Z for a greater amount £z. If X fails to deliver, then although Y saves the amount £x, he or she loses the profit, but may also be sued by Z for damages.

The general ruling is that a contractual obligation is absolute. If a party wishes to be protected against subsequent difficulties in performance, that party should stipulate for that protection. However, the doctrine of frustration has been developed to handle some exceptions to this ruling. The doctrine operates on the basis of that, if due to some event, the fundamental purpose of the contract becomes frustrated or rendered impossible of performance, so that attempted performance would amount to something quite different from what must have been contemplated by the parties when they made their contract. Such events are typically:

– Where there is total or partial destruction of some object necessary to the performance of the contract
– Where legislative change makes performance of the contract illegal
– Where death or illness prevents a party from fulfilling the contract
– Where an event which is fundamental to the contract does not occur.

The doctrine cannot apply to the following:

– Where there is an absolute undertaking for the contract to be performed in any event
– Where the event is covered by an express provision in the contract (for instance where the event is for example more catastrophic than envisaged, the contract may be frustrated).

If the event is introduced by one of the parties where the burden of proof is on the party making the allegation.

DISCHARGE BY BREACH

If one party breaks a condition of the contract, the other party may treat the contract as discharged. The injured party however, may (he or she has the option) treat the contract as still continuing and claim damages for loss. This principle is applicable in the broad sense but has faltered when applied to employment contracts.

Remedies

DAMAGES

Damages are defined as a sum of money awarded by a court as compensation for a breach of contract. Their purpose is to put the plaintiff in the position he or she would have been in if the contract had been fulfilled. However, this is controlled by the remoteness of damage; the extent to which the defendant is liable for the consequences of the breach. The defendant is liable, only if it was in his or her reasonable contemplation.

This means that the defendant has most likely contemplated the damage likely to result from the breach according to the usual course of events. Unusual damage arising from special circumstances is regarded within the defendant's contemplation if a reasonable man knowing what he knew or ought to have known, would have thought it liable to result. Damages are typically awarded as a lump sum where the plaintiff is entitled to full compensation for their losses. This is known as in *integrum resitutio*. Nominal damages are given for breach of contract as a token sum when a legal right has been infringed but no substantial loss has been incurred. Liquidated damages are a sum fixed in advance by the parties to a contract in the event of a breach. Unliquidated damages are a sum fixed by the court.

QUANTUM MERUIT

This particular claim is where a plaintiff sues to recover an unliquidated sum by way of payment for services rendered. This is a claim for reasonable remuneration. This remedy is appropriate under the following circumstances:

- Where there is an express or implied contract to render services, but no agreement as to remuneration, reasonable remuneration is payable. The latter is decided by the court (Case 18.5).
- Where contractual terms have been altered.
- Where the plaintiff has done work under a contract believing that it is valid while it is later proved to be void.

Case 18.5 Upton RDC v. Powell (1942)

There was an implied contract between P and the Fire Brigade for the services of the brigade.
Held Remuneration was payable by P to U for the services he had received.

SPECIFIC PERFORMANCE AND INJUNCTION

The court may order the defendant to perform his or her part of the brief instead of buying out of the contract by paying damages for breach. This typically applies to situations where the contract concerns the sale of land or one-off items that have little comparative commercial value to anyone outside the contract.

LIMITATION

The right to sue for breach becomes statute barred after six years from the date of the breach (or 12 years after the breach if the breach is under seal). The plaintiff's rights cease to be enforceable at law. A right to a liquidated sum, however, may be revived by acknowledgement in writing of the part of the debtor even after the limitation period has expired. If the defendant conceals the right of action by fraud (conduct judged to be unfair) the six year period only begins to run from when the plaintiff discovered or could by reasonable diligence have discovered the fraud. If the plaintiff is a minor or otherwise has a disability the breach of the contract only begins to run when the disability ceases.

Conclusion – a word of warning

The maxim which best applies to the use of law is prevention is better than cure. The time when a dispute passes through into the courts both parties have lost. In reality the strength in law lies in its deterrent value. The English legal system, which relies on case history, has with it an inherent risk of not going the way that subjective logic thinks that it should. Ultimately, using law to provide a mutually acceptable performance criterion and adhering closely to those conditions provides a process that is generally fair and equitable.

18.4 Impact of EU legislation

European Union (EU) legislation has a significant impact on the operation of both buyers and suppliers. It is important to have an understanding of some of the key articles of the Treaty of Rome, and of the directives of the European Commission as they can have a significant impact on the procurement policies of an organization. In particular, two directives, The Directive on Supplies and Services and the Directive of Construction Works, control procurement in the public sector, and the Utilities Directive controls procurement by the public utilities. In this section we consider:

– Community law versus national law
– The Treaty of Rome
– Directives relating to the supply of goods and services.

Community law versus national law

It has been established that where there is a conflict, Community law shall prevail over national laws. Nevertheless, the two systems complement each other. Community law and domestic law are interlocked and mutually dependent on one another.

An example of the relationship between the two legal orders is provided by the system of preliminary rulings introduced by the Treaties. When a national court is in doubt as to the interpretation of the Treaties (or with measures taken by the institutions), it may or must (depending upon the level of the national court involved) apply to the Court in Luxembourg for a preliminary ruling to clarify the meaning of Community law. This system helps to avoid conflicting interpretations of the provisions of the Treaties or the acts of the institution. Provisions of Community law are thus an integral part of and take precedence in the legal order applicable in the territory of each Member State.

Moreover, there is a principle of direct applicability of Community law; in certain instances, Community law confers rights and imposes obligations directly on Community citizens, as well as on Community institutions and the Member States. It has been one of the outstanding achievements of the Court of Justice to have enforced the direct applicability of some provisions of Community law despite the initial resistance of certain Member States: this has guaranteed the existence of the Community legal order.

Treaty of Rome

Many of the articles of the Treaty of Rome relate to the procurement of goods and services, and lay the foundation for the internal market. Some of the key articles and their impact are listed in Table 18.1.

Directives relating to the supply of goods and services

There are four directives relating to the supply of goods and services (Table 18.2).

THE SUPPLIES AND SERVICES DIRECTIVES

These control the procurement of goods, supplies and services in the public sector.

1. *Contract award procedures* Purchasers may use open or restricted procedures or, exceptionally, negotiated procedures with or without a call for competition. Negotiated procedures without a call for competition may only be used when:
   - No tenders are received under an open or restricted procedure.
   - Goods are for research and development purposes only.
   - Goods may only be supplied by a particular supplier for technical or artistic reasons or for reasons of exclusive rights.

Table 18.1   Impact articles of the Treaty of Rome relating to the procurement of good and services

Article	Impact
Article 3	Establishes the free market
Article 7	Prohibits discrimination on national grounds
Article 8a	Eliminates frontiers, allowing free movement of goods, persons, services and capital
Articles 30 and 31	Prohibits restrictions on imports between Member States
Article 37	Requires the progressive elimination of discrimination through state monopolies
Article 48	Secures freedom of movement for workers
Article 52	Allows nationals of Member States free movement
Article 57	Requires mutual recognition of academic qualifications
Article 59	Removes restrictions on freedom to provide services
Article 80	Outlaws imposition of transport restrictions
Article 85	Outlaws cartels
Article 86	Outlaws monopolistic practices
Article 90	Imposes the rules of the Treaty on state monopolies
Article 92	Outlaws state subsidies which distort competition
Article 95	Outlaws the use of internal taxation to distort competition
Article 100	Empowers the Council to issue directives
Article 113	Imposes a common approach to tariff and trade agreements
Article 189	Empowers the Commission to issue directives

- Extreme urgency resulting from unforeseeable events is involved.
- Additional deliveries are sought from a particular supplier because of the need for compatibility with existing goods or for technical reasons.
  The reasons for using restricted or negotiated procedures must be recorded by the purchasers and made available to the Commission on request.
2. *Advertising* Central government purchasers are required to publish advance notice of their procurement plans by product area, where purchases above the thresholds in each area concerned are likely to exceed 750 000 ECU (£562 500) per year in total. A contract notice advertising individual contracts must be placed in the *Official Journal of the European Communities* before the selection of applicants can begin or tenders be received, except in certain circumstances under the negotiated procedures. This notice must be in a standard format. When a contract has been awarded, the purchaser must also declare the result in the *Official Journal* in a contract award notice.
3. *Minimum time limits in award procedures* When open procedures are used, there must be at least 52 days between the dispatch of an invitation to tender and the deadline for the submission of tenders. In restricted and negotiated procedures, at least 37 days must elapse between the dispatch

Table 18.2 Four directives relating to the supply of goods and services

Directive	Type of supply	Lower limits ECU	£	Type of organization	Exclusions
Supplies	Purchase, lease or hire of goods	134 000 200 000	100 000 150 000	National government Local/regional government, QUANGOs	WETT Nationalized industry National security
Services	Procurement of services	134 000 200 000	100 000 150 000	National government Local/regional government, QUANGOs	WETT Nationalized industry National security
Works	Letting contracts for construction or civil engineering works	5.0 million	3.75 million	National/Local/ Regional government, QUANGOs Police forces	WETT Nationalized industry National security
Utilities	Supplies Works	400 000 5.0 million	300 000 3.75 million	Water, energy transport and telecommunications (WETT)	See 'Exclusions' on page 293

of a notice and the deadline for receipt of requests to participate. In restricted procedures, at least 40 days must be allowed between the date of dispatch of a written invitation to tender and the deadline for the receipt of bids.

THE WORKS DIRECTIVE

This controls the letting of contracts for construction or civil engineering works in the public sector.

1. *Contract award procedures* At present, purchasers may award contracts according to open or restricted procedures, although contracts may be let without the use of these procedures when:
   - No suitable tenders are received.
   - Only one contractor may carry out the works for technical or artistic reasons or reasons to do with the protection of exclusive rights.
   - Works are purely for research and development.
   - Extreme urgency resulting from unforeseeable events is involved.
   - Additional works cannot be separated from a main contract.
   - Under certain specified circumstances works repeat a previous contract.

- Exceptionally, works cannot be priced overall before the contract. From mid-1990, the use of single tendering was further limited by the introduction of negotiated procedures with one or more suppliers. Purchasers will have to keep a record of their reasons for using restricted or negotiated procedures and make this information available to the Commission on request. Contract award criteria imposed by the EU are listed in Table 18.3.

2. *Advertising* Purchasers are required to advertise individual contracts falling above the threshold of 5 million ECU (£3.75 million). They are also required to publish contract award notices. This applies even if the work is divided into lots, although lots worth less than 1 million ECU (£750 000) will be exempt if they total less than 20 per cent of the value of the work as a whole.

3. *Minimum time limits in award procedures* These are as above. However, in restricted procedures, the period between the date of dispatch of a written invitation to tender and the deadline for the receipt of bids must be least 40 days, although 24 days is allowed if advance notice has been given.

UTILITIES DIRECTIVE

The Utilities Directive differs from other directives in that it does not just apply to public sector bodies. It covers procurement of both supplies and works by public and private contracting authorities in water, energy, transportation and telecommunication, the WETT sectors, and was extended to cover procurement of services in 1994. The appropriate contract award procedures, requirements for advertising and minimum time limits in award procedures apply for supplies, services and works as above.

1. *Relevant activities* These are effectively the provision of WETT. In the area of energy, more detailed definitions are given:
   - The provision or operation of fixed networks intended to provide a service to the public in connection with the production, transportation or distribution of drinking water, electricity, gas or heat, or their supply to the networks;
   - The exploitation of a geographical area for the purpose of exploring for, or extracting, oil, gas, coal or other solid fuel, or the provision of terminal facilities to carriers by air, sea, or inland waterways.

2. *Exclusions* Various contracts are excluded from the provisions. The most significant are:
   - Contracts relating to the provision of water, electricity, gas or heat as an ancillary to another activity – water or electricity sales must not exceed 30 per cent of production and gas and heat sales 20 per cent.

Table 18.3   EU contract award criteria

Type	Objective	Criteria
Core (mandatory)		Whole life costs
		Technical specification compliance
		Acceptance delivery programme
		Appropriate quality
		Mutual acceptance of terms
		and conditions of contract
Options (at buyer's discretion)		
	Delivery	Lead time
		Completion date
		Acceptance project plan
		Start/completion dates
		Flexibility in delivery
		Delivered cost
	Quality	Certification
		References/recommendations
		Reliability
		Project quality plan
	Financial	Financial rating
		Currency considerations
	Technical	Production and design resources
		Proven competence
		Environmentally responsible
		Compatibility
		State of the art
		Proven technology
		Level of technical compliance
		Proposal verification costs
	Post-contract	Warranty
		Spares support
		Distribution (spares and service)
		Maintainability
		Initial training
		Drawings and manuals
		After sales and service
		Licence agreements (rate of royalties)
		Commissioning support
	People	Qualifications
		Manpower
		Attitude/past experience
		Project management capability
		Use of local labour

Table 18.3   EU contract award criteria (cont.)

Type	Objective	Criteria
Options (at buyer's discretion)		
	General	Safety
		Design rights and patents
		Political
		Subcontracting – how much, who to?
		National legislation
		Ease of communication
		Breadth of service offered
		Security of supply
		Tenders reputation for
		Making additional claims
		Country of origin
		Confidentiality agreement
		Options offered and flexibility
	Terms and conditions	Acceptance of client's T&C's
		Performance bonds
		Guarantees
		Liquidated damages
		Contact price adjustment
		Legal form of bidder
		(consortium etc.)
	Price	Whole life costs
		Price stability
		Currency
		Disposal cost
		Spares price
		Payment schedule

- Contracts for the exploitation of oil, gas and coal may be exempt if the Member State establishes with the EU Commission that the authorization to exploit was granted on the basis of objective criteria in a non-discriminatory manner.
3. *Significance for collaborative arrangements* In Chapters 7 and 8 we discussed collaborative and partnering arrangements. There is a view, sometimes expressed, that these are contrary to this directive. The situation is as follows:
  - *Single project partnering arrangements* Here the procedures laid down apply as they would for any lump sum contract.
  - *Long-term contracts* Here the directives and regulations recognize that utilities may wish to establish stable working relationships with a single contractor for a series of contracts. There are guidelines published by

the commission for 'Framework Agreements' that enable such a structure to be established. The Framework Agreement itself must be awarded in accordance with the procedures of the directive, details must be published in the *Official Journal*. Contracts can then be awarded under the Framework Agreement, without applying the regulations imposed by the directive. However, the Framework Agreement establishes rather a rigid partnering arrangement which may not suit the requirements of many utilities for stable, long-term arrangements with their contractors. Hence, the facility to award contracts on this basis may not prove as valuable as you might first think.

18.5 Summary

1. There are two types of law:
   - Criminal law
   - Civil law.
   Civil law is divided into:
   - Contract law
   - The law of torts.
2. Essential sources of English law include:
   - Common law
   - Equity
   - Judicial precedent
   - Statute.
3. A contract is a bargain made between two parties through an offer and an acceptance. One party, the seller, makes a promise, and the other, the buyer, gives a consideration for that promise. A contract has three functions:
   - Define normal performance.
   - Share risk.
   - Define mechanisms for dealing with problems.
4. The law of contracts defines:
   - Validity of a contract
   - The sources of mistakes in contracts
   - Duress and undue influence
   - Terms and representations
   - Termination of obligations
   - Remedies.
5. Where there is a conflict, European Union Law prevails over national law. Many of the articles of the Treaty of Rome establishing the European Community deal with procurement and establish the free market. There are four directives dealing with procurement:

- The Supplies Directive
- The Services Directive
- The Works Directive
- The Utilities Directive.

References

1. Wright, D., Contract law and contract formulation, lecture notes communicated privately, 1994.

19

The procurement process: selecting contractors and consultants

Rodney Turner, David Topping, Malcolm Watkinson and John Dingle

19.1 Introduction

Over this chapter and the next, we describe how the contractual relationship is entered into, first from the client's viewpoint, and then, in Chapter 20, from the contractor's viewpoint. Before choosing the contractors and consultants, the client must develop a procurement or contract strategy, and there are two steps in that:

– Defining the roles and responsibilities of the parties involved, and their likely contractual relationship.
– Choosing appropriate types of contract for the project.

We start this chapter by describing the roles and responsibilities of the parties to a contract and then how to choose an appropriate contract strategy. We then explain the process of selecting contractors and consultants.

19.2 Roles and responsibilities in project contract procurement

The traditional form of procurement, used in the construction industry, involves a client in a contract with a single contractor through a tightly drawn, inflexible form of contract.[1,2] The client is advised by, and the contractor supervised by, an independent professional architect or engineer. The professional is not a party to the contract but has a separate arrangement with the client, and has a role stated within the construction contract. Most often the professional has also been responsible for the design of the works and for producing the contract documents. Typical contracts of this type are the Institution of Civil Engineer's standard form of contract[3] used on civil engineering contracts and the Joint Contracts Tribunal Standard Forms[4] used on building works, and written by the Royal Institute of British Architects. The premisses upon which they were based, and indeed continue to serve well when used appropriately are:

- A well-defined project with detailed design substantially completed prior to commencing construction.
- Work types of general nature not requiring many specialist subcontractors.
- Low risk in design, materials, location (particularly ground conditions).
- Relatively short construction period (less than two years).

Although such contracts make some provision for design changes, subcontracting or unforeseen circumstances, their effectiveness is limited and use of these provisions is used sparingly or only when problems arise during construction. Increasingly, the limitations of such forms of contract have become apparent and since the 1970s interest has centred on contract forms which address the demands of modern construction procurement such as the ICE's new engineering contract.[3] This has led to different contractual and organizational relationships between clients, their professional advisers and contractors (Fig. 17.1). Nunos and Wearne[5] provide a more extensive model of the parties involved in a project and their contractual relationships (Fig. 19.1). This indicates the many different organizations, as distinct from departments within the client organization, that are likely to be involved in a contract. Hence, the development of an effective definition of these relationships is key to project success. There are three aspects to this: definition, allocation and communication:

- Correctly defining the *tasks* involved in design, construction and in all decision-making processes leading to commissioning of the project.
- Identifying an individual, department or organization uniquely and comprehensively with each task.
- Defining and creating the communication channels between individuals, departments and organizations which will ensure that project information is generated, communicated and acted upon correctly.

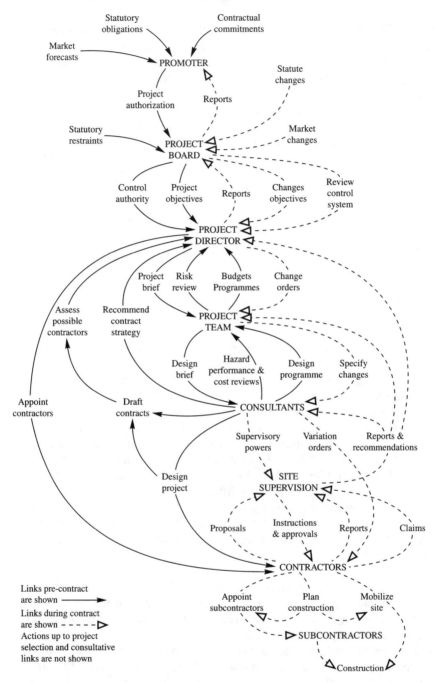

Figure 19.1 Responsibilities for construction

Each party must be given a brief specifying this as it relates to him or her. The brief may be a simple letter or a complicated as a set of contract documents in many volumes. It is instructive to note how the project management objectives flow through the hierarchy illustrated by Fig. 19.1. Project definition, for example, is indicated by:

- Project authorization between promoter and board
- Project objectives between board and director
- Project brief between director and team
- Design brief between team and consultant
- Contract drafting and contractor appointment between consultant/team/ contractor
- Subcontractor appointment between contractor and subcontractor.

Similar tracking of other aspects of the project in this traditional client/ engineer/contractor system illustrates technical and financial control and review procedures, as well as risk or hazard assessment.

On more recent forms of contract, such as target, cost reimbursable, construction management and management contract forms, the need for clear definition of responsibilities is even greater because these forms are not in general founded on the client/engineer/contractor principle. In the CIRIA report on management contracting,[2] considerable space is devoted to this issue. In CSSC's Report into Construction Management,[6] Part II – Guidance Notes – gives schedules of duties for each of four parties – the designer, construction manager, works contractors and clients. Different standard forms of contract translate these concepts into working practices in different ways:

New engineering contract[3]

Stated in the 'Core Clauses' of this form of contract are the names of the project manager, supervisor and adjudicator. The contractor is required to provide the names of up to three 'key people', their job descriptions, responsibilities, experience and qualifications. The core clauses go on to define the meaning of terms used in the contract, the manner of interpretation of the conditions, the form and status of formal communications, the status and powers of the project manager and the purpose of representation at management meetings. This leads on to a definition of the contractor's responsibilities, a requirement to cooperate with others involved in the contract, and limitations on scope for subcontracting (should trouble arise, which may not directly be the fault of any party to the contract). Disputes, arbitration and contract termination are dealt with in a separate section. Responsibilities for providing insurance are spelt out, as are procedures for payment.

A key feature of the new engineering contract is that the traditional role of engineer as designer, contract administrator and construction supervisor has been revised and there are now four recognized individuals; the project manager, designer, supervisor of construction and adjudicator of disputes. This policy was adopted to enable the modular form of the NEC to cover all forms of contract in which these tasks are combined in various ways. It also injects a greater degree of independence and freedom into the activities of the project manager, to remove conflicts of interest which could arise and allow more proactive approaches to achieving the client's aims. The core clauses of the six modular forms of the contract have sections defining the duties and responsibilities of these parties. There is nothing to stop a particular firm of professionals fulfilling more than one role, but the fact that the duties are separated allows individuals to focus attention on their particular role. (The ascendancy of project management throughout all industrial and service sectors of the economy, both public and private, will have been noted by the majority of managers at all levels.)

Institution of Chemical Engineer's model form[7]

This form begins with definitions, interpretation, contractors responsibilities and other general clauses. Clause 4.2 reads as follows:

> The Purchaser, through the Engineer, shall provide the Contractor with all such drawings, if any, as are to be provided by the Purchaser under the Contract and with all such further information and instructions as are necessary to be provided by the Purchaser to permit the Contractor to execute and complete the Works at the times specified in the Contract. ...

Schedules 1–3 which are provided under the contract provide a description of the works, drawings and operation manuals. Schedules are a typical and useful way of listing items of contractual importance or providing other contract-specific information.

The FIDIC Digest[8]

The FIDIC form is substantially the same as the ICE 6th edition, having 63 clauses. All these 'traditional' forms provide contract conditions based on clear definition of liabilities and responsibilities between three parties (employer, engineer and contractor). Actions in the event that the client changes his or her mind about the requirements, or the engineer (as designer) has made a mistake, or unforeseen weather or ground conditions arise, are dealt with as 'variations', and the procedure for dealing with them is well documented. The FIDIC form remains the most widely used form for major construction projects internationally. The *Digest* explains the many and varied clauses which define contract responsibilities, such as:

- *Clause 1.5* The Employer must provide in writing all notices which are his or her responsibility, and not unreasonably withhold or delay them.
- *Clause 2.5* The Engineer must give instructions in writing and to confirm any oral instructions in writing. The Contractor may confirm in writing any oral instructions of the Engineer.
- *Clause 5.2* The Engineer must explain and adjust ambiguities and discrepancies in the Contract Documents.
- *Clause 8.1* The Contractor must, with due care and diligence design (to the extent provided for by the contract), execute and complete the works and remedy any defects therein, in accordance with the Provisions of the Contract.
- *Clause 8.2* The Contractor must take full responsibility for the adequacy, stability and safety of all site operations and methods of construction.

RICS Project Management Agreement and Conditions of Engagement[9]

The Agreement is based upon a schedule of services to be provided for the management of building projects. The client and project manager agree a selection from 16 services (to which more may be added if required), from advising on site selection and the need for any initial feasibility studies, through appointment of consultants for design, financial management, construction management and securing tenancies for the building. Many of the services are those identified with the project manager and supervisor of construction defined in the NEC which is intended for civil engineering as distinct from building projects. This Agreement could be considered by any client wishing to engage professionals to assist with, for example, a project to build a new office or factory where the client's own organization lacks the resources to manage such a project effectively. The distinguishing feature of this form of agreement is that it envisages project management as being used at the very earliest stages in the project's life when critical decisions are being made by the client. Most other forms assume that the client has made the decision to build and defined to a large degree what his or her objectives are, before formal project management begins as part of the procurement process.

19.3 Contract strategy

Having identified the parties involved in the project, the client must choose an appropriate contract strategy, defining the type and form of contract to be used. In order to do this you need to:

- Select the procurement path.
- Draw up a contract plan.

Select the procurement path

One of the first client guides published on project contract procurement was produced by NEDO.[10] This publication suggested that when selecting the appropriate type of contract for project procurement, you use the following eight *Procurement Assessment Criteria*, (PAC). Table 19.1 shows appropriate forms of contract which should be used depending on which of these criteria are significant in the current project.

1. *Programme (timing)* NEDO[11] reported that, compared to contractors abroad, the United Kingdom built too slowly. There are two considerations:
   - Completion } The standard forms of contract say
   - Before completion } 'on or before the date of completion'.
2. *Variations* This can become an emotive issue as the causes of changes are brought about for the following reasons (Chapters 21 and 22):
   - *Client* Changes of mind, rethinks; reappraisals afterthoughts; add-ons; take-offs.
   - *Inadequacy of design* The thrust of CPI (Section 11.7) is to eliminate this high risk area.
   Both areas will result in extra costs and claims will occur, particularly in a low supply/high demand market.
3. *Complexity* Complexity is usually obvious and can be broken down into three main categories:
   - *Highly complex buildings* are structures such as hospitals, chemical plants, power stations, some processing plants.
   - *Medium complex buildings* will be high tech building, advanced services, signalling centres, bridges.
   - *Low complex buildings* are factories, warehouses, houses, retail units, railway stations.
4. *Product (quality)* This area is extremely subjective and subdivides into quality of:
   - Design
   - Materials and workmanship.
   NEDO (1985)[10]suggested three levels of measurement:
   - Basic competence
   - Good but not special
   - Prestige.

Table 19.1 Appropriate forms of contract to use depending on the relevant procurement assessment criteria

Procurement assessment		Appropriate form of contract	Qualification
Criteria	Sub-criteria		
Programme (timing)	Two-stage, complex	Design and build	
	Large, complex	Management contracting	
	Design complete }	Traditional	With CPI
		Accelerated traditional	By negotiation
Variations	Changes likely }	Management contracting	
		Traditional	
		Design and build	Expensive changes
Complexity	Highly complex	Management contracting	
		Construction management	
	Medium complexity	Traditional	
	Low complexity	Design and build	
Product (quality)	Prestigious	Management contracting	with CPI
	Good but not special	Traditional	with CPI
	Basic competence	Design and build	
Price	Unknown	Management contracting	
		Construction management	
	Uncertain	Traditional	
	Certain	Design and build	Turnkey
Competition	Low (novel product)	Management contracting	
		Construction management	
	High (routine product)	Traditional	
		Design and build	Turnkey
Responsibility		See Figs 17.1 and 19.1	
Risk (Balance of product/ programme/ price)	In balance	Traditional	
	Product wins	Fee based	
		Management contracting	
	Programme wins	Design and build	
		Management contracting	
	Price wins	Traditional	By negotiation
		Cost Plus	

CPI, Coordinated Project Information (see Chapter 11).

Quality of design Like all organizations, architects, engineers and quantity surveyors rely on the *people* involved. Track record is therefore a vital issue in assessing the organization. However, in terms of administering and checking the quality and readiness of the design, there can be no better off-the-shelf system than using coordinated project information. This will allow the project manager to spot check his or her consultant's performance.

Quality of materials and workmanship BS 5750 can be referred to in the contract documentation. Currently very few contractors are accredited. It is, therefore, not recommended to be obligatory in contract documentation. However, many contractors are developing systems to meet the standard, and evidence of the existence of a quality process should be part of the contractor pre-selection process.

5. *Price* With price, the type of contract more determines the price strategy, than vice versa. The price will be certain, predictable but uncertain, or unknown depending on the type of contract (Tables 17.3 and 19.1).

6. *Competition* The level of competition will, to a certain extent, be determined by the novelty of the facility, which in turn will affect the choice of contract form:
   - If the facility is novel, the bid will require considerable design work, and so few contractors should be asked to bid – if large numbers are asked to bid, each will put in inadequate design effort to make the bid as the risk of failure is too high to justify the cost. Competition will therefore be low, and a flexible contract form should be used.
   - If the facility is routine, it will not require much design before bidding. Large numbers of contractors can be asked to bid. Competition will be high, and lump sum forms of contract can be used.

7. *Responsibility* The contract form will also determine the lines of responsibility and contractual relationships between the owner, contractor and subcontractors (Figs 17.1 and 19.1).

8. *Risk (the summation of the other seven)* Construction involves risk and is at best a compromise of existing circumstances consisting of:
   - Product
   - Programme
   - Price.

Achieving the correct balance is the essence of procurement. Table 17.3 also shows how the choice of contract strategy is affected by how risk is shared between the parties.

The contract plan

Having identified the parties involved in a contract, their roles, responsibilities and relationships, and having identified the procurement assessment criteria, you are able to draw up your contract plan:

- This plan should be developed early, as an integral part of planning in development of the project.
- The plan should take account of the project's context, and the influence these factors have on the project strategy.
- It should set out the way the project will be divided into contract packages, the interfaces between these, their relation to sources of supply, and the general method of managing contracts.
- The plan should consider alternatives, evaluating each in terms of resources, schedules, budgets, finance and risk.
- The plan should state preferences for contract types and aims, together with fall-back positions, in order to achieve the project objectives.
- It should indicate the required management organization in relation to the types of contracts foreseen, and a shortlist of preferred contractors, thus establishing the initial guidelines for negotiation.

19.4 Choosing contractors

Choosing contractors is about matching a contractor's resources to a particular project, and since the orientation of their resources is affected by their business culture, the methods we adopt to choose the best contractor for a job are not simply to do with quantitative measures of their resources (including the price they put on them). When we evaluate their response to the invitation to tender, ITT, we shall be looking to assess their attitudes to the project – their *capability* as well as their *capacity*. Contractors can have a range of business approaches, including:

- We sell what we can build.
  or
- We build what we can sell.
- Most of our profit comes from margin on what we supply, so we are interested in turnkey projects.
  or
- Most of our profit comes from variations, so we should mostly offer minimum scope.
- The contract price is the sum of costs, overheads, contingencies and profit.
  or
- The contract price is what the market will bear.

It is essential that contractor selection is carried out fairly, with rigorous adherence to a pre-defined procedure. Failure to do so can result in a loss of reputation for the client and his or her professional advisers, and ultimately increased costs. Managing the tender process is the duty of the engineer in traditional forms of procurement, or of the client's own departments or of the project manager in more recent forms. Any one project may require the letting of many contracts for different elements of work to a variety of contractors. On large projects such as power stations and process plants, the contract administration team will be a large department within the client or project manager's organization set up purely to carry out the administration process, including contractor selection, tendering and letting of contracts and may then go on to deal with payments, insurance and bonds required under the contract.

The steps in the process of contractor selection are:[12]

− Prequalification of bidders
− Issue of the invitation to tender, ITT, to selected bidders
− Tender assessment
− Contract negotiation and award.

Prequalification of bidders

The first step is to reduce the number of contractors asked to bid to between four and eight. The reason is simple: the more tenderers there are, the lower their chances of success and therefore the likelihood of them putting adequate resources into preparation, to reduce their bid to the minimum, is reduced. The client therefore fails to achieve the objective of obtaining the works for the minimum cost. Some clients, especially in the public sector, in pursuit of 'fairness', open every contract tender to all comers. This is not fair:

− To the contractors, who must invest a significant amount of time and cost in making a bid, with little chance of success.
− To the client, who must invest an inordinate amount of time fully evaluating every bid.

There are two approaches to prequalification:

OPEN TENDERING

Advertisements are placed in appropriate publications inviting prospective tenderers to write to the client or project manager expressing an interest in tendering for the works, which are briefly described in terms of content, location and estimated value. Often a prequalification form is required to be completed. From the response, which typically in the United Kingdom for public works may number up to 100, the select list is drawn up. This in itself is a time consuming process requiring subjective and objective judgements to be made regarding the suitability of each applicant. We saw in the last chapter that this approach is compulsory in a lot of circumstances under four directives from the European Commission.

SELECTIVE TENDERING

Because the open tendering process is time consuming, many clients maintain select lists for various types of work and ranges of contract values, from which to select, on a rotating basis, contractors to be invited to tender for a particular contract. Some client companies set up a 'contractor evaluation unit' to operate the data bank. Contractors are encouraged to keep the unit informed about recent project experience, changes in management and specializations, and other events which relate to the contractor's capability. The unit will re-evaluate contractors in the data bank whenever a particular project is in view, advising the client's project management department on those considered likely contenders for the job. The unit will also assist in the eventual final selection. Preliminary assessment will be against three key criteria:

1. The contractors must be financially sound, capable of interim funding of the works as required by the payment procedure of the contract, and not unduly exposed to outstanding debts and claims from other contracts to the extent that they could risk insolvency during the contract.
2. They must be technically capable of carrying out the works as demonstrated by a track record in the industry and the resources currently available to them, and have the organizational ability.
3. They should have a general performance record which is acceptable.

Secondary criteria which support the above include:

- Ownership, including parent/subsidiary relationships
- Management structure, with main lines of responsibility and communication
- Staff numbers and disciplines
- Proportion and assignment of temporary versus permanent staff
- Resumés of key people
- Work capacity of the main departments
- Current and projected workloads
- Location and type of offices and other facilities.

To assess these requirements, the client may need to obtain company accounts, commercially available financial reports, letters from the contractor's bank and possibly insurers, evidence from the contractor that he or she has the required experience and, where the contractor is not well known, an interview may be required.

Issue of the invitation to tender, ITT

Once the select list has been drawn up, each tenderer is issued with at least two sets of tender documents (one to return, priced; one to keep). The tender documents will comprise a variety of separate forms,[1] including:

- Design details or requirements
- Drawings
- Specifications
- Instructions on bid presentation
- Contract conditions.

Clearly, great care is needed in preparing the tender documents to describe what is required to be provided in the technical proposal. Recently, a government body in response to the first ever ITT received prices ranging from £17 000 to over £100 000 for what was ostensibly the same consulting engineering services. In such cases, it is apparent that the definition of what was required to be provided under the contract was inadequate and resulted in many different interpretations.

It is essential to state the date and time by which tenders are to be returned (any tenderer who does not comply should not be considered), and to maintain secrecy regarding the names of the tenderers (so that collusion is avoided). Queries arising from the tender documents should be answered by letter (or fax) and any substantive change which arises from a query or amendment during the tender period must be communicated to all tenderers. Construction contracts normally allow a minimum of one month, and up to two may be allowed where there is a contractor's design element involved. Contractors are always free to propose alternatives. However, they should be required to comply with the bid documents (including alternatives) and be required to explain the reasons for alternatives.

While the contractors are preparing their tenders, the owner should prepare their own, including an estimate of how much the work will cost, called a Fair Price Estimate, FPE. This dummy tender will be used as a yardstick to judge the bidders tenders.

Evaluation of tenders

Once the priced tenders have been returned the contract administrator must carry out an appraisal of the bids. Appraisal may be against two or three key criteria, respectively:

- Compliance with the bid
- Price
- Compatibility.

A detailed list of criteria acceptable to the European Commission is given in Table 18.3.

1. *Compliance* The bids should be checked to ensure they are technically compliant. If one is not compliant it can be rejected outright. If the contractor has put forward a good argument why the proposal is acceptable, and it is decided to accept the change, then to be fair, you must offer the other bidders the chance to revise their bids against the change.

2. *Price* If the tender is on a single payment, lump sum basis then there is little to do. If, however, a complicated pricing system such as a full bill of quantities is used, which may have hundreds or possibly thousands of items of work individually priced, appraisal takes some time. Note that the EU contract award criteria actually say life cycle cost, not price. Hence you are allowed to take account of the quality of the product, and its availability, reliability and maintainability, ARM. You expect the prices to be similar. Assuming that the bids do comply with the ITT, that is, they cover the same scope of work and extent of supply, the bid prices may differ for a variety of reasons. Among the most common are:

- Something has been omitted from the bid price.
- Allowances and/or contingencies have been wrongly estimated.
- Financing proposals are inappropriate.

Since these, and similar factors, may feature in one, several, or all of the bids received, their existence may be identified by the owner comparing with his or her own estimate of how much the work should cost, the FPE. If something has been omitted, it may be due to a misunderstanding, or carelessness, or deliberate intent. In any case, it is better to clear up the reason in discussion, not to try to take advantage later. (Deliberate omission of items in the bid price may be construed as an attempt to win later on 'variations to contract', or change orders, and dealt with accordingly!)

Allowances and contingencies are the contractors' confessions of ignorance, sometimes about circumstances where they have insufficient information (and where the owner should be willing to provide, if possible, additional information so as to reduce the allowance), sometimes about circumstances where their experience leads them to expect some additional costs (quite usual: only the amount of the contingency may be disputed). Often however, the total of allowances and contingencies includes double (even triple) counting, as when the project manager adds his percentage to the estimator's, and the managing director adds his on top. Comparison with the FPE helps to pinpoint these signs of risk management *non*-capability.

Increasingly, contractors' bids include proposals for financing the project. From the owner's point of view, the total price (i.e., including the cost of finance) is one thing, while the cash flow of funds to the project is another. Funds are required to match the phasing of project expenditures. If they do not, the project schedule is at risk. If they are more generous than the project requires, the contractor is financing something other than the project, almost certainly at an eventual cost which is higher than necessary. In some cases – as in export credit finance – the owner may gain from a disguised subsidy, but this has more to do with assessing the motives of politicians than with the merits of the contractor.

Some people argue that you should ignore the cheapest bid, as the bidder has almost certainly missed something (see Case 19.1). This is a sort of Butler Scoring approach to price assessment. Another practice you should beware of is to put in a bid with a very short validity period, shorter than the likely evaluation time. Sharp contractors will use this as a ploy of finding out what all the other contractors have bid, and then putting in a revised, higher bid, just under what the next cheapest contractor has tendered.

Case Study 19.1 Concrete at the Dead Sea

Contractors bidding for a construction job near the Dead Sea sought bids for the price of ready-mixed concrete, and received tenders of $US80, $US200, $US220, $US240 and $US400 per tonne. Clearly the fifth subcontractor did not want the work. However, the contractors thought they had struck lucky, and accepted the lowest bid, which they incorporated into their fixed price tender. When they came to take delivery, the subcontractor told them there was a delivery charge of $US180 per tonne from Tel Aviv!

3. *Compatibility* This has much to do with ensuring good communications. Many experienced project managers consider good communications to be

the most important single factor in running a successful project. It is easy to see how difficult it may be to achieve good communications in a project if you consider the flow of information between those who originate it and those who use it. Suppose there are n sources/users of information: then there will be $(n - 1)n/2$ interfaces between them. The number of interfaces grows very rapidly as n increases, and so does the number of opportunities for information to go wrong! Good communication underpins many of the factors to be taken into account in the bid evaluation, such as the method of project implementation, the use of resources, the organization and the project schedule.

Where tenderers have been asked to carry out some design work, for instance in submitting design-and-build proposals, the proposals will also require technical vetting to ensure that the proposed design and methods of working will meet the client's objectives. The client's contract administrator must take care during this period to restrict communication with any tenderer to those of clarification, if necessary; and in no way to negotiate a change to proposals or prices. If he or she believes that such is necessary, then he or she must do so with all tenderers on an equal basis. Once the choice of contractor is made, the outcome of the tendering process should be communicated to all tenderers. A legally binding contract is formed when an official letter of acceptance is written from or on behalf of the client.

Inexperienced clients often fail to understand that preparation of tenders is a time-consuming and expensive activity, both for the contract administrator and for the contractors invited to tender. In a recent tender for supply of engineering design services to a government body, 16 firms of consulting engineers were invited to tender. Each tenderer would have spent approximately £5000 of engineer's time in bid preparation. The cost of the employer's personnel in drawing up the tender and appraising the returns was around £25 000. Therefore the total cost to the industry was approximately £100 000. The services to be provided were valued at only £250 000. By contrast, the cost of preparing a bid for construction of a North Sea oil rig was recently put at over £1 million, but as there were only two contractors involved and the value of the work was hundreds of millions, this was considered an acceptable cost and risk by both tenderers.

Finally, we mention the 'two-envelope' system. This is a means of adding 'quality' to the competitive process as well as price, and is most commonly found in design-and-build forms of contract. The tenderer prepares a technical proposal which includes outline drawings, specifications and other information, to meet the client's stated objectives of functionality, appearance or other technical requirement. The client, in consultation with the contract administrator, selects *either* all those proposals which meet the requirements *or* only those which they particularly favour. The tenderers must know beforehand which criterion for choosing the technical proposals will be used. The latter is most commonly used when design competitions are held. Then, a straight choice on minimum construction cost is made from the selected second, financial proposals contained in a separate envelope. Those not considered on technical grounds should be returned unopened.

Contract negotiation

It is common in the private sector to choose from the tenders two contractors for final negotiation, and to enter detailed negotiation of their respective tenders against the contract award criteria. As this may involve the contractor in considerable additional work, you should impose the following self-discipline:

- No more than two contractors should be chosen for this stage.
- It should be clearly communicated to the contractors that you have entered this stage.
- No other contractors should be allowed to come in with a late revision to their bid.

The steps involved in this stage are described in the next chapter from the viewpoint of the contractor.

19.5 Choosing consultants

We have seen that consulting engineers, acting in the capacity of 'owner's engineer', have a position in the management of projects which is so well established that they have sections to themselves in many standard forms of contract. The new engineering contract identifies the 'Engineer's' role as:

- Project manager
- Design manager
- Site supervisor
- Arbiter.

The first is mandatory; the other three are optional. However, their role can be much wider. In this section we consider how to choose consultants and how to structure the assignment to monitor their performance, we identify standard terms of reference for consultancy assignments, and explain how to obtain value for money from consultancy assignments.

What kind of people?

The word 'consultant' is rather a catch-all title, and so it is worth considering what type of people are available, and pre-selecting the source before moving into the selection procedure proper.

1. *Body-shoppers* A form of 'consultancy' that flourishes in times of instability when either there is a surplus of qualified labour, or a shortage, body-shoppers offer to supply (or place) human resources. They usually accept no responsibility for the quality of the resource they offer, and for that reason alone should not be considered for any real consultancy work.
2. *Gurus* Occasionally, individuals arise whose every pronouncement seems to have the immediate authority of holy writ. They attract the simple-minded, and their casual remarks become the corner-stones of new ideologies. They may or may not say anything useful: that is not important. What is important is that *they* said it. Every ambitious consultant hopes to become a guru – preferably while they are alive.
3. *Employees* Large companies often employ in-house consultants. In fact, every 'staff' job is essentially an advisory role, and in companies which do not move people from 'staff' to 'line' assignments these are sought after by employees of a ratiocinative turn of mind. Contractor and equipment vendor companies (among others) also employ 'consultants' – often with that job title – in a sales role, providing advice to potential customers. It will be obvious that these consultants are not independent. Their advice is often valuable, when it concerns particular items of information to which they have privileged access, but it should be seen as inevitably biased.
4. *Academics* A special kind of employee consultant is the academic, who is available for consultancy work as a break from normal duties of teaching and research. Academics are useful for assignments: for example, those where the academic's speciality is directly relevant. However, academic eminence in a particular specialization is liable to spill over into more general pontification, which is always confusing and often dangerous, so that academics should be used as consultants only within the scope of a very clearly defined brief.
5. *Ex-employees* There are two classes of ex-employee consultants:
   – Those who have retired, and want to continue working, but part-time.
   – Those who have lost their normal employment, and have to do something while they look for another full-time job.
   Both may be competent, but are likely to be motivated in ways not entirely in line with their clients' needs. Retirees very quickly get out-of-date, unless they work hard at keeping themselves informed. This is easier for technical specialists than general managers. Indeed, the latter may

simply perpetuate the strategies which led to their retirement. In general, retirees can be extremely useful as members of consultancy teams where their separate skills can be blended and balanced for greatest effectiveness.

6. *Independents* In principle, independent consultants should be the ideal source of advisory services. They are motivated – so it would seem – exclusively by their clients' interests, and since they have chosen to leave the security of the corporate nest to fly alone, they must be pretty good at their job. Many clients do in fact take this Panglossian view of the world of consultants. The following short checklist may help to moderate any residual *naïveté*:
   - Is the 'independent' consultant an agent for any other business enterprise?
   - Are they a member of a partnership or association, and if so, how does this affect their personal responsibility for their professional performance?
   - How much of their work is for one client?
   - How much of their work is 'repeat' assignments?
   - What do they think about assignments involving a potential conflict of interest?

7. *Firms* Of course, many consultancies are *firms*. Firms, whether they are corporations or partnerships or other forms of association, are only as competent and capable as their people. If the association cultivates synergy between the individuals who make it up, it will be good (it will be 'greater than the sum of its parts'). Many consulting firms are subsidiaries of organizations whose main interests may well be inimical to objective advice. Consultancy about a project which may be constructed by the firm's contractor-parent could hardly be regarded as wholly independent. Indeed, this kind of linkage is often forbidden by the terms of reference for consultancy services, by which the successful bidder for consultancy is excluded from bidding for subsequent design or construction work on the same project.

Consulting firms often find it too expensive to retain the services of specialist consultants when they are seldom used. So they bring in – from classes (1) to (5) above – specialists on temporary, project-by-project assignments. In the extreme, a 'firm' might consist of a few high-powered salespeople and a good address book. This emphasizes the importance of assessing the *individuals* who will actually carry out the consultancy assignment, as well as the actual team organization in which the work will be managed.

The advantages of the consultancy firm are – or should be – to do with cultivating the synergy mentioned above. Continuity of experience – including the accumulation of relevant data – and consistency of management style, are instances. So is the availability of back-up resources and, if things go badly wrong, the resources to rectify or accept liability.

Making the choice (1) – Basic considerations

Whether clients are looking for an individual consultant or a team, they have a hard choice to make, and one where, if they get it wrong, they may cause major problems for their organization. What can clients do to make as sure as possible that their choice is the right one?

First of all, perhaps we should clear up the question of size. Clients, especially those that are unsure of themselves, often believe that they have to choose 'Big Name' consultancies, meaning those that have grown so large that their fee-income gets quoted in newspaper league tables. From the client's point of view, this may offer a let-out if (or when) the consultants' advice proves to be wrong as well as expensive. There is in fact no inherent advantage to the client in the size of consultancy. The client is paying for the quality of advice: and that relates only to the quality of the consultants working on their assignment, as individuals and as a team.

The Management Consultants Association has produced a set of guidelines, which is the basis of the following observations. Note that they all concern the *client's* attitudes of mind: if the client understands his or her side of the assignment, the chances are the assignment will go well and be productive: if not it almost certainly will not!

1. Accept that no consultancy can do everything. Any one that offers to do so should be treated with suspicion.
2. Understand that consultancies are also businesses. Find out how the consultants propose to manage their business while they are advising yours.
3. Meet the key people in the consultancy who will be responsible for your assignment, and make sure the people you meet are in fact the people who will do the work.
4. Be prepared to be quite open and frank in discussing the assignment with the consultants. Expect the consultants to be equally open and frank with you.
5. Realize that the only assignments which are free from conflict are trivial ones. In particular, several people on your side – including you – may resent what the consultants are doing. If you are not ready for this, you are not ready to place the assignment. If the consultants are not ready for it, they are not fit for the assignment.
6. Avoid open-ended assignments, which are bad for both the consultancy (which loses objectivity) and your own people (who get to be dependent

on the consultants) alike. One way to deal with large, ongoing assignments is to break them up into separate phases. Each phase is separately costed, and the next phase is authorized only on the basis of the progress demonstrated in the current phase.

7. Do not accept that the cheapest quotation is necessarily the best offer of consultancy services. Price alone is not the best criterion of choice for most things. It has to be taken into account of course, but in the case of the consultancy, it weighs rather little in comparison with factors such as capability, relevant experience and track-record, each of which, however, is extremely difficult to measure. This simply means that you are going to have to do some hard work in selecting consultants. In this connection, note that client pressures and the other forces of competition tend to lead both parties to underestimate the cost of consultancy assignments. Remember the old tag, 'you can have it by tomorrow, or you can have it right'. The best way to reach a reasonable balance between pressure of time and pressure of cost is wholehearted commitment by the client to the aims of the assignment. Sometimes this takes the form of a client's project leader (perhaps with his or her own team) who manages the assignment on the client's side, or the secondment of one or several client's people to the consultancy team, or simply providing the consultant's team leader with a company 'anchor' person who can set up meetings and generally get things done within the client organization.

Defining the assignment

Consultancy assignments tend to stretch, like elastic. It is important to define them so that this property can be utilized when it is advantageous to do so, but is rigorously controlled otherwise. For most reasonably substantial assignments, this is best done by preparing terms of reference for the assignment, which eventually become the basis of inviting detailed proposals from a short-list of consultants. The task of preparing terms of reference is in itself quite arduous. Sometimes, clients assign this work to consultants (who then must forgo bidding for the assignment to which the terms of reference apply). Whether undertaken in-house or assigned to an outside consultancy, a useful approach to writing terms of reference is to treat this like an engineering job: define the battery limits of the project (i.e. its concepts and objectives in time and space) and its tie-in points (i.e. where it interfaces with the rest of the organization and the outside world).

The terms of reference should contain enough information for the bidders to be able to show:

– How they propose to undertake the assignment
– Who they propose to do it

- The proposed programme of work, and schedule for delivery
- The quotation for fees and for other costs
- What are their requirements from the client organization
- Any differences in their concept from the terms of reference, their reasons, and how they propose to accommodate these differences.

It is in fact quite rare for honest consultants to have absolutely no difficulties in meeting clients' original terms of reference, so it makes sense to set up meetings with the possible contenders for a consultancy assignment to discuss all and any issues raised by the terms. Needless to say, clients must be prepared to provide the most complete information at these discussions.

The terms of reference for an assignment may contain the following sections:

- *Introduction* Provides a general review of the client's reasons for wanting the assignment carried out. It is usually very brief, and is intended merely to set the tone for the eventual enquiry.
- *Objectives of the assignment* Sets out as clearly and with as much detail as possible the client's view of the aims of the assignment. It may also specify supplementary objectives which concern long-term or peripheral aims of the client.
- *Basis of the assignment* Essentially sets out the client's view of the present business, and the organization's strengths and weaknesses, the resources available and any constraints affecting the eventual implementation of the consultant's recommendations. Further details may be given in appendices.
- *Scope of work* Simply specifies what the consultant is expected to do in the assignment. In addition to defining the conceptual scope of the work, the geographical and time horizon of the assignment should be stated. It is important that the expected *depth* of investigation should be specified: some assignments ask for detailed examination of short-term, but only superficial consideration of long-term, factors.
- *Proposed methodology* Requires consultants to indicate how they intend to carry out the assignment, and should indicate what details the client needs to be able to assess the validity of their approach. Consultants should specify here what resources they may need from the client in the course of performing the assignment.
- *Consultant team* Specifies details required of key team members, team organization and management.
- *Consultant's credentials* Specifies what details are required of the consultant firm's background, including references. If the consultant firm proposes to carry out the assignment in a joint venture with another firm, details of this – especially as they affect professional responsibility – will be called for in this section.

- *Assignment programme* Specifies required delivery of reports, review meetings, and other 'milestones' for completion of the assignment.
- *Fees and terms* Specifies the client's requirements as to timing of payments, conversion from per diem rates to firm fee basis, control of variations or extensions to the assignment, method, place and currency of payments, for fees and expenses. This section should also indicate the required period of validity of consultants' bids.
- *Confidentiality* This sets out the client's requirements for keeping assignment information confidential.
- *General considerations* This usually refers to general legal requirements (*force majeure*, proper law, etc.) but will also specify items such as: method of terminating the contract; procedure in the event of disputes; closing date for submitting bids; reasons for disqualifying bidders; procedure for selecting and announcing the successful bidder; addresses.

Short-listing

Defining the assignment is tantamount to allocating priorities to the problem which the assignment is designed to solve. A corollary of this is short-listing consultants. Just as with contracts, it is counter-productive to issue invitations to bid (ITTs) to all and sundry. Hence, prospective bidders should be prequalified, or *short*-listed. Short-listing implies an obligation on client organizations to know enough about prospective consultants to be able to construct a short list for any likely assignment. Client organizations are notoriously lazy about maintaining this kind of information: this explains why a large proportion of assignments are wasted or, at best, show poor value for money.

Making the choice (2) – Selection from the short list

Supposing that proposals are received from a properly drawn-up short list of consultants, how should one go about evaluating the proposals? There are a few basic criteria:

1. Does the proposal show that the consultants understand the terms of reference? There are, in effect, three levels on which this should be judged:
   - With respect to the assignment
   - With respect to the client organization, in particular its 'business culture', the opinions and attitudes of the decision makers which condition the way the client looks at its own business
   - With respect to the 'external environment': that is, the multiplicity of factors which influence the client's business without being in any way controllable by the client.

2. Does the proposed scope of work correspond with the terms of reference? If not, why not? The consultants may have very good, and acceptable, reasons for proposing work that does not precisely correspond with the TOR. These reasons must be made clear, and consequences explained, for otherwise it will prove difficult if not impossible to monitor and control the consultants' work.

3. Is the proposed methodology, programme of work, and method of reporting consistent with the proposed scope of the assignment and with the client's terms of reference (modified if need be)? In other words, if the consultants cannot show how they will undertake the assignment, it is not very likely that they will be able to carry it out satisfactorily.

4. Is the proposed consultancy team credible? This means, are the qualifications and experience of the proposed key members relevant and appropriate? Note that neither qualifications nor experience need be identical to the client's supposed requirements, but they should provide credible evidence of capability – especially ability to show insight – in the field under study. Of particular importance is to be sure of who will actually do the work. Most consultants can produce the CVs of a few distinguished individuals: what clients need to know is exactly who will be attending to *their* problem.

5. Is the consultant firm credible? This question mainly concerns formal responsibility for satisfactory performance of work. It is more to do with management experience of consultancy assignments (which is categorically different from management of, say, product marketing or project construction) and the organizational capability of the firm. For example, how will it cope with the unavoidable non-availability of one or more of its key team members? The consultant firm's credibility also depends on its background experience of working with similar clients – even your own competitors. In addition to the consultants' own representations, their credibility should be ascertained from other references: do not rely on what may appear in consultant registration documents.

6. Commercial terms. The consultants' proposal will (or should) contain references to items such as 'confidentiality', administration of the assignment, and the way any disputes should be managed. In practice, most client organizations are so much more powerful than most consultancies that the clients can always dictate these terms if they wish to do so. But the consultants' proposals in these respects are valuable pointers as to their attitude to the job. If the consultants demonstrate practical common sense in these areas, there is a good chance that they will handle the assignment in a similar vein.

7. Fees and costs. We have already discussed the pros and cons of low quotations. Basically, there are very few ways in which fees and costs can be proposed, and the essential guidelines are:

- If the scope of the assignment can be reasonably clearly agreed, the consultancy should be prepared to quote a firm fee.
- If the scope of the assignment cannot be defined (often the case in the initial phase of 'unstructured' problems) the client should be prepared to pay fees on a per diem rate basis. But this should be converted to firm fees as soon as agreement can be reached on definition of the scope of the assignment.
- In very few cases (typically long-term strategy development assignments, or assignments related to training) it makes sense to agree a retainer with consultants. The objective of a retainer is to give clients a priority claim on the availability of consultants when both the scope and the timing of the assignment are in doubt. When these unknowns are defined, the assignment should be brought within the framework of a firm fee or per diem rate agreement. (In other words, good consultants should try to work themselves out of their retainer agreements, despite its obvious attraction!)
- Expenses (typically for travel, accommodation and subsistence, but sometimes including items such as communications, computer time, and purchased services) should be reimbursable at net cost to the consultants. Clients who insist that these expenses should be borne by the consultants within their total price will pay more than they need: these expenses are not within the consultants' control, so if they have to provide for them, they will add in a contingency to cover the risk.

Clients should appreciate that consultants are not in business to provide financial credit. The phasing of payments to consultants should to ensure the assignment is effectively self-financing. If clients insist on a schedule of payments which undermines this principle, they, the clients, will eventually pay the cost, which is likely to be considerably higher than the cost of money to finance proper payments.

In making this choice, you also need to consider how these criteria are to be weighted. This will depend very much on how the client organization sees its own part in the assignment, for consultants rarely work in total isolation from the client. As an illustration, the weightings in Table 19.2 are fairly typical in the case of an 'arm's-length' assignment for a fairly enlightened client.

This procedure is by no means universally accepted. Some clients adopt a two-stage evaluation process, similar to the two envelope system described above, in which:

Step 1 The consultants' technical submissions are evaluated and ranked in order of technical acceptability.

Step 2 A separate evaluation team negotiates the price with the best

Table 19.2 Weightings of assessment criteria

Criteria	Sub-criteria	Weightings (%)
Understand terms of reference	The assignment The client organization The outside world	15
Scope of work matches TOR	If not, why not Is that reasonable/sensible	15
Proposed methodology	Schedule of work Arrangements for reporting	15
Appropriate team	Qualifications Experience Credibility	20
Firm credible	Credentials Organization Management Support Background Ownership	10
Contract proposals	Confidentiality Administrative provisions Resolution of disputes	15
Price	Fees Expenses Phasing of payments	10

technical bidder, and – if that negotiation fails – tries again with the next best technical bidder and so on until a satisfactory agreement is reached.

This two stage approach can lead to an unsatisfactory assignment, because it tends to lead to price haggling in which the technically superior bidders are invited to reduce their price to match that of technically inferior bids. Eventually, price reductions can be effected only at the sacrifice of quality. If you feel that quality is the prime requisite in consultancy assignments, you will judge this tendency to be unsatisfactory.

Monitoring consultants' performance

It is common sense for any buyer to take care that what they buy corresponds to what they were offered when the deal was struck. Clients for consultancy services often fail to do this, or try to monitor consultants' performance so closely that they actually interfere with the work in hand. In any substantial assignment there should be provision for the consultants to report on the status of their work at reasonable intervals. In short-term assignments this may not be feasible, but even then it is sensible for clients to see a draft report and discuss it with the consultants before the final report is completed. Note, this is *not* an occasion for browbeating consultants into changing their minds, or for leaping to premature conclusions. It is an opportunity to review data, and particularly to bring out into the open any assumptions that need to be made explicit.

In the main, interim reports are a nuisance and should be avoided. They prejudice the formation of well-founded conclusions, and they waste the time of consultants who should be doing serious work on the assignment. A better way for clients to keep abreast of progress is to hold fairly frequent progress meetings at which the consultants' project leader presents a verbal status report (with perhaps a simple one-page written summary) stating what has been achieved to date, and what the aims are for the period up to the next progress meeting. Note that phased payments are often linked to performance as marked by these progress meetings. This helps to ensure that they are taken seriously by the consultants.

No respectable consultants want to be associated with failure or poor value for money. No respectable consultants will therefore object if you want to monitor their work – although they will certainly object, and tell you so loudly, if your attempts to monitor get in the way of proper performance. The sensible approach is cooperation, not confrontation: this is perhaps the most important criterion affecting your use of consultants.

Value for money

How do you judge whether the proposal from your consultants is good value for money? So many variables affect the cost of consultancy services that it is almost impossible to give any guidelines for what costs 'should' be. Technical management consultancy is particularly difficult to generalize about: each assignment has to be assessed on its own scope and duration. However, the cost of studies for project investment relate to the cost of the project itself, for example:

- A 'scoping' or 'opportunity' study: 0.2 to 1.0 per cent.
- Pre-feasibility study: 0.25 to 1.5 per cent.
- Feasibility study (small-scale industries): 1.0 to 3.0 per cent.
- Feasibility study (major project): 1.0 to 5.0 per cent.

19.6 Summary

1. Before selecting contractors and consultants, you should develop a contract procurement plan. This should be based on:
   - An understanding of the roles, responsibilities and relationships

- The procurement assessment criteria.
2. Roles, responsibilities and relationships are identified. Appropriate assessment criteria include:
- Programme (timing)
- Variations
- Complexity
- Product (quality)
- Price
- Competition
- Responsibility
- Risk (the summation of the other seven).
3. The contract plan will identify the types and forms of contract to be used. It should:
- Be developed early
- Take account of the project's context
- Set out how the project will be divided into contract packages
- Identify the interfaces between these
- Consider alternatives
- Evaluate these by resources, schedules, budgets, finance and risk
- State preferences for contract types and aims
- Indicate the required management organization
- Establish the initial guidelines for negotiation.
4. The steps of contractor selection are:
- Prequalification of bidders
- Issue of the invitation to tender, ITT, to selected bidders
- Tender assessment
- Contract negotiation and award.
5. The steps in consultant selection and management are:
- Identify the consultants
- Set basic considerations
- Define the assignment
- Choose a shortlist
- Make the choice
- Monitor performance
- Obtain value for money.

References

1. Wearne, S.H., *Civil Engineering Contracts*, Thomas Telford, 1989.
2. CIRIA 85, *Target and Cost Reimbursable Construction Contracts*, Construction Industry Research and Information Association, Report No. 85, 1981.
   CIRIA 100, *Management Contracting*, Construction Industry Research and Information Association, Report No. 100, 1983.

3. Institution of Civil Engineers, *Conditions of Contract and Forms of Tenders, Agreement and Bond (6th Edition) for Use in Connection with Works of Civil Engineering Construction*, Thomas Telford, 1991.
   Institution of Civil Engineers, *New Style Engineering Contract*, Thomas Telford, 1992.
4. JCT 63, *Joint Construction Tribunal Standard Forms of Contract*, Royal Institute of British Architects, 1963.
   JCT 80, *Joint Construction Tribunal Standard Forms of Contract*, 2nd edition, Royal Institute of British Architects, 1980.
5. Nunos, G.E. and Wearne, S.H., *Responsibilities for Project Control During Construction*, School of Technological Management, University of Bradford, 1984.
6. Jones, R. (ed.), *Construction Management Forum: Report and guidance*, University of Reading, Centre for Strategic Studies in Construction, 1991.
7. Institution of Chemical Engineers, *Model Form of Conditions of Contract for Process Plants: Lump-sum Contracts (Red Book)*, 2nd edition, Institution of Chemical Engineers, 1981.
8. Sawyer, J.G. and Gillott, C.A., *The FIDIC Digest: Contractual relationships, responsibilities and claims under the fourth edition of the FIDIC conditions*, Federation Internationale des Ingénieurs Conseils, Thomas Telford, 1990.
9. Royal Institute of Chartered Surveyors, *Project Management Agreement and Conditions of Engagement*, 2nd edition, Royal Institute of Chartered Surveyors, 1992.
10. NEDO, *Thinking about Building*, National Economic Development Office, 1985.
11. NEDO, *Factor Building for Industry*, National Economic Development Office, 1989.
12. Institution of Civil Engineers, *Guidance on the Preparation, Submission and Consideration of Tenders for Civil Engineering Contracts*, Thomas Telford, 1981.

Bibliography

1. Burbridge, R.N.G. (ed.), *Perspectives on Project Management*, Peter Perigrinus Ltd (for the Institution of Electrical Engineers), 1988.
2. Kubr, M. (ed.), *Management Consulting – A Guide to the Profession*, International Labour Office, Geneva, 2nd (revised) edition, 1986.
3. Macomber, J.D., 'You *can* manage construction projects', *Harvard Business Review*, March/April 1989.

20
Winning contracts

Bart Bernink

20.1 Introduction

To be successful in winning contracts you need:

1. To know as much as possible about:
   - *The customer* Their needs, decision process and criteria, decision team, evaluation team, in-house supporters, preferences, etc.
   - *The customer's market* Its trends, what keeps the customer awake at night, his or her problems and needs.
   - *The competition* Their relationship with the customer, their available products and services, their position in the market segment, their previous experiences in similar projects in this market segment and outside, and how can both be converted into our benefit.
   - *Your own organization* Your relationship with the customer, the available products, services and resources, your position in the market segment, and your experience in doing similar projects in this market segment and outside.
2. To convert this information into themes to be used to define a winning strategy that will be saved in the 'win' plan.
3. To have a well-defined bid process which consists of information gathering, customer influence, proposal development and publication, and contract negotiation activities.
4. To have the properly trained people to do the job.
5. To have clearly defined roles and responsibilities.
6. To have well-qualified third parties and/or subcontractors.

Figure 20.1 describes the ideal process for winning a contract. The first three steps are similar to the first three steps of Coopers & Lybrand's *Contract Control Review Guide* (Fig. 20.2).[1,2] A guide to the tendering process has been published by the Institution of Civil Engineers.[3]

Potential bidders should also be aware that: 'unidentified RFPs are born

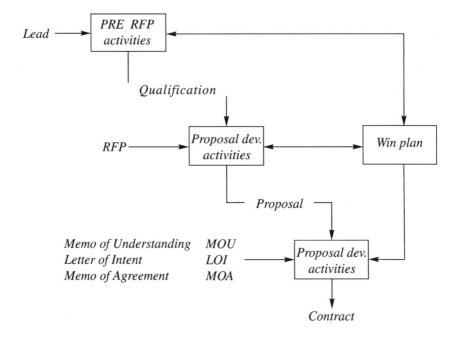

Figure 20.1 Ideal bid process

losers'. If a Request for Proposal (RFP) or Invitation to Tender (ITT) arrives unexpectedly in the post, the competition has already tried, more or less successfully, to influence the customer during the time they were writing the RFP.

The bid process can be divided into three phases:

- *Pre-RFP phase* To influence a customer as much as possible when the customer is writing the request for proposal (RFP).
- *Proposal development phase* To develop and present a winning proposal and execute the post-proposal submission activities.
- *Contract negotiation* To get the best contract for the company.

In this chapter we describe how to make successful bids. In the next two sections we introduce 'themes' and the 'win plan' as the backbone of your proposal. The bid process itself is explained in Section 20.4, and in Section 20.5 we describe post-bid reviews.

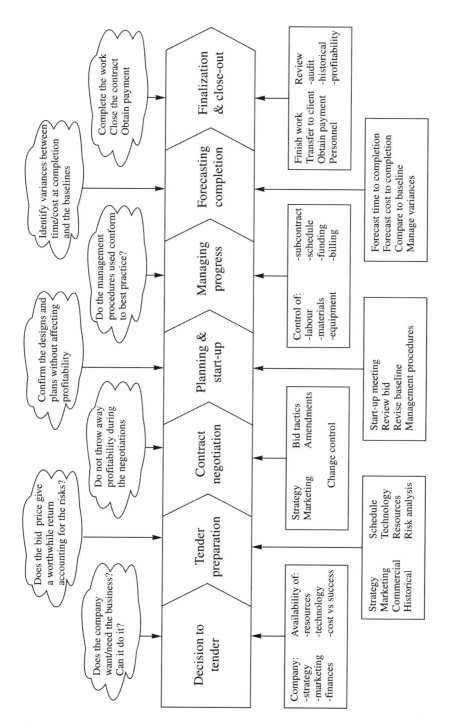

Figure 20.2 Coopers & Lybrand's *Contract Control Review Guide*

327

20.2 Themes

Themes are the conclusive reasons why the customer should select your company and not your competitors. The themes you define will all be used when writing your proposal and proposal presentation. They will set their tone, and identify your company's unique selling points. They are saved in the 'win plan' and will be continuously updated as a result of getting more information about the customer and the competition. There are three different types of theme:

1. *Common themes* These are customer driven, derived from the customer requirements and wish lists, and are common to all real competitors.
2. *Unique themes* These are contractor driven and derived from your SWOT analysis, and are unique for you.
3. *Competitive themes* These are competitor driven and used to neutralize your competitor's SWOT analysis.

The competitive themes will be used, if possible, during discussions with the customers before and after presenting the proposal. Possible themes are:

- A recurring thought
- A strength
- A major disclosure
- A discriminator
- A sound argument
- A platform
- A unique feature
- A competitor's disadvantage
- System integration capabilities
- Your reference list.

20.3 Win plan

Before you start the actual work, you have to develop a strategy that will help you to win the business. The win plan, sometimes called capture plan, contains your strategy for this opportunity. Therefore each opportunity has its own win plan. The win plan is a living document and therefore will be updated whenever it is necessary. The plan should contain the following information:

- Themes
- Circles of influence
- Customer contact plan

- SWOT analysis of you and your competition
- Customer seduction and intelligence gathering
- Influence strategy
- Influence the RFP writing activities
- Subcontracting
- Proposal development plan and corresponding schedule
- Proposal submission strategy
- Financial plan for developing the proposal.

You may need to update the win plan, for the following reasons:

- During interviews with one or more decision makers you find hidden needs – converted to themes.
- You obtain new information about the competition or action taken by the competition, customer decision criteria, decision team composition, etc.
- New products and/or services by the competition or your own organization are announced.
- Subcontractor teaming agreements are made.
- Team resources change.
- Budgets change.

The plan will initially be defined and maintained by the sales manager. As soon as you have been appointed as project/proposal manager, it is a joined responsibility. The sales manager manages the strategy part of the plan, you as a project manager will manage the actual work to be done.

20.4 Bid process

The bid process is the process to come to a winning bid (Fig. 20.3). It contains activities which start as soon as a lead has been detected and finishes after winning or losing the opportunity. You can therefore divide the process into three stages:

Stage 1: Pre-RFP When you try to influence the customer writing the RFP and to define the strategy after reception of the RFP. Your ultimate goal in this phase is to become the 'solid sound' and if that is impossible, to influence the writing of the RFP as much as possible so it will fit your company the most.

Stage 2: Proposal preparation and publication When you create a proposal, which is 100 per cent compliant with the RFP, and a proposal presentation, and you execute the post-proposal submission strategy defined in the 'win' plan. The goal of all these activities is to become the selected supplier.

Stage 3: Contract negotiations phase When you come to an implementation

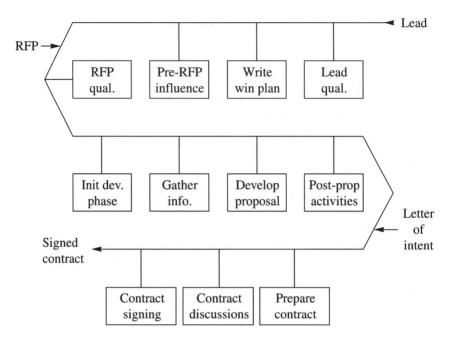

Figure 20.3   Major activities within the bid process

agreement with the most favourable terms and conditions for your company. The ultimate goal of this phase is a contract for designing and implementing the proposed solution.

The bid process will always finish with a post-bid review.

Managing the bid process

Because the total bid process is a project on its own, it should be managed by an experienced proposal manager. If you do not have dedicated proposal managers, the implementation manager should also manage the proposal development and contract negotiations. The account manager in this case will be responsible for the pre-RFP phase. Sometimes in small-scale proposals the account manager or account consultant can act as the proposal manager assisted by technical people. However, as you can imagine, this is not advisable because their primary job is selling and not managing project activities. However the overall responsibility is always with the account manager.

The project manager, who is responsible for implementing the proposed solution, must be part of the bid team, so that he or she understands the reasons for:

- Selecting a particular solution
- The implementation timetable
- Selecting particular subcontractor(s)
- Certain contracting aspects.

The implementation manager will present the proposal to the customer. From experience, a good presentation performed by the implementation manager will give the customer confidence that you and your company know the business and can implement the proposed solution within the proposed time frame and proposed quality.

Pre-RFP stage

The purpose of this stage is to define a strategy which will be used in the first place to influence the customer during the writing of the RFP and secondly to define a strategy for winning the business. Figure 20.4 shows the flow of activities through this stage.

QUALIFY THE LEAD

Projects involve taking risks – not only technical risks but also business risks. Therefore you should qualify each lead to identify possible risks. For each identified risk a contingency plan should be made. After you have performed the qualification, you must consider if it is worth while to continue. It is of course the management who makes the final decision. The qualification is a continuous activity. Whenever you receive more information, a better and more reliable qualification can be performed. Based on the outcome of each qualification you should ask yourself the question: 'shall we continue or shall we stop because we are wasting our time and money?'

Typical qualification areas and subsidiary topics might include:

1. For your own organization:
   - Do we have the resources available for proposal preparation project?
   - Do we have the resources available for implementing the proposed solution?
   - How strong is the competition?
   - Do we have a solution?
   - Do we have standard products and services?
   - Does it match future products and services?

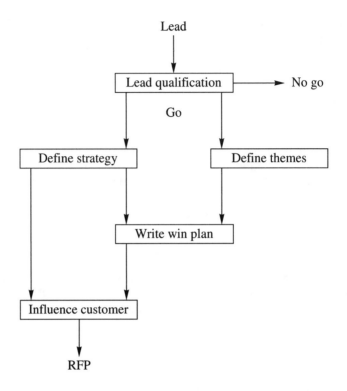

Figure 20.4 Pre-RFP activity flow

- Are there high performance requirements?
- Is compliance required with a particular standard such as ISO 9000, IEEE, etc.?
2. For subcontractors:
    - What is their financial situation?
    - Do they have a solution?
    - What is our experience with this subcontractor?
    - Is the subcontractor a preferred subcontractor by the customer?
3. For the customer:
    - Does the customer have a budget?
    - Does the customer knows what he or she wants?
    - Who are the in-house supporters?
    - Is the customer cooperative?
    - Are there special quality standards required?
    - Are there in-house references?

4. For the business area:
   – Does the opportunity fit in with our market strategy?
   – Do we have references in the market?
   – Are we known in this market?
   – Is this a new market?
5. For the terms and conditions of the contract:
   – Are there complex acceptance criteria expected?
   – Is a third party involved?
   – Are there special terms and conditions?
   – Do we have turnkey responsibility?
   – Do we have subcontractor responsibility?

DEFINE THEMES

Based on the existing information the first common, unique and competitive themes are defined. More themes can be added, existing themes can be deleted or modified, if more information becomes available.

DEFINE STRATEGY

This step is one of the most important steps within the pre-RFP phase. Consider what will happen if you did not do your homework well. You give the competition the opportunity to fully influence the customer when writing the RFP and even during the decision-making period. You can divide your strategy into three parts:

Part 1 : Influencing the customer during the writing of the RFP This part is used to brief the customer on your proposed technical approach and technology, to find out the customer's hidden needs and to offset the competition. Ways in which you can influence the customer might include:

– Making site visit and executive tours.
– Getting more in-house supporters/sponsors.
– Giving presentations and demonstration.
– Inviting the customer to conferences and/or seminars.
– Emphasizing your experience on similar types of job.
– *Writing your own RFP*: any question bubbling up can be asked of the customer. He or she may answer the questions or tell you that he (or she) did not think about this problem. In that case you have scored a point.

Part 2: Proposal preparation To keep the customer involved during the writing and publication of the proposal. Sometimes it is forbidden to contact the customer after the RFP has been submitted. If you have the possibility to contact the customer you should:

- Start second team activities: the second team consists of top management which have at least the same level as the decision maker(s).
- Discuss the solution with the right people in the customer's organization to find out if the solution is the one they expect.
- Ask your major sponsor to come over to your premises and discuss with him your proposal and the proposal presentation.
- Continuously build on the relationship with the decision makers.
- Write press articles.

Part 3: Post-proposal submission strategy This convinces the customer that you are continuously working on the solution and that you are the best partner for him or her. Actions that can be taken, are:

- Increase second team activities.
- Write final letter to the sponsor(s) indicating why their organization should choose your company and not the competitor.
- Prepare a proposal and pricing update plan.
- Respond to all customer's questions.

Your defined strategy will never stay the same during the bid. There are reasons enough which will influence your strategy resulting in updating your strategy plan and the implementation of that plan.

WRITE WIN PLAN

Based on the information from the previous activities you can write the win plan for this lead. This plan will be the formal vehicle to guide all activities related to this opportunity. Table 20.1 gives a possible table of contents for a win plan.

CUSTOMER INFLUENCE

In this activity you will start the previously defined pre-RFP customer influence strategy with the ultimate goal: to become the only company, or one of the few companies to receive the RFP. After the RFP has been issued, you continue to influence the customer but now according to the proposal development strategy. Influencing the customer should be done at all levels within the customer organization (Fig. 20.5):

- End users
- Department management
- Directors
- Technical specialists.

Table 20.1   Table of contents for a win plan

No	Chapter	Section	Contents
1.0	General		
1.1		Technical plans	Defines the technical baseline for the programme
1.2		Themes	Contains at least 20 themes for this bid equally divided into common, unique and competitive types
2.0	Customer		
2.1		Customer contact plan	Contact plan for all key persons within the customer organizations
2.2		RFP influence strategy	Contains the specific actions to be performed to influence the customer during the writing of the RFP
2.3		Proposal development plan	Contains the strategy which will be followed during the proposal development period
2.4		Post proposal submission	Contains the specific actions which will be performed after the proposal has been submitted and before the customer makes the final decision.
2.5		Information gathering	Specific seduction and information-gathering activities to be performed for this programme
3.0	Competition		
3.1		SWOT analysis	Results of a SWOT analysis of major competition
3.2		Competition offset	A pre-planned programme to offset the competition
4.0	Company		
4.1		Pricing strategy	Contains strategy that you have ascertained is necessary to win
4.2		Teaming plan	A specific plan and activities to be taken to develop the best team to win the contract
4.3		Proposal development plan	Contains a top level proposal development and publishing plan including an overall financial spending plan
5.0	Subcontracting		
5.1		Third parties	Describes the third party strategy necessary to win
5.2		Suppliers	Describes product strategy to follow, to win the contract

All people of your company visiting the customer should help you, not only members of the account. However, do not forget to give them the right information and emphasize the importance of the possible project.

Proposal preparation and publication

The purpose of this stage is to define a compliant solution based on the information in the RFP and to deliver a quality proposal indicating your

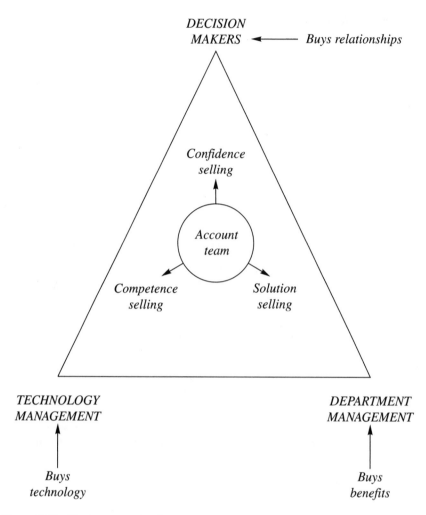

Figure 20.5 Customer contracts

company as most suitable business partner. Figure 20.6 shows the flow of proposal development.

QUALIFY THE OPPORTUNITY

The RFP has been received and contains more information and requirements. Therefore you should perform another qualification. Because the RFP is more emphasized on technical aspects, the qualification should be performed by the account team supported by the project/proposal

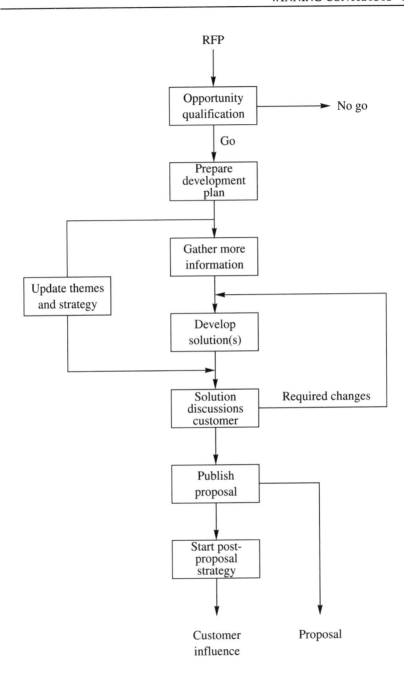

Figure 20.6 Proposal development flow

manager and technical solution specialists. At this point in the bid process you have, as a team, still the possibility to decide not to bid. Possible reasons for deciding not to bid at this stage are:

- Lack of resources to do the bid
- Lack of resources to implement the solution
- Risks too high
- Competition too strong
- No proper solution
- Customer preferred subcontractor not available
- Profit margin too low compared with the identified risks
- Bid costs too high
- Win chance too low.

PREPARE PROPOSAL DEVELOPMENT PLAN

Planning a proposal development and publication effort is in many ways like planning any other project. The primary differences are immovable deadlines and high financial stakes. These differences demand that plans should be designed and maintained in such a way that changes to the plan involve how something gets done rather than extending the final deadline. This can be accomplished by performing only a late date schedule (scheduling backwards). You can resolve the problem from a negative slack when scheduling backwards by:

- Overlapping tasks
- Adding more human resources
- Planning for contingencies
- Finding alternative technical solutions
- Finding alternative more expensive proposal development and publication solution.

The proposal development plan includes at least the following sections:

- An opportunity overview
- An available resource overview
- A resource responsibility list
- A proposal budget and spending plan
- An overall project timeline for this phase in the bid process
- Risks and dependencies
- Review criteria
- Change management.

When preparing the proposal, the types of resources you may use are:

- Graphics design specialist(s)
- Editor(s)
- Technical writer(s)
- Solution specialist
- Publishing department people
- Legal experts
- Volume managers for large proposals
- Review people
- Finance expert(s)
- Quality expert(s)
- Equipment
- Materials.

PERFORM KICK-OFF MEETING

All members of the development team need to know where they are going, how they are going to get there, what is expected along the way, and what the final result is going to be. At the end of the meeting all participants commit themselves to the proposal development and publishing plan. Who should you invite for a kick-off meeting beside yourself? All participants contributing in the proposal development, the person responsible for managing the publishing activities and the account manager. The meeting is usually run by the account manager and the proposal manager. The proposal manager controls the agenda and the use of time. A possible agenda can be:

1. Introduction
2. Review of the opportunity
3. Review of the account relationship
4. Overview proposal effort
5. Ground rules
6. Commitments
7. Publication overview.

As a result of the kick-off meeting the original proposal development and publication plan will be updated to reflect the comments given during the meeting.

GATHER INFORMATION

Based on the information in the RFP it is often required to get additional information concerning:

- The customer via interviews, sometimes bidding conference and previous experiences
- The possible subcontractors via interviews and previous experiences
- Your own company via second opinions
- The competition via detailed study and previous experiences.

The information received will be used:

- To perform a more detailed qualification
- To update the themes and strategy in the win plan
- To update the proposal development and publishing plan
- To develop the most suitable solution.

UPDATE THEMES AND STRATEGY

Because more information becomes available, the themes and strategy chapters in the win plan will continuously be updated by the proposal manager.

SOLUTION DEVELOPMENT

The developed solution should always be compliant with what has been requested in the RFP. As well as the technical solution, it will also contain:

- Financial solution
- Contractual solution
- Organizational change solution
- Quality assurance solution
- Implementation solution.

The first check you can perform on a proposed solution is an informal review of the complete solution or one or more chapters of the solution description. The review is performed by other solution developers within your proposal team. They review the draft to discover contradictions and to ensure consistency. The second round of reviews will be performed by technical specialists who are not part of the proposal development team. Based on the comments made, you revise the draft.

SOLUTION DISCUSSIONS WITH CUSTOMER

If you have the possibility to discuss the solution with the customer use the opportunity. Discuss all aspects of the solution with the relevant people within the customer's organization. Based on the comments received you can update the proposed solution.

PROPOSAL PUBLICATION

You have designed the solution, it is now time to write the proposal. If you did your homework well, you know the customer's decision makers, evaluation team members and their selection and evaluation criteria. Possible sources of information for use in preparing the proposal are:

- RFP information (layout, publishing requirements, etc.)
- Company standards (publishing standards, layout standards, etc.)
- Win plan (themes and strategy)
- Bid plan (resources, planning)
- Solution design
- Previous proposals written for this customer (win and lost ones) and their post bid review reports.

Figure 20.7 shows the proposal publication procedure.

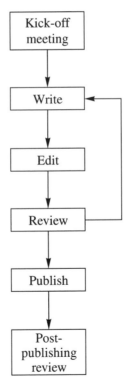

Figure 20.7 Proposal publication flow

1. *Kick-off meeting with publication team* The first and most important step in the proposal publication activity is to perform a kick-off meeting. Your goal as proposal manager for this meeting is:
   - To provide the necessary information about publication effort, reaffirmation of commitments and available resources, explanation of limitations, etc.
   - To establish publication guidelines as far as it concerns consistency (one theme, one writer), submitting of materials, reviews, available tools, etc.
   - To gather information about a solid understanding of the themes, names and locations of content providers and other key people, the expected delivery date and time, a clearer picture of the resources required and resources available, etc.
2. *Write chapters/volumes* The actual writing of the proposal is, as you can imagine, a staggered, cyclical process. Like other living documents it will grow in time and therefore you must manage that growth so that 80 per cent of the final product resembles the original concept. Based on the proposed solution and corresponding themes, the actual writing of the corresponding proposal volumes/chapters will start. Sometimes and maybe also in your company (technical) writers will do this job. However, before the volume/chapter will be send to the editor, the content provider must perform a review to check if the contents are still correct. Figure 20.8 shows a suggested layout for a proposal. A proven order in writing a proposal is:
   Step 1 Write, edit and review various solution volumes.
   Step 2 Develop proposal presentation.
   Step 3 Write management summary.
   Step 4 Write executive summary.
   Step 5 Write cover letter.
3. *Edit chapters/volumes* Winning proposals are not written in one shot. You will rewrite, and rewrite, and rewrite ... them. Each chapter/volume will be edited. The job of the editor is to see that the theme developed is maintained throughout the document and that the writing style matches what has been requested in the proposal guidelines. Any changes made by the editor must be reviewed by the content provider.
4. *Review* After each volume/chapter has been written and edited, the planned formal review must be performed. The review may be conducted by two review teams:
   - One review team poses as the customer evaluation team. This team is sometimes called the RED team. The team should consist of highly qualified and objective personnel who were not involved in preparing the proposal. The reviewers examine the proposal and offer solutions and suggestions for improvement. You as proposal manager, may or

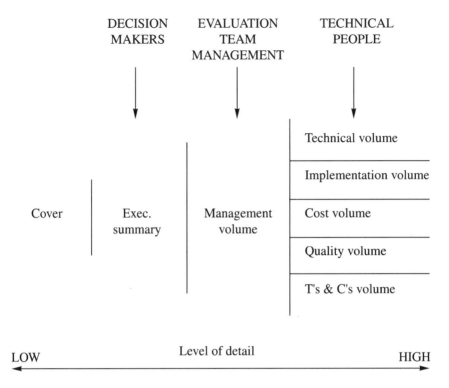

Figure 20.8   Proposal layout

may not accept the suggested revisions, but the input should be evaluated seriously.

– Another review team (BLUE team) focuses on the business aspects of the solution, that are not reviewed by the red team.

The final chapters have been reviewed and approved, graphics have been integrated, and the document is ready to be printed. Now the team can look at the document as a whole. Before handing the document to the publisher, you will do a consistency and completeness check, comprising:

– Compile and print all volumes/chapters.

– Review document for heading levels, page numbers, references, and appendixes.

– Verify all page numbers with the table of contents.

– Produce cover letters on stationery and have each one individually signed.

– Make a copy of the proposal for yourself.

Because you planned ahead your publishing order is expected. Therefore no delays are accepted. Before sending the requested number of

proposals to the customer you should do a final check on:
- Correct page order
- Finger prints
- Torn paper
- Upside down pages.

5. *Post-publication review meeting* As you know, proposal preparation and publication efforts are always intense efforts. There is usually no time during the process to step back and reflect on what has gone on. Therefore the purpose of a review meeting is to analyse and share observations of the effort and to provide closure to it. The outcome of this meeting is very useful when you plan your next proposal development effort. Topics for such a meeting are:
- Proposal completeness and quality
- Process analysis for timeless, quality of experience, etc.
- Problems and issues evaluation
- Participants recognitions for their good work, long hours and though situation
- A party.

Participants in a review meeting can be:
- Contents developers
- Technical writers
- Editors
- Reviewers
- Publishing
- Account manager
- Proposal manager.

The conclusions of the review meeting will be documented and sent to the participants of the meeting, management and your 'methods and tools' department.

POST-PROPOSAL SUBMISSION

After the proposal has been submitted, there is no time for a rest. The previous defined post-proposal submission strategy will come into operation. The purpose of the strategy is to get ready for possible discussions with the customer. The discussions can be oral or written discussions. Post-proposal submission activities are:

- Prepare for possible audits, presentations, etc.
- Find weak points in your own proposal and take steps to strengthen your position.
- Get more information about the competition proposed solution and if there is a new strength, prepare a plan to match or beat it.

- Prepare yourself for the best and final offer.
- Write the 'last' letter.

During this stage in the bid process it is not necessary to have the complete proposal development team on board. However, the key players within the team must stay. Key players are the account manager, account consultant, at least one senior technical specialist and the implementation manager.

Contract negotiations

The actual contract negotiations will start as soon as your company has been selected as preferred supplier. However, as part of your post-proposal strategy you can start with the contract information-gathering activities as soon as you submitted the proposal. The purpose of this phase within the bid process is to create a contract which is acceptable for both the customer and your own company. The contract should be clear, concise and written in a contractual language to facilitate administration of the agreement. The flow of contract negotiations is shown in Fig. 20.9.

PREPARE FOR NEGOTIATIONS

In this first activity within the contract negotiations stage you are going:

- To gather more information from previous occasions, your own internal and eternal contact network, business information resources, etc.
- To learn more about the negotiation style of the customer, the negotiation team and objectives, organizational culture, political agendas, etc.
- To define a preliminary strategy based on issues likely to come up during the negotiations.
- To set up your negotiation team.
- To plan logistics such as support resources and equipment, meeting rooms, etc.
- To write a draft contract based on the terms and conditions volume in the proposal and to discuss the contract with your team members and others within your company.

A typical negotiation team will consist of:

- Account manager
- Legal expert(s)
- Proposal manager
- Implementation manager.

LOI, MOU, MOA

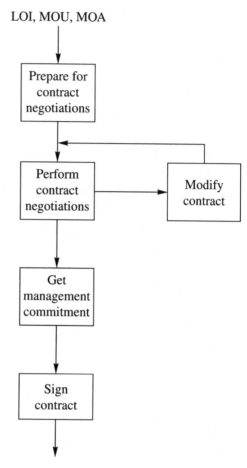

Implementation contract

Figure 20.9 Contract negotiations flow

PERFORM NEGOTIATIONS

The purpose of this activity is to get the best deal obtainable, not the perfect solution. The negotiations will never be completed in one session. As you may have experienced, contract negotiations will take time (weeks sometimes months). Often too long in your opinion. However, you should always remember that having a well-defined contract will save you time and money during the implementation and acceptation of the solution.

During the first session you should discuss logistics, collect information, get comments on the draft contract and ask if there are possible issues. If there are issues, you should develop a precise understanding of what the customer means regarding each issue.

During the actual negotiations, you should set specific goals for each session. Once issues are identified, you negotiate a solution. Possible tactics you can follow, are:

– Generating alternatives
– 'Make me an offer'
– 'Take it or else' (risky)
– The strategic recess.

Once you came to an agreement during a session, you must, back in the office, first analyse the agreement for possible business and technology implications, before you sign the agreement. If there are business and/or technical implications you should discuss these with the specialists in your company, define alternatives and inform senior management to get approval. If the impact is too high you should go back to the customer and explain to him or her why the impact is too high for your company and negotiate a better deal.

GET MANAGEMENT COMMITMENT

Before signing the final contract you ask senior management, both business management and legal management, for an approval of the total contract.

SIGNING THE CONTRACT

If senior management from the customer and your company have approved the contract, the contract can be signed by top management. Top management should sign the contract in order to:

– Get top management involved (see responsibility above).
– Give an indication to the customer that the project is strategic for your company.
– Build a relation if not already done, between top management of both parties.

As you know, signing the contract is never the end of conflicts. Conflicts will always come during the implementation of the solution. It is advisable that you should attach summaries of major points of agreement (history of the deal) to the contract. Save all versions of the agreement for reference use.

20.5 Post-bid reviews

At the end of each bid, lost or won, a post-bid review should be performed. During the review you have the opportunity to evaluate the total bid effort: strategy planning, execution, results and opportunities to improve the way you are doing business. The review should be started before members of the bid team disperse and then completed as soon as possible. One of the most important elements of the review is a meeting with the customer. Participating in this meeting are the sales manager and the bid manager. The kind of information you want to get from the customer at this meeting includes:

– Why did the customer choose or did not choose for your company?
– Was the customer satisfied with the proposal and the proposal presentation?
– Was your company approach the correct one?
– Was the offered solution suitable?
– Was the offered time correct.

After you have had your meeting with the customer, you can hold the formal review meeting. All members of the bid team are expected to participate fully and be available as needed for the review. Others who can be present are quality assurance personnel, as well as third-party and if possible, customer representatives.

After the review meeting the bid manager writes the bid review report and sends the report to your company's management.

20.6 Summary

1. Before bidding, you must gain as much information as possible about:
   – The customer
   – The customer's market
   – The competition
   – Your own organization.
2. If the invitation to tender turns up unexpectedly, perform a detailed qualification and proceed with great caution.
3. There are three stages of bidding:
   – Prior to receiving the invitation to tender
   – Proposal development
   – Contract negotiation.
4. Themes are the conclusive reason why the customer should select your bid. There are three types of theme:
   – Common themes
   – Unique themes
   – Competitive themes.

5. Before starting work on the bid, you should develop a win plan.
6. There are five activities in the Pre-ITT stage:
   - Lead qualification
   - Define themes
   - Define strategy
   - Write win plan
   - Influence customer.
7. There are eight steps to writing the proposal:
   - Opportunity qualification
   - Development planning
   - Information gathering
   - Themes and strategy update
   - Solution development
   - Solution discussion with customer
   - Proposal publication
   - Post-proposal strategy.
8. There are five steps to publishing the proposal:
   - Kick-off meeting
   - Write
   - Edit
   - Review
   - Publish.
9. There are five steps in contract negotiation:
   - Prepare
   - Negotiate
   - Modify contract
   - Get top management commitment
   - Sign.
10. Conduct a post-bid review, and ask the customer:
   - Why did the customer choose (or did not choose) your company?
   - Was the customer satisfied with the proposal and the proposal presentation?
   - Was your company approach the correct one?
   - Was the offered solution suitable?
   - Was the offered time correct?

References

1. Derby, P., Stirling, D. and Turner, J.R., *Contract Control Review Guide*, Coopers & Lybrand, 1987.
2. Turner, J.R., *The Handbook of Project-based Management*, McGraw-Hill, 1993.
3. Institution of Civil Engineers, *Guidance on the Preparation, Submission and Consideration of Tenders for Civil Engineering Contracts*, Thomas Telford, 1981.

21

Contract administration

Geoff Quaife and Rodney Turner

21.1 Introduction

In this chapter, we consider the administration of contracts and the management of the client/contractor interface. We consider how clients issue variations on the contract to the contractor, how clients make interim payments, and the issue of completion certificates and the payment of the final account.

The client and the contractor are the parties to the contract, which will be signed on their behalf by directors. However, the administration of the contract and the management of the project will normally be delegated to named individuals, typically a project manager or engineer. Both companies will delegate powers, duties and responsibilities to this individual, and empower him or her to act on their behalf. In this chapter we do not differentiate between the party to the contract or the party's representative, except where necessary.

21.2 Managing the client/contractor interface

As work on the contract starts, the client and contractor must put in place an administrative procedure to manage the contract. There are three essential elements of this procedure:

- Appropriate review meetings
- A document control procedure
- Structured contacts between client and contractor personnel at all levels of management.

Appropriate review meetings

Review meetings should be agreed and scheduled from the start of the contract and should indeed form part of it. Attendance should be compulsory. There is a view that they should not be scheduled on Mondays and Fridays, to avoid long weekends. There are three fundamental levels of review meeting:

- Strategy review meetings between client and contractor directors
- Progress review meetings between client and contractor project managers
- Technical review meetings (design or compliance review) between engineers during contract execution (design or delivery respectively).

The review meetings should be linked to a predetermined control cycle.[1]

Document control

A document control procedure is essential to protect the positions of both the client and contractor organizations. Both should maintain a single point of contact for all documents passing between the two organizations, and they should log all documents in and out. Engineers should not be allowed to send documents between each other without them first going through the document control point. This prevents conflicting instructions being issued, avoids confusion and abortive work, and hence cost escalation, and ensures coordination of information release. It is also essential if the contract comes to arbitration or litigation. There must be a complete record of all documents. This can be a double-edged sword as all documents are admissible in evidence. There is a story of a contractor's project manager ringing a day in his site diary in black, and writing something to the effect that this was the day he lost control. This destroyed his employer's case in the subsequent litigation. (This is similar to former US Secretary of Defense Caspar Weinberger who risked being charged with an imprisonable offence because he allegedly shredded personal documents.)

Building relationships

In spite of the need for strict document control, the building of relationships between the two organizations is also essential:

- This helps to build mutual understanding, and increases the likelihood of a successful outcome.
- Either project manager can be very exposed to slander by the other if they are the only point of contact between the two organizations.

While it is important to have contact at all levels, it must be recognized that only written documents from authorized personnel can change the scope or terms of the contract (see Section 21.3 below). There is a growing recognition that a good working relationship between client and contractor personnel can increase the likelihood of a successful out-turn for both the client and contractor. This concept is being developed into a concept called *partnering*, in which the two organizations take a win–win approach, rather than a win–lose approach, to the contract. Partnering means the two organizations work together so that they both achieve a better result from the contract. Gray and Larson[2] propose a model for partnering (Fig. 21.1).

PRE-PROJECT

As soon as the directors of the two organizations agree to use a partnering approach, they begin to build the collaborative arrangement between the two organizations. For managers experienced in this sort of approach, this will involve little more than agreeing how the procedures are to work on this contract. For inexperienced managers it may involve some training. This may involve client and contractor managers working together to build mutual respect. The next step is to roll the partnering out to lower levels of

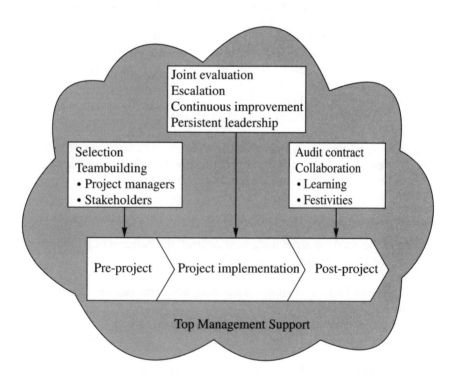

Figure 21.1 Project partnering

management, through *project start-up workshops* perhaps lasting several days and involving personnel from both organizations.[1] The workshops focus on:

- Agreeing the project objectives
- Identifying barriers to effective communication
- Identifying potential sources of conflict
- Agreeing collaborative problem-solving procedures.

Overall, the workshops aim to produce a cohesive, cooperative team with a common set of objectives and agreed procedures for managing the project. It is common for the workshops to deliver a charter through which the client and contractor personnel agree how they are going to work together.

PROJECT IMPLEMENTATION

The cooperative mechanisms agreed during the pre-project stage will include:

- *Joint evaluation* The partners assess each other's performance according to predetermined criteria.
- *Problem resolution* Procedures are agreed whereby problems are solved at the lowest possible level, within a given time frame, or escalated to the next level of management.
- *Continuous improvement* Like all quality organizations the partnership aims for rapid and continuous improvement.
- *Persistent leadership* Managers at all levels lead by example, showing a collaborative response to problem solving, and recognize those of their staff who contribute to the process.

Some people also view this as a way of increasing productivity, by having only one person doing each job, instead of having every contractors' engineer shadowed by a client engineer repeating his or her work.

POST-PROJECT

Project close-out is a collaborative process whereby the two organizations learn better how to work together for future collaborative arrangements.

21.3 Variations and instructions

During the course of executing the work of a contract, either the client or the contractor may decide that a matter requires clarifying, or a change in work is necessary. This additional work may arise from:

- Changes in the specification, design or required functionality
- Errors made in the design or work executed so far
- Quality problems.

Not all instructions lead to a variation in the contract, for instance the clarifying of paint colour from a range of options would not, unless it caused a delay. If the change is due to a mistake or omission by the contractors, the client will expect them to pay for the extra work, whether the contract is fixed price or cost plus. If it is due to a mistake or omission by the client, the contractor will expect to be reimbursed for the additional work, again whether the contract is fixed price or cost plus. Indeed, on fixed price contracts, contractors often bid the jobs on little or no profit margin in order to win the work, and then expect to make their profit on the additional work resulting from errors or omissions by the client. If the mistake or omission by the client is first noticed by the contractors, then they will make a claim on the client. Claims are the subject of the next chapter. If the omission or change is first noticed by the client, then he or she will issue a variation order or instruction to the contractor. These are handled under the contract administration procedure set up be the client.

Variations or instructions will usually arise from some change to the specification or design of the facility in order to meet the required or revised functionality, or to meet their quality, safety or environmental standards. There are three essential steps in the issuing of variation orders or instructions:

- They must be issued in writing, by an appropriate authority.
- The contractor must acknowledge their receipt.
- The cost of the additional work must be agreed.

Issuing variations and instructions

The orders must be issued in writing, by the appropriate authority as defined in the contract, as:

- Revised drawings, design proposals or specifications.
- Letters.
- Variation orders or change orders on a standard form.
- Written instructions.

Variations or instructions should not be actioned by the contractor if they are issued:

- Orally
- By the incorrect authority within the client organization
- By the managing contractor without authority.

An example of the first two is of a variation being issued by junior engineers at progress control or design review meetings. Often junior engineers can be commercially naive, with damaging consequences for their employer, whether the client or contractor. It has been known for them to throw away the contractor's profit margins by accepting changes outside the original scope of supply. Worse still, if the client has a history of cost-plus contracts, the engineers can sometimes behave as if they have the right to change the specification or design. That can result in either:

- The contractor organization accepting the changes without recompense because of the power the client organization has over them.
- The client's project manager discovering that the contractor has accepted costly variations without proper authorization, and is charging for them in full.

To avoid delays which excessively bureaucratic, written procedures can cause, administration procedures have evolved which allow later written confirmation of verbal instructions. However, this is risky.

Accepting variations and instructions

There should also be some procedure in place by which the contractor acknowledges receipt of variation orders. There are two reasons for this:

- To initiate the procedure where the cost of the variation is assessed, and a price agreed.
- To ensure that the contractor has received the variation, taken account of its contents, and does not undertake further work which will be rendered redundant by the change.

It seems obvious, but without such a procedure it is easy for the contractor to continue working on an old design, and eventually repeat more work than would otherwise have been necessary. Such an event can have an adverse effect on the client/contractor interface, as they argue about who should pay for the wasted work. With a procedure in place whereby a contractor must acknowledge receipt of a variation, by responding in writing, the client must ensure the response is received within a given time period, and establish procedures to deal with lack of acknowledgement. Unless instructed otherwise, the contractor usually has a reasonable time to respond and action a variation order or instruction. If there is a need to action the change quickly, this must be allowed for when agreeing a price for the variation.

Valuing variations

How the variation is valued will depend on whether or not the amount of work can be measured and quantified before execution. Where the contract work is tangible (bricks and mortar), the contract documentation and variations to it can usually be valued in a tangible way. Where the contract deliverable is less tangible (a service), the contract work and changes are less easy to quantify, and more likely to be reimbursed on a lump sum or time and materials basis.

WORK QUANTIFIABLE

If the work is quantifiable, then its cost will be estimated and a price agreed.

- If the work is similar in all respects to work undertaken elsewhere on the contract, the previously agreed contract rates will be used to assess the price for the new work.
- If the work is similar, but the conditions are different, then contract rates will form the basis for the estimate, but allowances will be made for the different conditions.
- If the work is different, then fair rates must be agreed. The basis for these may have been written into the original contract.

WORK NOT QUANTIFIABLE

If the work is not quantifiable, a lump sum may be agreed or the contractor will be paid for the work as it is done. The rates of pay will be daywork rates for labour, materials, subcontract, etc., using rates or a mechanism for establishing rates which should be written into the original contract. This situation exposes the client to the greatest risk as the commitment is almost open ended. There is added risk that the contractor will try to absorb non-recoverable overspend elsewhere on the contract, by including it within the daysheets for the extra work. Because the contractor is paid for all the effort and materials expended, there is little incentive for him to be efficient. The situation must therefore be carefully monitored by the client. It is this suspicion which leads to the terrible relationships within the construction industries.

21.4 Valuations and interim payments

English contract law merely makes provision for payment on completion. It is common, however, for contracts to have provisions enabling the client to make interim payment to the contractor during the progression of the work. This will help the contractor's cash flow, and enable the contractor to pay for materials, labour and subcontract costs. Somebody has to raise the finance for the project:

– If the client raises the finance, then he or she will make interim payments to the contractor.
– If the contractor raises the finance, then quite clearly he or she will add the financing charges to the overall price for the works.

We looked at buyer and supplier credit in previous chapters.
Interim payments can be made in one of two ways:

– Against predefined milestones
– Against valuations of the work to date.

Against predefined milestones

Interim payments are made at predefined milestones. It is assumed in the initial contract that to reach each milestone, a predetermined amount of work must have been done, and a payment is made for that assumed amount of work. This approach is often used in the shipbuilding and engineering construction industries. It can lead to uses and abuses.

1. The most common abuse is for a milestone to be nominally achieved even though much of the assumed work is incomplete. In the shipbuilding industry, for instance, launch is a fairly visible milestone, but is in fact a fairly insignificant step in the overall network. It is not a major bottleneck. Hence it is quite easy for work which is assumed to have been done before launch to be delayed until after launch.
2. An effective use of this approach was illustrated on the later stations in the Nuclear Power Programme in the United Kingdom.[3] Payments were only made to contractors at six monthly intervals. They were paid against milestones completed in the last six months. If they were just a day late on a milestone at the end of the six monthly period, then they would have to wait six months before receiving payment. Nothing concentrates the mind more, and ensures the job receives high-level attention within a contracting organization than hitting the cash flow in this way.

Interim valuations

The other approach is to make interim valuations of the work in progress, and to pay the contractor against those valuations. This approach is commonly used in the building industry. On a cost-plus or time and materials contract the valuation is aimed at determining how much work has been done in the period, and then how much it cost to do that work. The components of cost are listed in Section 3.3, and include labour, materials, overheads, etc. On a cost-plus contract the contractor will be paid costs plus a fixed percentage. On a time and materials contract, the contractor will be paid costs plus a fixed fee for the period. On a fixed price contract, the valuation is aimed at determining how much work has been done, and what it was estimated that work would cost (including the contractors' profit), by reference to the tender price as stated in the contract documents. Irrespective of the method of calculation, it is normal for the contractor only to be paid a proportion of the moneys due. A small, agreed percentage (often 5 per cent) is held back as retention against satisfactory completion of the work. In making interim valuations and payments you need to consider:

- The obligations of the parties involved
- How the valuations are made
- Allowing for the effect of inflation
- The ownership of materials on site and the retention of title.

OBLIGATIONS OF THE PARTIES INVOLVED

All the parties involved in a contract have obligations in the making of interim valuations and payments:

- *The client's quantity surveyor or cost engineer* prepares the valuation of work in progress.
- *The contractor* aids the QS in the valuation. If nominated subcontractors are used, then they should pay them within an agreed time period, typically 17 days.
- *The designer or managing contractor* must issue certificates at agreed intervals, and check payments are being made to nominated subcontractors.
- *The client* must pay the certificates within an agreed period, typically 14 days.

MAKING VALUATIONS

Valuations should include an assessment of all work in progress. Some of this work will be subjected to retentions, and some not. (Retentions are money held over by the client until issue of the final completion certificates to cover any default by the contractor.) Work valued and which is subject to retention includes:

- Work properly executed
- Materials on site
- Materials off site (when agreed by the client)
- Nominated subcontractor values including contractor's profit.

Work valued and which is not subject to retention includes:

- Statutory fees, royalties and similar items
- Reimbursement of loss and expense
- Final payment to nominated subcontractors
- Price fluctuations
- Similar expenses incurred by nominated subcontractors, including the contractor's profit.

THE EFFECT OF INFLATION

Should the contract conditions so require, when making a valuation of work on a fixed price contract, it is necessary to allow for inflation. The valuation is then the original estimate plus the allowance made for inflation. There are several ways of allowing for inflation:

- The contractor estimates the likely effects of inflation at the tender stage, and includes it in the fixed price: the risk is the contractor's that inflation will be greater or less than the estimate.
- The contract sum is escalated by the known increases in costs of materials and labour since the date of tender. This can be very time consuming as the estimate must almost be repeated for each valuation period. The risk is entirely the owner's that inflation will be greater or less than assumed in the investment appraisal.
- The contract sum is escalated, but only to include changes in costs arising from the action of government, which usually means changes in tax or duty – the risk is the owner's again.
- Standard escalation formulae are used to calculate the escalation. It is assumed that labour and materials are a fixed proportion of the contract value throughout the work, and published indices are used to calculate the increase of labour and material costs in this period, assuming they are that fixed percentage. The risk is primarily the owner's, although the contractor takes the risk that the simplifying assumptions still provide a realistic estimate of the increase.

In contracts with local or national government, a non-adjustable element is often added to the contract. Typically escalations are reduced by 10 per cent from the estimate. This can be self-defeating, because contractors just allow for it in their tenders.

MATERIALS ON SITE AND RETENTION OF TITLE

Following the delivery of materials to site, the question can arise as to who owns them. This can become more important in the case of liquidation or bankruptcy of either party. Many suppliers and clients incorporate into contracts clauses known as 'retention of title'. Depending on the author, these seek either to ensure that ownership will only pass to the purchaser on payment in full, or that ownership passes on delivery. Such clauses are, however, often found to be inadequately drafted, and so offer no protection (see Case 21.1). Many standard forms of contract contain clauses on retention of title. This is a complex issue of law, and many of these clauses are dubious. If faced with a problem of retention of title it is advisable to seek expert advice.[4]

Case 21.1 Dawber Williamson Roofing Ltd v. *Humberside County Council* (1979)

DWR were subcontractors. They delivered roofing slates to site. The valuation of the slates was included in a valuation certificate issued under the main contract, and the certificate was paid. However, the main contractor went into liquidation before paying the subcontractor. HCC claimed the slates were theirs, and therefore refused to allow the plaintiff to remove them from site.
Held The court ruled that ownership of the slates had not passed from subcontractor to main contractor as the former had not been paid, and thus ownership could not have passed from main contractor to client under the valuation certificate. This was because the plaintiffs as subcontractors were not party to the main contract, and therefore not bound by it.

21.5 Completion and final account

Completion under English law is recognized as a single event, when the contractor has completed his or her obligations to undertake the work and the client has paid the contract sum. On complex projects, this is seen as too simplistic. While construction may cease abruptly, other obligations of the parties may be phased out more slowly, reflecting the complexity of verifying completion and contract compliance. A contract does not finally come to an end until the client, or the client's agent (the managing contractor or the designer), issues the final completion certificate.

Completion can take place in several stages:

- Practical completion
- Sectional completion
- Partial possession
- Defects and making good
- The final account.

Practical completion

Practical completion of the work is the stage of the contract when, in the opinion of the client or client's agent, the works including authorized variations are substantially complete and have been carried out in accordance with the contract documents. On practical completion the client will issue the first completion certificate to the contractor. This action has an important effect on the contract and any legal dispute that may arise. Very often the facility is ready for use, although a number of minor items have yet to be completed. The implications of issuing the certificates must be considered. For example, the contractor's difficulty in returning to finish incomplete work once the facility is in full use. On issue of the certificates at this stage, one-half of the retention fund will be paid. The retention fund remaining is only intended to cover defects discovered after practical completion for the agreed duration of the defects liability period. It is not intended that retention should cover future payment of incomplete works. It is therefore important that the only outstanding work is of a very minor nature. When the practical completion certificates are issued, various provisions of the contract take effect, including:

- Issue of one-half of the retention moneys.
- Release of the contractor from obligation to insure.
- Start of the defects liability period.
- Start of arbitration proceedings.

1. *Half retention* One-half of the retention money held against satisfactory completion must be released to the contractor with the first interim certificate after practical completion.
2. *Insurance* The contractor is released from his or her obligation to insure the facility on the date of issue of the practical completion certificates.
3. *Defects liability* The defects liability period begins on the date named in the practical completion certificate. The six-month period in which the contractor must usually provide all documents necessary to compute the final account also commences.
4. *Arbitration proceedings* When practical completion is reached, certain

arbitration on matters which cannot be pursued prior to practical completion can be opened. These include disputes on extensions of time or the level of liquidated and ascertained damages.

Sectional completion

Sectional completion is completion in agreed phases or sections, and so is an alternative to completing the whole project at one time. This situation arises from a planned programme of work which was previously incorporated into the contract documents by use of a sectional completion supplement. This supplement makes amendments to the contract, and also sets requirements to be met on completion of each section of the facility. These requirements include:

– The value of the work
– The dates for possession and completion
– The defects liability period
– The amount of liquidated and ascertained damages.

The client, or client's agent, will issue a certificate of practical completion on completion of each section. The certificate for the final section will be the certificate of practical completion for the entire contract. Effectively, each section is treated as a contract within a contract. Hence, at practical completion of a section, the provisions of the contract which apply at practical completion take effect for that section, including the four items (1) to (4) above.

Partial possession

An unplanned, *ad hoc* version of sectional completion is known as partial possession. This is when the client decides to take possession of part of the facility during the contract. If the client, by agreement with the contractor, takes possession of a part of the facility at a date before practical completion of the whole works, then partial possession of that part can occur. The contract administrator is required to issue, immediately after possession has been taken, a statement giving an estimate of the value of this part and the date of possession. The contractor is then entitled to one-half the retention money relating to that portion of the cost of the total works, and the defects liability period commences on that part of the building. However, arbitration cannot begin until practical completion of the entire facility.

At the time of partial possession of any part of the facility, the value of insurance and the amount of liquidated damages for non-completion must be reviewed. These will generally be reduced pro rata to the value of the portion of the facility handed over. Because the contractor has possession of the site, the client must seek the contractor's permission for this *ad hoc* arrangement. In a recent court case, it was held that the client had sought and been granted 'use' of an area (not partial possession) and so the contractor was still liable for protection and insurance of the areas involved. Thus, should this situation arise, always carefully check what rights are actually being granted to the employer.

Defects and making good

During the defects liability period, any defects, which appear in the facility and are due to the use of materials or workmanship not in accordance with the contract, are listed by the client or the client's agent in a schedule of defects. This list is sometimes called a *snagging list*. The contractor must rectify these defects in a reasonable time, at his or her own expense. If the contractor fails to rectify the defects within a reasonable time, the client or client's agent may instruct another contractor to do the work, and deduct the amount charged by the second contractor from the final account, or recover the moneys as a debt. When the client or client's agent is satisfied that all defective work has been made good, a completion certificate must be issued to that effect. This is called the *Certificate of Completion of Making Good Defects*. The final retention is released to the contractor on issue of this certificate.

The final account

If proper records have been kept and interim valuations made during the course of the contract, there should be little delay in completing the final account. In particular:

1. Provisional quantities should have been re-measured as work progressed, and provisional sums omitted or expended against written instructions from the designer or managing contractor.
2. Prime costs should have been substituted by the final accounts of nominated subcontractors.
3. Daywork sheets should have been annotated to show the source of instruction for the work they record. Any sheets recording work which has not previously been valued by other means should be extended, priced and checked before inclusion in the final account. Daywork sheets relating to a subcontract are usually required to be submitted for inclusion in the main contract within a week of the work to which they relate being done. In any case, it is advisable that they should be submitted as soon as possible after the work being done.

We referred earlier to site diaries. Information in these diaries should record the variations which occurred. These may have been initiated by:

- Architects' written instructions
- Drawing revisions
- Clients' letters
- Contractors' letters
- Written directives from the client's agent (designer or managing contractor).

When your work on a project has been completed, it is a good idea to read quickly through the files to ensure that all additional chargeable work is included in the final account. Do not be dismayed if, at that stage, you find evidence of a variation which has not yet been the subject of a written instruction. The designer or managing contractor is usually empowered to confirm such in writing at any time prior to issuing of the final certificate. If not, then this variation should become the subject of a claim – and that leads us into the chapter, Chapter 22.

21.6 Summary

1. Managing the client/contractor interface requires:
   - Appropriate review meetings
   - A document control procedure
   - Structured contacts between client and contractor personnel at all levels of management.
2. Single project partnering is an approach to building collaborative contacts between client and contractor. This requires close working pre-project, during project implementation and post-project. Pre-project client and contractor should:
   - Agree the project objectives
   - Identify barriers to effective communication
   - Identify potential sources of conflict
   - Agree collaborative problem-solving procedures.
   During the project they should have mechanisms for:
   - Joint evaluation
   - Problem resolution
   - Continuous improvement
   - Persistent leadership
   - Productivity improvement.
3. Variations are changes to the contract issued by the client. There should be defined mechanisms for:
   - Issuing variations

- Acknowledging and accepting variations
- Valuing variations.
4. Interim payments may be made against:
- Milestones
- Interim valuations.
5. Completion may take place in several stages:
- Practical completion
- Sectional completion
- Partial possession
- Defects and making good
- The final account.

References

1. Turner, J.R., *The Handbook of Project-based Management*, McGraw-Hill, 1993.
2. Gray, C. and Larson, E., 'Partnering in the construction Industry', in *Proceedings of the International Conference Management by Projects in Practice*, Vienna, 24–25 June, Gareis, R. (ed.), Project Management Austria, 1993.
3. Morris, P.W.G. and Hough, G., *The Anatomy of Major Projects: a study of the reality of project management*, Wiley, 1987.
4. Parris, J., *Effective Retention of Title Clauses*, Collins, 1984.

22
Dispute resolution

Frank Thomas and Tim Adams

22.1 Introduction

The effect of claims has brought major national projects to their knees,[1] and caused well-conceived schemes to be abandoned altogether. Within major projects, international contractors can founder, and small highly skilled subcontractors go to the wall simply as a result of claims. However, one thing is certain, claims are a fact of life on most projects, and so we must have an efficient, contractual mechanism for dealing with them:

1. The wise client carefully considers the estimated allowance for claims in his or her project budget and reckons that the cumulative value of claims from all sources may be very substantial in relation to the estimated overall project cost.
2. The astute contractor when bidding for work recognizes that negotiating adequate reimbursement for claims is the essence of good management and survival. However, if the contractor overdoes the estimated allowance for unidentified items when tendering, the result may be failure to secure the business in the first place. Far better, perhaps, to concentrate on fielding a strong management team to execute the work, and reducing their contingency margin in order to win the contract.

This chapter describes claims and their management. The chapter is written with a contractor bias, as it is they who usually initiate claims, and normally the majority of claims arise on the job-site. The client should define requirements so that any post-award scope, specification or schedule changes are issued to the contractor in the form of variation orders. If the contractor fails to perform or meet his guarantees, the client will resort to other commercial devices to obtain redress. On the other hand, it is worth emphasizing that, if the contractor's ultimate business objectives are 'to do a good job', make a reasonable profit and end up with a happy client, a sure way of failing on all counts is to saturate a project with claims.

In the next section we define claims, and identify types of claims. We then describe ways of minimizing the potential for claims. We explain how to manage claims, estimate their cost and identify potential risk areas; and describe how they can be reduced. We close the chapter by describing alternative dispute resolution as a way of avoiding costly legal processes as a result of claims. We try to present the subject in a way which offers practical guidance to assist the student in preparing project-specific procedures, should these be required.

22.2 Definitions of claims

Claims are raised by contractors. They are the procedure by which contractors formally seek financial compensation for having to make (unforeseen) adjustments to pre-arranged methods, work plans and rates specified in a contract. A claim will protect a contractor's cash flow. Without having the ability to claim for legitimate recompense, a contractor may go into liquidation to the disadvantage of the project as a whole. Resolution of a claim may be in two parts:

- Settlement or interim settlement of the basic claim to allow work to proceed.
- Issue of a variation order by the client to address changes or restructuring of the remaining scope of work.

Contractors need their clients' formal recognition of proven changes to contract scope and price. The mechanism is often referred to as change control and associated terms such as compensation event, written instruction and variation order are in common use. These variation orders are prepared by the client (Chapter 21) and may result in the adjustment of a contract price (up or down).

To manage claims and satisfy modern quality auditing requirements (BS 5750) organizations need well-defined procedures. Standard forms of contract, including those from the Institution of Civil Engineers,[2] describe general principles for handling claims, and these can provide the framework and form the basis of procedures for many organizations.

Claims are raised by a contractor for a variety of reasons, and they are discussed in this section. Claims fall into two basic categories:

- Claims based on adjustment to the contract rates
- Claims for additional payment for defined reasons.

Claims for changes in rates

If the contractor finds that the work being undertaken is of a dissimilar character to that addressed in the bills of quantities, or where the quantities of work to be accomplished are significantly different from those stated in the contract, a re-evaluation of the relevant contract rates is admissible. When situations of this nature arise the contractor is obliged to give the client advance notice (typically 28 days) of his or her intention to claim a higher rate. Clearly this type of claim is not likely to have an immediate or restraining effect on the contractor's ability to advance the work.

Claims for additional payments

The situation here is more complex. Claims for additional payments can arise from:

- Perceived scope changes
- Changes to schedule
- Schedule restraints.

PERCEIVED SCOPE CHANGES

Contracts may be let on the basis that the contractor will deliver a series of defined packages known overall as the *scope of work*. A typical Engineer/ Procure/Construct (EPC) contract would comprise several elements as listed in Table 22.1. The contractor may raise a claim for changes to the scope of work in any of these deliverables and for any associated consequential costs.

Table 22.1 Typical elements of an EPC contract

Deliverable	Price basis	Location
Detailed designs	Man-hours	Home office
Working drawings and documentation	Man-hours and documents	Home office
Procured equipment	Lump sum	Home office
Procured materials	Bills of quantities	Home office
Shipping and transportation	Lump sum	Home office
Installation services	Man-hours	Site
Installation materials	Bills of quantities	Site
Commissioning services	Man-hours	Site

Changes to schedule introduced by a client may have a profound effect on a contractor's cost. If, for example, a client decides after contract award to delay full commencement of detailed design work, this could have a disruptive effect on the contractor's total in-house work programme for which the contractor is entitled to receive recompense. If such a delay is also not accompanied by an extension to the contract work schedule equal to the front-end delay the contractor may need to accelerate the estimated rate of production and thus incur extra costs to meet the contract completion date. A claim would be fully justified in this type of situation.

SCHEDULE RESTRAINTS

Any experienced contractor will always be alert to the straightforward claim arising from changes to the scope or schedule as just described. However, contractors must also protect themselves against other more sinister effects; namely, the outside forces which could prevent them from performing and progressing the work as set out in their contract schedule.

Figure 22.1 shows typical EPC contract key milestone activities above a line which represents 'progress', moving from left to right. Illustrated below the line are some typical *external restraints* which could develop if the client or other parties involved fail to provide specified information or hardware to the contractor on time.

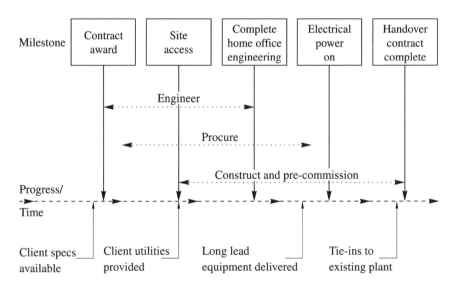

Figure 22.1 Schedule restraint diagram for EPC projects

To amplify this important point the following is an expanded list of typical restraints which often occur during the site phase of a contract:

- Delayed initial access to site due to non-availability of road systems and setting out data
- Lack of working drawings and data scheduled for provision by other parties
- Late delivery of free-issue materials
- On-site clashes with other contractors due to out-of-sequence activities
- Client instructions involving disruption or delay
- Late access to perform pre-commissioning tasks
- Temporary suspension of the works.

To overcome these situations the contractor may incur additional costs for:

- Changing installation methods
- Double-handling materials
- Using additional construction plant
- Loss of productivity and the consequent need to introduce additional manpower
- Working additional overtime or shift hours at premium rates to recover the lost time.

In any such circumstances the contractor is entitled to raise a claim and would expect recompense for remedial action which is beneficial to the project overall.

22.3 Minimizing potential for claims

We have briefly examined *what* claims are. We consider *how* to minimize the potential for claims, following the simple philosophy that 'prevention is better than cure'. The action to minimize claims potential must commence in the pre-award stage of a contract and be directed towards:

- Avoiding ambiguity and misunderstanding through a formal process of bid clarification
- Identifying significant milestone markers
- Seeking definition of terminology by using accepted technical terms amplified as necessary into project-specific language.

Avoiding ambiguity

Contractors must strive to obtain the best possible understanding of the scope of work to which they will be committed before they sign the contract.

Since enquiry documents often contain a requirement that the contractor shall identify any ambiguity or discrepancy during the tendering period and seek clarification, the onus is on that contractor to take positive action. The prudent company will therefore ensure, to the best of its ability, that its bid documents, including any descriptive narrative, are completely understood by the client.

This objective will best be accomplished by means of pre-award bid clarification meetings between expert representatives of the parties. The minutes of these formal meetings should form appendices to the contract.

Identifying significant milestone markers

Consider Figure 22.1 and the key milestone markers which are above the progress line. It is apparent that any ambiguity or misunderstanding as to *their meaning* will also cause confusion, create restraints and introduce claims potential.

Take for example 'Site access'. This is a crucial date from the contractors' viewpoint, since it will determine their ability to mobilize their facilities and workforce. A precise definition of the contractors' entitlements at access date are therefore of the utmost importance and a clear listing accompanied by sketch plans, etc., must be included in the contract documentation.

The discipline of seeking definition is equally important at the 'Hand-over' milestone. The parties must understand mutually what this implies, otherwise the contractor will be put in a disadvantageous position giving rise to needless claims and frustration at the end of the job.

Definition of terminology

We see that even in the definition of these milestone markers there is some potential for misunderstanding through the use of differing terminology between client and contractor. Fortunately, milestones such as 'Mechanical completion' and 'Ready for operation', are well-known technical terms having a high degree of definition in the engineering construction industry. It is, nevertheless, important that they be developed into project-specific detail as necessary.

22.4 Managing claims

In this section we consider:

- How claims can be classified according to the ease of resolution.
- The adoption of suitable organizations by both the client and contractor for claims management.
- The adoption of appropriate procedures for managing claims.

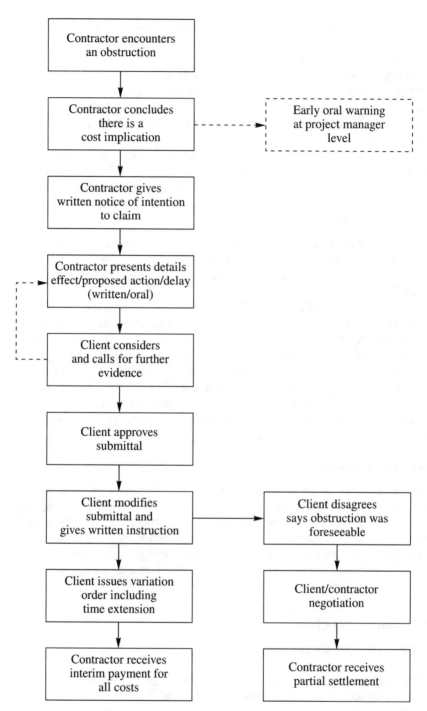

Figure 22.2 Problematical claims – sequence of events

Classifying claims

Clients and contractors alike have a common interest in progressing claims through to final settlement with the minimum of delay. Their joint objective should be to 'keep the job moving'. Non-settlement of claims in some circumstances will embarrass a client as well as a contractor, who may be engaged on an activity which is on the critical path.

Assuming the client's commercial organization is shrewd enough to detect and quickly rebut an over-zealous contractor or the occasional 'frivolous' claim, the resolution of claims usually progresses in one of two ways:

− The claim succeeds and is quickly resolved.
− The claim is problematical and follows a negotiation procedure.

THE CLAIM SUCCEEDS

Examples of straightforward claims which succeed without recourse to lengthy negotiation or the need for clarification or re-submittal are:

1. Changes in the contractor's schedules of rates for installing, say, concrete, structural steel, pipe, or cable, provided the contractor can demonstrate that the quantity of materials or the character of the work has changed significantly (see Section 22.3).
2. Changes in manual man-hour rates arising from national wage awards. These are usually based on price adjustment formulae which are agreed and included in the contract document.

In these circumstances contractors would be obliged to give clients an agreed notice period of their intention to raise a claim. In the meanwhile there should be no restraining effect on the schedule.

THE CLAIM FOLLOWS A TORTUOUS ROUTE

The problematical claim usually follows a more tortuous route, introducing serious delays unless it receives close attention and is progressed vigorously by both the parties. In civil engineering works, for example, on-site delays are commonly encountered when the contractor meets a physical ground condition or obstruction which could not reasonably have been foreseen. This will trigger a series of events such as depicted in Fig. 22.2. Clearly, in view of the delay potential, it behoves the contractor to notify the client as quickly as possible regarding complex claims of this nature.

Organizational requirements

We now consider the type of organization which is required to put into effect the pre-planning, procedural and executive actions which are required to ensure the most cost-effective handling of claims. In Section 22.3 we showed that it is important that the client and contractor have a common understanding of terminology. It is equally important to be quite specific about the structure of the organization which is required to execute the plan, and to be accurate regarding the roles which individuals should perform.

In a contractor/client relationship a clearly delineated organization must be created. There must be a single-point contact on each side near the top of the structure with responsibility for the handling and resolution of claims, together with the necessary defined channels of communication. It is now common for the system to be defined to satisfy a quality audit procedure.

On the contractor's side the organization must be capable of executing the following functions:-

– Pre-planning
– Identification of claims potential
– Assembly of claims, including quantity survey, schedule/cost impact, documentation
– Submission (written/oral)
– Tracking and expediting
– Negotiation
– Implementation
– Records.

On the client's side the organization must be capable of executing the following functions:

– Receival (written/oral)
– Prioritizing
– Examination and response
– Negotiation
– Resolution (initial/final)
– Approval and certification
– Records.

The contractor's organization chart (Fig. 22.3) is an extract from an overall project organization. It is adapted to show the commercial operation (continuous lines) within which claims are handled together with the various supporting functions. Each one of the personnel portrayed has an involvement in the assembly of a claim. For simplicity, industrial

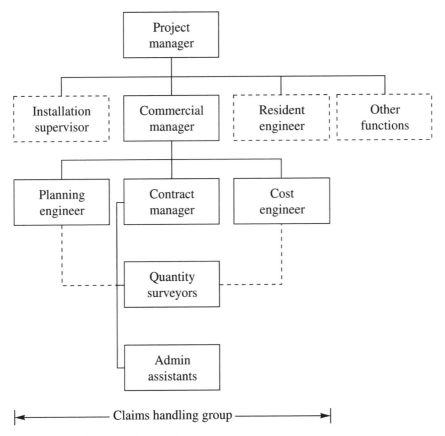

Figure 22.3 Contractor's organization chart

relations, safety, QA/QC, and legal specialists are omitted. For smaller projects the organization will be reduced in numbers but the functions indicated above must still be covered.

The client and contractor must identify the single point contact within their respective organizations for handling and expediting claims. The organization chart (Fig. 22.3) places the contract manager in this position for the contractor. He or she will receive delegated financial authority limits sufficient to deal with all day-to-day claims in conjunction with his or her opposite number on the client's side. In the event that claims are estimated to exceed this authorized level, he or she will prepare the case in conjunction with the commercial manager.

Clearly there is a limit to the financial authority of even the most senior representative on a project both for the client and the contractor. However, in setting up the organization and the procedures, it is strongly recommended that where feasible, the project/site organization is given substantial autonomy to obviate external approval loops which introduce delays.

Implementing procedures

Having identified the organizational structure, it may be necessary to prepare project-specific procedures. It makes sense, however, to avoid separate procedures covering a particular subject which merely duplicate what is already well covered in the Contract.

On many projects a high level of quality assurance, QA, incorporating the relevant principles of BS 5750 is a requirement spelled out in the contract.[3] Such a project organization will probably include a project QA manager who will have a direct reporting line to a corporate QA manager. It is, therefore, the ultimate responsibility of a contractor's QA department in conjunction with the client, to establish project policy regarding procedures prior to contract award.

The following headings address some of the key areas where specific procedures are considered beneficial:

- Approvals
- Early warning systems
- Presentation and progressing of claims
- Arbitration.

APPROVALS

We described above the flow paths of claims to and from contractor and client. The recommended procedure should address:

- Single-point contact and nominees (contractor and client)
- Levels of delegated financial authority for the above personnel
- Organization chart and job descriptions
- Methods of communication.

EARLY WARNING SYSTEMS

As described above, a simple early warning procedure must be set up to alert a client to those impending claims which a contractor considers to be of significant value or to have project-wide consequences. This will minimize potential delays and allow maximum time to consider changes in scheduling strategy should this be contemplated.

The successful resolution of a claim, particularly a major claim, depends upon the quality and manner of its presentation to the client. The homework must be done in detail and the contractor must be ready to be cross-examined on every aspect of his or her submission by a panel of client's experts. A standardized format to regulate the way in which claims are compiled and presented is advantageous to both contractor and client. The following is an example of the required index:

- Summary
- Reference drawings
- Perceived impact on others
- Schedule impact
- Schedule recovery proposals
- IR implications
- Safety implications
- Inspection and test plans
- Estimated cost
- Authorization.

The number of claims in the system will probably increase as the project advances. The contract manager must therefore monitor claims progress and produce periodic status reports for presentation at formal progress meetings.

ARBITRATION

The procedure for settling disputes of any kind between client and contractor will normally be addressed within the overall contract. It is to be hoped that on every project all claims will be resolved, if necessary by negotiation, within the project organization. Should there be any exception the contractor should carefully observe the notice periods and time limitations that apply. Should they fail to act within the stipulated period they may find that their right to raise the issue in arbitration is time-barred.

22.5 Estimating the cost of claims

We said above that the expeditious and successful resolution of a claim usually depends upon the quality of the claim and the manner in which it is packaged and presented. The client will scrutinize the make-up of cost in detail, and it is quite normal for estimators and quantity surveyors to be called upon to substantiate their calculations. In this section, we draw attention to some of the pitfalls which abound and suggest ways of improving the accuracy of claims evaluation.

The word *definition* keeps cropping up in this chapter. Accurate estimates in which a contractor has a high degree of confidence stem from *understanding* the scope of work as defined by drawings, specifications, quantities of materials, bought out items, man-hours of effort, etc., as described in Section 22.2. The need for definition starts when the contractor is tendering and continues until the contract price is agreed.

The quest for definition continues with every claim that is raised and the problem does not necessarily become any easier as the project advances.

It should be borne in mind that when a project is underway we are, in effect, attempting to freeze it at the instant when the claims occurrence is first perceived and take a snapshot of the whole scene. It is only then that the estimator can evaluate the consequential costs.

For example, if there are 1500 manual workers involved in the claim area of work the consequential cost of suspending work or diverting the workforce to other tasks could be very considerable indeed. The Estimator would postulate that in order to replace £30,000 worth of legitimate claim entitlement not resolved, his or her company would have to undertake some £1 000 000 worth of averagely profitable work to make up the difference.

This anecdote helps to put the contractor's cash flow risks into perspective and demonstrates the need for experience and perception skills of a high order in the commercial team in which claims are handled (Section 22.4).

The moving target analogy also focuses attention on the need for constant review and awareness in all the following areas:

- Monitoring project status by recording the accumulation of all manual and non-manual man-hours.
- Monitoring project status and progress by periodic measurement of all installed quantities (cubic metres of concrete, tonnes of structural steel, metres of pipe, cable, etc.).
- Comparing estimated and actual productivity.
- Plotting actual progress versus estimated values to determine trends.
- A visual appreciation of activities in the work area including photographic records.

The availability of current records in the above areas permits the estimator to view a claim relative to a real cut-off point. Current – not historical – productivity data are essential for making sound judgements for the scheduling and costing of future recovery predictions.

22.6 Risk areas

It can be argued that the incidence of the contractor's claims on a project is in direct proportion to the risks which the client takes on board when developing the project concept and strategy. If we consider the overall number of claims, those totally reimbursed are paid for from the client's contingency fund and those which are not, or only in part, are met mainly out of contractor's contingency; more precisely as a deduction from the contractor's potential profit margin.

When studying risk areas it is more correct to think in terms of project risk. There are no winners. Table 22.2 sets out an action plan to minimize claims occurrences and suggests the degree of risk in each case. As we might expect the claims exposure from the client's viewpoint is greatest on the prototype, one-off and retrofit projects where scope definition is difficult to achieve at the time of contract award. Conversely, claims potential should reduce on repeat or duplicate projects.

Finally, from the prudent contractor's viewpoint it is worthy of note that in the absence of definitive information, a clear listing of areas and activities which are *excluded* from the tender documents will assist in minimizing claims occurrences and improve client relations during the project execution phase.

22.7 Alternative dispute resolution

The preceding sections described how claims for additional payment can easily and frequently arise during the construction phase of a project and indicated how these situations may be managed in order to secure an outcome that is satisfactory to both parties. Sometimes, and ever increasingly, it is difficult for the two parties to agree a settlement to their dispute and this has traditionally resulted in the need to resort to legal processes such as arbitration or litigation. Both these approaches, which seek to have a legally binding decision on the dispute made by either an arbitrator or the courts, have in recent years evolved into extremely expensive and risky courses of action. Lawyers have developed what were originally straightforward procedures into protracted and complex legal actions which incur significant costs with no guarantee of success. Because of this, many lawsuits relating to construction claims settle on the steps of the court but not before both parties have spent considerable time and money in the preliminary stages of the process.

A situation of ever increasing legal costs and an industry prone to confrontation lead, in the United States, to the development of other 'alternative' dispute resolution (ADR) techniques with the aim of encouraging the amicable, non-legally-assisted settlement of contractual

Table 22.2 **Minimizing the risk of claims**

Risk area	Effect	Required action	Action by	Degree of risk
Inadequate scope definition	Ambiguity Misunderstanding Delay	Bid clarification Pre-planning	Joint	Med–High
Not recognizing claims potential	Project delay Contractor's profitability	Better organization	Contractor	Low–Med
Lack of flexibility of the parties	Project delay Bad relationships	Better organization	Joint	Low
Prototype/one-off project	Ambiguity Misunderstanding	Bid clarification Pre-planning	Client and joint	High
Retrofit project	Ambiguity Misunderstanding Restraints	Bid clarification Pre-planning	Client and joint	High
Accumulation, slow response to claims	Project delay Bad relationships	Better procedures	Client	Low
Inadequate claims submissions	Project delay Contractor's profitability	Better procedures	Contractor	Low–Med
Inexperienced contractors	Project delay Contractor's profitability	Assist contractor	Client and main contractor	Low–Med
Unscrupulous contractor or subcontractor	Project delay	Cancel contract Remove from bidders' list	Client and main contractor	Low

disputes. In the 15 years since its official inception, the use of ADR has enjoyed 'organic' growth in the United States and it is now being actively promoted in the United Kingdom. With strong support in the judiciary and many official bodies representing industry and general commerce, the use of ADR to achieve cheap, fast and equitable solutions to contractual disputes is going to increase and its possible mandatory inclusion in the legal framework suggests that it should be considered when faced with a claims situation in deadlock.

In this section we describe the various techniques of ADR, describe the relative merits and drawbacks of an ADR approach, explain when and why ADR may be considered, to explain how ADR may be initiated and used. It is intended that the subject should be covered in sufficient detail to provide a good understanding of what ADR is such that an objective decision can be reached on the possible benefits of its use in a given circumstance either by suggesting or agreeing to partake in an ADR process.

The machinery of ADR

The flexibility of ADR has led to the proliferation of many variations and hybrids of the basic techniques involved, all of which purport to be ADR in some form or other. It is therefore important to establish a definition of ADR in order to appreciate the essence of the approach and how it is fundamentally different from traditional methods. A suitable definition,[4] is as follows:

> Alternative Dispute Resolution (ADR) means dispute resolution by processes:
> (a) which encourage disputants to reach their own solution and
> (b) in which the primary role of the third party neutral is to facilitate the disputants to do so.

There are three main types of ADR: mediation, conciliation and the mini-trial. Other procedures frequently described as ADR include expert appraisal, adjudication and dispute resolution panels but are not ADR in its pure form as they have evolved to give a definitive binding result based on the decision of the third party.

All three mainstream ADR approaches require the use of a 'neutral' or third party whose main function is to act as a catalyst in enabling the parties to identify common ground. The role of the neutral is vital to the outcome of the attempted settlement process and great emphasis is placed on selecting suitably experienced and trained professionals for the task. It is not considered that neutrals should be lawyers as others may have more relevant knowledge of the issues involved and the possible solutions to the dispute should not be constrained in any way by aspects of the law. Neutrals should aim (either as mediators or conciliators) to participate in the resolution process with the following objectives in mind:

- to establish a constructive ambience for negotiation;
- to collect and judiciously communicate selective confidential material;
- to help parties clarify their values;
- to deflate unreasonable claims and loosen positions;
- to seek joint gains;
- to keep negotiations going;
- to articulate the rationale for agreement.

The three main forms of ADR are now examined in more detail.

MEDIATION

In the mediation process, the mediator will meet with each of the parties separately in an informal environment to try to assist them in focusing on

382 THE COMMERCIAL PROJECT MANAGER

the real issues of the dispute. As progress is made towards an acceptable solution the mediator will 'shuttle' between the parties in an attempt to bring the matter to a conclusion. The mediator will have some form of expert knowledge in the subject area and each party must be represented by a person with the requisite authority to settle the dispute. Following on from individual meetings, the mediator may then try to bring the parties together whereupon both sides have the opportunity to describe their respective views on the dispute itself and their criteria for an acceptable settlement. This allows them to analyse their position in the light of the other party's such that they may more readily identify the relative strengths or weaknesses of their own case. Further individual meetings may then take place, with the mediator discussing the possibility of offers of settlement without influencing the process with his or her own opinions. If a dialogue of offer and counter offer is sustained via the mediator, the parties may reach a common position, the conditions pertaining to which may then be committed to paper. Under some conditions of contract the mediator is given the power to make a binding decision based on his assessment if there is no settlement as a result of the mediation process. It should however be remembered that the basic principle of ADR is that the parties find their own agreement retaining the decision-making process under their own control. Even an unsuccessful mediation will probably have narrowed the gap between the parties and will have maintained an open channel of communication in the meanwhile.

CONCILIATION

While the objective of the conciliator remains the same as that of the mediator, it is the forum in which a settlement is sought that is slightly different. In conciliation, there are no private meetings between the parties and the conciliator but instead the proceedings are conducted with everyone 'round the table'. The role of the conciliator is often described as being less 'interventionist' than the mediator, but the conciliator will participate in the negotiations by contributing to the discussions and offering his or her opinions on the strengths and weaknesses of each party's case. By so doing, it is intended that the parties will be able to address the main issues of the dispute and thereby progress towards a solution to the problem.

THE MINI-TRIAL

This is the least common approach although it has seen significant success especially in the United States. Unlike both mediation and conciliation, it can take place at a relatively late stage in the dispute when proceedings in court have already been commenced. A mini-trial is a presentation of each case before a panel comprised of one person of authority from each party and an appointed neutral who may act as chairman. The two parties are each represented by one lawyer who makes a speech giving details of the client's case. Following this, the executives from each party discuss with their own advisers the merits of their opponent's case and then meet together to try and reach a settlement. The neutral may give his or her views if desired by either party, which may include advice on the likely outcome of litigation, but the neutral acts without binding authority over the parties. If a solution is achieved, it can be set out in a legally enforceable document.

Of the three types of ADR described, experience has shown that mediation is by far the most popular accounting for over 90 per cent of all successful resolutions.

Advantages and disadvantages of ADR

ADR has attracted both supporters and critics in the legal and business fields and as such it is important to note both the positive and negative aspects of its use. The list is not comprehensive as an ADR approach may have unique drawbacks in any particular set of circumstances but it does provide an overview of the pros and cons to be weighed up. The advantages of ADR are:

– It keeps the decision making process in the hands of the parties most affected by it.
– It enables settlements to be reached under very flexible terms involving issues such as future work.
– It can assist in maintaining business relationships between the parties.
– It can achieve very quick solutions to disputes.
– It is very cheap compared to arbitration or litigation.
– It involves senior management in disputes at an early stage and exposes both parties to each other's arguments.
– It is a totally confidential process.
– It does not prejudice further legal action.

The advantages of ADR are generally described relative to the traditional legal processes and, as it in no way jeopardizes the use of such methods at a later stage, there is in fact very little to lose in attempting to find a solution by this route. The disadvantages of ADR are:

– It is a non-binding process and cannot be instigated by one party alone.
– It requires both parties to want to achieve a settlement.
– It cannot guarantee a resolution to the dispute.
– It can over-simplify complex cases.

- It can be used as a delaying tactic.
- It can be a disadvantage in later legal proceedings.

While all the above are potentially very real drawbacks to the use of an ADR, fundamentally it is the abuse of the approach by one or other of the parties that poses the biggest threat to achieving a successful resolution.

When and how to use ADR

It is increasingly common for the use of ADR to be prescribed as one of the stages of resolution in the conditions of contract. This may appear in a very large variety of forms from a simple 'the parties shall attempt to resolve all disputes by negotiation' to more complex procedures detailing precise timescales for the process, the method of selection and powers of the neutral. It is likely that if such a mandatory procedure is in place then the neutral will have the authority to make a binding recommendation should the parties be unable to agree, whereupon the approach to the ADR requires careful consideration.

There is evidence to suggest that if ADR is compulsory, either by virtue of the conditions of contract or if, as in some countries, it is court assisted, there is a lower chance of achieving success. Consequently, the use of *ad hoc* ADR in response to its suggestion by one of the parties is generally more likely to result in a satisfactory resolution.

There are no hard and fast rules as to when to try ADR but the basic condition that both sides are actively seeking a resolution (albeit that they may have become entrenched in their respective positions) is a prerequisite if it is to stand any chance at all. However, there are certain circumstances in which ADR is not appropriate and in which only the traditional legal methods will yield results. ADR is unsuitable if any of the following criteria apply:

- The jurisdiction or sanction of the court is essential, for example one party needs to seek an injunction or set a precedent.
- Where one party wants to be publicly vindicated.
- Where one party has no motivation for settling short of a trial.

Equally, a dispute might be particularly likely to benefit from an ADR approach such as disagreements on simple issues between parties with a long-standing relationship where the sums at stake are not great.

ADR can be initiated very simply either on a formal or informal basis. Having agreed to partake in the ADR, the parties can decide whether to use a commercial ADR service, where the proceedings will be orchestrated by a third party, or develop rules for the ADR mutually and follow them through to a natural conclusion. ADR is offered by a range of organizations including legal firms, claims consultants, and such as the Centre for Dispute Resolution (CEDR) and IDR Europe. All these organizations retain a long list of trained neutrals experienced in a wide variety of commercial fields. They will also act as liaison between parties, establishing the procedure to be followed, the timing and coordination of the process. The cost of this service is shared equally between the disputants and is not normally high compared with other legal services. If the two parties can easily agree on a neutral and the format of the ADR, then it can proceed forthwith with no need for any referral to a formal commercial service. It should be noted that it is in selecting the neutral that most parties find it difficult to agree and this accounts for why most expedient ADR resolutions are achieved with formal assistance.

Concluding remarks

The use of ADR is already widespread in many countries and it is increasing rapidly in all areas of industry and commerce. This coupled with the momentum driving it into the legal framework means that there will be in future an ever greater chance of having to undergo such procedures as part of the protocol of resolving claims and contractual disputes. Furthermore, there is a real possibility that ADR may in fact save both time and money in finding efficient solutions and indeed it is worthy of consideration at every stage as part of the effective management of claims by both sides to a contract.

22.8 Summary

1. Settlement of a claim may be in two parts:
   - Interim settlement to allow work to proceed
   - Issue of a variation order.
2. Claims can arise from:
   - Changes in rates
   - Perceived scope changes
   - Changes to schedule
   - Schedule restraints.
3. The potential for claims is minimized by:
   - Avoiding ambiguity
   - Using milestone markers
   - Defining terminology.
4. There are three types of ADR procedure:
   - Mediation
   - Conciliation
   - Mini-trial.

References

1. Morris, P.W.G. and Hough G.H., *The Anatomy of Major Projects: a study of the reality of project management*, Wiley, 1987.
2. Institution of Civil Engineers, *Conditions of Contract and Forms of Tenders, Agreement and Bond (6th Edition) for Use on Connection with Works of Civil Engineering Construction*, Thomas Telford, 1991.
   Institution of Civil Engineers, *New Style Engineering Contract*, Thomas Telford, 1992.
3. Turner, J.R., *The Handbook of Project-based Management*, McGraw-Hill, 1993.
4. Newman, P., 'Alternative dispute resolution: a viable alternative to arbitration or litigation', *Construction Law*, **4**(2), 1993.

Subject Index

Accidents (*see* Safety)
Accounting
  practice and standards, 110, 117
  project, 248
Accounting rate of return (*see*
  Investment appraisal,
  techniques)
Acts of Parliament, 233, 237, 279
  Alkali Act, 224
  Companies Act (1985), 111
    Articles of Association, 279
  Consumer Credit Act (1974), 272
  Control of Pollution Act (1974), 205–
    207
  Environmental Protection Act (1990),
    199–200, 205–207
  Goods and Services Act (1982), 283
  Health and Safety at Work Act
    (1974), 207, 224, 269
  Infants Relief Act, 279
  Minors Contracts Act (1987), 279
  private bills, 233
  Resale of Goods Act, 272
  Restrictive Trade Practices Act, 272
  Sale of Goods Act (1979), 282
  Water Resources Act (1991), 205
  (*see also* Government policy and
    regulation; Legislation)
Adjudication, 262–263, 300, 381
ADR (*see* Alternative Dispute
  Resolution)
Agreement (*see* Contract)
Aid, 80, 84–87, 99, 112–116, 177, 182,
  189–190
  agencies, 189–190
  project and programme aid, 86
  soft loans, 87, 189–190

(*see also* Banks, international
  investment institutions;
  Finance, sources of)
Alternative Dispute Resolution (ADR),
  xxii, 126, 242, 366, 379–385
  Centre for Dispute Resolution
    (CEDR), 385
  Institute for Dispute Resolution,
    Europe (IDR), 385
  types, conciliation, mediation, and
    mini–trial, 381–385
Ansoff matrix (*see* Marketing)
Arbitrage, 180
Arbitration, 113, 262–263, 273, 297, 312,
  351, 361–362, 376–379, 383
  International Chamber of Commerce,
    273
  London Arbitration Centre, 273
ARR (*see* Investment appraisal,
  techniques)
Availability, reliability and
  maintainability (ARM), 16,
  309
Audit, 58, 247, 327, 352, 373

Balance sheet, 132
  (*see also* Finance, off–balance sheet)
Banks, xvii, 80–84, 89–96, 136–138, 178–
  179, 185–189
  clearing banks, 179
  Eurobank, 180
  international investment institutions,
    83, 95, 140, 177–182, 193
  International Finance Corporation,
    98
  Islamic banks, 88–91
  merchant banks, 83–85, 179, 191

Author and Source Index

Project and Country Index